PLASTIC ADDITIVES TECHNOLOGY HAND BOOK

LIST OF PUBLICATIONS/BOOKS PUBLISHED BY

ENGINEERS INDIA RESEARCH INSTITUTE 4449, NAI SARAK, MAIN ROAD, DELHI - 6 (INDIA)

DAIRY FARMING & MILK PROCESSING & ICE CREAM

Name of Books	₹	US$
* Dairy Formulations Processes & Milk Processing Industries	750/-	75
* Milk Processing and Dairy Products Industries	750/-	75
* Hand Book of Dairy Farming	375/-	50
* Hand Book of Ice Cream Technology and Formulae	525/-	75
* H.B.Milk Processing, Dairy Products and Packaging Technology	975/-	100

HERBS CULTIVATION/MEDICINES

Name of Books	₹	US$
* Herbs, Medicinal & Aromatic Plants Cultivation	650/-	65
* औषधीयए वंस ुगन्धितप ेधोंक ा व्यवसायिकक ृषिकरण(हिन्दी)	800/-	80
* Hand Book of Medicinal & Aromatic Plants	875/-	90
* Hand Book of Aromatic & Plants and Biodiesel (Jatropha)	1100/-	110

FOOD PROCESSING, PRESERVATION, FOOD DEHYDRATION, SNACK FOOD, MEAT PROCESSING

Name of Books	₹	US$
* Fruits & Vegetables Processing Hand Book	750/-	75
* Food Processing & Agro Based Industries	975/-	100
* Manufacture of Snacks Food, Namkeen,Pappad & Potato Products	750/-	75
* Agro Based and Food Processing with E.O.U	1300/-	130
* Preservation & Canning of Fruits and Vegetables	900/-	90
* Hand Book of Food Dehydration and Drying	650/-	65
* Meat Processing & Meat Products Hand Book	900/-	90
* Technology of Food Preservation and Processing	950/-	100
* Agro Based & Processed Food Products	1100/-	110
* Hand Book of Mushroom Cultivation, Processing & Packaging	550/-	60
* Potato & Potato Processing Technology	750/-	75
* Technology of Maize & Allied & Allied Corn Products	650/-	65
* Fruit Beverage & Processing with Mango Products	750/-	75
* Technology of Food Processing Indu.	975/-	100
* Technology of Sweets (Mithai) with Formulae	1050/-	105
* Citrus Fruits Cultivation and Processing Technology	1000/-	100

HOSIERY/TEXTILES/GARMENTS

Name of Books	₹	US$
* Hosiery, Ready-Made Garments & Textile Projects	1300/-	130
* Technology of Textiles (Spinning & Weaving, Dyeing, Scouring, Drying, Printing and Bleaching)	900/-	90
* Hand Book of Garments Manufacturing Technology	900/-	90

PRODUCT FROM WASTE

Name of Books	₹	US$
* Technology of Products From Waste	900/-	90

SOAP & DETERGENTS ACID SLURRY

Name of Books	₹	US$
* Household Soaps, Toilet Soaps & Other Soaps	750/-	75
* Profitable Small Scale Manufacture of Soaps & Detergents	375/-	40
* Hand Book of Synthetic Detergents with Formulations	900/-	90
* Modern Technology of Acid Slurry, Surfactants, Soap and Detergents with Formulae	900/-	90

COSMETIC (SYNTHETIC & HERBAL)

Name of Books	₹	US$
* Cosmetics Processes & Formulations Hand Book	900/-	90
* Herbal Cosmetics & Beauty Products with Formulations	750/-	75
* Profitable Small Scale Manufacture of Cosmetics (Synthetic & Herbal)	950/-	95
* Hand Book of Synthetic and Herbal Cosmetics	575/-	60
* Technology of Herbals Cosmetics & Toiletries Products with Formulae	1100/-	110

ESSENTIAL OILS & AROMATIC PLANTS

Name of Books	₹	US$
* Hand Book of Essential Oils Mfg. & Aromatic Plants	650/-	65
* Essential Oils Processes and Formulations Hand Book	650/-	65
* Modern Technology of Essential Oils	850/-	85
* Technology of Perfumes, Flavours & Essentials Oil	1175/-	120

PERFUMES AND FLAVOURS

Name of Books	₹	US$
* Hand Book of Perfumes & Flavours	600/-	60
* Technology of Perfumes & Flavours and Essential Oils	1175/-	120
* Hand Book of Perfumes with Formulations	750/-	75
* Hand Book of Flavour Technology	750/-	75
* Hand Book of Flavour & Food Colourants Technology	1400/-	140

OIL AND FATS

Name of Books	₹	US$
* Oils, Fats and Derivatives with Refining & Packaging Technology	950/-	95

BUILDING MATERIALS & CHEMICALS

Name of Books	₹	US$
* Technology of Building Materials & Chemicals with Processes	950/-	95

AGRO CULTIVATION, ANIMAL FARMING, AGRO PLANTATION & AGRO CHEMICAL/PESTICIDES

Name of Books	₹	US$
* Hand Book of Tree Farming	800/-	80
* Hand Book of Poultry Farming and Feed Formulations	450/-	45
* Hand Book of Pig Farming	400/-	40
* Agro Based H.B. of Plantation, Cultivation & Farming	500/-	50
* Agro-Based Plantation Cultivation & Farming	475/-	50
* Agro Based Industries (Plantation & Farming)	1300/-	130
* Technology of Modern Rice Milling and Basmati Rice	600/-	60
* Floriculture Hand Book (Flowers Growing Technology)	1000/-	100
* Hand Book of Goat Farming	450/-	45
* Modern Bee Keeping & Honey Processing	375/-	45

PLASTIC ADDITIVES TECHNOLOGY HAND BOOK

Written By

Dr. Himadri Panda, Ph.D., F.I.C., F.I.C.S.

Industrial Consultant

Fellow of the Essential Association of India
Fellow of the Indian Pulp & Paper Technical Association of India
Fellow of the Indian National Science Congress
Fellow of the Oil & Colour Chemist's Association, U.K.
Member of Chinese Academy of Forests
Former Chemist, I.T.R. Co. Ltd., Bareilly (U.P.)
Former Chief Chemist (Q.C. & R & D) Tarpina Pvt. Ltd., Ramnagar, Uttrakhand

ENGINEERS INDIA RESEARCH INSTITUTE

4449, Nai Sarak, Main Road, Delhi - 110006 (India)
Ph: +91-11-23918117, 23916431, 45120361, 23947058
*** E-Mail: eiribooks@yahoo.com**
***Website: www.eiriindia.org**

PRINTED & PUBLISHED BY

ENGINEERS INDIA RESEARCH INSTITUTE

4449, Nai Sarak, Main Road, Delhi - 110006 (India)
Ph: +91-11-23918117, 23916431, 45120361, 23947058
* E-Mail: eiribooks@yahoo.com
*Website: www.eiriindia.org

Sole Distributors:

EIRI PROJECT CONSULTANTS AND PUBLISHERS
4/54 Roop Nagar, Delhi-110007

ISBN: 9789380772127

Printed in New Delhi (INDIA)

₹ 950/-

Printed & Published by Sudhir Gupta for "Engineers India Research Institute", 4449 Nai Sarak, Main Road, New Delhi -110006

Preface

Every activity in modern life is influenced by plastics and many depend entirely on plastics products. Imagine cars without synthetic bumper, dashboards, steering wheels and switches; medicine without plastic hypodermic syringes and artificial hip joints. And what about telecommunications, dependent on plastic telephones, circuit boards and cable insulation. Our entertainment and leisure relies on the unique combination of characteristics offered by plastics in sports equipment and clothing, CDs, video and audio tape, television and cinema - indeed you wouldn't be able to read this over the internet without plastics!

All these plastics products are made from the essential polymer mixed with a complex blend of materials known collectively as additives. Without additives, plastics would not work, but with them they can be made safer, cleaner, tougher and more colourful. Additives cost money, of course, but by reducing production costs and making products last longer, they help us to save money and conserve the world's precious raw material reserves. In fact, our world today would be a lot less safe, a lot more expensive and a great deal duller without the additives that turn basic polymers in to useful plastics.

One way to improve the performance characteristics of plastic products is to compound resins with additives and fillers. Additives help fight against factors such as heat, chemicals or light. There are thousands of additives/fillers on the market today. Below are some of the most common ones used in manufacturing:

- **Antimicrobials**: Used to control the build up of bacteria, fungi and algae on the surface of plastic products. A wide range of chemical and natural compounds are used as antimicrobials. An example would be naturally occurring silver ions used in products such as cell phones or organic acids in food-related products.

- **Antioxidants**: Used to control the degradation of products due to exposure to air.

- **Antistatics**: Used to minimize static electricity. These types of additives can be mixed with the resin or applied to the surface of the product. Antistatic additives are common to a wide variety of products ranging from cosmetics to industrial goods to sensitive electronic parts.

- **Electrostatic Induction**: Used for the economical and even application of polyurethane paints to consumer goods such as automobiles, bicycles and others.

- **Fibers**: Used to increase strength and stiffness. The most common type of fibers added for strength would be carbon and glass. Glass-reinforced plastic is more commonly known and marketed as fiberglass.

- **Conductive fibers**: Used to provide special properties for certain applications.

- **Lubricants**: Used for easier molding or for increased adhesion and viscosity of the molded parts.

- **UV stabilizers**: Used for the protection of the resin's mechanical properties by absorbing selective UV rays resulting in less degradation.

- **Flame retardants/ Smoke suppressants**: A variety of chemicals that can be added to resins to eliminate its tendency to burn. For polyethylene and similar resins, chemicals such as antimony trioxide and chlorinated paraffin are useful.

Author

Contents-cum-Index

1

Introduction

Plastic additives represent a broad range of chemicals used by resin manufacturers, compounders, and fabricators to improve the properties, processing, and performance of polymers. From the earliest days of the plastics industry, additives have been used initially to aid these materials in processing and then to improve their properties. Plastics additives have grown with the overall industry and currently represent over $16 billion in global sales.

Scope

This chapter includes all of the major chemical additives for plastics that are consumed worldwide.

Definitions

To ensure understanding we will define the terms additives and plastics.

Additives

Plastic additives are comprised of an extremely diverse group of materials. Some are complex organic molecules (antioxidants and light stabilizers for example) designed to achieve dramatic results at very low loadings. At the opposite extreme are a few commodity materials (talc and glyceryl monostearate) which also can impart significant property improvements.

Adding to this complexity is the fact that many varied chemical materials can, and frequently do, compete in the same function. Also, the same material type may perform more than one function in a host plastic. An example would include the many surfactant type materials based on fatty acid chemistry which could impart lubricant, antistatic, mold release, and/or slip properties to a plastic matrix, depending upon the materials involved, loading level, processing conditions, and application. Given the range of materials used, plastic additives are generally classified by their function rather than chemistry.

Plastics

Plastics denotes the matrix thermoplastic or thermoset materials in which additives are used to improve the performance of the total system. There are many different types of plastics that use large volumes of chemical additives including (in order of total additive consumption): polyvinyl chloride (PVC), the polyolefins [polyethylene (PE) and polypropylene (PP)], the styrenics, [polystyrene (PS) and acrylonitrile butadiene styrene (ABS)], and engineering resins such as polycarbonate and nylon.

Chemical structure of Different Types of Plastic Additives

Plastic Additives are used to either aid in the processing of the material, ot to make the final product more appealing, durable or useful. Many of these compounds can be used for multiple functions and many of them interact synergistically to protect against heat, light, and oxidation.

We have listed the compounds by the most common uses. If you cannot find a particular compound, or are interested in a custom solvent, concentration, or a custom solution containing more that one compound please call our Technical Service Department for a quotation.

ACCELERATORS

Accelerators are additives that, as the name implies, accelerate or speed up the chemical reaction or the curing of the polymers into the final plastic. Accelerators are also sometimes called promoters, in rubbers accelerators are used to increase the crosslinking reaction with sulfur in the vulcanization of rubber.

Accelerator BBTS

N-(1,1-dimethylethyl)2-benzothiazolesulfenamide

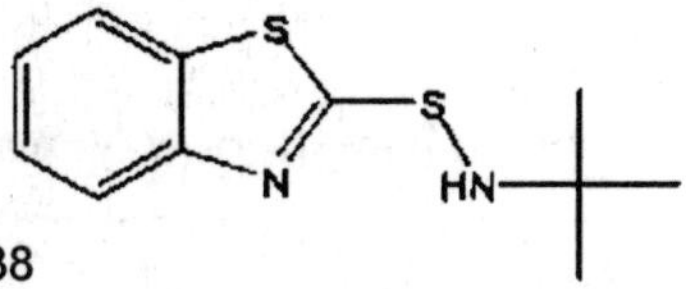

CAS 95-31-8 **MF** $C_{11}H_{14}N_2S_2$ **MW** 238.38

Matrix	Cat. No.	Unit
1000 μg/mL in Hexane	PLAS-AC-003S	1 mL
NEAT	PLAS-AC-003N	50 mg

Accelerator MBT, MBT/MG

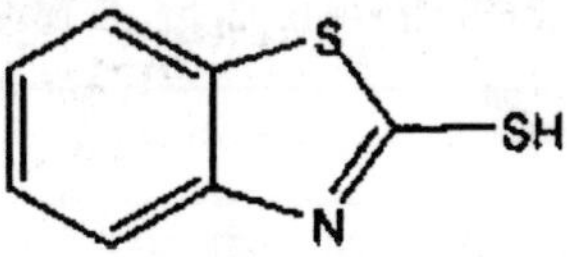

2-Mercaptobenzothiazole

CAS 149-30-4 **MF** $C_7H_5S_2N$ **MW** 167.25

Matrix	Cat. No.	Unit
1000 μg/mL in Hexane	PLAS-AC-001S	1 mL
NEAT	PLAS-AC-001N	50 mg

Akroform ETU-22 PM

Ethylene thiourea

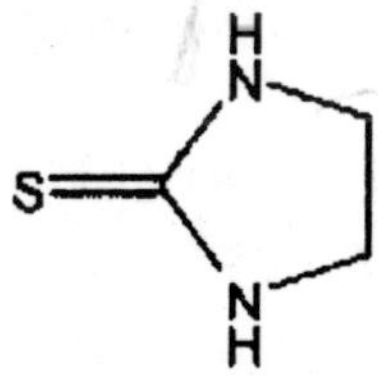

CAS 96-45-7 **MF** $C_3H_6N_2S$ **MW** 102.11

Matrix	Cat. No.	Unit
1000 μg/mL in Hexane	PLAS-AC-002S	1 mL
NEAT	PLAS-AC-002N	50 mg

Accelerator CBTS *NEW*

N-cyclohexyl-2-benzothioazole sulfenamide

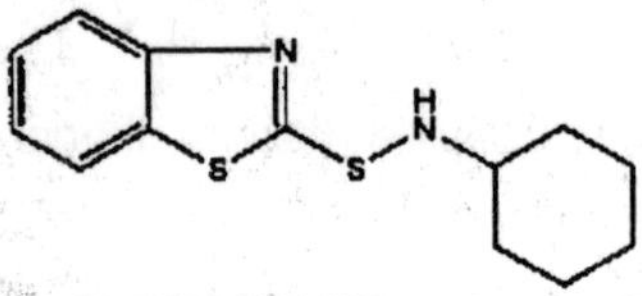

CAS 95-33-0 **MF** $C_{13}H_{16}N_2S_2$ **MW** 264.41

Matrix	Cat. No.	Unit
NEAT	PLAS-AC-007N	50 mg

Activator OT Urea

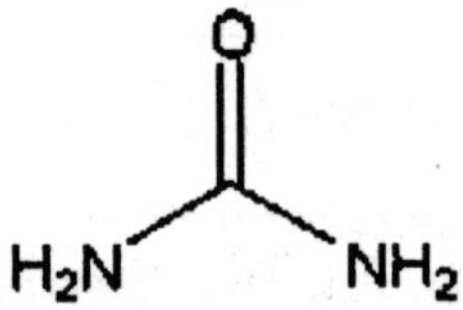

Urea

CAS 57-13-6 **MF** CH_4N_2O **MW** 60.07

Matrix	Cat. No.	Unit
1000 µg/mL in Acetone	PLAS-AC-005S-A	1 mL
NEAT	PLAS-AC-005N	50 mg

Cure-Rite® IBT

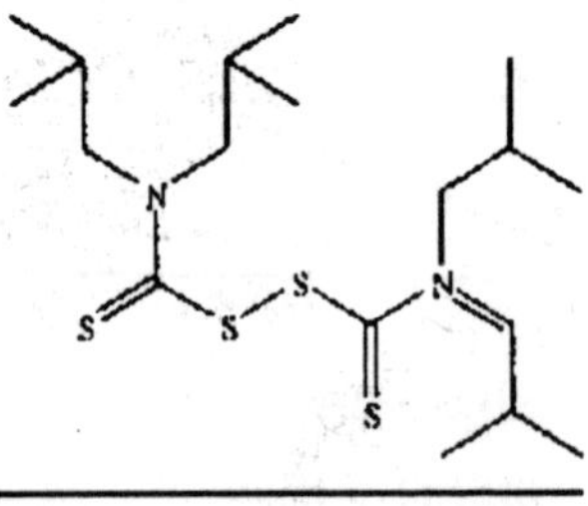

tetraisobutylthiuram disulfide

CAS 3064-73-1 **MF** $C_{18}H_{36}N_2S_4$ **MW** 408.76

Matrix	Cat. No.	Unit
1000 µg/mL in Hexane	PLAS-AC-004S	1 mL
NEAT	PLAS-AC-004N	50 mg

Accelerator EZ & EZ-SP

Zinc diethyldithiocarbamate

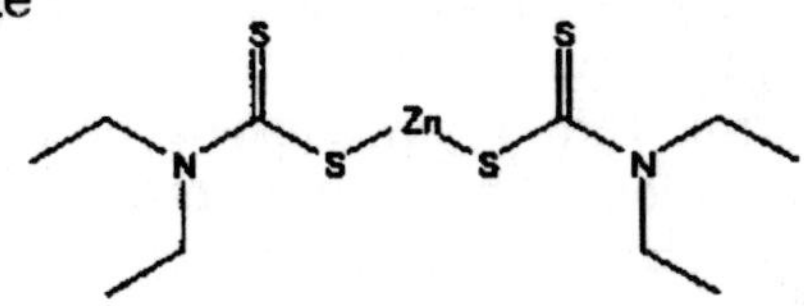

CAS 14324-55-1 **MF** $C_{10}H_{20}N_2S_4 \cdot Zn$ **MW** 361.93

Matrix	Cat. No.	Unit
1000 µg/mL in Hexane	PLAS-AC-006S	1 mL
NEAT	PLAS-AC-006N	50 mg

ANTIFOAMS

Antifoaming agents (sometimes called defoamers) act to stop foaming during processing. Foaming can cause both processing problems as well as weak spots in the final product.

Antifoaming agents typically work by reducing surface tension breaking up the foam. There are many different types of antifoaming agents such as silicones, polysiloxane oils, surfactants, or fatty acids.

SF100

Dimethyl silicone fluid

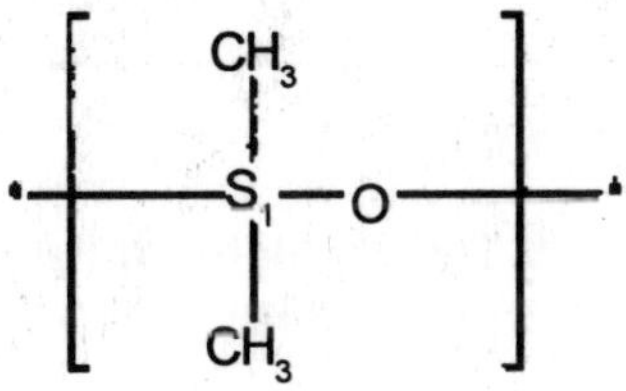

GE Silicons

CAS 9016-00-6 **MF** $(C_2H_6OSi)n$ **MW** N/A

Matrix	Cat. No.	Unit
1000 µg/mL in Hexane	PLAS-AF-001S	1 mL
NEAT	PLAS-AF-001N	50 mg

ANTIDEGRADANTS

Antidegradants include a broad category of additives used in compounding to slow deterioration that can occur due to oxidation, ozon. light or any combination of these conditions. It is basically a generic term for additives that include antioxidants, antiozonants, and UV Stabilizers.

Akrochem Antiox 12

Butylated reaction product of p-cresol and dicyclopentadiene

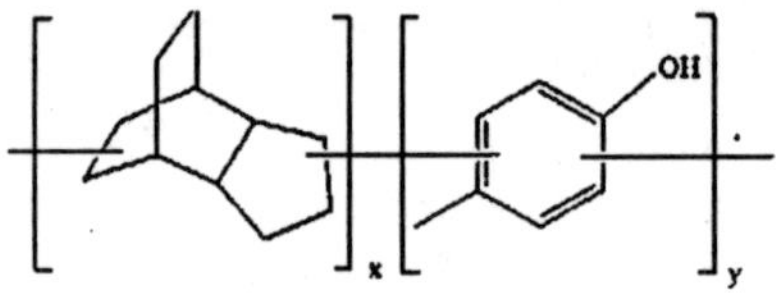

Goodyear Tire & Rubber Company

CAS 68610-51-5 **MF** $C_{11}H_{20}OH \cdot C_{12}H_{23}OH]\ nC_4H_9$ **MW** 600-800

Matrix	Cat. No.	Unit
1000 µg/mL in Hexane	PLAS-AC-001S	1 mL
NEAT	PLAS-AC-001N	50 mg

Ethanox® 314

1,3,5-Tris(3,5-di-tert-butyl-4-hydroxybenzyl)-1,3,5-triazine-2,4,6-(1H,3H,5H)-trione

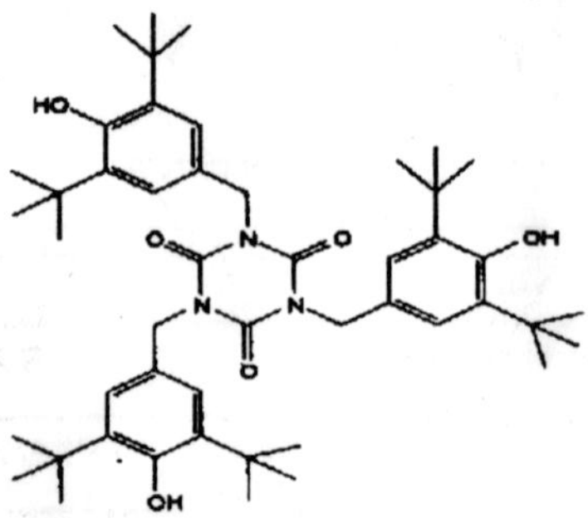

Akrochem Corporation

CAS 27676-62-6 **MF** $C_{48}H_{69}N_3O_6$ **MW** 784.08

Matrix	Cat. No.	Unit
1000 μg/mL in Hexane	PLAS-AX-084S	1 mL
NEAT	PLAS-AC-084N	50 mg

Santoflex® IPPD

N-(1,3-Dimethylbutyl)-N'-phenyl-p-phenylenediamine

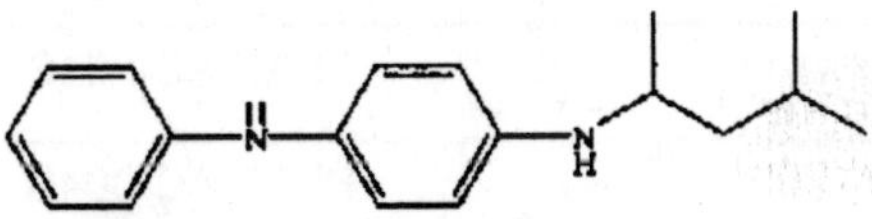

Flexsys

CAS 793-24-8 **MF** $C_{18}H_{24}N_2$ **MW** 268.40

Matrix	Cat. No.	Unit
1000 μg/mL in Hexane:Acetone 8:2	PLAS-AC-003S	1 mL
NEAT	PLAS-AC-003N	50 mg

Santoflex® 77PD

N,N'-bis(1,4-dimethylpentyl)-p-phenylenediamine

Flexsys

CAS 3081-14-9 **MF** $C_{20}H_{36}N_2$ **MW** 304.51

Matrix	Cat. No.	Unit
1000 μg/mL in Hexane	PLAS-AD-002S	1 mL
NEAT	PLAS-AD-002N	50 mg

Santoflex® 6PPD

N-(1,3-Dimethylbutyl)-N'-phenyl-p-phenylenediamine

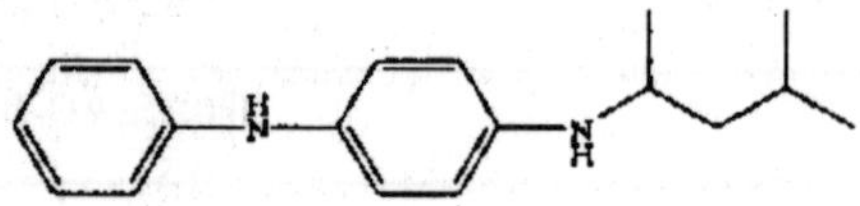

Flexsys

CAS 793-24-8 **MF** $C_{18}H_{24}N_2$ **MW** 268.40

Matrix	Cat. No.	Unit
1000 µg/mL in Hexane	PLAS-AC-004S	1 mL
NEAT	PLAS-AC-004N	50 mg

ANTIOXIDANTS

Oxidation during compounding or processing can cause problems such as: loss of strength, breakdown or discoloration. Oxidation can also occur in the final product causing discoloration, scratching, and loss of strength, flexibility, stiffness or gloss.

Antioxidants are used in most hydrocarbon polymers including polyethylene, polypropylene, polystyrene, and ABS.

Antioxidants work to slow down the oxidation cycle, usually by scavenging free radicals. Some types of antioxidants are: organophosphites, sterically hindered phenols, amines, and thioesters.

Alkanox® P27

bis(2,4-di-tert-butylphenyl)pentaerythritol diphosphate and magnesium aluminum hydroxy carbonate hydrate

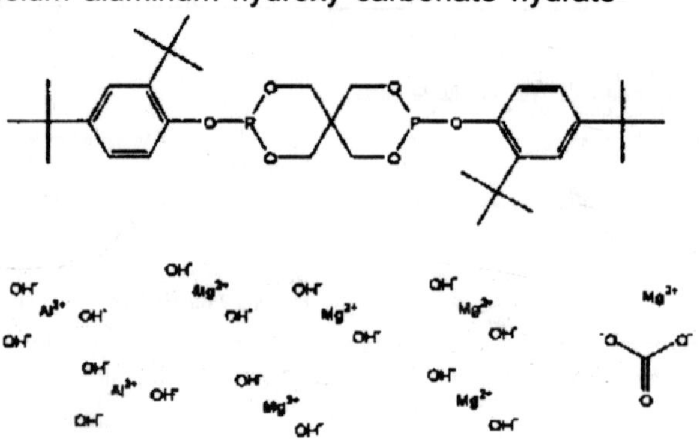

Chemtura Corporation

CAS 26741-53-7 / 11097-59-9 **MF** $C_{33}H_{50}O_6P_2 \cdot H_{16}Al_2Mg_6O_{19}$ **MW**

Matrix	Cat. No.	Unit
NEAT	PLAS-AX-032N	50 mg

Antioxidant 60

2H-benzimidazole-2-thione, 1,3-di-hydro-4(or 5)-methyl

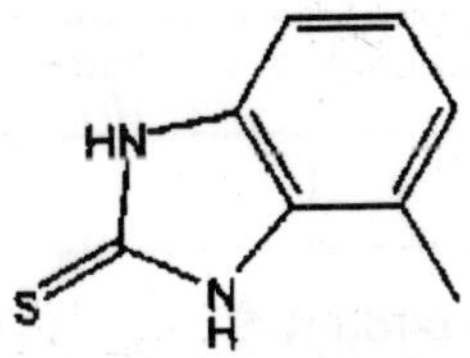

Akrochem Corporation

CAS 53988-10-6 **MF** $C_8H_8N_2S$ **MW** 164.23

Matrix	Cat. No.	Unit
1000 µg/mL in Methanol	PLAS-AX-019S-M	1 mL
NEAT	PLAS-AX-019N	50 mg

BLS® 234 *NEW*

2-[2-Hydroxy-3,5-di-(1,1-dimethylbenzyl)]-2Hbenzotriazole

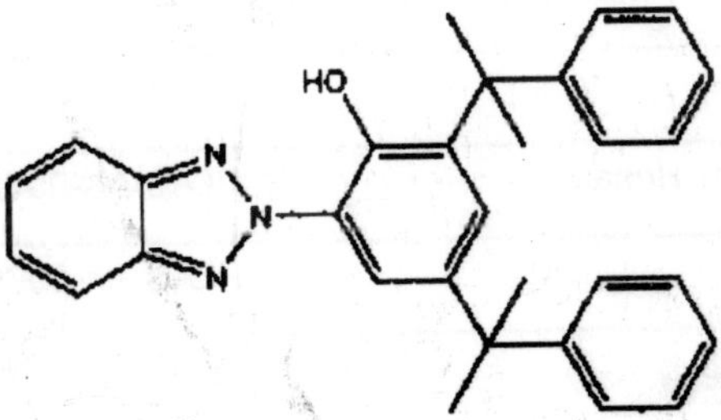

CAS 70321-86-7 **MF** $C_{30}H_{29}N_3O$ **MW** 447.57

Matrix	Cat. No.	Unit
NEAT	PLAS-AX-088N	50 mg

Alkanox® TNPP

tris(mono-nonylphenyl) phosphite with up to 1% triisopropanol amine

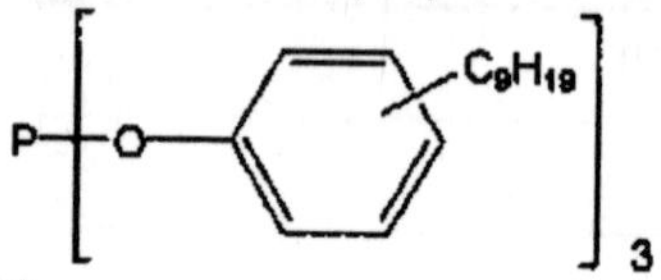

Chemtura Corporation
CAS 26523-78-4 **MF** $C_{45}H_{69}O_3P$ **MW** 689

Matrix	Cat. No.	Unit
1000 µg/mL in Hexane	PLAS-AX-077S	1 mL
NEAT	PLAS-AX-077N	50 mg

Antioxidant S

Benzenamine, N-phenyl, reaction products with 2,4,4-trimethyl-pentene

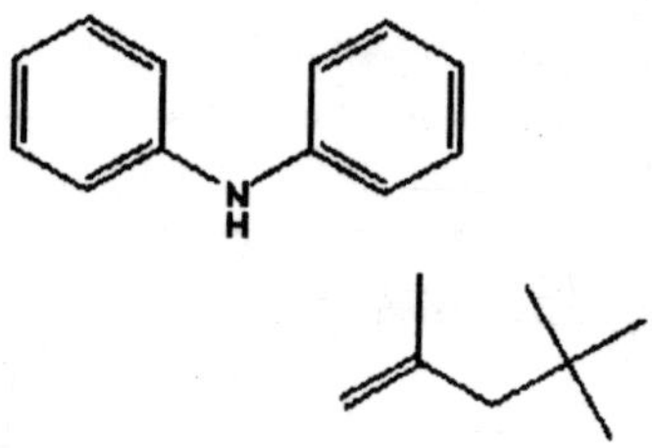

Akrochem Corporation
CAS 68411-46-1 **MF** $C_{12}H_{11}N \cdot C_8H_{16}$ **MW** 393.66

Matrix	Cat. No.	Unit
1000 µg/mL in Hexane	PLAS-AX-057S	1 mL
NEAT	PLAS-AX-057N	50 mg

BLS® 292 NEW

bis(1,2,2,6,6-pentamethyl-4-piperidinyl)sebacate and

Methyl(1,2,2,6,6-pentamethyl-4-piperidinyl)sebacate

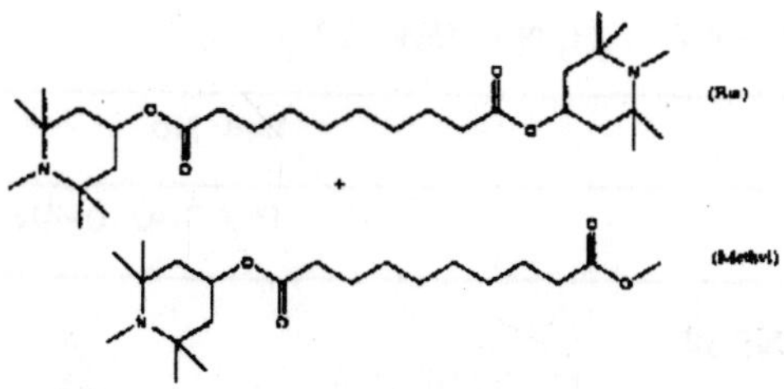

CAS 41556-26-7/8219-37-7 **MF** $C_{30}H_{56}N_2O_4/C_{21}H_{39}NO4$
MW 508.78/369.54

Matrix	Cat. No.	Unit
NEAT	PLAS-AX-089N	50 mg

Alox® PP18 NEW

Octadecyl 3-(3,5-ditert-butyl-4-hydroxyphenyl) propanoate

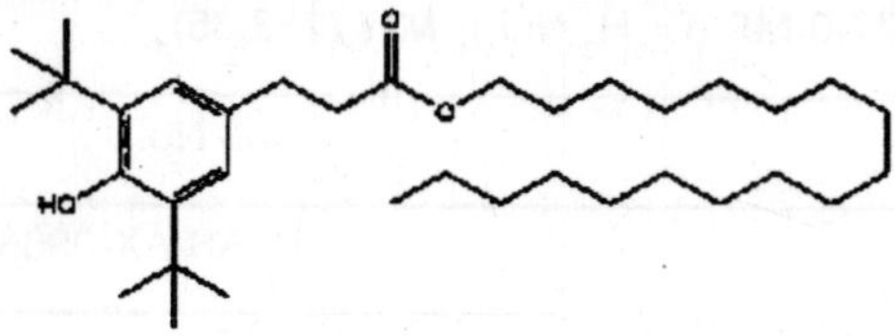

CAS 2082-79-3 **MF** $C_{35}H_{62}O_3$ **MW** 530.86

Matrix	Cat. No.	Unit
NEAT	PLAS-AX-114N	50 mg

2-(2H-Benzotriazol-2-yl)-4,6-bis(1-methyl-1-phenylethyl)phenol *NEW*

2-(benzotriazol-2-yl)-4-(2,4,4-trimethylpentan-2-yl) phenol

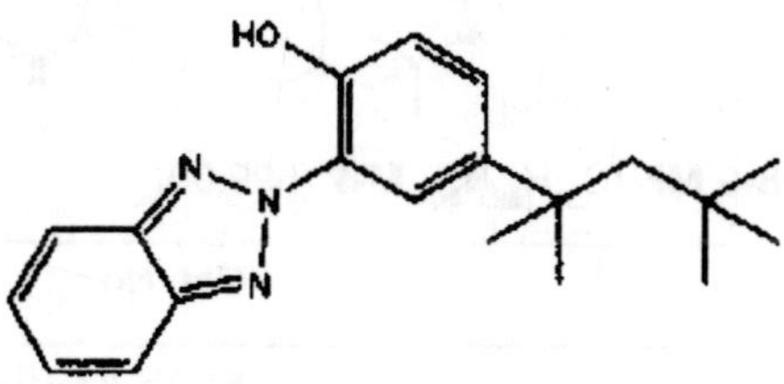

CAS 3147-75-9 **MF** $C_{20}H_{25}N_3O$ **MW** 323.43

Matrix	Cat. No.	Unit
NEAT	PLAS-AX-094N	50 mg

BLS® 1622 NEW

Dimethyl soccinate polymer with 4-hydroxy-2,2,6,6-tetramethyl-1-piperidine ethanol

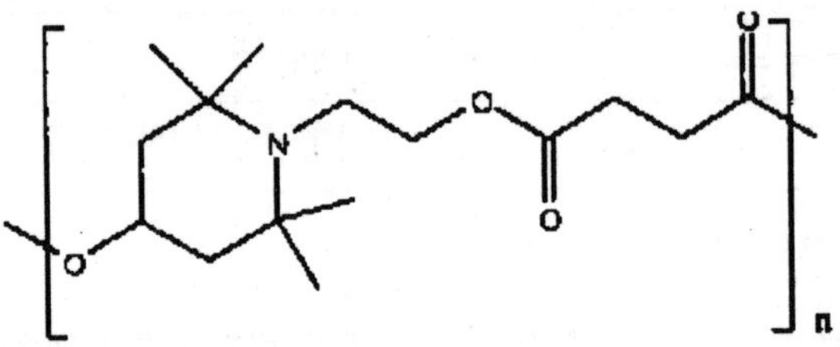

CAS 65447-77-0 **MF** $(C_{15}H_{25}NO_4)_n$ **MW** $(283.35)_n$

Matrix	Cat. No.	Unit
NEAT	PLAS-AX-096N	50 mg

BLS® 1944 NEW

Poly[[6-[(1,1,3,3-tetramethylbutyl)aminol]-s-triazine-2,4-diyl][(2,2,6,6-tetramethyl-4-piperidyl)imino]]hexamethylylene[(2,2,6,6-tetramethyl-4-piperidyl)imino

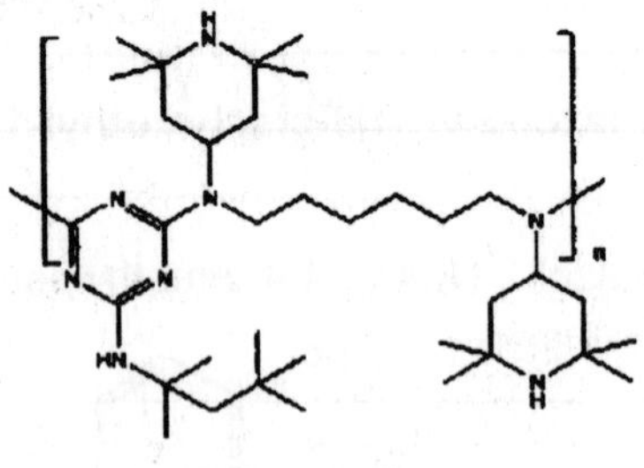

CAS 70624-18-9 **MF** $(C_{35}H_{66}N_8)_n$ **MW** $(599.09)_n$

Matrix	Cat. No.	Unit
NEAT	PLAS-AX-090N	50 mg

2-tert-Butyl-6-(5-chloro-2H-benzotriazol-2-yl)-4-methylphenol NEW

2-tert-butyl-6-(5-chlorobenzotriazol-2-yl)-4-methylphenol

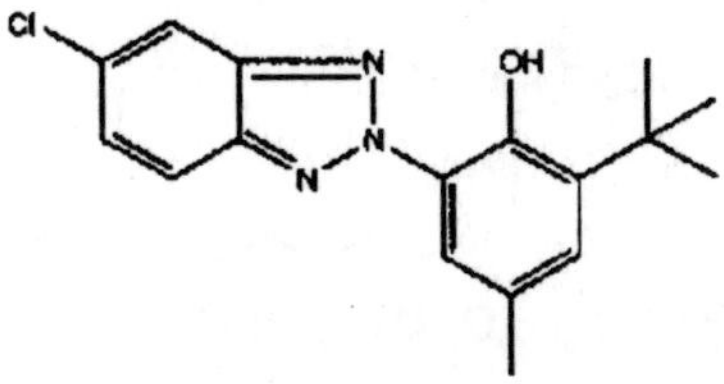

CAS 3896-11-5 **MF** $C_{17}H_{18}ClN_3O$ **MW** 315.80

Matrix	Cat. No.	Unit
NEAT	PLAS-AX-093N	50 mg

Cyanox® 1790

1,3,5-tris(4-tert-butyl-3-hydroxy-2,6-dimethylbenzyl)-1,3,5-triazine-2,4,6-(1h, 3h,5h)-trione

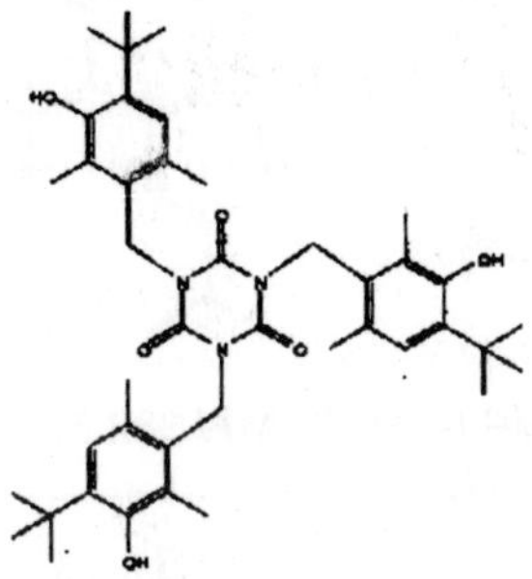

Cytec Technology

CAS 40601-76-1 **MF** $C_{42}H_{57}N_3O_6$ **MW** 699.92

Matrix	Cat. No.	Unit
1000 µg/mL in Hexane	PLAS-AX-005S	1 mL
NEAT	PLAS-AX-005N	50 mg

BNX 1077 NEW

Benzenepropanoic acid, 3,5-bis(1,1-dimethylethyl)-4-hydroxy-, isotridecyl ester

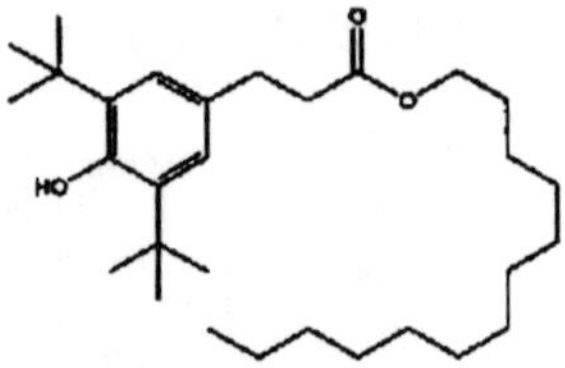

CAS 847488-62-4 **MF** $C_{30}H_{52}O_3$ **MW** 460.73

Matrix	Cat. No.	Unit
NEAT	PLAS-AX-087N	50 mg

4,4'-Butylidenebis(6-tert-butyl-mcresol) NEW

6,6'-di-tert-butyl-4,4'-butylidene di-m-cresol

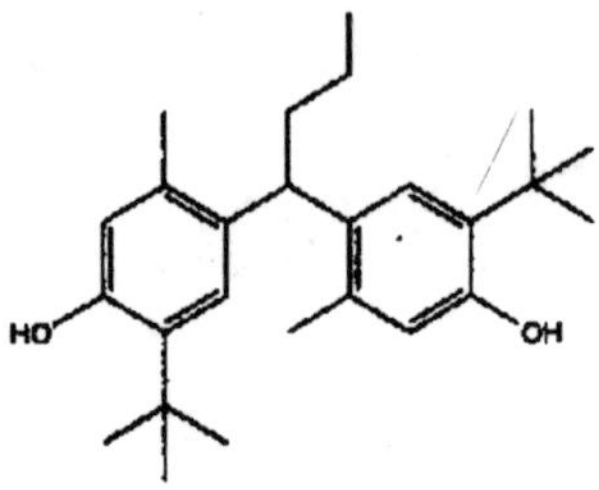

CAS 85-60-9 **MF** $C_{26}H_{38}O_2$ **MW** 382.58

Matrix	Cat. No.	Unit
NEAT	PLAS-AX-105N	50 mg

Cyanox® 2246

2,2'-methylene-bis-(4-methyl-6-tert-butyl-phenol)

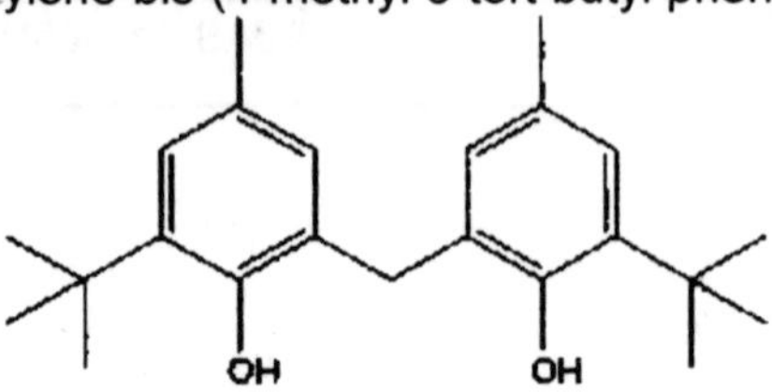

Cytec Technology
CAS 119-47-1 **MF** $C_{23}H_{32}O_2$ **MW** 340.55

Matrix	Cat. No.	Unit
1000 μg/mL in Hexane	PLAS-AX-013S	1 mL
NEAT	PLAS-AX-013N	50 mg

BNX 1225TPR NEW

Blend of BNX®1010, Benefos®1680 and SIS Block Copolymer

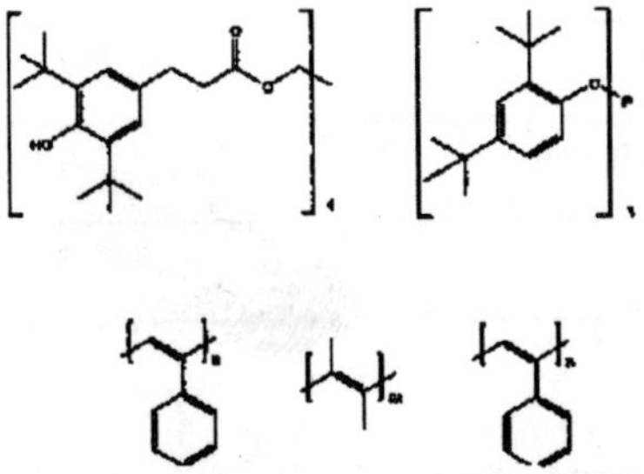

CAS 6683-19-8/31570-04-4/25038-32-8 **MF** N/A **MW** N/A

Matrix	Cat. No.	Unit
NEAT	PLAS-AX-091N	50 mg

Cyanox® 1212

lauryl stearylthiopropionate

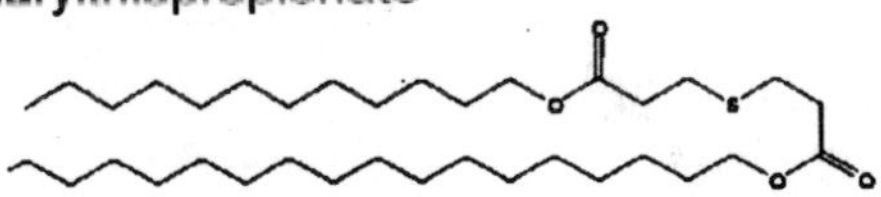

Cytec Technology
CAS 13103-52-1 **MF** $C_{36}H_{70}O_4S$ **MW** 599.00

Matrix	Cat. No.	Unit
1000 μg/mL in Hexane	PLAS-AX-047S	1 mL
NEAT	PLAS-AX-047N	50 mg

Cyanox® 425

2,2'-methylene-bis-(4-ethyl-6-tert-butyl-phenol)

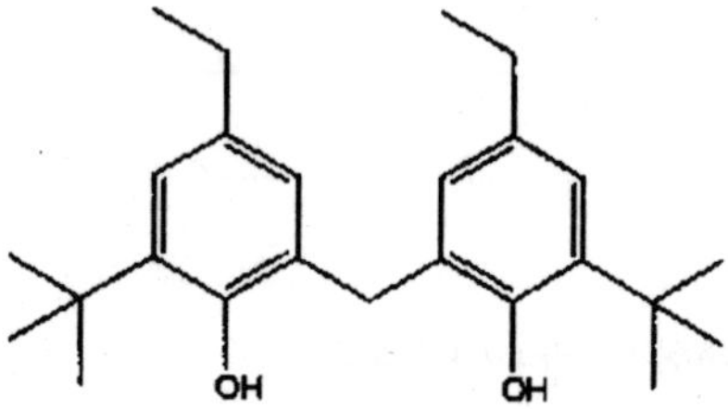

Cytec Technology

CAS 88-24-4 **MF** $C_{25}H_{36}O_2$ **MW** 368.55

Matrix	Cat. No.	Unit
1000 µg/mL in Hexane	PLAS-AX-012S	1 mL
NEAT	PLAS-AX-012N	50 mg

Cyanox® LTDP

dilaurylthiopropionate

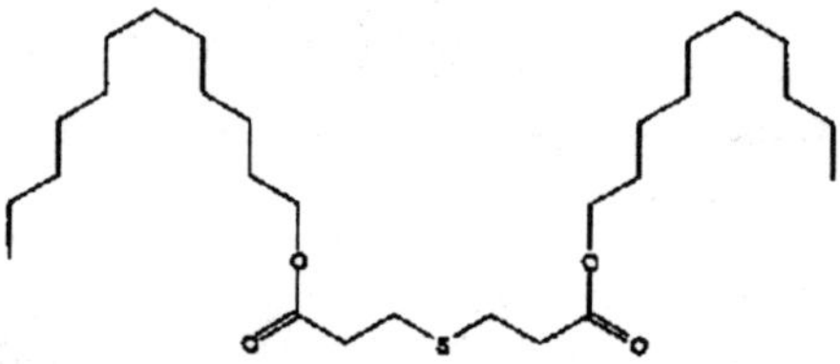

Cytec Technology

CAS 123-28-4 **MF** $C_{30}H_{58}O_4S$ **MW** 514.85

Matrix	Cat. No.	Unit
1000 µg/mL in Hexane	PLAS-AX-041S	1 mL
NEAT	PLAS-AX-041N	50 mg

Diethyl 3,5-Di-tert-butyl-4-hydroxybenzylphosphonate NEW

2,6-ditert-butyl-4-(diethoxyphosphorylmethyl)phenol

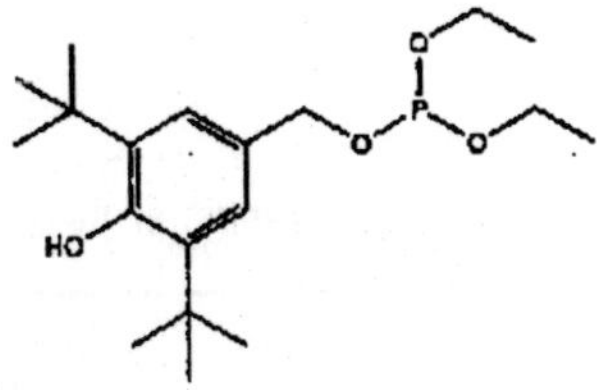

CAS 976-56-7 **MF** $C_{19}H_{33}O4P$ **MW** 356.44

Matrix	Cat. No.	Unit
NEAT	PLAS-AX-110N	50 mg

1,3-Diphenyl-2-thiourea NEW

1,3-di(phenyl)thiourea

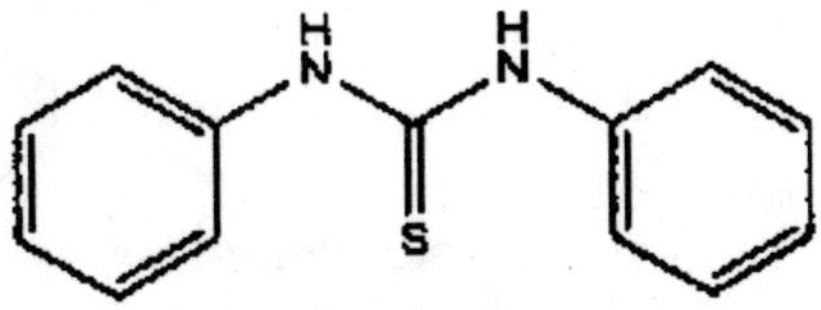

CAS 102-08-9 **MF** $C_{13}H_{12}N_2S$ **MW** 228.31

Matrix	Cat. No.	Unit
NEAT	PLAS-AX-100N	50 mg

Cyanox® STDP

distearylthiopropionate

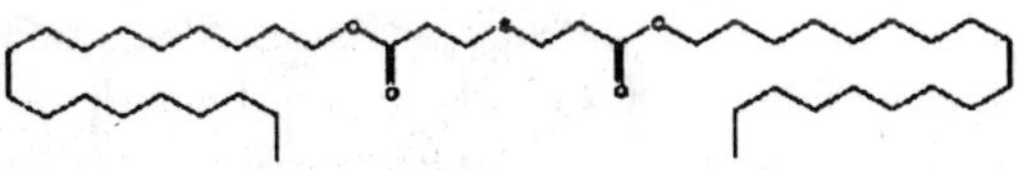

Cytec Technology
CAS 693-36-7 **MF** $C_{42}H_{82}O_4S$ **MW** 683.3

Matrix	Cat. No.	Unit
1000 µg/mL in Hexane	PLAS-AX-044S	1 mL
NEAT	PLAS-AX-044N	50 mg

N,N'-Diethylthiourea NEW

1,3-Diethyl-2-thiourea

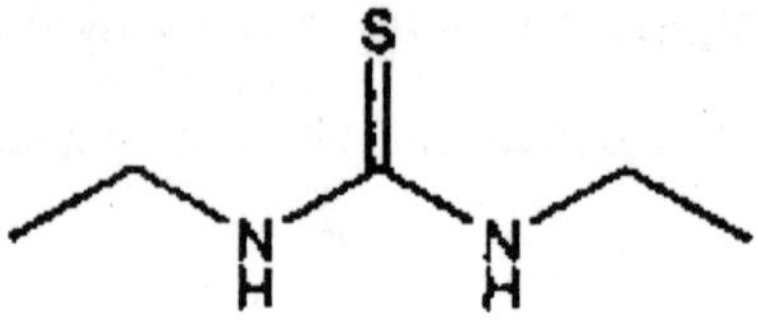

CAS 105-55-5 **MF** $C_5H_{12}N_2S$ **MW** 132.23

Matrix	Cat. No.	Unit
NEAT	PLAS-AX-103N	50 mg

Distyryl biphenyl NEW

Disodium 4,4'-Bis(2-sulfonatostyryl)biphenyl

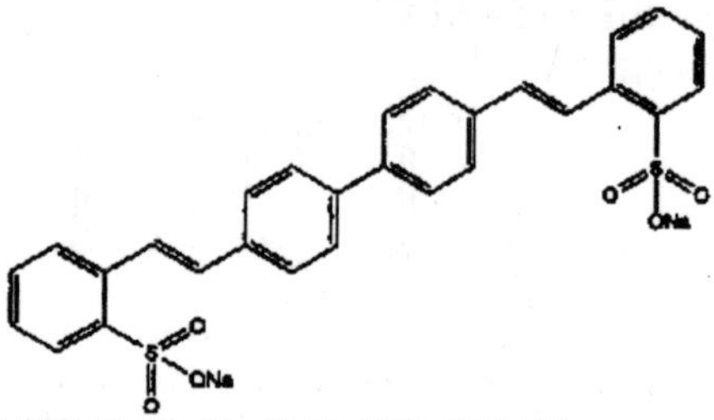

CAS 27344-41-8 **MF** $C_{28}H_{20}Na_2O_6S_2$ **MW** 562.57

Matrix	Cat. No.	Unit
NEAT	PLAS-AX-099N	50 mg

Dibenzylhydroxylamine NEW

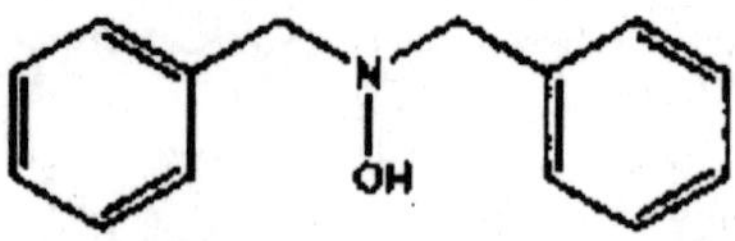

CAS 621-07-8 **MF** $C_{14}H_{15}NO$ **MW** 213.28

Matrix	Cat. No.	Unit
NEAT	PLAS-AX-092N	50 mg

O,O'-Dioctadecylpentaerythritol distearyl bis(phosphile) NEW

Distearyl pentaerythritol bis(phosphile)

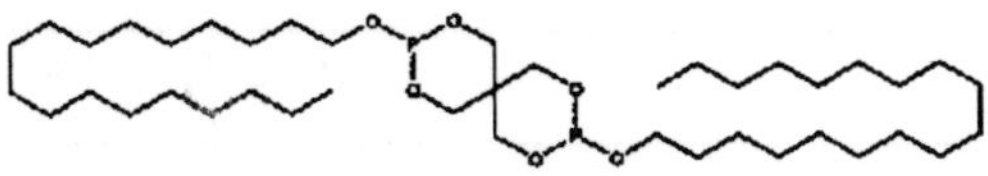

CAS 3806-34-6 **MF** $C_{41}H_{82}O_6P_2$ **MW** 733.03

Matrix	Cat. No.	Unit
NEAT	PLAS-AX-108N	50 mg

1,3-Di-o-tolylguanidine NEW

1,2-bis(2-methylphenyl)guanidine

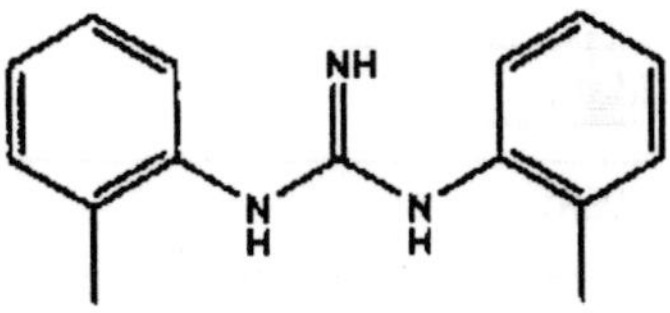

CAS 97-39-2 **MF** $C_{15}H_{17}N_3$ **MW** 239.32

Matrix	Cat. No.	Unit
NEAT	PLAS-AX-101N	50 mg

3,9-Bis(2,4-dicumylphenoxy)-2,4,8,10-tetraoxa-3,9-diphosphaspiro[5,5] undecane NEW

3,9-bis[2,4-bis(2-phenylpropan-2-yl)phenoxy]- 2,4,8,10-tetraoxa-3,9-diphosphaspiro[5,5]undecane

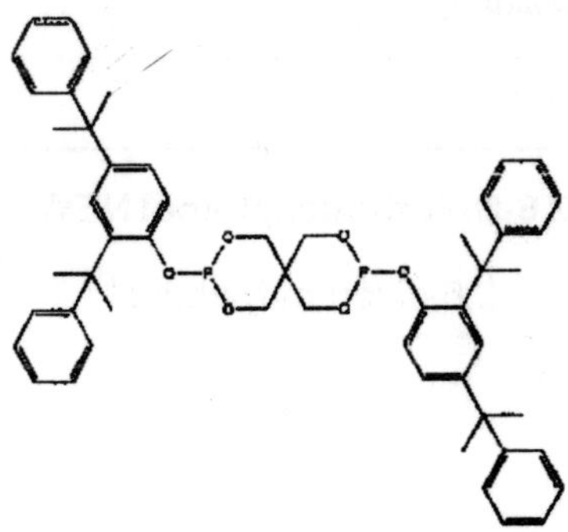

CAS 154862-43-8 **MF** $C_{53}H_{58}O_6P_2$ **MW** 852.97

Matrix	Cat. No.	Unit
NEAT	PLAS-AX-111N	50 mg

Dipentamethylenethiuram tetrasulfide NEW

Piperidine, 1,1'-(tetrathiodicarbonothioyl)-bis-

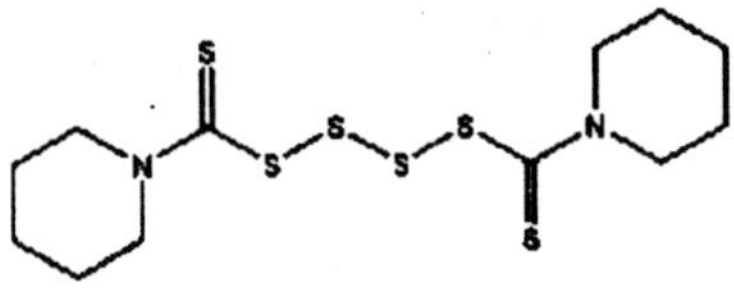

CAS 120-54-7 **MF** $C_{12}H_{20}N_2S_6$ **MW** 384.70

Matrix	Cat. No.	Unit
NEAT	PLAS-AX-104N	50 mg

2,6-Di-tert-butyl-4-ethylphenol NEW

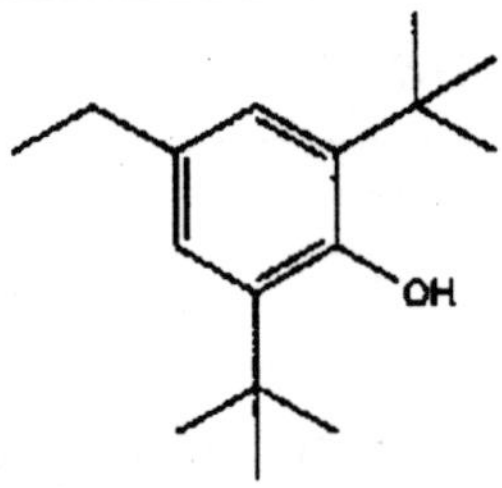

2,6-Bis(1,1-dimethylethyl)-4-ethylphenol

CAS 4130-42-1 **MF** $C_{16}H_{26}O$ **MW** 234.38

Matrix	Cat. No.	Unit
NEAT	PLAS-AX-107N	50 mg

2,6-Di-tert-butylphenol NEW

2,6-di-tert-butylphenol

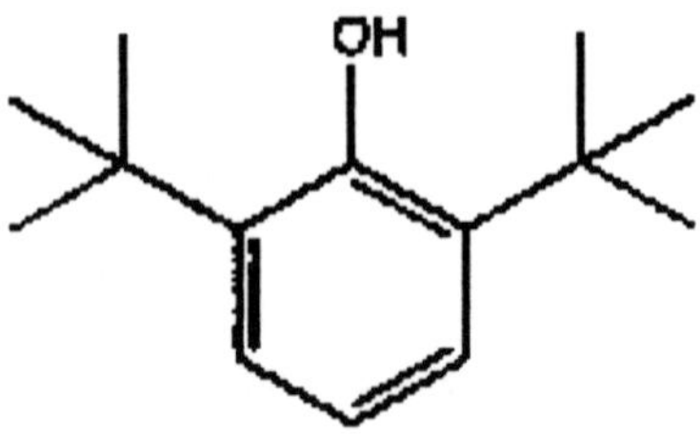

CAS 128-39-2 **MF** $C_{14}H_{22}O$ MW 206.32

Matrix	Cat. No.	Unit
NEAT	PLAS-AX-112N	50 mg

Ethanox® 330

1,3,5-trimethyl-2,4,6-tris(3,5-di-tert-butyl-4-hydroxybenzyl) benzene

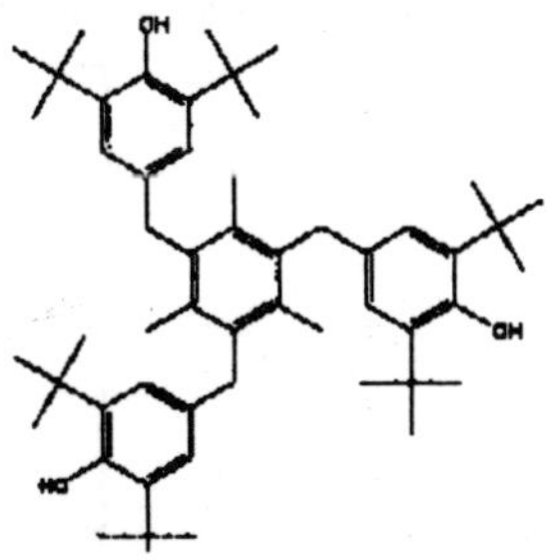

Albemarle Corporation
CAS 1709-70-2 **MF** $C_{54}H_{78}O_3$ **MW** 775.32

Matrix	Cat. No.	Unit
1000 µg/mL in Hexane	PLAS-AX-021S	1 mL
NEAT	PLAS-AX-021N	50 mg

Ethaphos® 368

tris(2,4-di-tert-butylphenyl) phosphite

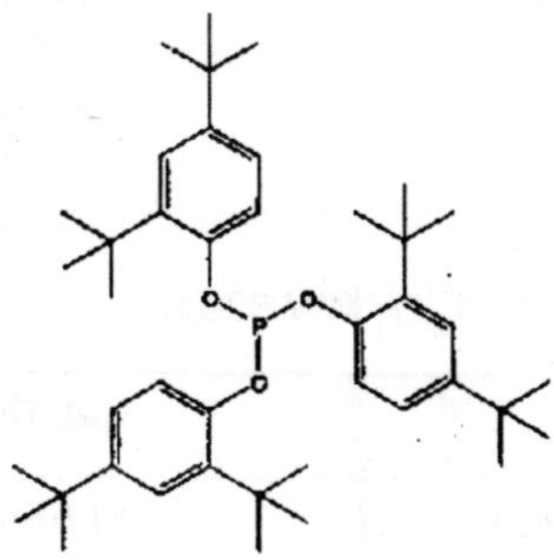

Albemarle Corporation
CAS 31570-04-4 **MF** $C_{42}H_{63}O_3P$ **MW** 646.92

Matrix	Cat. No.	Unit
1000 µg/mL in Hexane	PLAS-AX-074S	1 mL
NEAT	PLAS-AX-074N	50 mg

Ethanox® 310

penterythritol tetrakis (3-(3,5-di-t-butyl-4-hydroyphenyl) propionate)

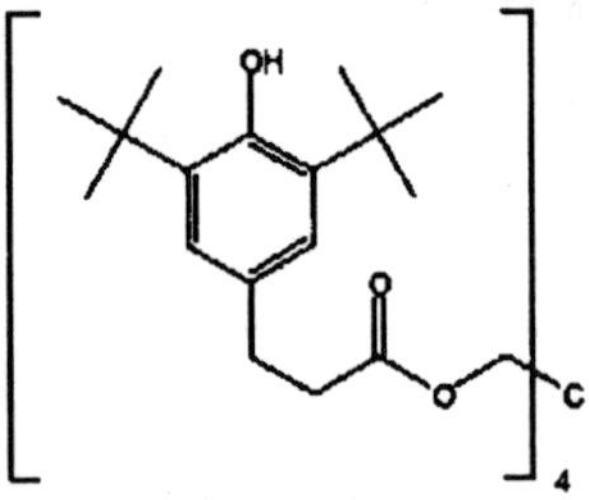

Albemarle Corporation

CAS 6683-19-8 **MF** $C_{73}H_{108}O_{12}$ **MW** 1177.65

Matrix	Cat. No.	Unit
1000 µg/mL in Hexane	PLAS-AX-086S	1 mL
NEAT	PLAS-AX-086N	50 mg

Ethanox® 376

3,5-di-tert-butyl-4-hydroxyhydrocinnamic acid, octadecyl ester

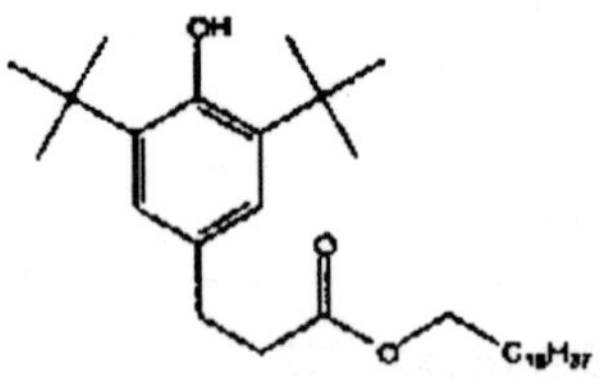

Albemarle Corporation

CAS 2082-79-3 **MF** $C_{35}H_{62}O_3$ **MW** 530.87

Matrix	Cat. No.	Unit
1000 µg/mL in Hexane	PLAS-AX-054S	1 mL
NEAT	PLAS-AX-054N	50 mg

2,2'-Ethylidene-bis(4,6-di-tert-butylphenol) NEW

Phenol, 2,2'-ethylidenebis[4,6-bis(1,1-dimethylethyl)-

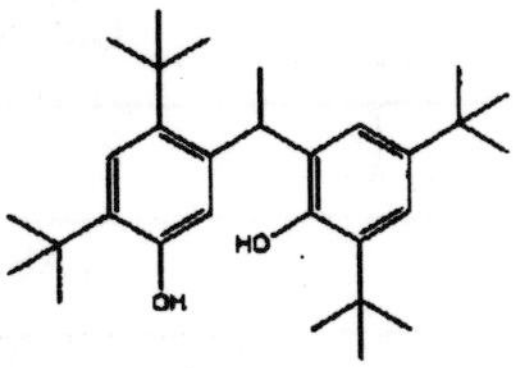

CAS 35958-30-6 **MF** $C_{30}H_{46}O_2$ **MW** 438.69

Matrix	Cat. No.	Unit
NEAT	PLAS-AX-106N	50 mg

Ethanox® 323

nonylphenol disulfide oligomer

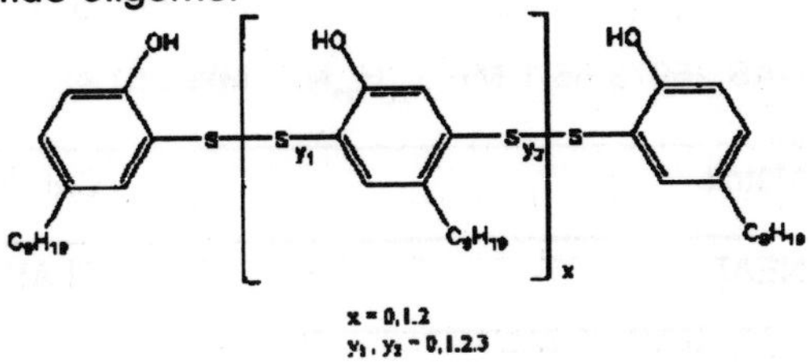

Albemarle Corporation

CAS MF MW

Matrix	Cat. No.	Unit
1000 μg/mL in Hexane	PLAS-AX-082S	1 mL
NEAT	PLAS-AX-082N	50 mg

Ethanox® 702

4,4'-methylene bis(2,6—di-tert-butylphenol)

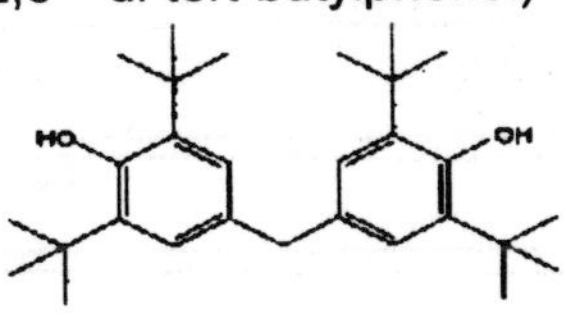

Albemarle Corporation

CAS 118-82-1 **MF** $C_{29}H_{44}O_2$ **MW** 424.66

Matrix	Cat. No.	Unit
1000 µg/mL in Hexane	PLAS-AX-025S	1 mL
NEAT	PLAS-AX-025N	50 mg

2-(2'-Hydroxy-3',5'-di-tert-amylphenyl) benzotriazole NEW

2-(benzotriazol-2-yl)-4,6-bis(2-methylbutan-2-yl) phenol

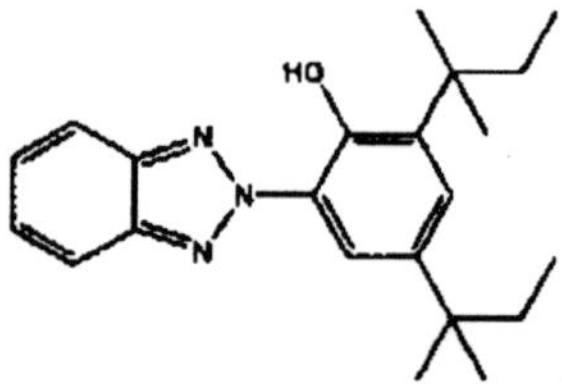

CAS 25973-55-1 **MF** $C_{22}H_{29}N_3O$ **MW** 351.49

Matrix	Cat. No.	Unit
NEAT	PLAS-AX-095N	50 mg

Ethanox® 703

2,6-di-tert-butyl-N,N-dimethylamino-p-cresol

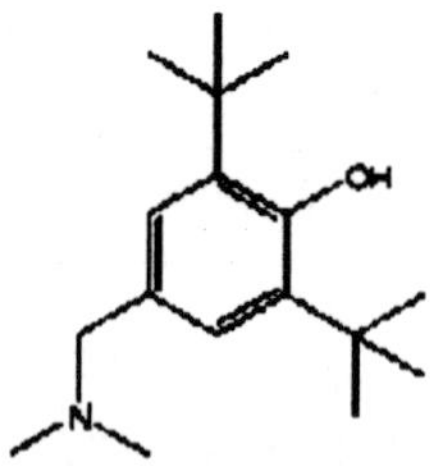

Albemarle Corporation

CAS 88-27-7 **MF** $C_{17}H_{29}NO$ **MW** 263.42

Matrix	Cat. No.	Unit
1000 µg/mL in Hexane	PLAS-AX-085S	1 mL
NEAT	PLAS-AX-085N	50 mg

Irganox® 245

triethyleneglycol bis[3-(3'-tert-butyl-4'hydroxy-5'-methylphenol) propionate]

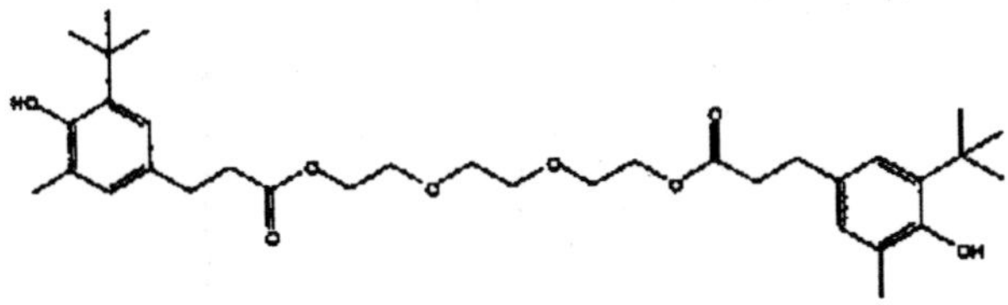

Ciba Specialty Chemicals

CAS 36443-68-2 **MF** $C_{34}H_{50}O_8$ **MW** 586.76

Matrix	Cat. No.	Unit
1000 µg/mL in Hexane	PLAS-AX-070S	1 mL
NEAT	PLAS-AX-070N	50 mg

Irganox® 1035

thiodiethylene bis(3,5-di-tert-butyl-4-hydroxyhydrocinnamate)

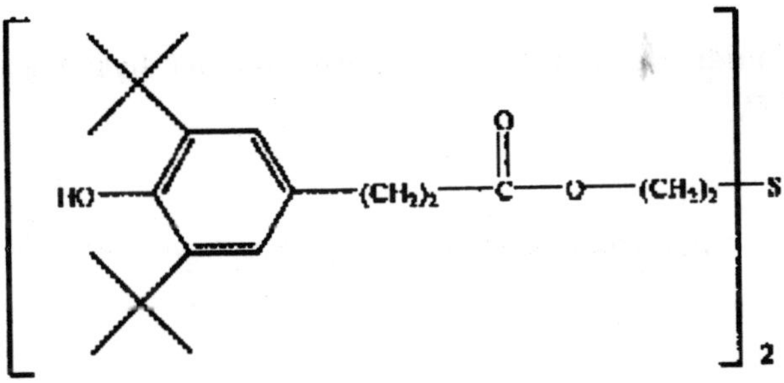

Ciba Specialty Chemicals

CAS 41484-35-9 **MF** $C_{38}H_{58}O_6S$ **MW** 642.93

Matrix	Cat. No.	Unit
1000 µg/mL in Hexane	PLAS-AX-069S	1 mL
NEAT	PLAS-AX-069N	50 mg

Irganox® 1425 WL

ethyl 3,5-di-tert-butyl-4-hydroxybenzylphosphonate, calcium salt and polyethylene-wax mixture

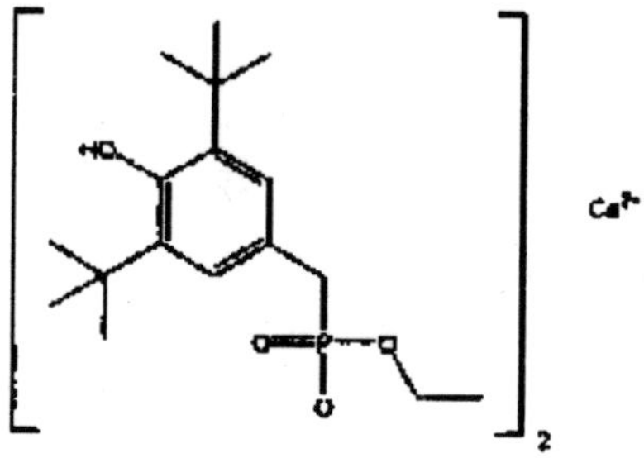

Ciba Specialty Chemicals

CAS 65140-91-2 / 9002-88-4 **MF** $2C_{17}H_{29}O_4P \cdot Ca(C_2H_4)x$ **MW** 695

Matrix	Cat. No.	Unit
NEAT	PLAS-AX-079N	50 mg

Irganox® 259

hexamethylene bis(3-(3,5-di-tert-butyl-4-hydroxyphenyl) propionate)

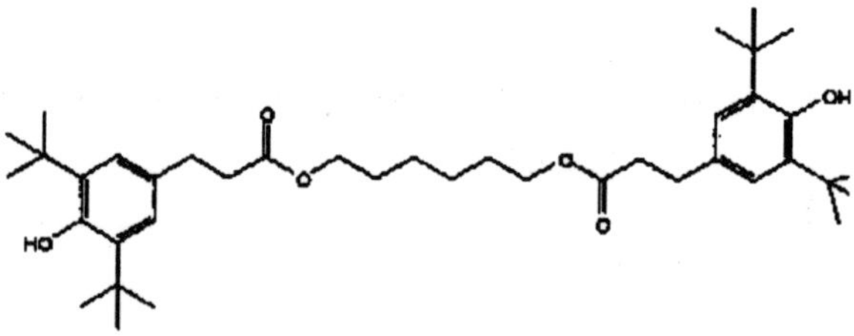

Ciba Specialty Chemicals

CAS 35074-77-2 **MF** $C_{40}H_{62}O_6$ **MW** 638.92

Matrix	Cat. No.	Unit
1000 μg/mL in Hexane	PLAS-AX-045S	1 mL
NEAT	PLAS-AX-045N	50 mg

Irganox® 1081

6,6'-di-tert-butyl-2,2'-thiodi-p-cresol

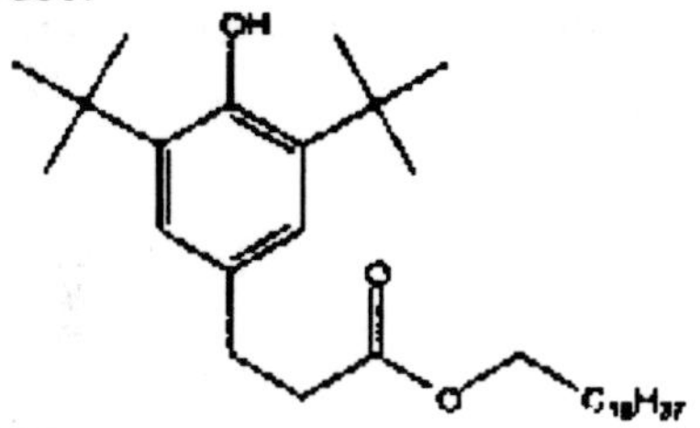

Ciba Specialty Chemicals

CAS 90-66-4 **MF** $C_{22}H_{30}O_2S$ **MW** 358.54

Matrix	Cat. No.	Unit
1000 µg/mL in Hexane	PLAS-AX-080S	1 mL
NEAT	PLAS-AX-080N	50 mg

Irganox® 3125

3,5-di-tert-butyl-4-hydroxyhydrocinnamic ester with 1,3,5-tris[2-hydroxyethyl]-s-triazine-2,4,6[1H,3H,5H]-trione

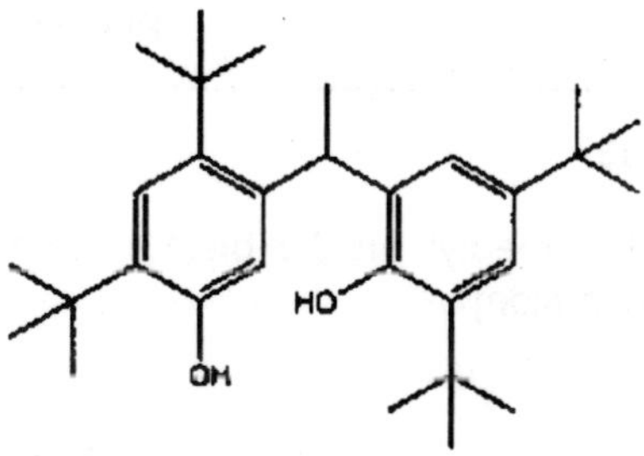

Ciba Specialty Chemicals

CAS 34137-09-2 **MF** $C_{60}H_{87}N_3O_{12}$ **MW** 1042.35

Matrix	Cat. No.	Unit
1000 µg/mL in Hexane:Acetone (95:5)	PLAS-AX-020S	1 mL
NEAT	PLAS-AX-020N	50 mg

Irganox® 565

2,4-bis(n-octylthio)-6-(4-hydroxy-3,5-di-tertbutylanilino)-1,3,5-triazine

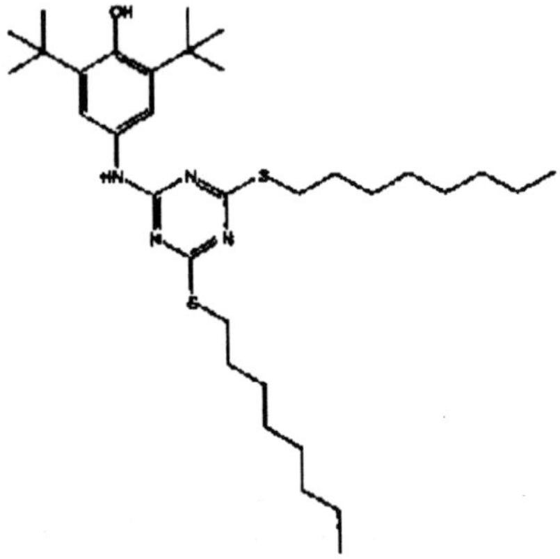

Ciba Specialty Chemicals

CAS 991-84-4 **MF** $C_{33}H_{56}N_4OS_2$ **MW** 588.96

Matrix	Cat. No.	Unit
1000 μg/mL in Hexane	PLAS-AX-014S	1 mL
NEAT	PLAS-AX-014N	50 mg

Irganox® 1098

N,N'-1,6-hexanediyl bis[3,5-bis(1,1-dimethylethyl)-4-hydroxy-benzenepropanamide]

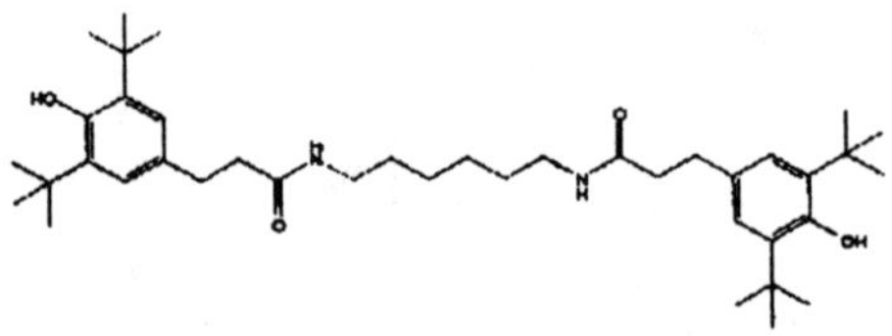

Ciba Specialty Chemicals

CAS 23128-74-7 **MF** $C_{40}H_{64}N_2O_4$ **MW** 636.95

Matrix	Cat. No.	Unit
1000 μg/mL in Hexane:Acetone 8:2	PLAS-AX-050S	1 mL
NEAT	PLAS-AX-050N	50 mg

Irganox® 3144 FF

1,3,5-Tris(3,5-di-tert-butyl-4-hydroxybenzyl)-1,3,5-triazine-2,4,6-(1H,3H,5H)-trione

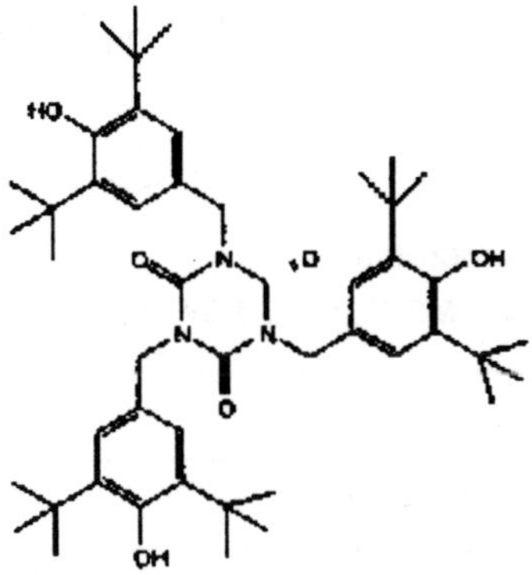

Ciba Specialty Chemicals

CAS 27676-62-6 **MF** $C_{48}H_{69}N_3O_6$ **MW** 784.08

Matrix	Cat. No.	Unit
1000 µg/mL in Hexane	PLAS-AX-078S	1 mL
NEAT	PLAS-AX-078N	50 mg

Irganox® E 201

alpha-tocopherol

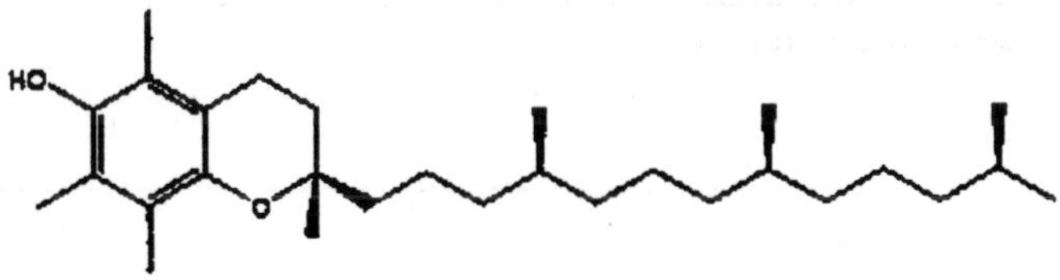

Ciba Specialty Chemicals

CAS 10191-41-0 **MF** $C_{29}H_{50}O_2$ **MW** 430.71

Matrix	Cat. No.	Unit
1000 µg/mL in Hexane	PLAS-AX-027S	1 mL
NEAT	PLAS-AX-027N	50 mg

Isonox® 232

2,6-di-tert-butyl-4-nonylphenol

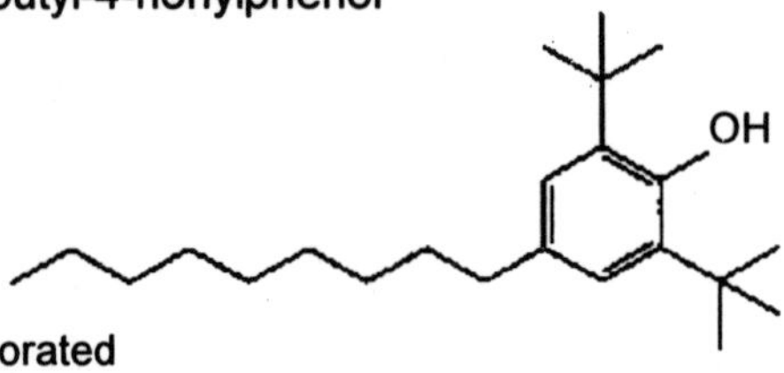

SI Group Incorporated

CAS 4306-88-1 **MF** $C_{23}H_{40}O$ **MW** 262.43

Matrix	Cat. No.	Unit
1000 µg/mL in Hexane	PLAS-AX-063S	1 mL
NEAT	PLAS-AX-063N	50 mg

Markstat® 60

Polyethylene glycol ether - contain < 20% sodium perchlorate

N/A

Chemtura Corporation

CAS N/A **MF** N/A **MW** N/A

Matrix	Cat. No.	Unit
1000 µg/mL in Hexane	PLAS-AX-028S	1 mL
NEAT	PLAS-AX-028N	50 mg

Irganox® MD 1024

1,2-bis(3,5-di-tert-butyl-4-hydroxyhydrocinnamoyl)hydrazide

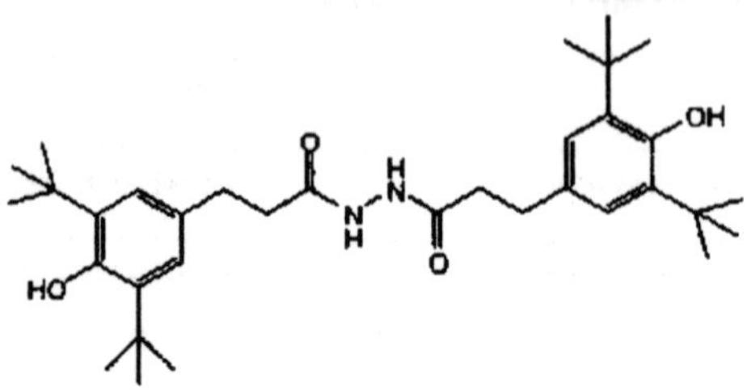

Ciba Specialty Chemicals

CAS 32687-78-8 **MF** $C_{34}H_{52}N_2O_4$ **MW** 552.79

Matrix	Cat. No.	Unit
1000 µg/mL in Hexane:Acetone 8:2	PLAS-AX-001S	1 mL
NEAT	PLAS-AX-001N	50 mg

Lowinox® AH25

2,5-bis(1,1-dimethylpropyl)-1,4-benzenediol

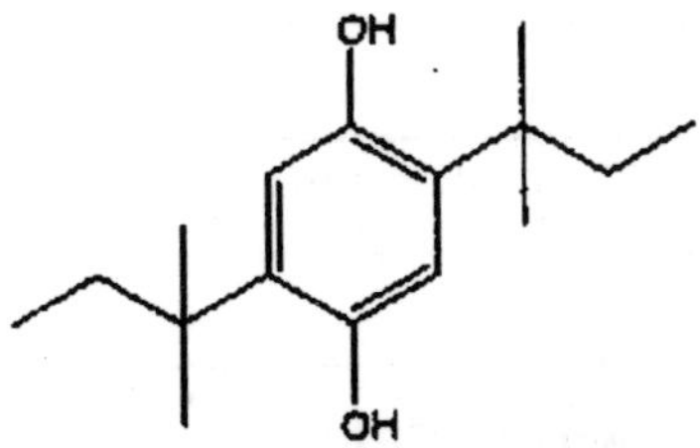

Chemtura Corporation

CAS 79-74-3 **MF** $C_{16}H_{26}O_2$ **MW** 250.38

Matrix	Cat. No.	Unit
1000 µg/mL in Hexane	PLAS-AX-016S	1 mL
NEAT	PLAS-AX-016N	50 mg

Naugard® 412S

beta-laurylthiopropionate

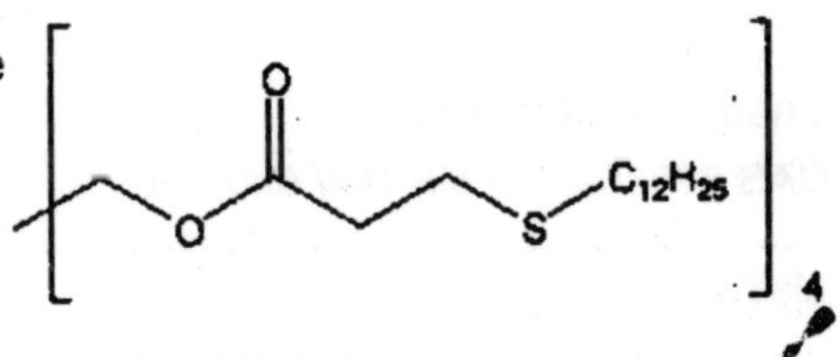

Chemtura Corporation

CAS 29598-76-3 **MF** $C_{65}H_{124}O_8S_4$ **MW** 1161.94

Matrix	Cat. No.	Unit
1000 µg/mL in Hexane	PLAS-AX-030S	1 mL
NEAT	PLAS-AX-030N	50 mg

Isonox® 132

2,6-di-tert-butyl-4-sec-butylphenol

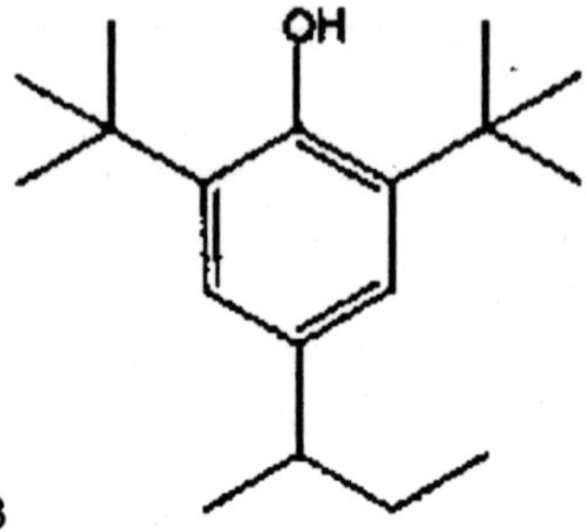

SI Group Incorporated

CAS 17540-75-9 **MF** $C_{18}H_{30}O$ **MW** 262.43

Matrix	Cat. No.	Unit
1000 µg/mL in Hexane	PLAS-AX-018S	1 mL
NEAT	PLAS-AX-018N	50 mg

Lowinox® CPL

Polymeric sterically hindered phenol

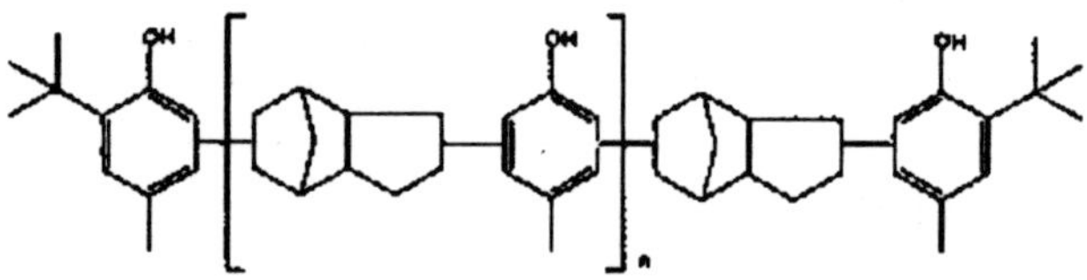

Chemtura Corporation

CAS 68610-51-5 **MF** **MW** 600-700

Matrix	Cat. No.	Unit
1000 µg/mL in Hexane	PLAS-AX-059S	1 mL
NEAT	PLAS-AX-059N	50 mg

Naugard® 445

4,4'-bis(alpha,alpha-dimethylbenzyl)diphenylamine

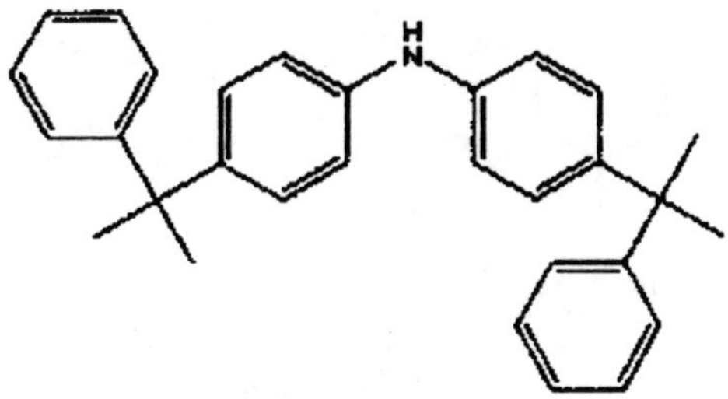

Chemtura Corporation

CAS 10081-67-1 **MF** $C_{30}H_{31}N$ **MW** 405.57

Matrix	Cat. No.	Unit
1000 µg/mL in Hexane	PLAS-AX-022S	1 mL
NEAT	PLAS-AX-022N	50 mg

Lowinox® TBM-6

4,4'-thiobis(2-tert-butyl-5-methylphenol)

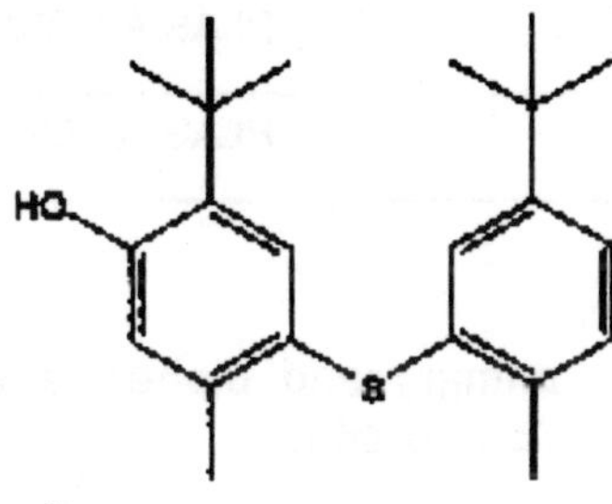

Chemtura Corporation

CAS 96-69-5 **MF** $C_{22}H_{30}O_2S$ **MW** 358.54

Matrix Cat. No. Unit		
1000 µg/mL in Hexane:Acetone(9:1)	PLAS-AX-024S	1 mL
NEAT	PLAS-AX-024N	50 mg

Naugard® 635 NEW

4-(1-phenylethyl)-N-[4-(1-phenylethyl)phenyl]aniline

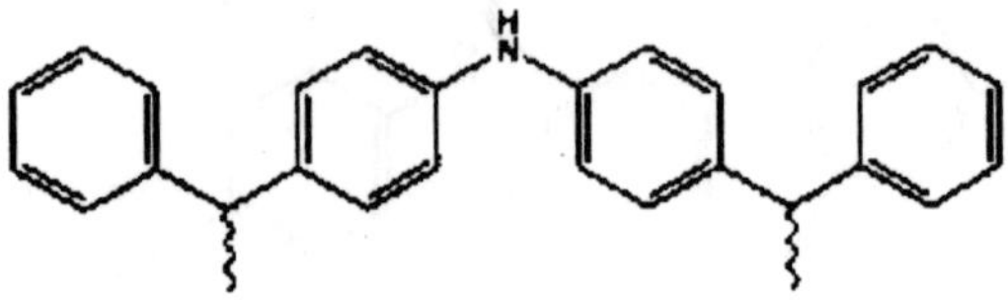

CAS 68442-68-2 **MF** $C_{38}H_{27}N$ **MW** 377.52

Matrix	Cat. No.	Unit
NEAT	PLAS-AX-113N	50 mg

Naugard® 956

proprietary blend of primary and secondary antioxidants

N/A

Chemtura Corporation

CAS MF MW

Matrix	Cat. No.	Unit
1000 µg/mL in Toluene	PLAS-AX-060S	1 mL
NEAT	PLAS-AX-060N	50 mg

Naugard® HM-22

blend of phenolic primary and diphenylamine secondary antioxidants (Naugards 76 and 445)

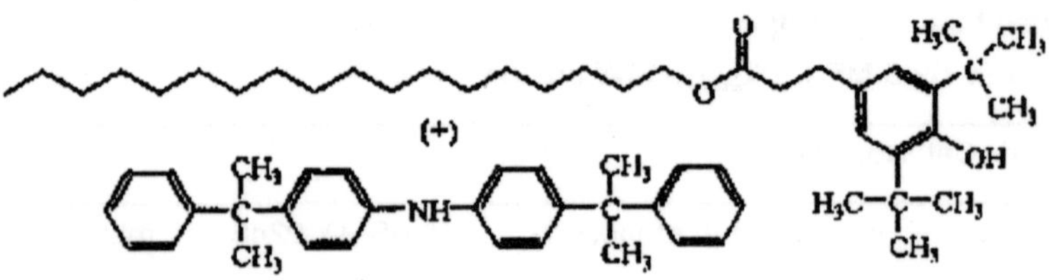

Chemtura Corporation

CAS 10081-67-1/2082-79-3 **MF** $C_{30}H_{31}N$ / $C_{35}H_{62}O_3$ **MW** 405.57/530.86

Matrix	Cat. No.	Unit
1000 μg/mL in Hexane	PLAS-AX-033S	1 mL
NEAT	PLAS-AX-033N	50 mg

Naugard® PHR

tris(mono-nonylphenyl) phosphite with up to 1% triisopropanol amine

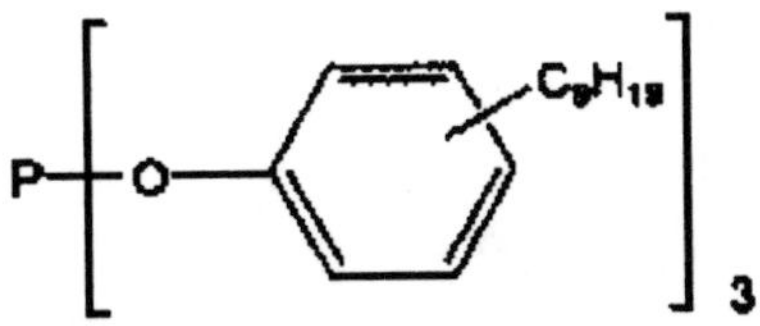

Chemtura Corporation

CAS 26523-78-4 **MF** C45H69O3P **MW** 689.00

Matrix	Cat. No.	Unit
1000 μg/mL in Hexane	PLAS-AX-076S	1 mL
NEAT	PLAS-AX-076N	50 mg

Naugard® A

acetone diphenylamine condensation products

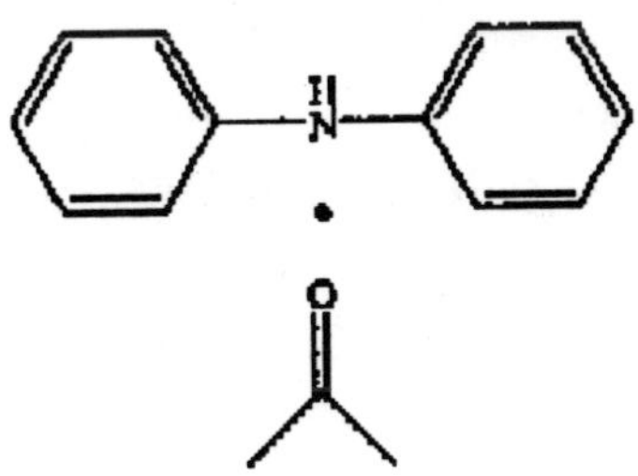

Chemtura Corporation

CAS 68412-48-6 **MF** $C_{12}H_{11}N \cdot C_3H_6O$ **MW** 227.31

Matrix	Cat. No.	Unit
1000 µg/mL in Hexane:Acetone (8:2)	PLAS-AX-026S	1 mL
NEAT	PLAS-AX-026N	50 mg

Naugard® J

N,N'-diphenyl-p-phenylenediamine

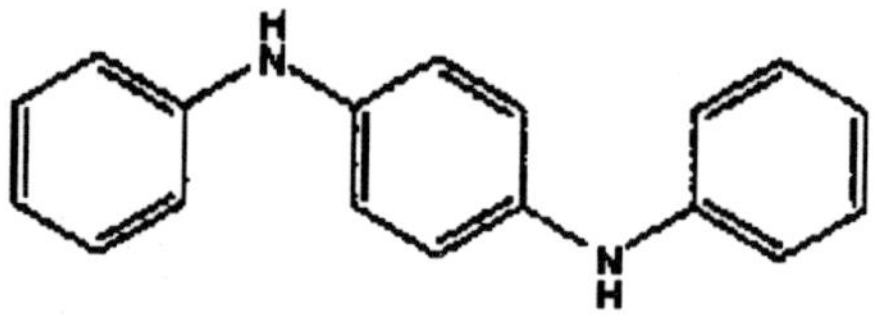

Chemtura Corporation

CAS 74-31-7 **MF** $C_{18}H_{16}N_2$ **MW** 260.36

Matrix	Cat. No.	Unit
1000 µg/mL in Hexane:Acetone(1:1)	PLAS-AX-048S	1 mL
NEAT	PLAS-AX-048N	50 mg

Naugard® PS-30

Benzenamine, N-phenyl, reaction products with 2,4,4-trimethy-lpentene

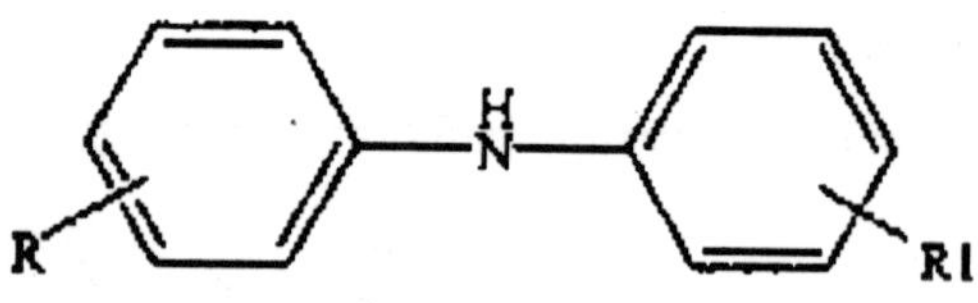

Chemtura Corporation

CAS 68411-46-1 **MF** $C_{12}H_{11}N \cdot C_8H_{16}$ **MW** N/A

Matrix	Cat. No.	Unit
1000 µg/mL in Hexane	PLAS-AX-038S	1 mL
NEAT	PLAS-AX-038N	50 mg

Naugard® B-25

1:1 blend of Naugard 10 & Naugard 424

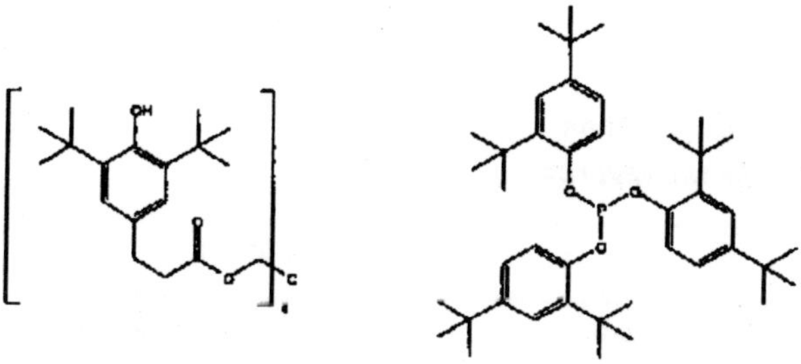

Chemtura Corporation

CAS 6683-19-8/31570-04-4 **MF** $C_{73}H_{108}O_{12}$ • $C_{42}H_{63}O_{3}P$ **MW** 1177.65 / 646.92

Matrix	Cat. No.	Unit
1000 µg/mL in Hexane	PLAS-AX-061S	1 mL
NEAT	PLAS-AX-061N	50 mg

Naugard® NBC

nickel dibutyl dithiocarbamate

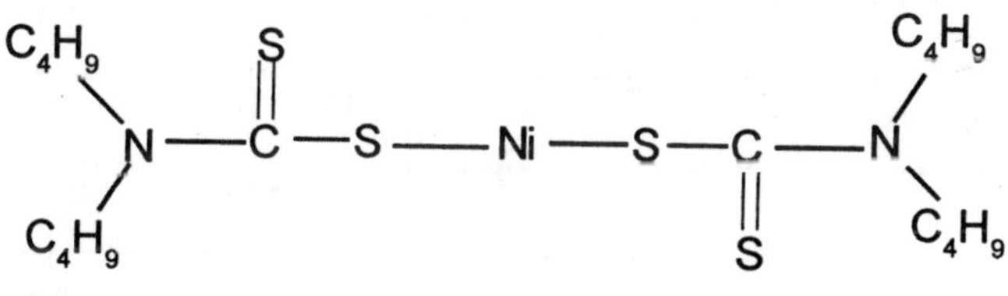

Chemtura Corporation

CAS 13927-77-0 **MF** $C_{18}H_{36}N_{2}NiS_{4}$ **MW** 467.45

Matrix	Cat. No.	Unit
1000 µg/mL in Hexane	PLAS-AX-051S	1 mL
NEAT	PLAS-AX-051N	50 mg

Naugard® PS-35

Butylated, octylated diphenylamine-2,6 di-tert-butyl-4-sec-butyl phenol

N/A

Chemtura Corporation

CAS N/A **MF** N/A **MW** N/A

Matrix	Cat.No.	Unit
1000 µg/mL in Hexane	PLAS-AX-046S	1 mL
NEAT	PLAS-AX-046N	50 mg

Naugard® BHT

2,6-di-tert-butyl-4-methylphenol

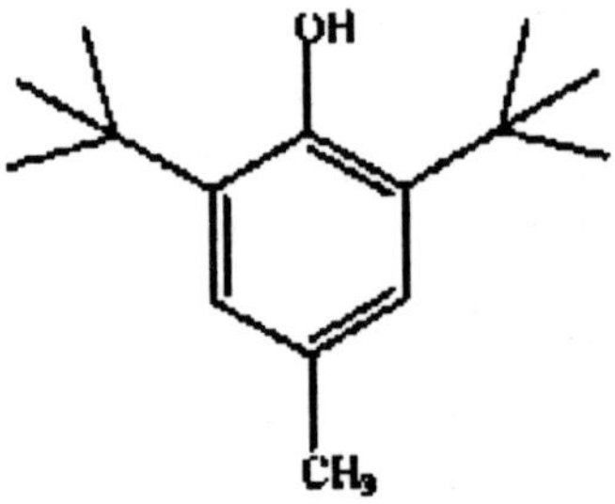

Chemtura Corporation

CAS 128-37-0 **MF** $C_{15}H_{24}O$ **MW** 220.35

Matrix	Cat. No.	Unit
1000 µg/mL in Hexane	PLAS-AX-017S	1 mL
NEAT	PLAS-AX-017N	50 mg

Naugard® PANA

N-phenyl-1-naphthylamine

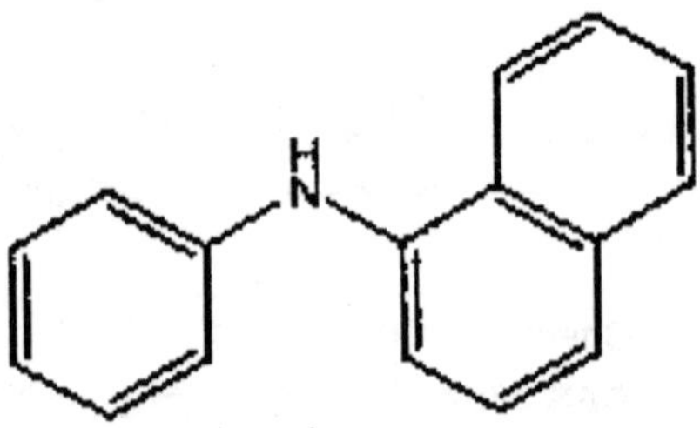

Chemtura Corporation

CAS 90-30-2 **MF** $C_{16}H_{13}N$ **MW** 219.28

Matrix	Cat. No.	Unit
1000 µg/mL in Hexane	PLAS-AX-058S	1 mL
NEAT	PLAS-AX-058N	50 mg

Naugard® Q Extra

1,2-dihydro-2,2,4-trimethylquinoline (polymerized)

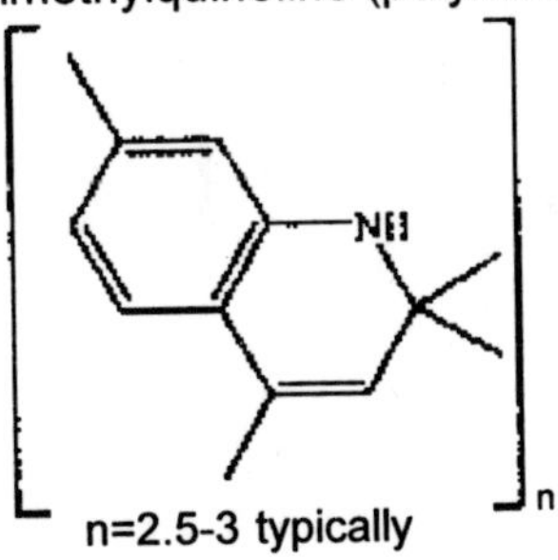

Chemtura Corporation

CAS 26780-96-1 **MF** $(C_{12}H_{15}N)_n$ **MW** (173.25)n

Matrix	Cat. No.	Unit
1000 µg/mL in Hexane	PLAS-AX-002S	1 mL
NEAT	PLAS-AX-002N	50 mg

Naugard® RM-51

Tris(mono-nonylphenyl)phosphite, 2,2'-methylene bis(4-methylene bis(4-methyl-6-nonylphenol)

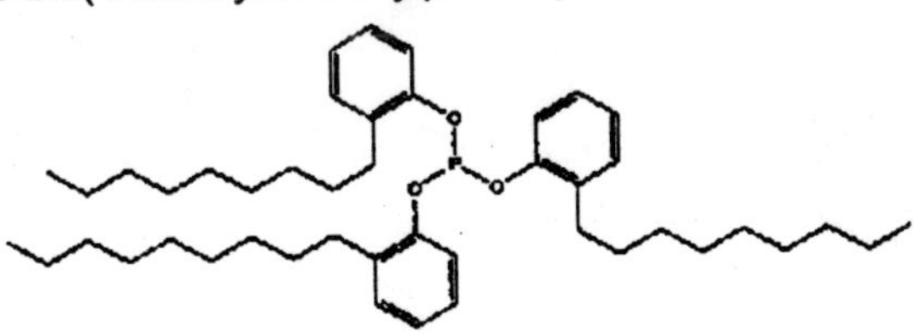

Chemtura Corporation

CAS 26523-78-4 **MF** $C_{45}H_{69}C_3P$ **MW** 689.00

Matrix	Cat. No.	Unit
1000 µg/mL in Hexane	PLAS-AX-034S	1 mL
NEAT	PLAS-AX-034N	50 mg

Naugard® XL-1

2,2'-oxamidobis[ethyl-3-(3,5-di-tert-butyl-4-hydroxyphenyl) propionate]

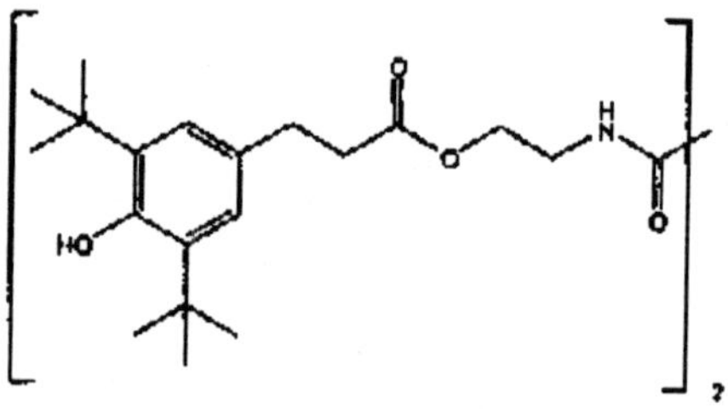

Chemtura Corporation

CAS 70331-94-1 **MF** $C_{40}H_{60}N_2O_8$ **MW** 697.00

Matrix	Cat. No.	Unit
1000 µg/mL in Hexane:Acetone 8:2	PLAS-AX-008S	1 mL
NEAT	PLAS-AX-008N	50 mg

Bis(2,2,6,6-tetramethyl-4-piperidyl) sebacate NEW

bis(2,2,6,6-tetramethylpiperidin-4-yl) decanedioate

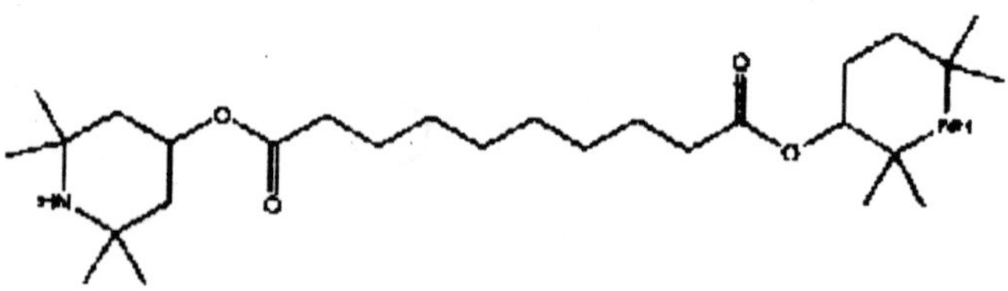

CAS 52829-07-9 **MF** $C_{28}H_{52}N_2O_4$ **MW** 480.72

Matrix	Cat. No.	Unit
NEAT	PLAS-AX-097N	50 mg

Naugard® Super Q

1,2-dihydro-2,2,4-trimethylquinoline (polymerized)

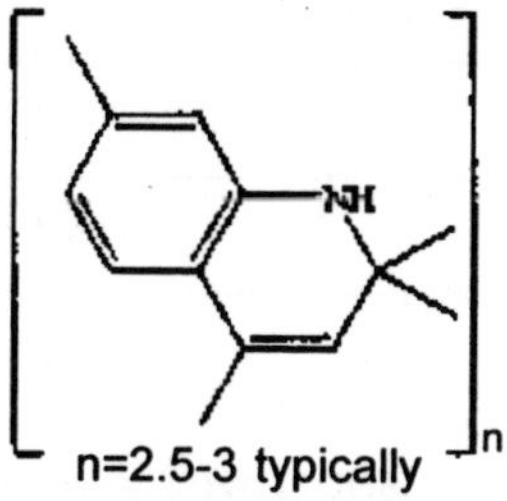

Chemtura Corporation

CAS 147-47-7 **MF** $(C_{12}H_{15}N)_n$ **MW** $(173.25)_n$

Matrix	Cat. No.	Unit
1000 μg/mL in Hexane	PLAS-AX-003S	1 mL
NEAT	PLAS-AX-003N	50 mg

Propyl gallate NEW

propyl 3,4,5-trihydroxybenzoate

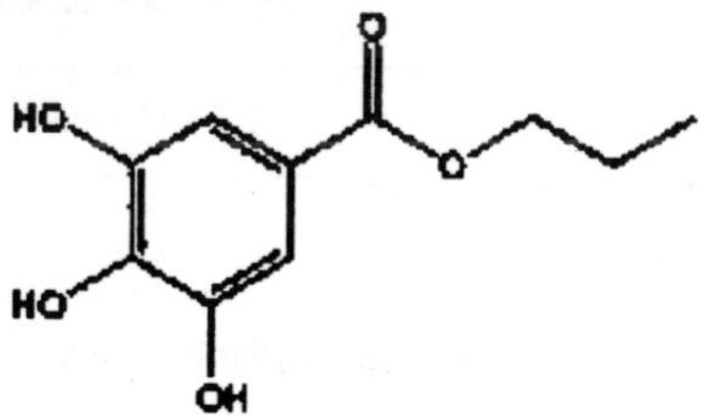

CAS 121-79-9 **MF** $C_{10}H_{12}O_5$ **MW** 212.20

Matrix	Cat. No.	Unit
NEAT	PLAS-AX-109N	50 mg

2,2'-(2,5-thiophenediyl)bis(5-tert-butylbenzoxazole) NEW

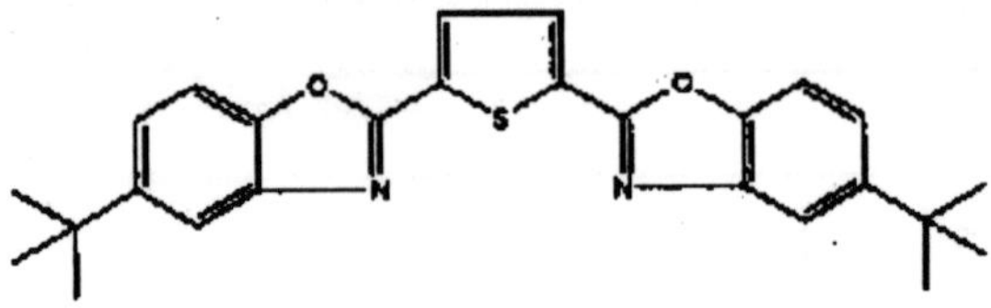

CAS 7128-64-5 **MF** $C_{26}H_{26}N_2O_2S$ **MW** 430.56

Matrix	Cat. No.	Unit
NEAT	PLAS-AX-098N	50 mg

Santicizer® 278

benzyl 3-isobutyrloxy-1-isopropyl-2,2-dimethylpropyl phthalate

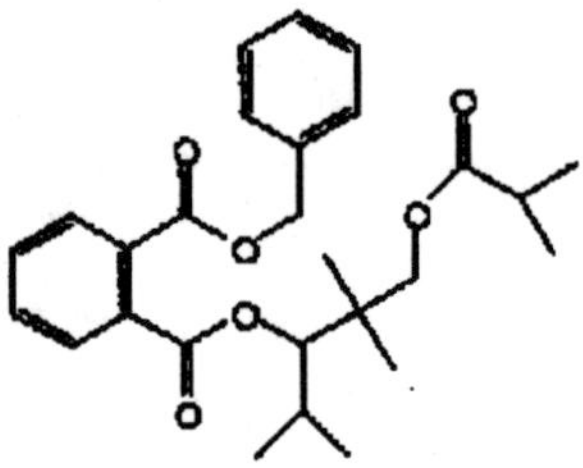

Chemtura Corporation

CAS 16883-83-3 **MF** $C_{27}H_{34}O_6$ **MW** 454.56

Matrix	Cat. No.	Unit
1000 µg/mL in Hexane	PLAS-AX-029S	1 mL
NEAT	PLAS-AX-029N	50 mg

Ultranox® 626

bis(2,4-di-tert-butylphenyl)pentaerythritol diphosphite

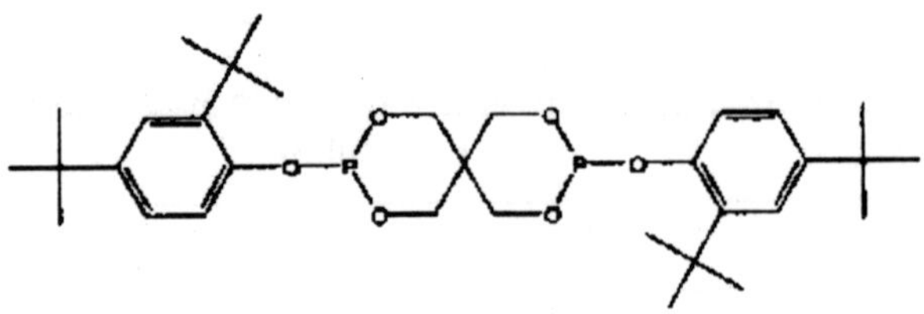

Chemtura Corporation

CAS 26741-53-7 **MF** $C_{33}H_{50}O_6P_2$ **MW** 604.62

Matrix	Cat. No.	Unit
1000 μg/mL in Hexane	PLAS-AX-031S	1 mL
NEAT	PLAS-AX-031N	50 mg

ANTIOZONANTS

Antiozonants are materials added to plastics to slow the deterioration of the finished product that occurs from exposure to ozone. Antiozonants typically work by migrating to the surface of the product and then create an ozone-impermeable barrier or skin on the surface.

Akrochem® NIBUD

nickel dibutyl dithiocarbamate

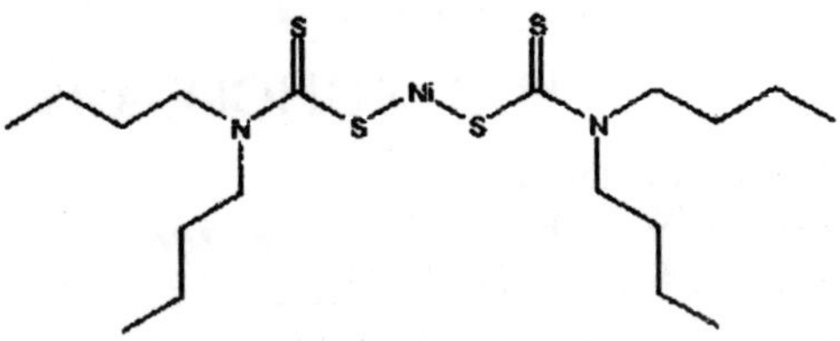

Akrochem Corporation

CAS 13927-77-0 **MF** $C_{18}H_{36}N_2NiS_4$ **MW** 467.45

Matrix	Cat. No.	Unit
1000 μg/mL in Hexane	PLAS-AZ-001S	1 mL
NEAT	PLAS-AZ-001N	50 mg

Akrowax™ 195 NEW

A highly refined petroleum wax which is comprised of long chain saturated hydrocarbon molecules

CAS 121-79-9 **MF** N/A **MW** N/A

Matrix	Cat. No.	Unit
NEAT	PLAS-AZ-002N	50 mg

BLOWING AGENTS/BLOWING AGENTS, PLASTICIZER

Blowing agents are sometimes also called chemical foaming agents. They are used to release gas into the plastic or resin. Blowing agents can be used to reduce weight, improve softness, provide insulation, add shock absorption properties or add resilience in the final product.

Chemical blowing agents (as opposed to physical blowing agents such as nitrogen gas) are principally organic chemicals that decompose at elevated temperatures to release a gas during decomposition that can add a cellular structure in the plastic.

CPW-100

chlorinated paraffin wax

$$H_3C-(CHCl)_n-CH_2-CH_3$$

Harwick Standard

CAS 63449-39-8 **MF** Unspecified **MW**

Matrix	Cat. No.	Unit
1000 µg/mL in Hexane	PLAS-BA-001S	1 mL
NEAT	PLAS-BA-001N	50 mg

Celogen® AZ

carbamoyliminourea

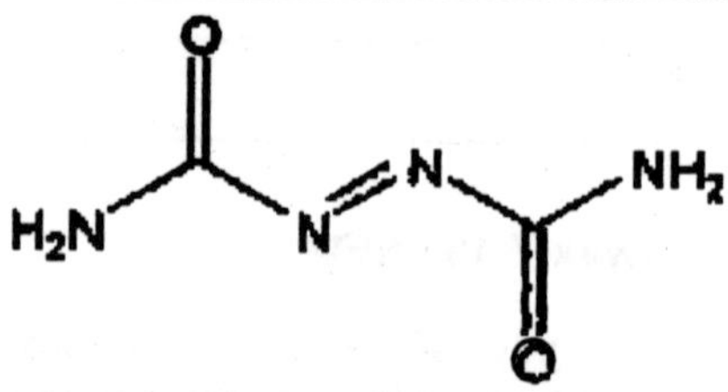

Chemtura Corporation

CAS 123-77-3 **MF** $C_2H_4N_4O_2$ **MW** 116.08

Matrix	Cat. No.	Unit
1000 μg/mL in DMSO	PLAS—BA-002=DMSO	1 mL
NEAT	PLAS-BA-002N	50 mg

Celogen® RA NEW

[(4-methylphenyl)sulfonylamino]urea

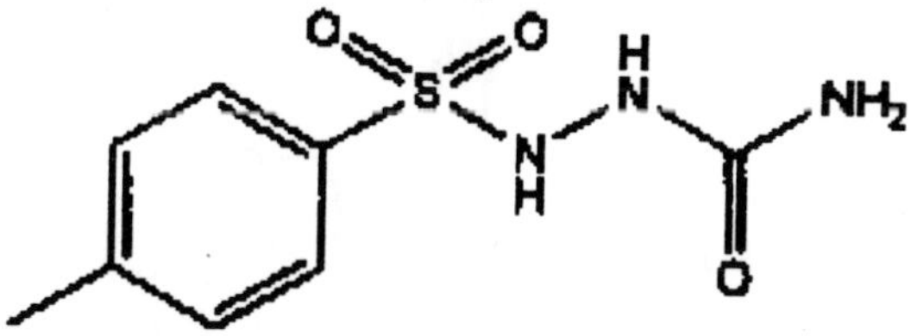

CAS 10396-10-8 **MF** $C_8H_{11}N_3O_3S$ **MW** 229.26

Matrix	Cat. No.	Unit
NEAT	PLAS-BA-003N	50 mg

COUPLING AGENTS

Coupling agents promote the physical or chemical interaction with the polymer.

Silquest® A-187

gamma-glycidoxypropyltrimethoxysilane

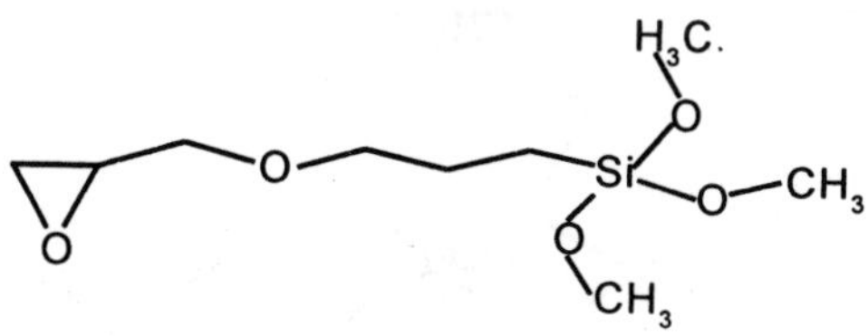

Chemtura Corporation

CAS 2530-83-8 **MF** $C_9H_{20}O_5Si$ **MW** 236.38

Matrix	Cat. No.	Unit
1000 µg/mL in Hexane	PLAS-CA-004S	1 mL
NEAT	PLAS-CA-004N	50 mg

Silquest® A-1102

gamma-aminopropyltriethoxysilane (Tech grade)

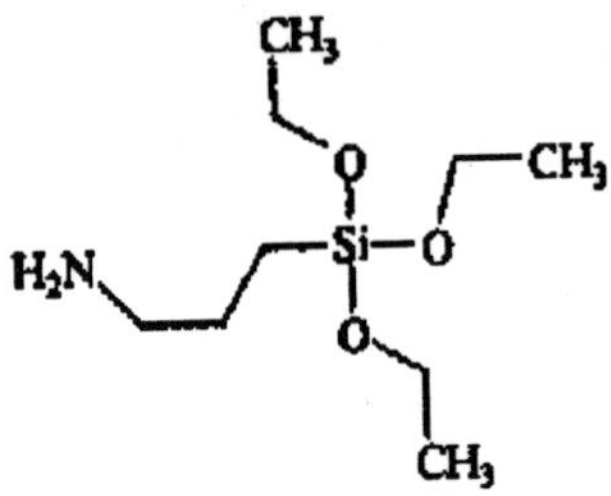

General Electric

CAS 919-30-2 **MF** $C_9H_{23}NO_3Si$ **MW** 221.37

Matrix	Cat. No.	Unit
1000 µg/mL in Hexane	PLAS-CA-003S	1 mL
NEAT	PLAS-CA-003N	50 mg

Silquest® A-137

octyltriethoxysilane

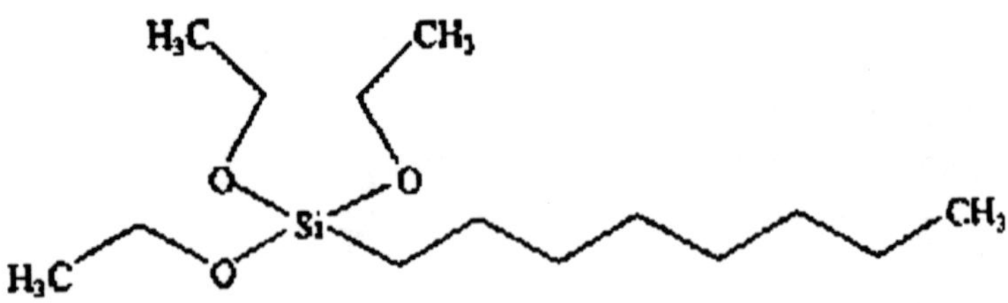

General Electric

CAS 2943-75-1 **MF** $C_{14}H_{32}O_3Si$ **MW** 276.55

Matrix	Cat. No.	Unit
1000 µg/mL in Hexane	PLAS-CA-005S	1 mL
NEAT	PLAS-CA-005N	50 mg

Silquest® A-1100

gamma-aminopropyltriethoxysilane

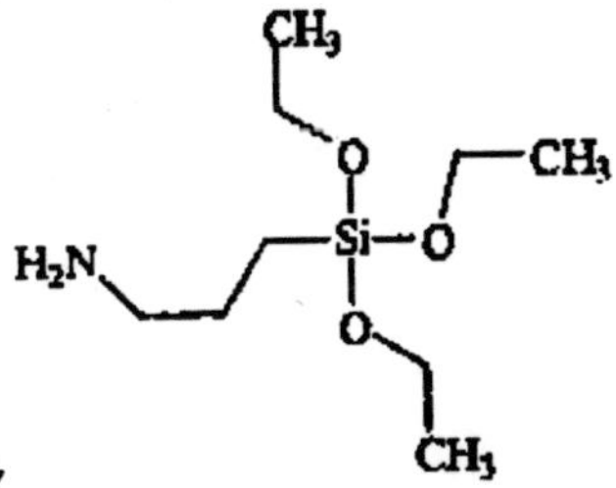

Chemtura Corporation

CAS 919-30-2 **MF** $C_9H_{23}NO_3Si$ **MW** 221.37

Matrix	Cat. No.	Unit
1000 µg/mL in Hexane	PLAS-CA-002S	1 mL
NEAT	PLAS-CA-002N	50 mg

Silquest® A-1289

bis-(triethoxysilypropyl)tetrasulfane

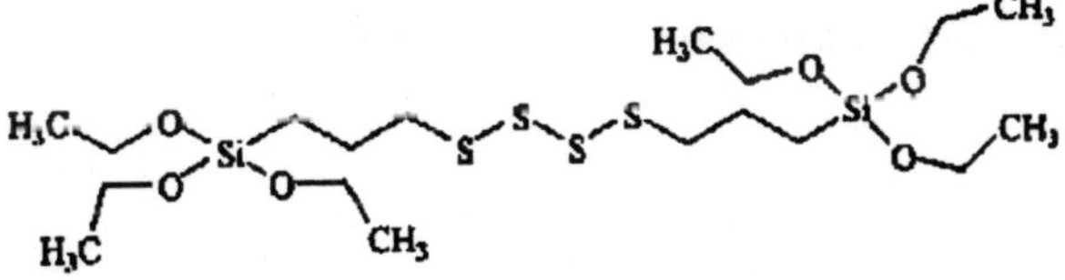

General Electric

CAS 211519-85-6 **MF** $C_{18}H_{42}O_6S_4Si_2$ **MW** 538.94

Matrix	Cat. No.	Unit
1000 µg/mL in Hexane	PLAS-CA-001S	1 mL
NEAT	PLAS-CA-001N	50 mg

Silquest® A-2171

vinylmethyldimethoxysilane

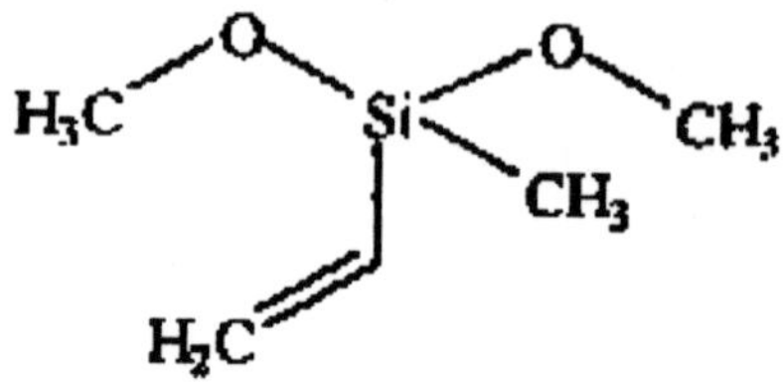

General Electric

CAS 16753-62-1 **MF** $C_5H_{12}O_2Si$ **MW** 132.24

Matrix	Cat. No.	Unit
1000 μg/mL in Hexane	PLAS-CA-006S	1 mL
NEAT	PLAS-CA-006N	50 mg

CROSS-LINKING AGENTS

Cross-linking is the polymerization reaction that branches out from the main molecular chain forming a network pattern of chemical bonds. Cross-linking agents enhance this crosslinking and bonding between polymer chains.

Cross-linking adds desirable properities such as: solidity, elasticity, impermeability to gases, and better electrical insulation. Cross-linking can also improve a rubber's resistance to chemicals, heat and abrasion.

F-300, F-1000, F-1500, F-2000, F-3000

stearic acid

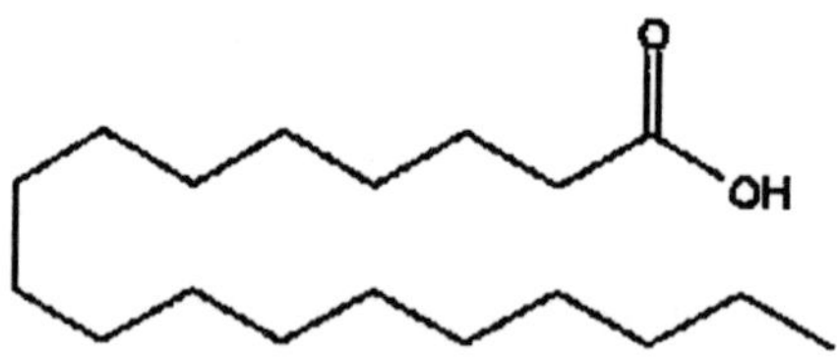

Harwick Standard

CAS 57-11-4 **MF** $C_{18}H_{36}O_2$ **MW** 284.48

Matrix	Cat. No.	Unit
1000 μg/mL in Hexane	PLAS-CL-006S	1 mL
NEAT	PLAS-CL-006N	50 mg

Perkacit® MBTS

2,2'-dithiobis(benzothiazole)

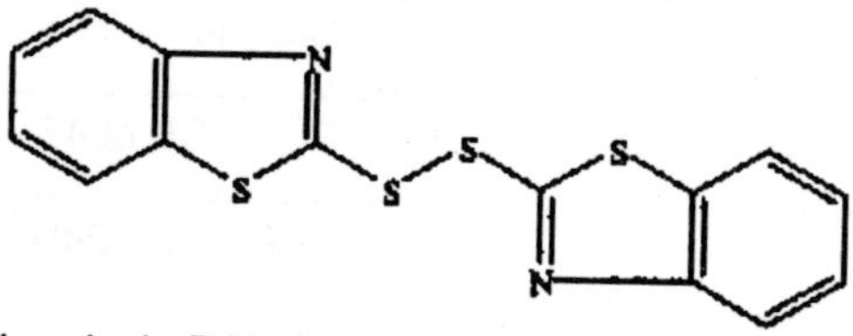

Akzo Nobel Chemicals B.V.

CAS 120-78-5 **MF** $C_{14}H_8N_2S_4$ **MW** 332.48

Matrix	Cat. No.	Unit
1000 µg/mL in Dichloromethane	PLAS-CL-001S-D	1 mL
NEAT	PLAS-CL-001N	50 mg

Perkacit® ZDEC

zinc diethyldithiocarbamate

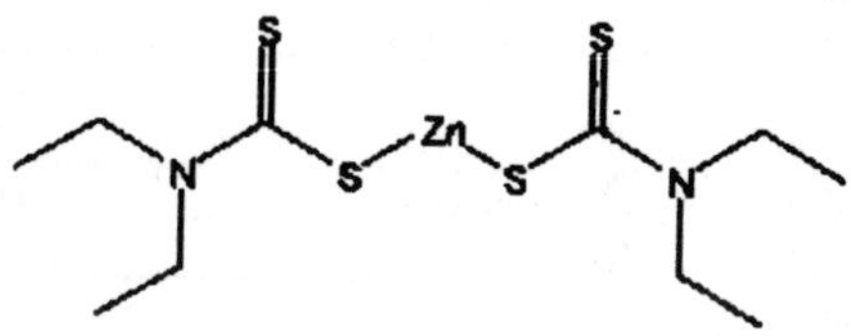

Akzo Nobel Chemicals B.V.

CAS 14324-55-1 **MF** $C_{10}H_{20}N_2S_2Zn$ **MW** 361.9

Matrix	Cat. No.	Unit
1000 µg/mL in Hexane	PLAS-CL-007S	1 mL
NEAT	PLAS-CL-007N	50 mg

Perkacit® DPG

N,N'-diphenylguanidine

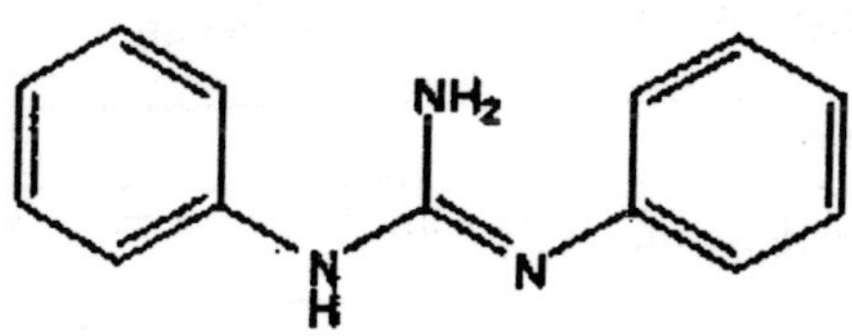

Akzo Nobel Chemicals B.V.

CAS 102-06-7 **MF** $C_{13}H_{13}N_3$ **MW** 211.27

Matrix	Cat. No.	Unit
1000 µg/mL in Hexane:Acetone(9:1)	PLAS-CL-004S	1 mL
NEAT	PLAS-CL-004N	50 mg

Perkacit® NDBC

nickel dibutyl dithiocarbamate

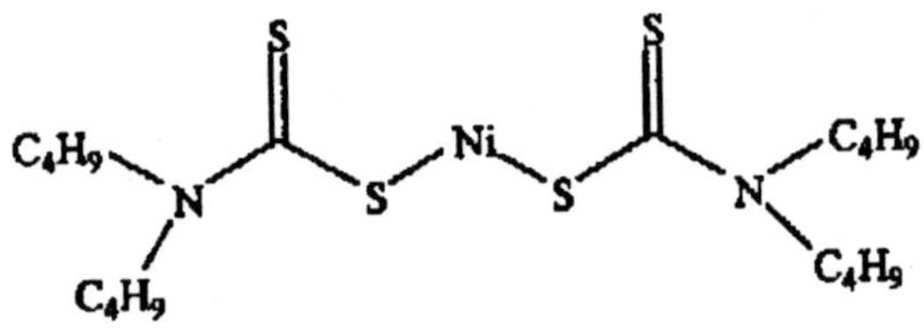

Akzo Nobel Chemicals B.V.

CAS 13927-77-0 **MF** $C_{18}H_{36}N_2NiS_4$ **MW** 467.45

Matrix	Cat. No.	Unit
1000 µg/mL in Hexane	PLAS-CL-005S	1 mL
NEAT	PLAS-CL-005N	50 mg

Perkacit® MBT

2-Mercaptobenzothiazole

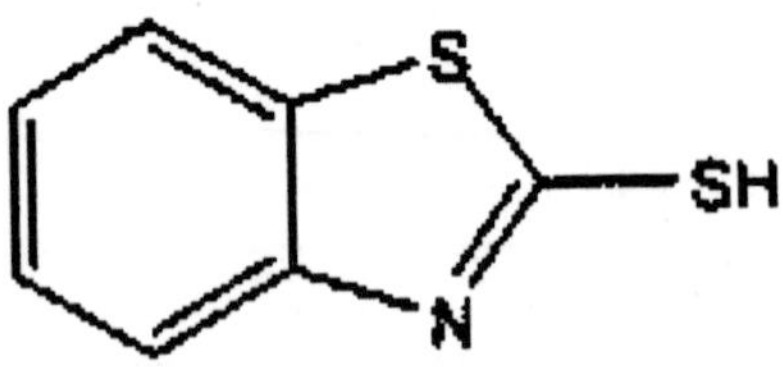

Akzo Nobel Chemicals B.V.

CAS 149-30-4 **MF** $C_7H_5S_2N$ **MW** 167.25

Matrix	Cat. No.	Unit
1000 µg/mL in Hexane	PLAS-CL-002S	1 mL
NEAT	PLAS-CL-002N	50 mg

Resimene® 3520

hexamethoxy methyl melamine

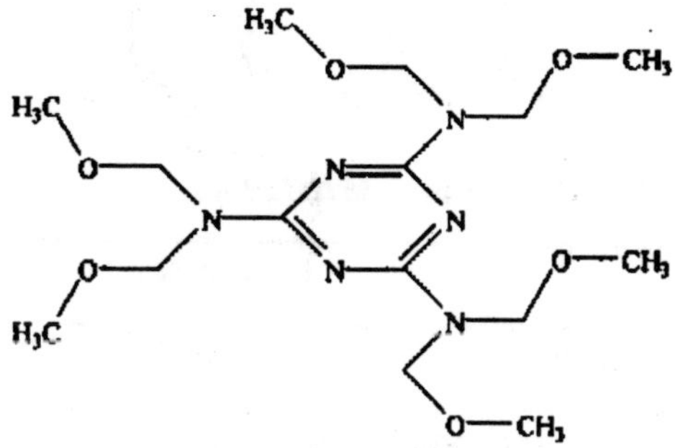

Cytec Surface Specialties

CAS 3089-11-0 **MF** $C_{15}H_{30}N_6O_6$ **MW** 390.51

Matrix	Cat. No.	Unit
1000 µg/mL in Hexane	PLAS-CL-003S	1 mL
NEAT	PLAS-CL-003N	50 mg

FLAME RETARDANTS

Flame retardants are added to inhibit ignition or the flammability of the end-use product. Flame retardants generally function by inhibiting the mechanisms of burning. Typical chemical elements found in compounds used as flame retardants are: aluminum, bromine, chorine, fluorine and sulfur.

Brominated flame retardants commonly used in polystyrene, polyesters, polyolefins, polyamides, epoxies and ABS. Decabromodiphenyl oxide is the most frequently used brominated flame retardant. The bromodiphenyl ethers are the most highly regulated of these compounds, and AccuStandard offers the most complete line of individual congeners available anywhere.

Some of these flame retardants are not typically added to polymers in processing, but can be found in a polymer matrix from leaching out of the contents. The largest example of this type is the Aroclors, which can often be found in a plastic matrix from having been in contact with a fluid containing these materials.

2,2',3,4,4',5',6-Heptabromodiphenyl ether

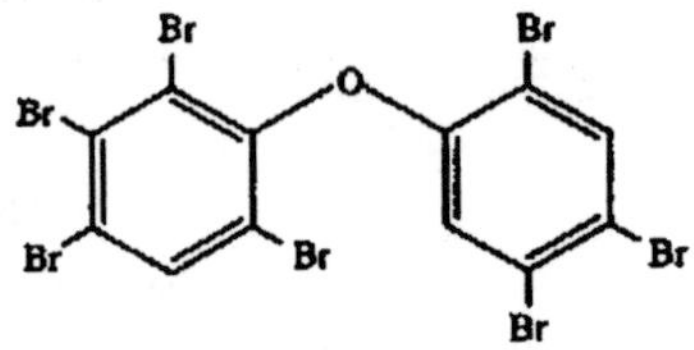

CAS 207122-16-5 **MF** $C_{12}H_3Br_7O$ **MW** 722.48

Matrix	Cat. No.	Unit
50 µg/mL in Isooctane	BDE-183S	1 mL

2,2',4,4',5,6'-Hexabromodiphenyl ether

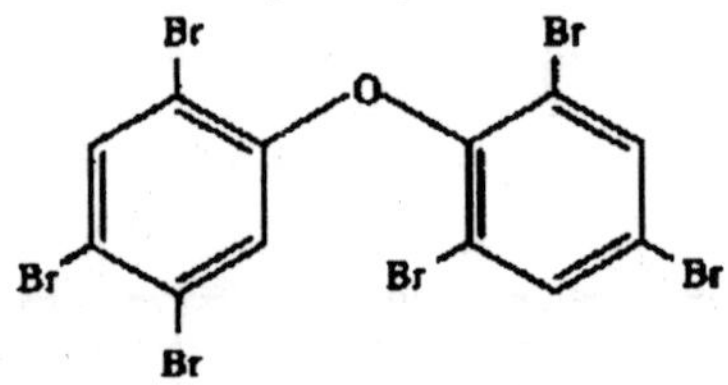

CAS 207122-15-4 **MF** $C_{12}H_4Br_6O$ **MW** 643.58

Matrix	Cat. No.	Unit
50 µg/mL in Isooctane	BDE-154S	1 mL

Aroclor® 1221

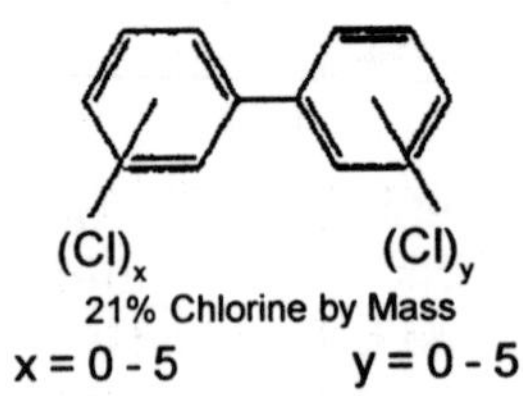

Monsanto

CAS 11104-28-2 **MF** Technical Mix **MW**

Matrix	Cat. No.	Unit
1000 μg/mL in Hexane	C-221S-H-10X	1 mL
NEAT	C-221N-50MG	50 mg

2,2',4,4'-Tetrabromodiphenyl ether

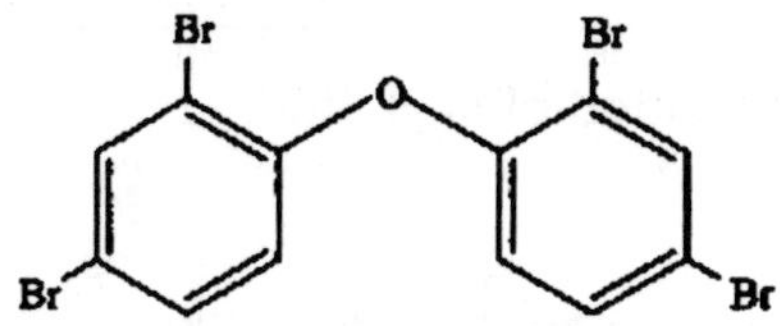

CAS 40088-47-9 **MF** $C_{12}H_6Br_4O$ **MW** 485.82

Matrix	Cat. No.	Unit
50 μg/mL in Isooctane	BDE-047S	1 mL

2,2',4,4',6-Pentabromodiphenyl ether

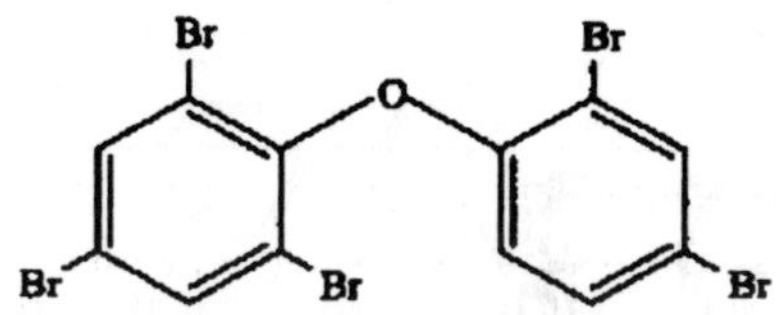

CAS 189084-64-8 **MF** $C_{12}H_5Br_5O$ **MW** 564.69

Matrix	Cat. No.	Unit
50 mg/mL in Isooctane	BDE-100S	1 mL

Aroclor® 1232

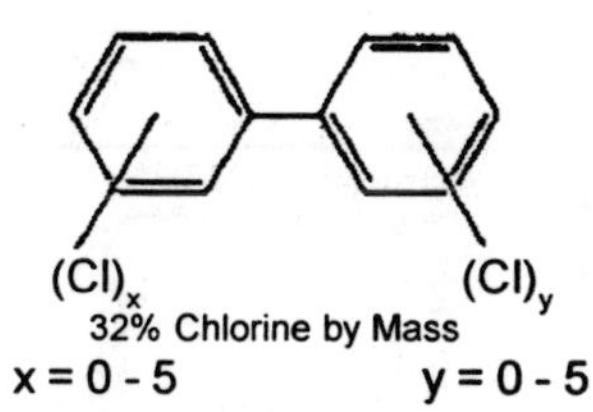

Monsanto

CAS 11141-16-5 **MF** Technical Mix **MW**

Matrix	Cat. No.	Unit
1000 µg/mL in Hexane	C-232S-H-10X	1 mL
NEAT	C-232N-50MG	50 mg

2,2',4,4',5-Pentabromodiphenyl ether

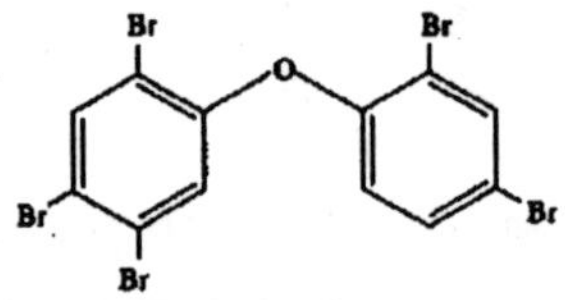

CAS 60348-60-9 **MF** $C_{12}H_5Br_5O$ **MW** 564.69

Matrix	Cat. No.	Unit
50 µg/mL in Isooctane	BDE-099S	1 mL

Aroclor® 1016

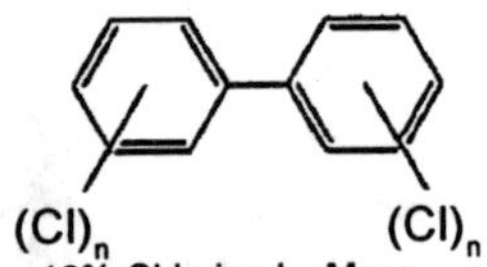

16% Chlorine by Mass

Monsanto

CAS 12674-11-2 **MF** Technical Mix **MW**

Matrix	Cat. No.	Unit
1000 µg/mL in Hexane	C-216S-H-10X	1 mL
NEAT	C-216N	100 mg

Aroclor® 1242

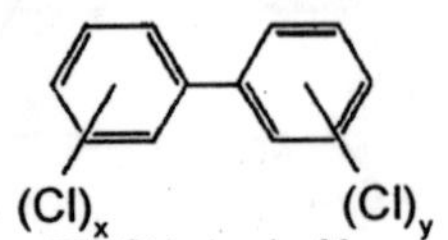

42% Chlorine by Mass

x = 0 - 5 y = 0 - 5

Monsanto

CAS 53469-21-9 **MF** Technical Mix **MW**

Matrix	Cat. No.	Unit
1000 µg/mL in Hexane	C-242S-H-10X	1 mL
NEAT	C-242N-50MG	50 mg

2,2',4,4',5,5'-Hexabromodiphenyl ether

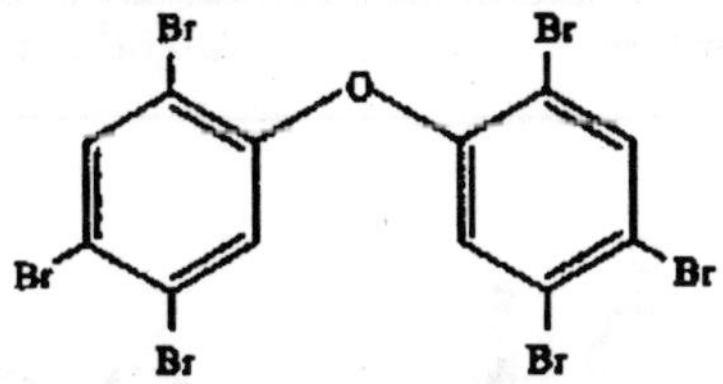

CAS 36483-60-0 **MF** $C_{12}H_4$-Br_6O **MW** 643.58

Matrix	Cat. No.	Unit
50 µg/mL in Isooctane	BDE-153S	1 mL

Aroclor® 1248

Monsanto

CAS 12672-29-6 **MF** Technical Mix **MW**

Matrix	Cat. No.	Unit
1000 µg/mL in Hexane	C-248S-H-10X	1 mL
NEAT	C-248N-50MG	50 mg

Aroclor® 1268

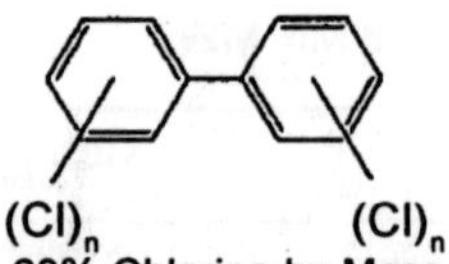

68% Chlorine by Mass

Monsanto

CAS 11100-14-4 **MF** Technical Mix **MW**

Matrix	Cat. No.	Unit
1000 μg/mL in Hexane	C-268S-H-10X	1 mL

Aroclor® 6050

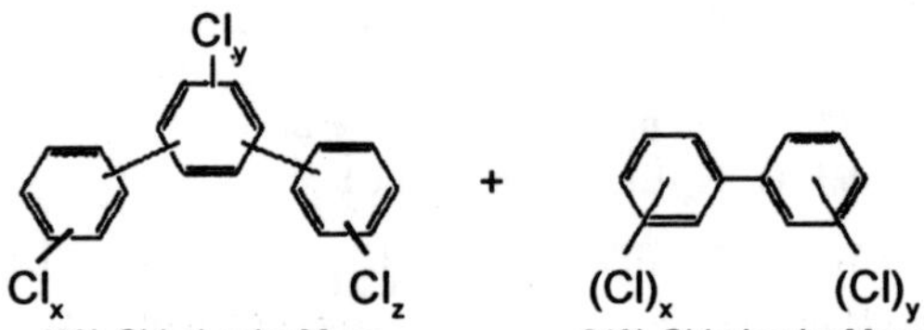

42% Chlorine by Mass   21% Chlorine by Mass

Monsanto

CAS **MF** Technical Mix **MW**

Matrix	Cat. No.	Unit
35 μg/mL in Toluene	T-6050S	1 mL

Aroclor® 1254

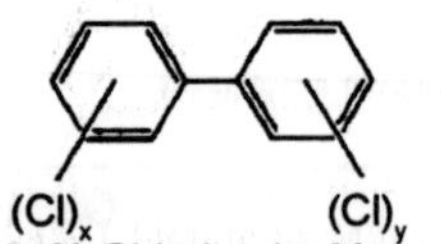

54% Chlorine by Mass

x = 0 - 5   y = 0 - 5

Monsanto

CAS 11097-69-1 **MF** Technical Mix **MW**

Matrix	Cat. No.	Unit
1000 μg/mL in Hexane	C-254S-H-10X	1 mL
NEAT	C-254N-50MG	50 mg

Aroclor® 5432

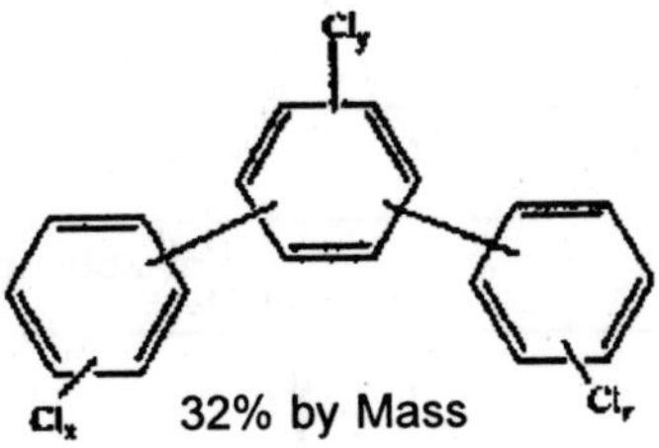

32% by Mass

Monsanto

CAS 63496-31-1 **MF** Technical Mix **MW**

Matrix	Cat. No.	Unit
35 µg/mL in Toluene	T-432S	1 mL

Decabromodiphenyl ether

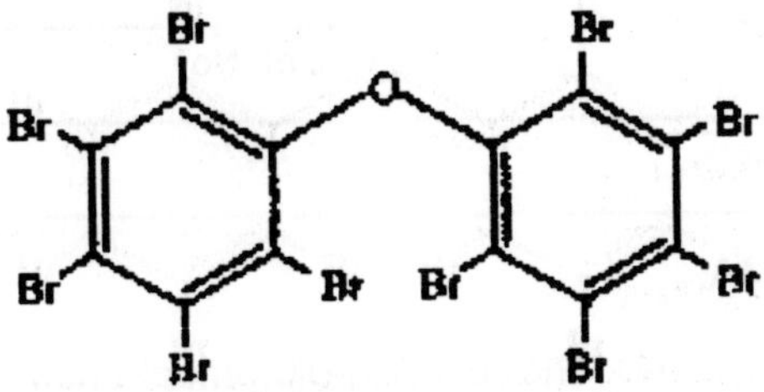

CAS 1163-19-5 **MF** $C_{12}Br_{10}O$ **MW** 959.22

Matrix	Cat. No.	Unit
50 µg/mL in Isooctane	BDE-209S	1 mL

Aroclor® 1260

Monsanto

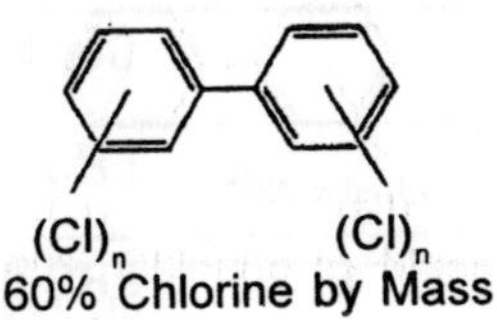

60% Chlorine by Mass

Monsanto

CAS 11096-82-5 **MF** Technical Mix **MW**

Matrix	Cat. No.	Unit
1000 µg/mL in Hexane	C-260S-H-10X	1 mL
NEAT	C-260N-50MG	50 mg

Aroclor® 5442

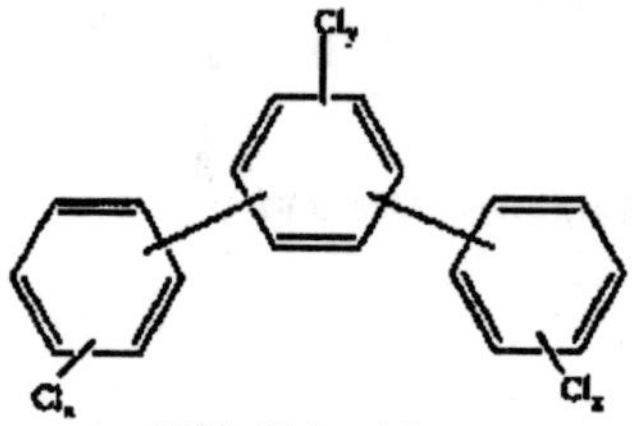

42% Cl by Mass

Monsanto

CAS 12642-23-8 **MF** Technical Mix **MW**

Matrix	Cat. No.	Unit
35 µg/mL in Toluene	T-442S	1 mL

Firemaster BP4A

4,4'-(1-methylethylidene) bis (2,6-dibromophenol)

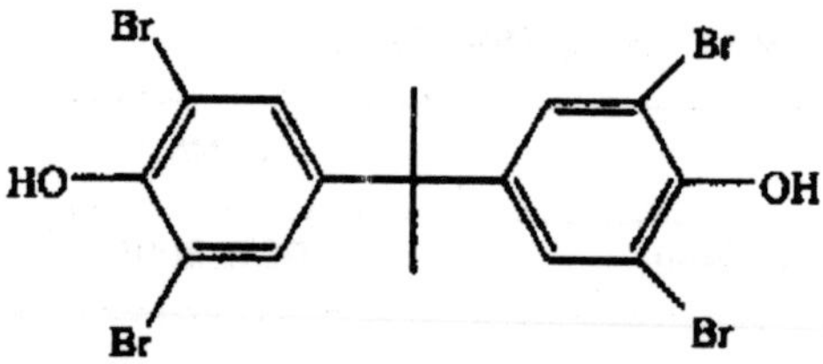

CAS 79-94-7 **MF** $C_{15}H_{12}Br_4O_2$ **MW** 543.91

Matrix	Cat. No.	Unit
100 µg/mL in Toluene	FRS-006S	1 mL
Neat	FRS-006N	10 mg

Aroclor® 1262

Monsanto

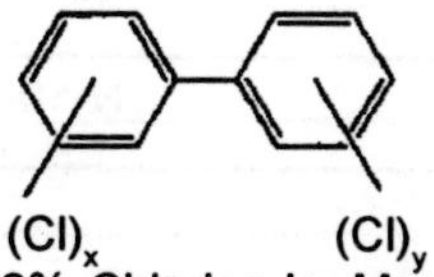

62% Chlorine by Mass

$x = 1 - 5$ $y = 1 - 5$

Monsanto

CAS 37324-23-5 **MF** Technical Mix **MW**

Matrix	Cat. No.	Unit
1000 μg/mL in Hexane	C-262S-H-10X	1 mL
NEAT	C-262N-50MG	50 mg

Aroclor® 5460

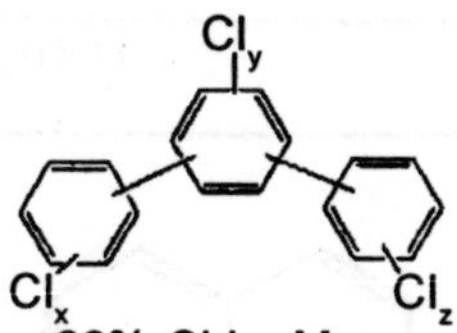

60% Cl by Mass

Monsanto

CAS 11126-42-4 **MF** Technical Mix **MW**

Matrix	Cat. No.	Unit
35 μg/mL in Toluene	T-460S	1 mL

Halowax 1000

Polychlorinated naphthalene

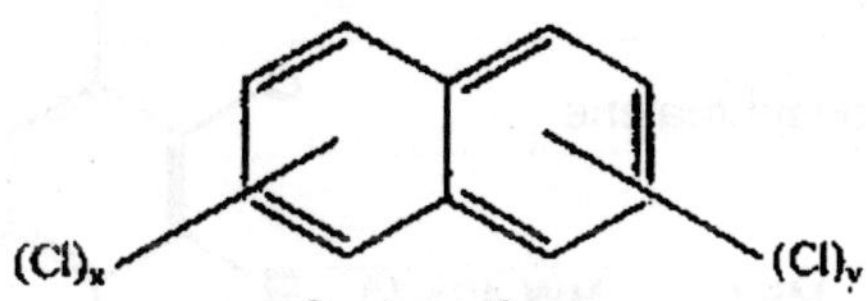

$x = 0 - 4$ $y = 0 - 4$

CAS 58718-66-4 **MF** Technical Mix **MW**

Matrix	Cat. No.	Unit
100 µg/mL in MeOH	N-1000S	1 mL

Halowax 1001

Polychlorinated naphthalene

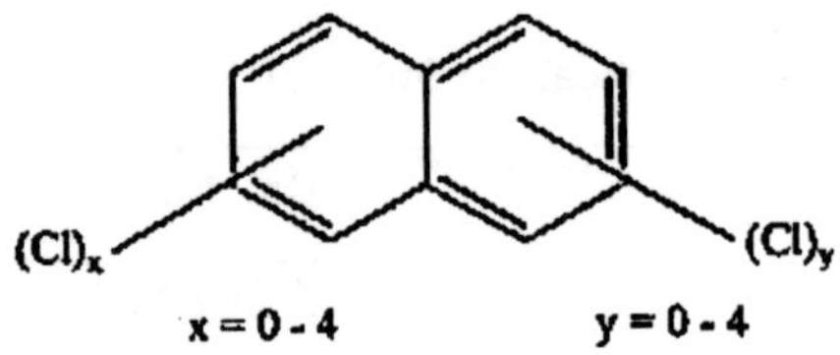

CAS 58718-67-5 **MF** Technical Mix **MW**

Matrix	Cat. No.	Unit
100 µg/mL in MeOH	N-1001S	1 mL

Halowax 1013

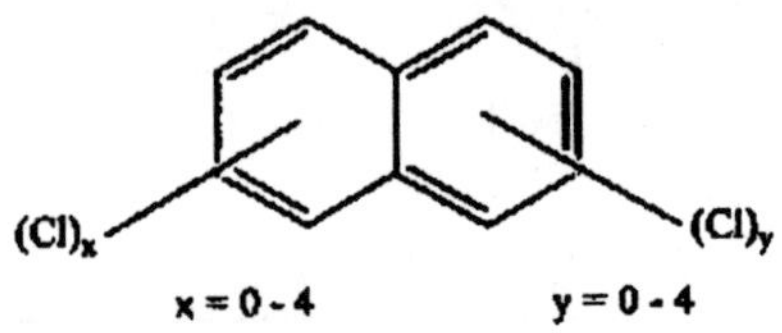

CAS 1321-64-8 **MF** Technical Mix **MW**

Matrix	Cat. No.	Unit
100 µg/mL in MeOH	N-1013S	1 mL

Halowax 1051

Octachoronaphthalene

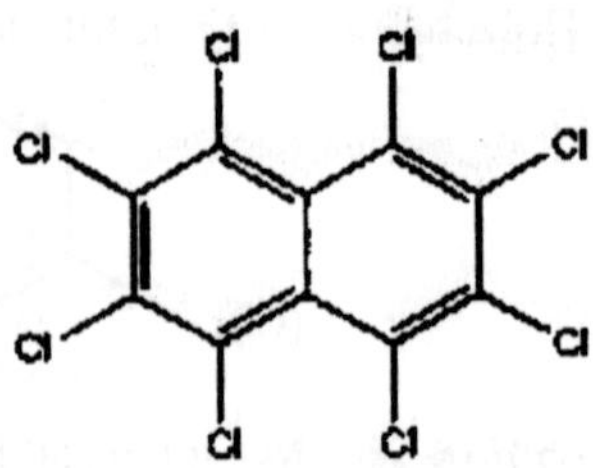

CAS 2234-13-1 **MF** $C_{10}C_{18}$ **MW** 403.73

Matrix	Cat. No.	Unit
100 μg/mL in MeOH	N-1051S 1 mL	

Halowax 1099

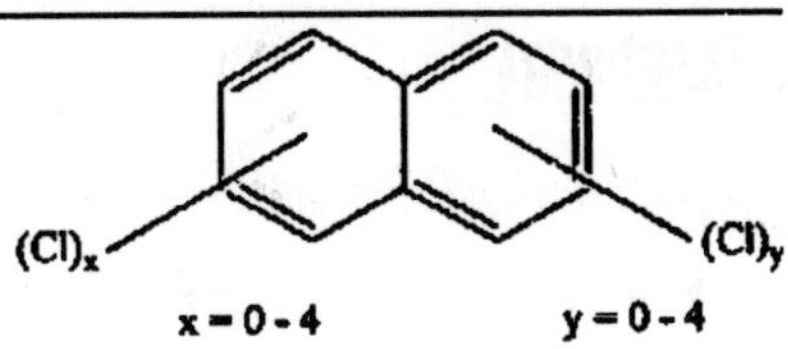

CAS 39450-05-0 **MF** Technical Mix **MW**

Matrix	Cat. No.	Unit
100 μg/mL in MeOH	N-1099S	1 mL

Saytex® 8010 NEW

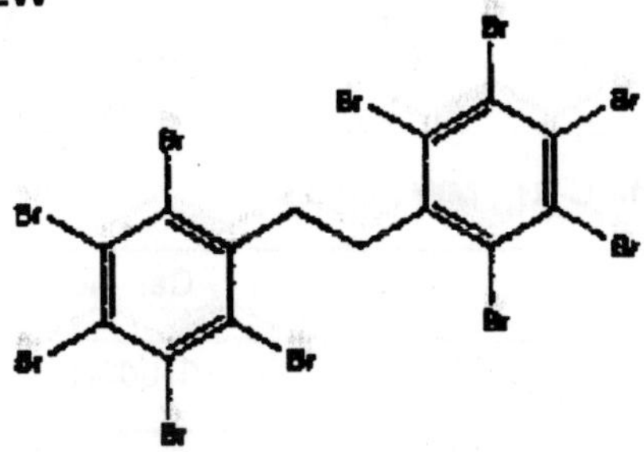

CAS 84852-53-9 **MF** $C_{14}H_4Br_{10}$ **MW** 971.22

Matrix	Cat. No.	Unit
NEAT	PLAS-FR-001N	50 mg

m-Terphenyl

1,3-diphenylbenzene

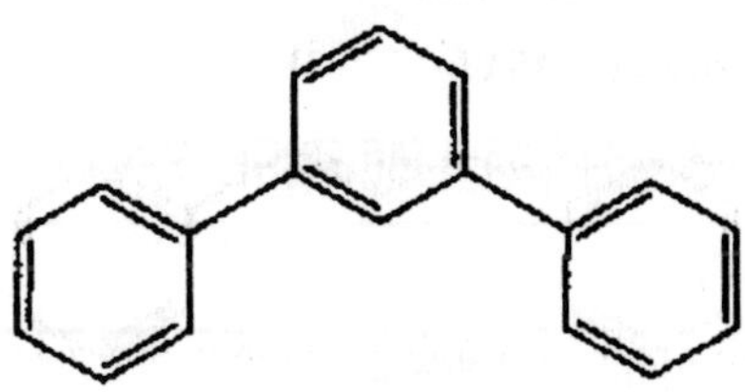

CAS 92-06-8 **MF** $C_6H_5C_6H_4C_6H_5$ **MW** 230.32

Matrix	Cat. No.	Unit
NEAT	T-002N	1 mL

o-Terphenyl

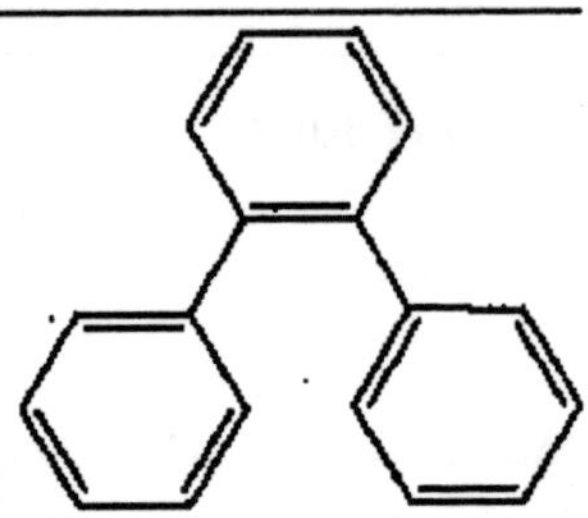

CAS 84-15-1 **MF** $C_6H_5C_6H_4C_6H_5$ **MW** 230.32

Matrix	Cat. No.	Unit
NEAT	T-001N	1 mL

p-Terphenyl

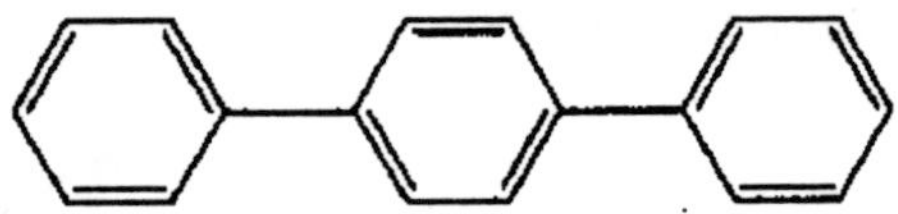

CAS 92-94-4 **MF** $C_{18}H_{14}$ **MW** 230.32

Matrix	Cat. No.	Unit
NEAT	T-003N	1 mL

Tetradecachloro-m-terphenyl

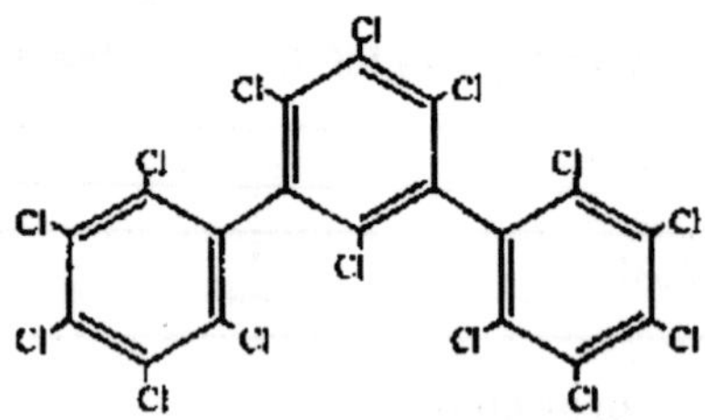

CAS 42429-88-9 **MF** $C_{18}Cl_{14}$ **MW** 712.48

Matrix	Cat. No.	Unit
35 μg/mL in Toluene	T-005S	1 mL

Tetradecachloro-o-terphenyl

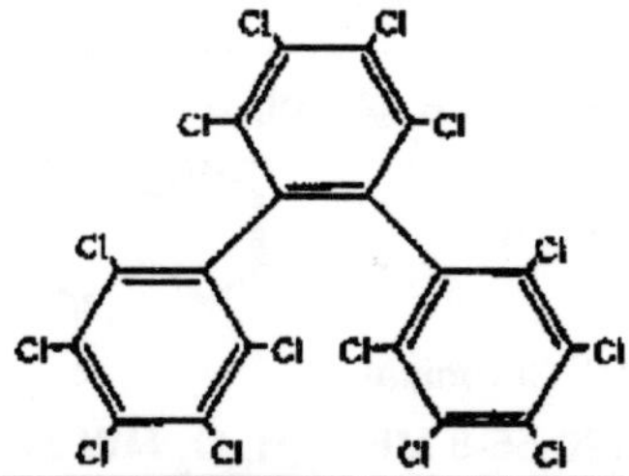

CAS MF $C_{18}Cl_{14}$ **MW** 712.48

Matrix	Cat. No.	Unit
35 µg/mL in Toluene	T-004S	1 mL

Tetradecachloro-p-terphenyl

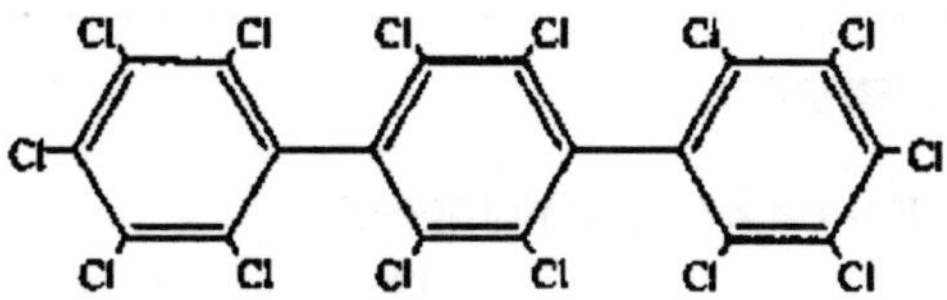

CAS MF $C_{18}Cl_{14}$ **MW** 712.48

Matrix	Cat. No.	Unit
100 µg/mL in MeOH	T-006S	1 mL

PLASTICIZERS

A plasticizer is a compound added to a material, usually a plastic, to make it flexible, resilient and easier to handle. Plasticizers are major components in plastics that determine the physical properties of polymer products.

Plasticizers are generally medium to high molecular weight esters of aliphatic or aromatic carboxylic acids, or sometimes of phosphoric acid. The phosphate esters are often also used for their flame retardant properties. Adipates and phthalates are also very common, but are becoming more highly regulated due to concern that they could act as endocrine disruptors.

The USEPA regulates many Phthalates and Adipates by Methods 606, 506-1 and 8061.

Benzoflex® 2-45

diethylene glycol, dibenzoate

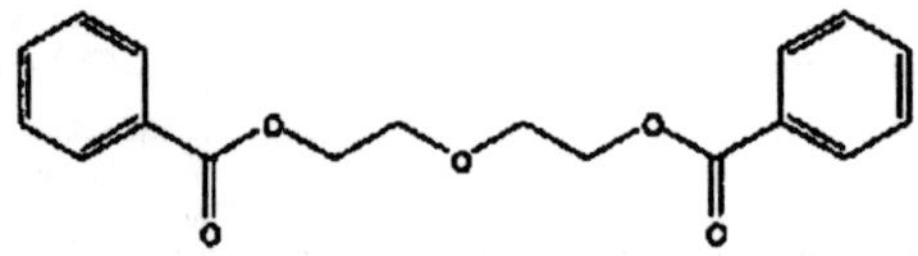

Velsicol Chemical

CAS 120-55-8 **MF** $C_{18}H_{18}O_5$ **MW** 314.33

Matrix	Cat. No.	Unit
1000 µg/mL in Hexane	PLAS-PL-015S	1 mL
NEAT	PLAS-PL-015N	50 mg

Bisphenol A (BPA)

4,4'-dihydroxy-2,2-diphenylpropane

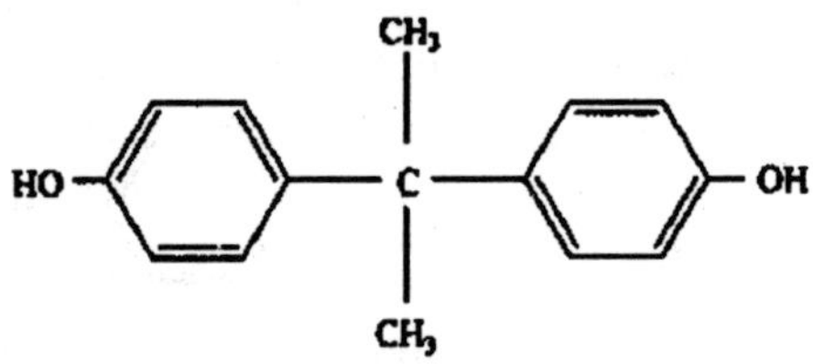

CAS 80-05-7 **MF** $C_{15}H_{16}O_2$ **MW** 228.29

Matrix	Cat. No.	Unit
1000 µg/mL in Methanol	M-1626-01S	1 mL

Celogen® SD-125

50% azodicarbonamide in a phthalate plasticizer

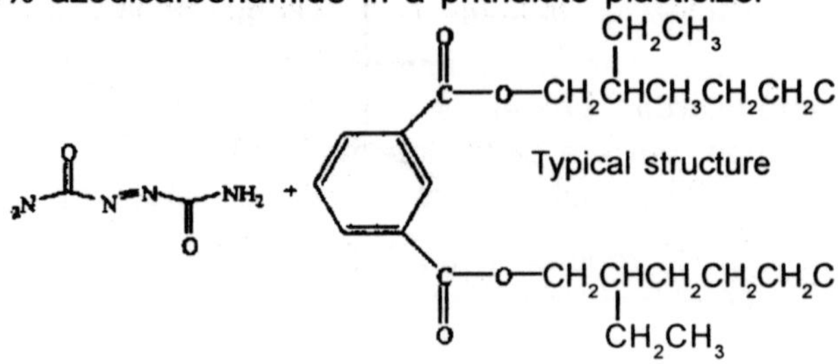

CAS N/A **MF** N/A **MW** N/A

Matrix	Cat. No.	Unit
1000 μg/mL in Hexane	PLAS-PL-009S	1 mL
NEAT	PLAS-PL-009N	50 mg

Citroflex 2

2-hydroxy-1,2,3-propanetricarboxylic acid, triethyl ester

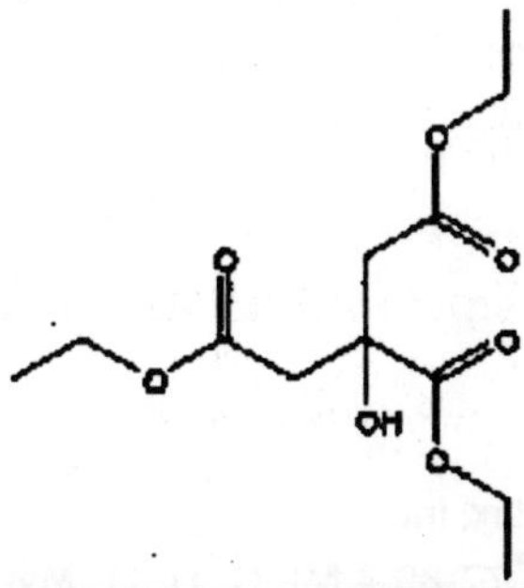

Morflex, Inc.

CAS 77-93-0 **MF** $C_{12}H_{20}O_7$ **MW** 276.32

Matrix	Cat. No.	Unit
1000 μg/mL in Hexane	PLAS-PL-028S	1 mL
NEAT	PLAS-PL-028N	50 mg

Citroflex 4

2-hydroxy-1,2,3-propanetricarboxylic acid, tributyl ester

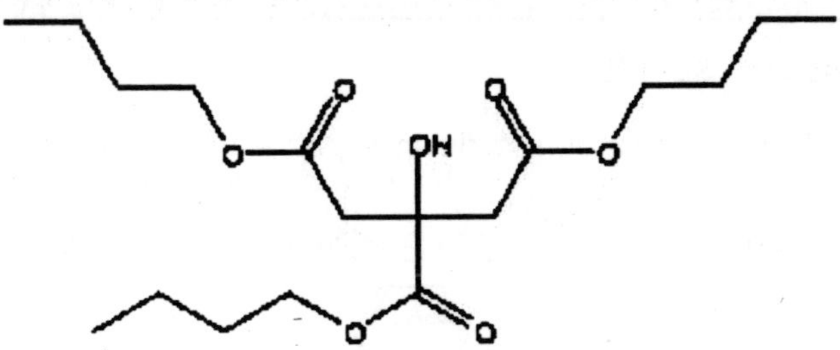

Morflex, Inc

CAS 77-94-1 **MF** $C_{18}H_{32}O_7$ **MW** 360.45

Matrix	Cat. No.	Unit
1000 µg/mL in Hexane	PLAS-PL-030S	1 mL
NEAT	PLAS-PL-030N	50 mg

Citroflex A-2

2-(acetyloxy)-1,2,3-propanetricarboxylic acid, triethyl ester

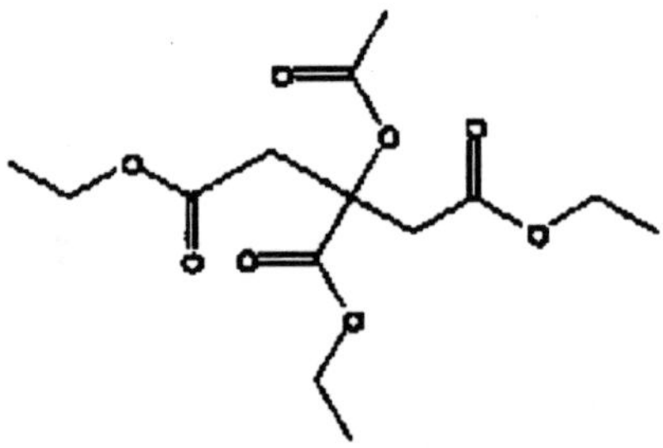

Morflex, Inc.

CAS 77-89-4 **MF** $C_{14}H_{22}O_8$ **MW** 318.32

Matrix	Cat. No.	Unit
1000 µg/mL in Hexane	PLAS-PL-001S	1 mL
NEAT	PLAS-PL-001N	50 mg

Citroflex A-4

2-Acetoxy-1,2,3-propanetricarboxylic acid, tributyl ester

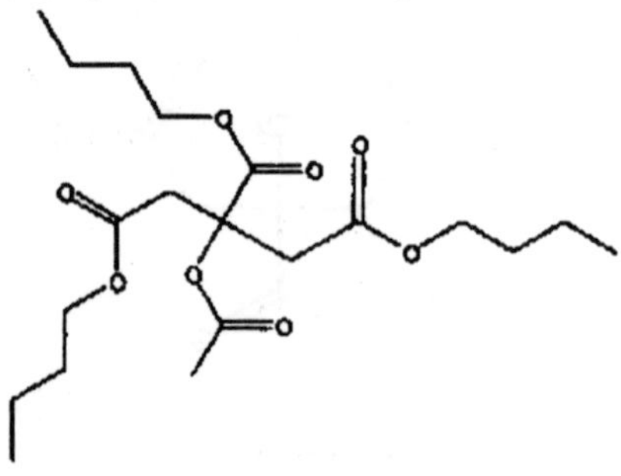

Morflex, Inc.

CAS 77-90-7 **MF** $C_{20}H_{34}O_8$ **MW** 402.54

Matrix	Cat. No.	Unit
1000 μg/mL in Hexane	PLAS-PL-002S	1 mL
NEAT	PLAS-PL-002N	50 mg

Citroflex B-6

n-butyltri-n-hexyl citrate

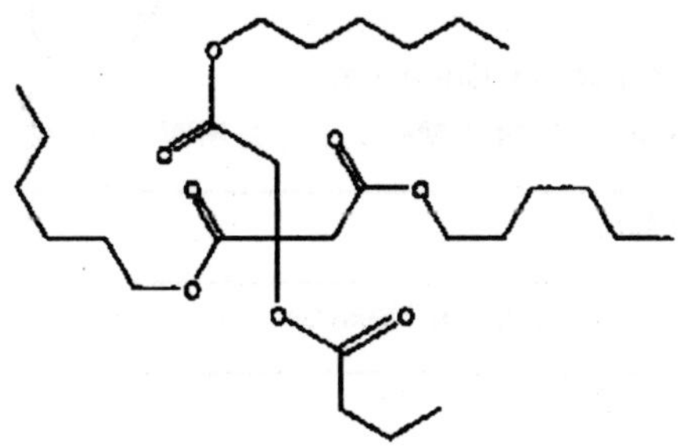

Morflex, Inc.

CAS 82469-79-2 **MF** $C_{28}H_{50}O_8$ **MW** 514.7

Matrix	Cat. No.	Unit
1000 μg/mL in Hexane	PLAS-PL-025S	1 mL
NEAT	PLAS-PL-025N	50 mg

Cresyl diphenyl phosphate NEW

(4-methylphenyl) diphenyl phosphate

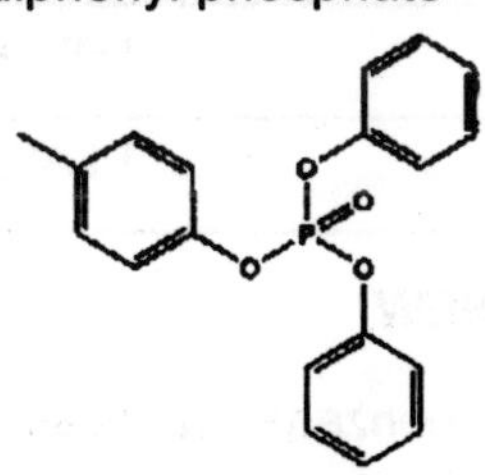

CAS 26444-49-5 **MF** $C_{19}H_{17}O_4P$ **MW** 340.31

Matrix	Cat. No.	Unit
NEAT	PLAS-PL-043N	50 mg

Dibutyl phthalate

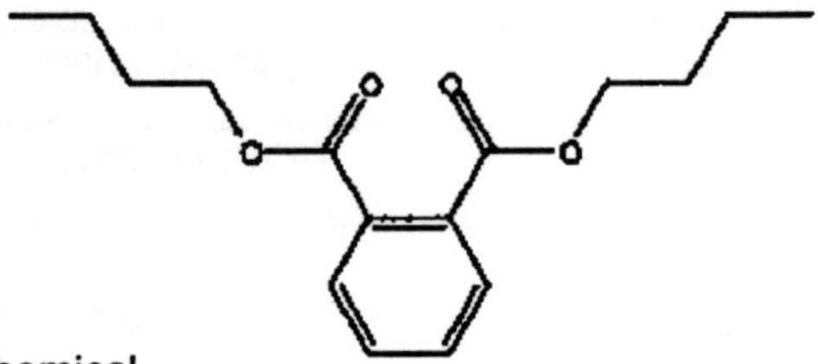

Houghton Chemical

CAS 84-74-2 **MF** $C_{16}H_{22}O_4$ **MW** 278.34

Matrix	Cat. No.	Unit
1000 µg/mL in Hexane	PLAS-PL-013S	1 mL
NEAT	PLAS-PL-013N	50 mg

Dibutyl sebacate NEW

Dibutyl decanedioate

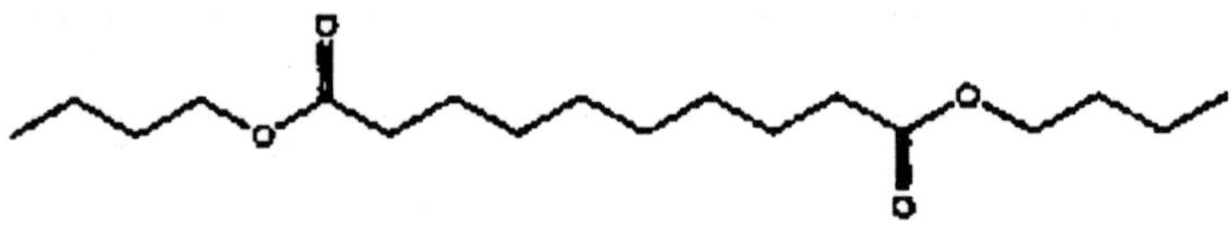

CAS 109-43-3 **MF** $C_{18}H_{34}O_4$ **MW** 314.46

Matrix	Cat. No.	Unit
Neat	PLAS-PL-041N	50 mg

Diisooctyl phthalate NEW

bis(6-methylheptyl) benzene-1,2-dicarboxylate

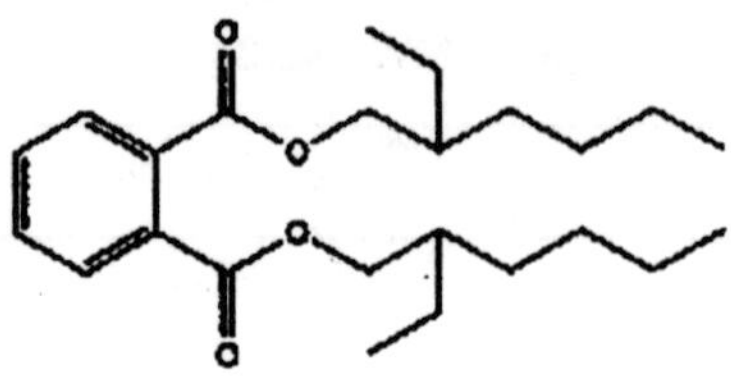

CAS 27554-26-3 **MF** $C_{24}H_{38}O_4$ **MW** 390.56

Matrix	Cat. No.	Unit
NEAT	PLAS-PL-051N	50 mg

Dimethyl adipate NEW

Dimethyl hexanedioate

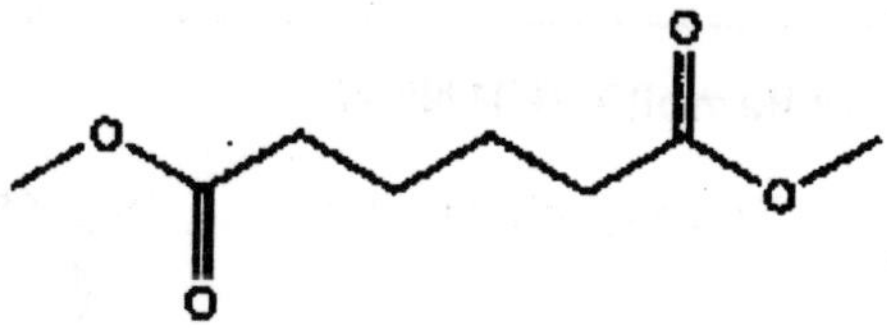

CAS 627-93-0 **MF** $C_8H_{14}O_4$ **MW** 174.19

Matrix	Cat. No.	Unit
NEAT	PLAS-PL-050N	50 mg

Dimethyl sebacate NEW

Dimethyl decanedioate

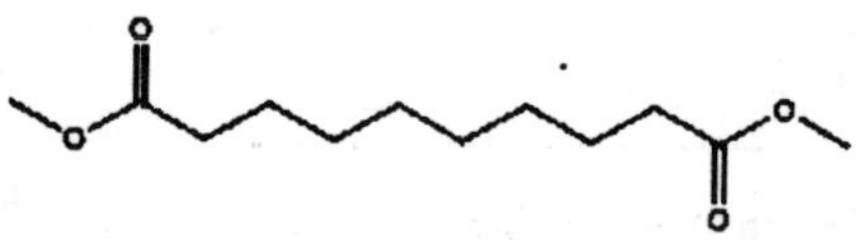

CAS 106-79-6 **MF** $C_{12}H_{22}O_4$ **MW** 230.30

Matrix	Cat. No.	Unit
NEAT	PLAS-PL-040N	50 mg

Dioctyl phthalate (DOP)

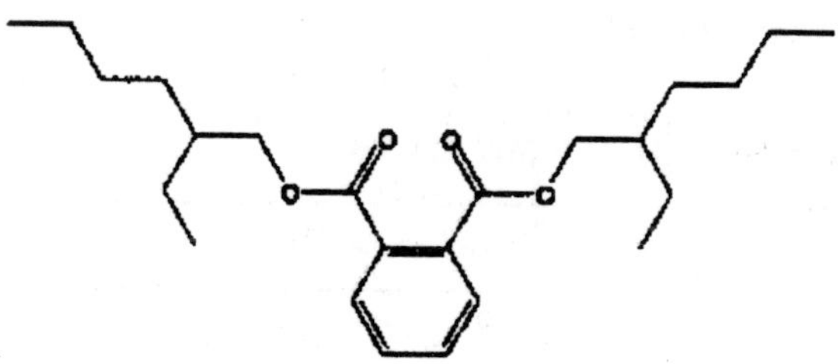

CAS 117-81-7 **MF** $C_{24}H_{38}O_4$ **MW** 390.56

Matrix	Cat. No.	Unit
1000 µg/mL in Hexane	PLAS-PL-019S	1 mL
NEAT	PLAS-PL-019N	50 mg

Disflamoll® TKP NEW

Tricresyl phosphate

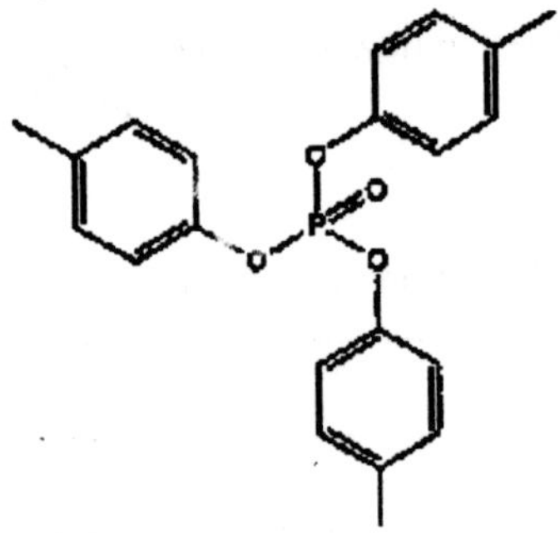

CAS 1330-78-5 **MF** $C_{21}H_{21}O_4P$ **MW** 368.36

Matrix	Cat. No.	Unit
NEAT	PLAS-PL-053N	50 mg

Disflamoll TP NEW

Triphenyl phosphate

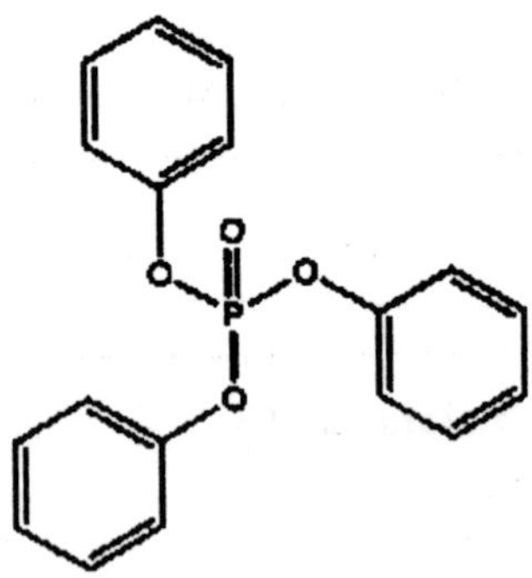

CAS 115-86-6 **MF** $C_{18}H_{15}O_4P$ **MW** 326.28

Matrix	Cat. No.	Unit
NEAT	PLAS-PL-049N	50 mg

2-Ethylhexyl sebacate NEW

bis(2-ethylhexyl) decanedioate

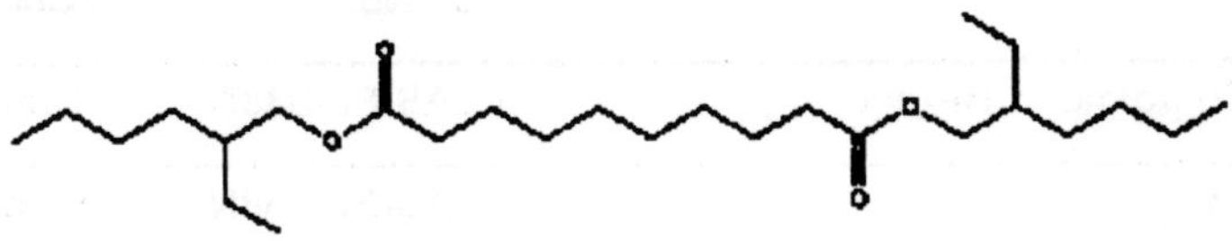

CAS 122-62-3 **MF** $C_{26}H_{50}O_4$ **MW** 426.67

Matrix	Cat. No.	Unit
NEAT	PLAS-PL-044N	50 mg

Bis(2-Ethylhexyl) terephthalate NEW

bis(2-ethylhexyl) benzene-1,4-dicarboxylate

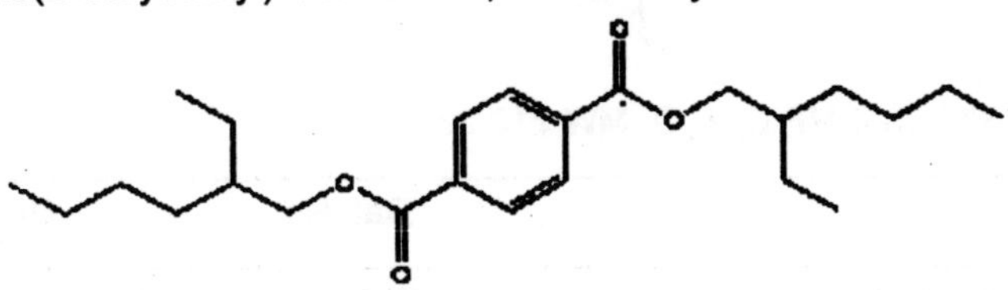

CAS 6422-86-2 **MF** $C_{24}H_{38}O_4$ **MW** 390.56

Matrix	Cat. No.	Unit
NEAT	PLAS-PL-045N	50 mg

Hercoflex® 900

1,3-Isobenzofurandione, polymer with 2,2'-(1,2-ethanediylbis (oxy))bis(ethanol), benzoate

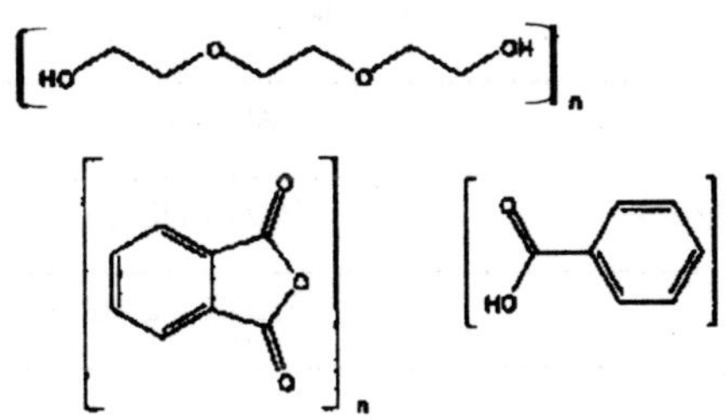

Hercules Incorporated

CAS 68186-30-1 **MF** $(C_8H_4O_3)_n$ $(C_6H_{14}O_4)_n$ $(C_7H_6O_2)_n$ **MW** N/A

Matrix	Cat. No.	Unit
1000 μg/mL in Hexane	PLAS-PL-038S	1 mL
NEAT	PLAS-PL-038N	50 mg

Hi-Point® 90

2-Butanone peroxide (in DMP)

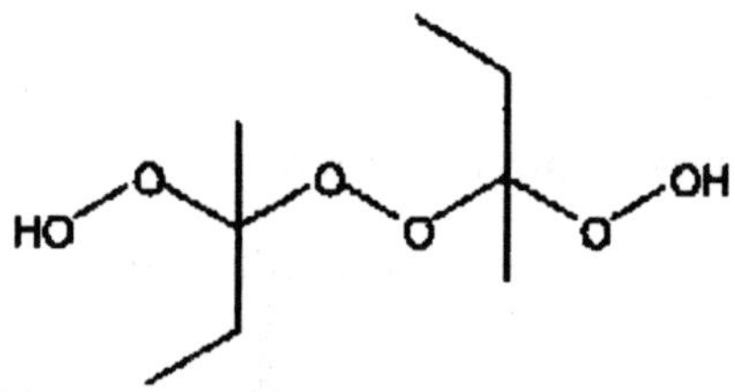

CAS 1338-23-4 **MF** $C_8H_{18}O_6$ **MW** 210.22

Matrix	Cat. No.	Unit
1000 μg/mL in Hexane	PLAS-PL-023S-R1	1 mL
NEAT	PLAS-PL-023N-R1	50 mg

HI-POINT PD-1

methyl ethyl ketone peroxide (CAS 1338-23-4) solution

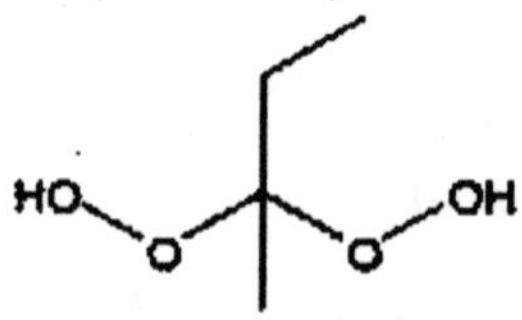

Matrix	Cat. No.	Unit
1000 μg/mL in Hexane	PLAS-PL-024S	1 mL
NEAT	PLAS-PL-024N	50 mg

Jayflex® 77

diisoheptyl phthalate

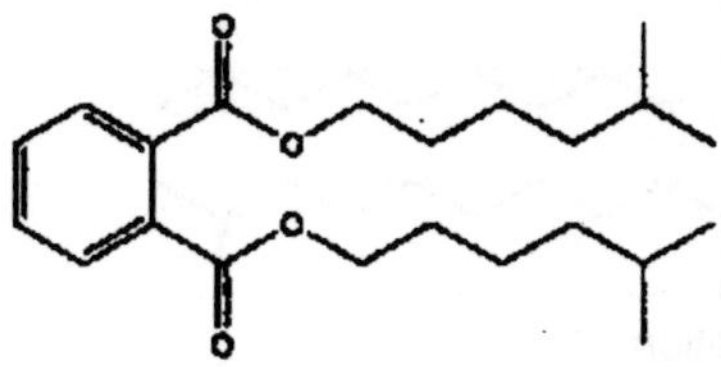

ExxonMobil Corporation

CAS 71888-89-6 **MF** $C_{22}H_{34}O_4$ **MW** 362.50

Matrix	Cat. No.	Unit
1000 μg/mL in Hexane	PLAS-PL-017S	1 mL
NEAT	PLAS-PL-017N	50 mg

Jayflex® DIDP

diisodecyl phthalate

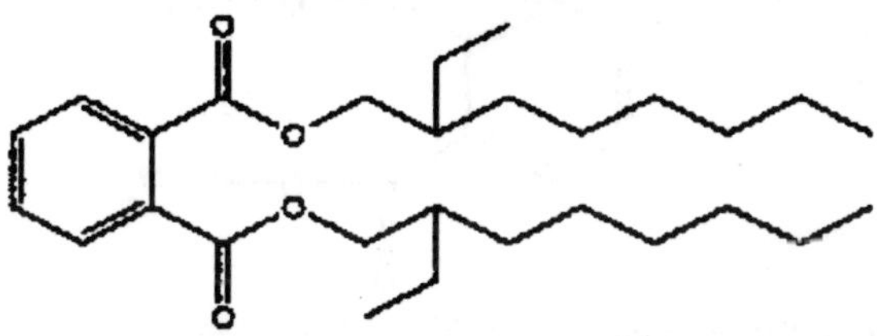

ExxonMobil Corporation

CAS 68515-49-1 **MF** $C_{28}H_{46}O_4$ **MW** 446.66

Matrix	Cat. No.	Unit
1000 μg/mL in Hexane	PLAS-PL-016S	1 mL
NEAT	PLAS-PL-016N	50 mg

Jayflex® DINP

diisononyl phthalate

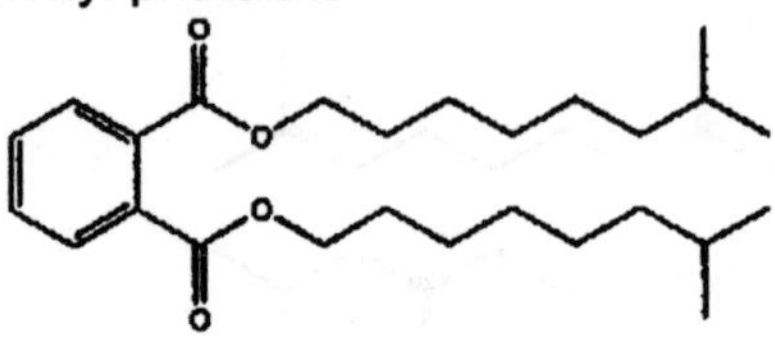

ExxonMobil Corporation

CAS 68515-48-0 **MF** $C_{26}H_{42}O_4$ **MW** 418.61

Matrix	Cat. No.	Unit
1000 µg/mL in Hexane	PLAS-PL-018S	1 mL
NEAT	PLAS-PL-018N	50 mg

Jayflex® DTDP

ditridecyl phthalate

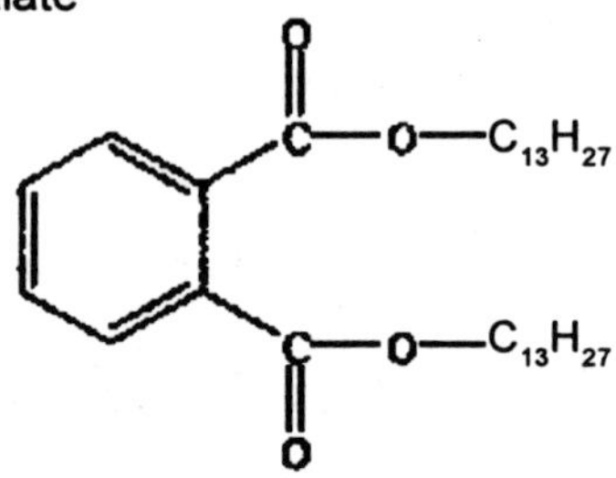

ExxonMobil Corporation

CAS 68515-47-9 **MF** $C_{34}H_{58}O_4$ **MW** 530.82

Matrix	Cat. No.	Unit
1000 µg/mL in Hexane	PLAS-PL-020S	1 mL
NEAT	PLAS-PL-020N	50 mg

Jayflex® L11P-E

diundecyl phthalate

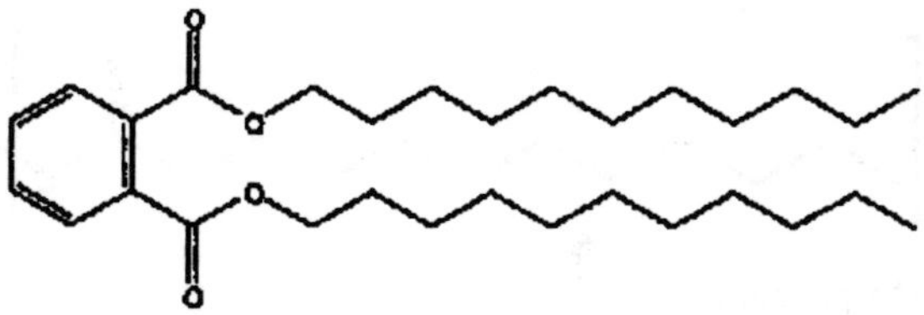

ExxonMobil Corporation

CAS 3648-20-2 **MF** $C_{30}H_{50}O_4$ **MW** 474.72

Matrix	Cat. No.	Unit
1000 µg/mL in Hexane	PLAS-PL-021S	1 mL
NEAT	PLAS-PL-021N	50 mg

Jayflex® TINTM

triisononyl trimellitate

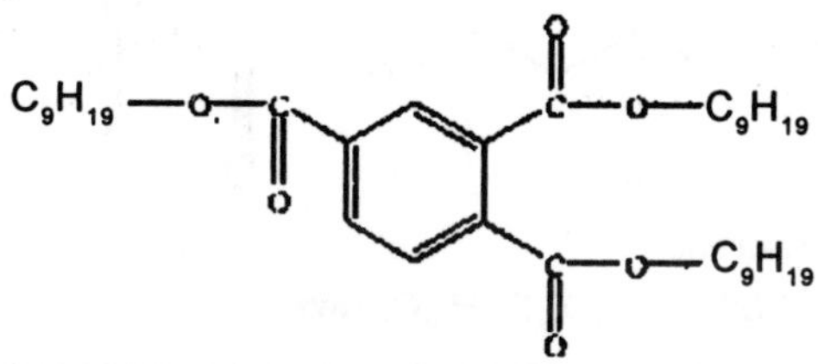

ExxonMobil Corporation

CAS 53894-23-8 **MF** $C_{36}H_{60}O_6$ **MW** 588.96

Matrix	Cat. No.	Unit
1000 µg/mL in Hexane	PLAS-PL-029S	1 mL
NEAT	PLAS-PL-029N	50 mg

Laurex®

zinc salt of lauric and related fatty acids

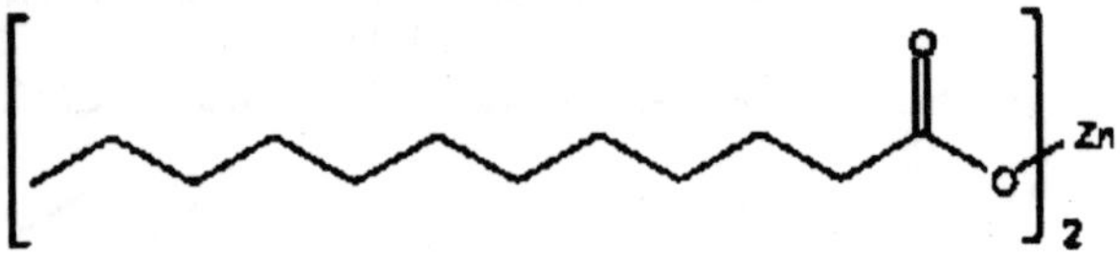

Chemtura Corporation

CAS MF $C_{24}H_{46}O_4Zn$ **MW** 464.01

Matrix	Cat. No.	Unit
1000 µg/mL in Hexane	PLAS-PL-032S	1 mL
NEAT	PLAS-PL-032N	50 mg

Markstat® 51

poly(ethylene glycol) monolaurate

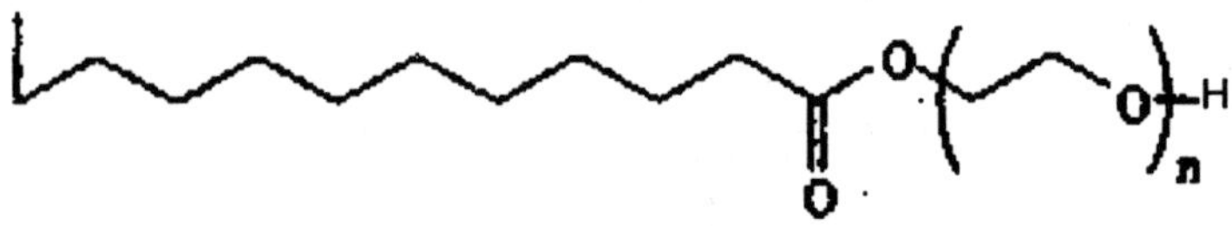

Chemtura Corporation

CAS 9004-81-3 **MF** $(C_2H_4O)_nC_{12}H_{24}O_2$ **MW**

Matrix	Cat. No.	Unit
1000 µg/mL in Hexane	PLAS-PL-003S	1 mL
NEAT	PLAS-PL-003N	50 mg

Methyl O-Acetylricinoleate NEW

Methyl (Z)-12-acetyloxy-octadec-9-enoate

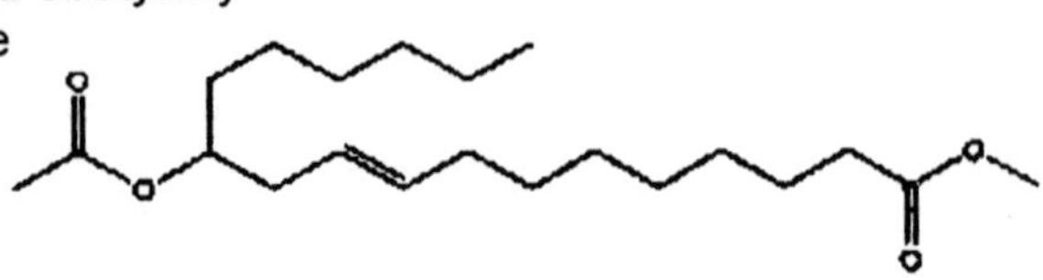

CAS 140-03-4 **MF** $C_{21}H_{38}O_4$ **MW** 354.52

Matrix	Cat. No.	Unit
NEAT	PLAS-PL-042N	50 mg

Morflex® 150

dicyclohexyl phthalate

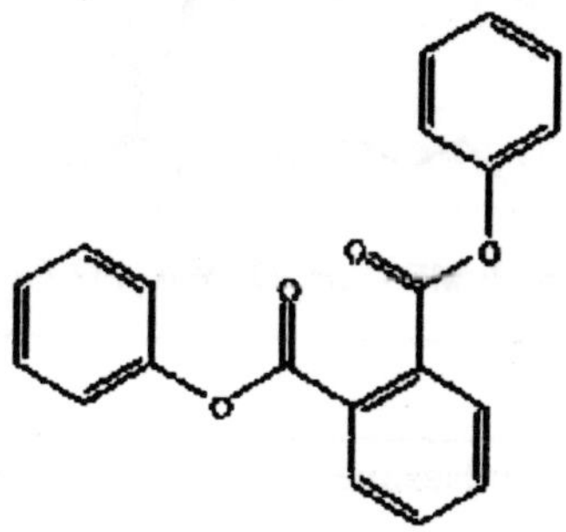

CAS 84-61-7 **MF** $C_{20}H_{26}O_4$ **MW** 330.46

Matrix	Cat. No.	Unit
1000 μg/mL in Hexane	PLAS-PL-014S	1 mL
NEAT	PLAS-PL-014N	50 mg

Morflex® 190

butylphthalyl butyl glycolate

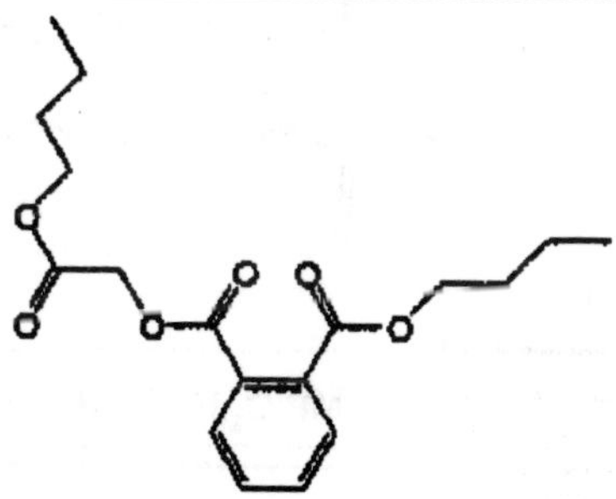

Morfex, Inc.

CAS 85-70-1 **MF** $C_{18}H_{24}O_6$ **MW** 336.38

Matrix	Cat. No.	Unit
1000 μg/mL in Hexane	PLAS-PL-008S	1 mL
NEAT	PLAS-PL-008N	50 mg

Morflex® 560

tri-n-hexyl trimellitate

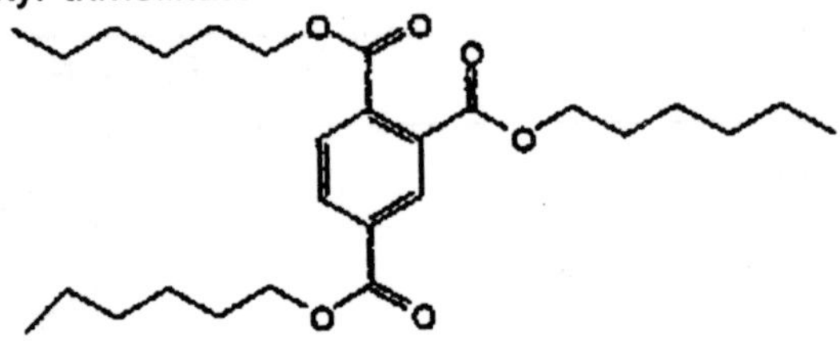

Morfex, Inc.

CAS 1528-49-0 **MF** $C_{27}H_{42}O_6$ **MW** 462.62

Matrix	Cat. No.	Unit
1000 µg/mL in Hexane	PLAS-PL-031S	1 mL
NEAT	PLAS-PL-031N	50 mg

Morflex® x-1125

1,2-benzenedicarboxylic acid, ditridecyl ester

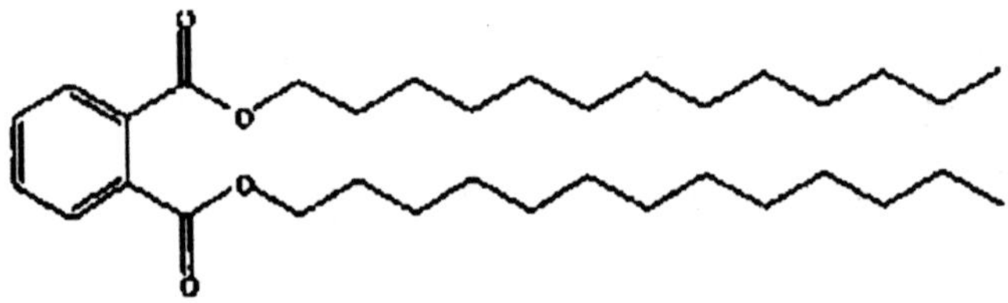

Morfex, Inc.

CAS 119-06-2 **MF** $C_{34}H_{58}O_4$ **MW** 530.83

Matrix	Cat. No.	Unit
1000 µg/mL in Hexane	PLAS-PL-033S	1 mL
NEAT	PLAS-PL-033N	50 mg

Paraplex® G-30

proprietary dibasic acid polyester mixture

N/A

CPH Innovations

CAS MF MW

Matrix	Cat. No.	Unit
1000 µg/mL in Hexane	PLAS-PL-027S	1 mL
NEAT	PLAS-PL-027N	50 mg

Plasthall® DINP plasticizer NEW

Diisononyl phthalate

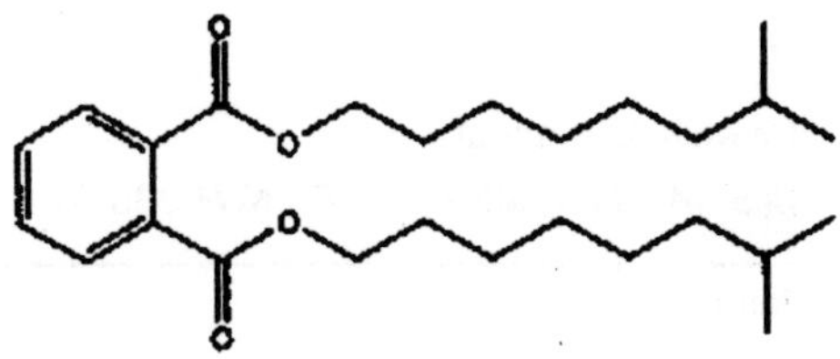

CAS 28553-12-0 **MF** $C_{26}H_{42}O_4$ **MW** 418.61

Matrix	Cat. No.	Unit
NEAT	PLAS-PL-052N	50 mg

Plasthall® ESO

epoxidized soybean oil

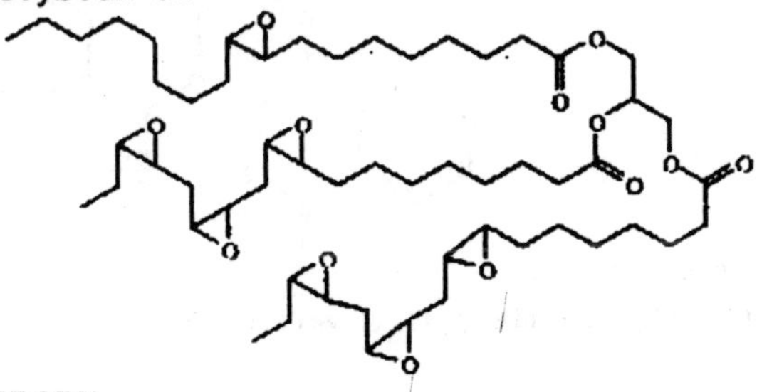

CPH Innovations

CAS 8013-07-8 **MF MW**

Matrix	Cat. No.	Unit
1000 µg/mL in Hexane	PLAS-PL-035S	1 mL
NEAT	PLAS-PL-035N	50 mg

Polycizer® butyl oleate

butyl oleate

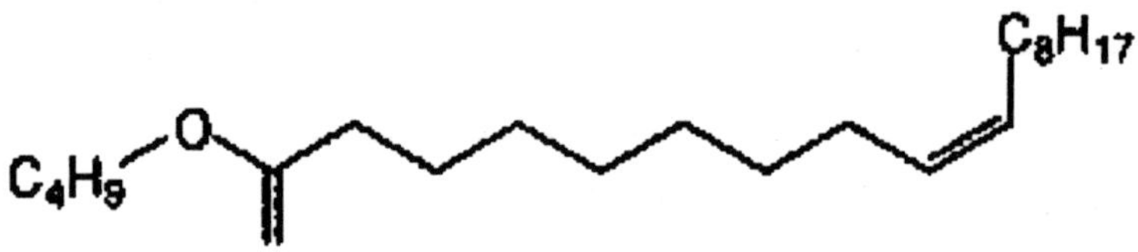

Harwick Chemical

CAS 142-77-8 **MF** $C_{22}H_{42}O_2$ **MW** 338.57

Matrix	Cat. No.	Unit
1000 µg/mL in Hexane	PLAS-PL-007S	1 mL
NEAT	PLAS-PL-007N	50 mg

Polycizer® DP 500

Dipropylene glycol dibenzoate

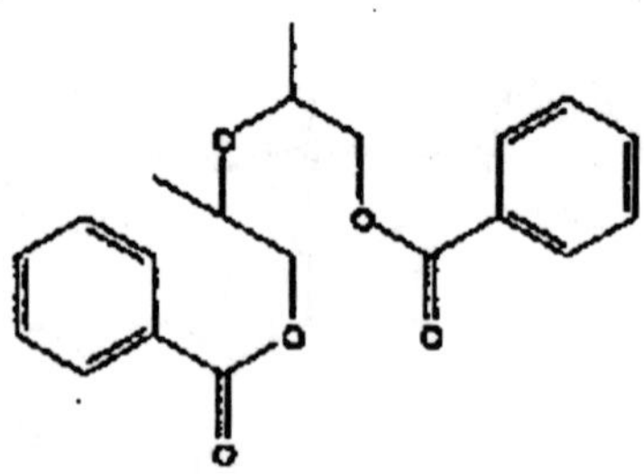

Harwick Chemical

CAS 27138-31-4 **MF** $C_{20}H_{22}O_5$ **MW** 342.39

Matrix	Cat. No.	Unit
1000 μg/mL in Hexane	PLAS-PL-011S	1 mL
NEAT	PLAS-PL-011N	50 mg

Santicizer® 141

2-Ethylhexyldiphenyl phosphate

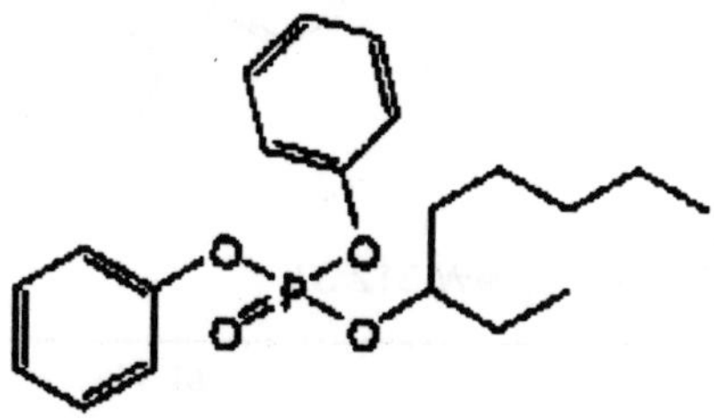

Solutia Inc.

CAS 1241-94-7 **MF** $C_{20}H_{27}O_4P$ **MW** 362.4

Matrix	Cat. No.	Unit
1000 μg/mL in Hexane	PLAS-PL-026S	1 mL
NEAT	PLAS-PL-026N	50 mg

Santicizer® 148

Mixture: isodecyldiphenyl phosphate (80-90%)/diisodecyl phenyl phosphate / triphenyl phosphate

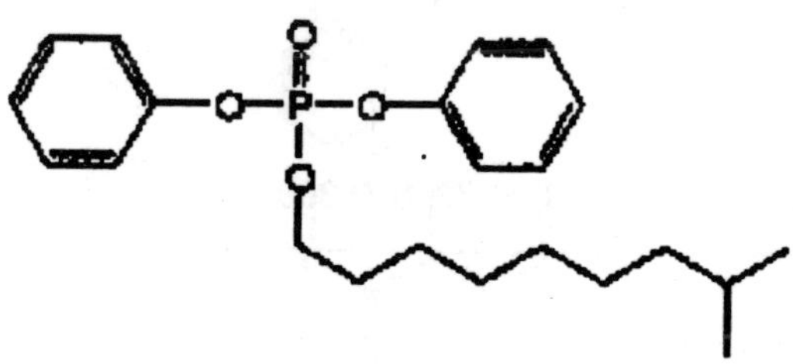

Solutia Inc.

CAS 29761-21-5 **MF** $C_{22}H_{31}O_4P$ **MW** 390.46

Matrix	Cat. No.	Unit
1000 µg/mL in Hexane	PLAS-PL-022S	1 mL
NEAT	PLAS-PL-022N	50 mg

Santicizer® 160

benzyl butyl phthalate

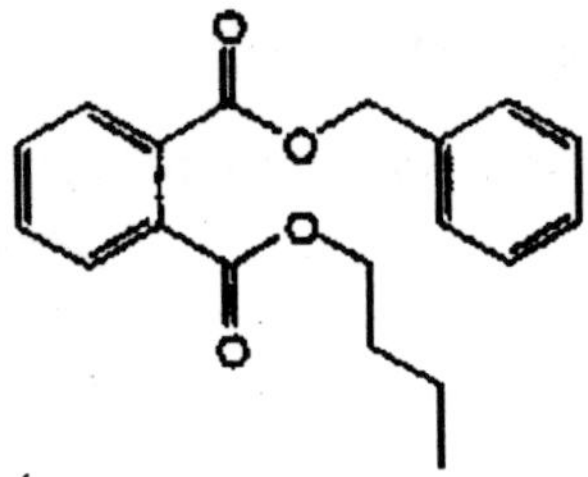

Solutia Inc.

CAS 85-68-7 **MF** $C_{19}H_{20}O_4$ **MW** 312.37

Matrix	Cat. No.	Unit
1000 µg/mL in Hexane	PLAS-PL-004S	1 mL
NEAT	PLAS-PL-004N	50 mg

Santicizer® 261

benzyl octyl phthalate

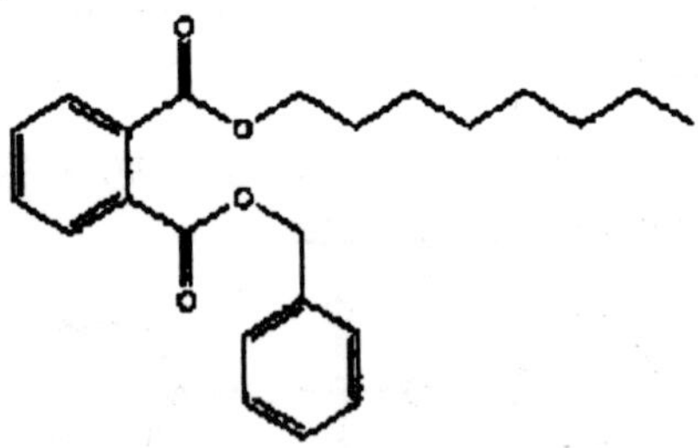

Solutia Inc.

CAS 68519-40-2 **MF** $C_{23}H_{28}O_4$ **MW** 368.47

Matrix	Cat. No.	Unit
1000 µg/mL in Hexane	PLAS-PL-005S	1 mL
NEAT	PLAS-PL-005N	50 mg

Tributylphosphate NEW

Tributyl phosphate

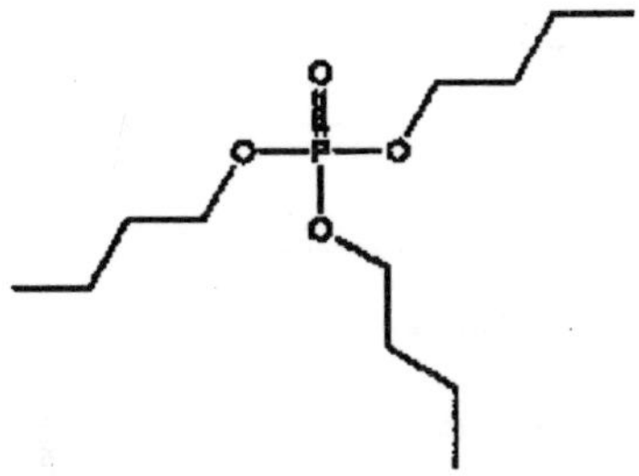

CAS 126-73-8 **MF** $C_{12}H_{27}O_4P$ **MW** 266.31

Matrix	Cat. No.	Unit
NEAT	PLAS-PL-048N	50 mg

Triethylphosphate NEW

Triethyl phosphate

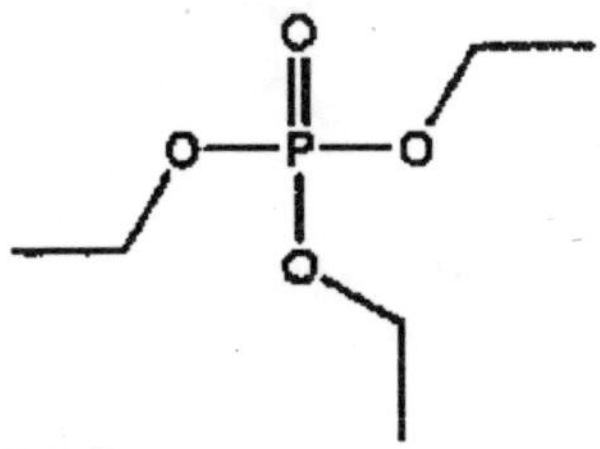

CAS 78-40-0 **MF** $C_6H_{15}O_4P$ **MW** 182.15

Matrix	Cat. No.	Unit
NEAT	PLAS-PL-047N	50 mg

2,2,4-Trimethyl-1,3-pentanediol-isobutyrate NEW

(3-hydroxy-2,2,4-trimethylpentyl) 2-methylpropanoate

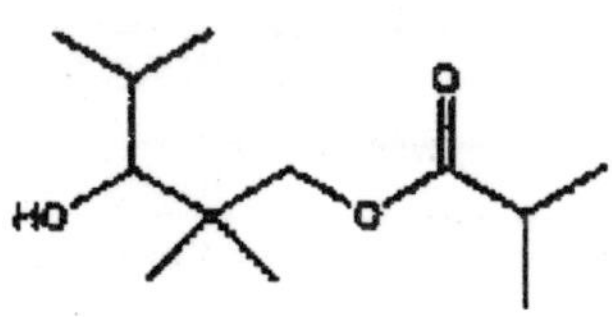

CAS 25265-77-4 **MF** $C_{12}H_{24}O_3$ **MW** 216.32

Matrix	Cat. No.	Unit
NEAT	PLAS-PL-046N	50 mg

Trimellitate NEW

1,2,4-Benzenetricarboxylic acid, tris(2-ethylhexyl) ester

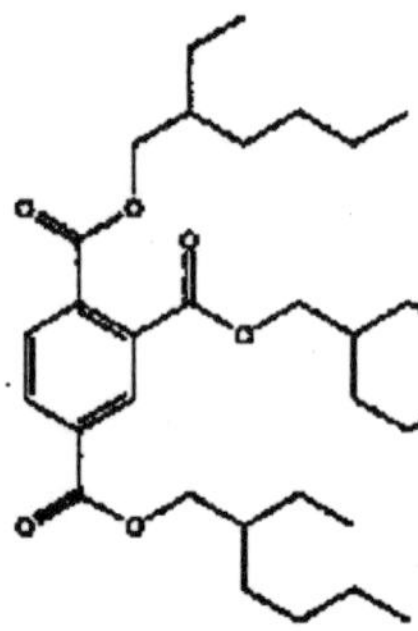

CAS 3319-31-1 **MF** $C_{33}H_{54}O_6$ **MW** 546.78

Matrix	Cat. No.	Unit
NEAT	PLAS-PL-039N	50 mg

VINSOL® POWDER

N/A

Hercules Incorporated
CAS 8050-09-7

Matrix	Cat. No.	Unit
1000 μg/mL in Hexane	PLAS-PL-037S	1 mL
NEAT	PLAS-PL-037N	50 mg

Vinsol® resin

gum rosin

N/A

Hercules Incorporated

CAS 8050-09-7

Matrix	Cat. No.	Unit
1000 µg/mL in Hexane	PLAS-PL-036S	1 mL
NEAT	PLAS-PL-036N	50 mg

PROCESSING AIDS

Processing aids are compounding materials that improve the processing of polymers by: creating better dispersion of dry materials, increasing extrusion rates, reducing powder consumption during mixing, promoting compound fusion, adding lubrication, improving knitting and creating a smoother surface on calendered and extruded products.

Akrochem® Ceresin Wax NEW

A complex combination of hydrocarbons produced by the purification of Ozocerite with Sulfuric acid and filtration through bone black to form waxy cakes

CAS 8001-75-0 **MF** N/A **MW** N/A

Matrix	Cat. No.	Unit
NEAT	PLAS-PL-002N	50 mg

Kemamide® E ultra

Erucamide

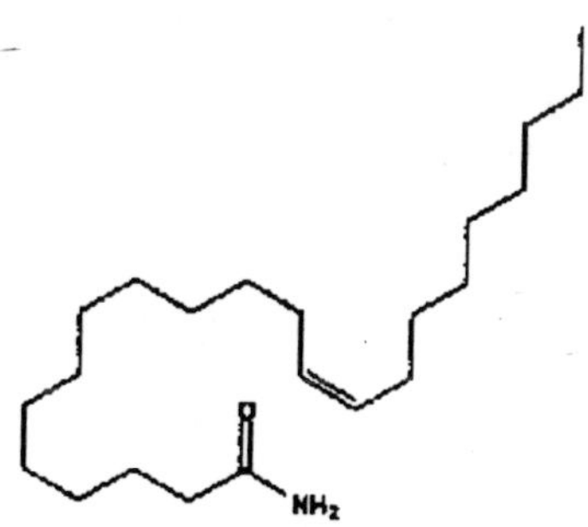

Chemtura Corporation.

CAS 112-84-5 **MF** $C_{22}H_{43}NO$ **MW** 337.58

Matrix	Cat. No.	Unit
1000 μg/mL in Hexane	PLAS-PA-001S	1 mL
NEAT	PLAS-PA-001N	50 mg

RETARDERS

Retarders are used to delay the onset of crosslinking and can be used to allow for longer processing times. They are also used to reduce scorching.

Akrochem® Retarder BAX NEW

N/A

CAS 65-85-0 **MF MW**

Matrix	Cat. No.	Unit
NEAT	PLAS-RT-011N	50 mg

2-Cyano-2-propyl benzodithioate NEW

Benzenecarbodithioicacid, 1-cyano-1-methylethyl ester

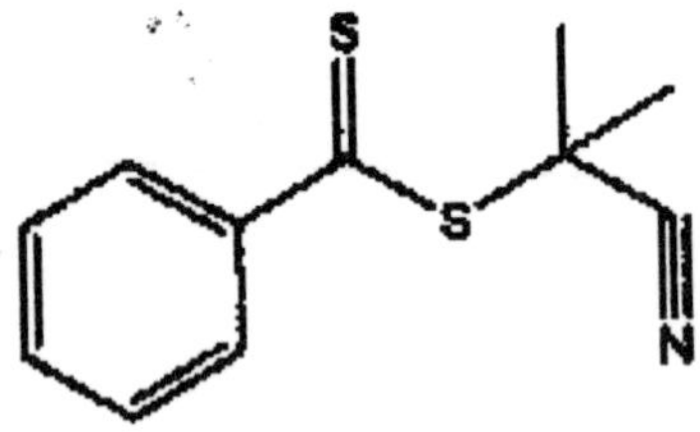

CAS 201611-85-0 **MF** $C_{11}H_{11}NS_2$ **MW** 221.34

Matrix	Cat. No.	Unit
1000 μg/mL in Hexane:Acetone(1:1)	PLAS-RT-002S	1 mL
NEAT	PLAS-RT-002N	50 mg

4-Cyano-4-(phenylcarbonothioylthio) pentanoic acid NEW

Pentanoicacid, 4-cyano-4-[(phenylthioxomethyl)thio]-

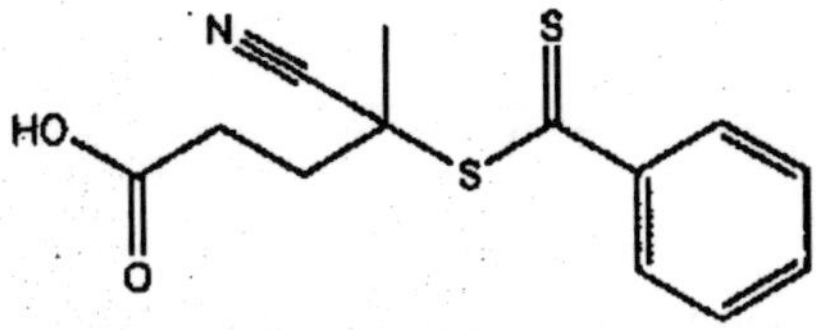

CAS 201611-92-9 **MF** $C_{13}H_{13}NO_2S_2$ **MW** 279.38

Matrix	Cat. No.	Unit
1000 μg/mL in Hexane	PLAS-RT-003S	1 mL
NEAT	PLAS-RT-003N	50 mg

2-Cyano-2-propyl dodecyl trithiocarbonate NEW

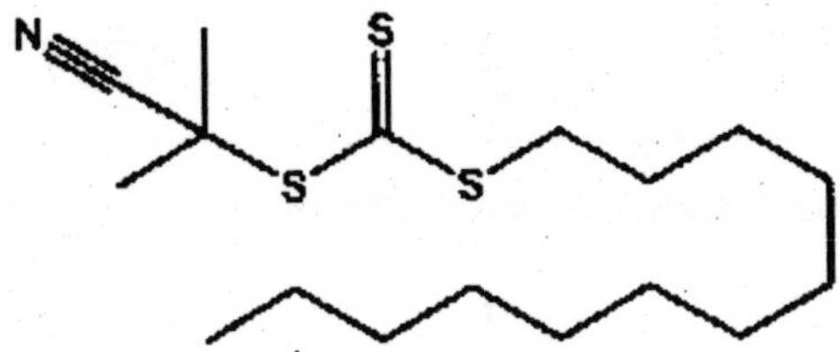

CAS 870196-83-1 **MF** $C_{17}H_{31}NS_3$ **MW** 345.63

Matrix	Cat. No.	Unit
1000 μg/mL in Hexane	PLAS-RT-004S	1 mL
NEAT	PLAS-RT-004N	50 mg

4-Cyano-4-[(dodecylsulfanylthiocarbonyl) sulfanyl]pentanoic acid NEW

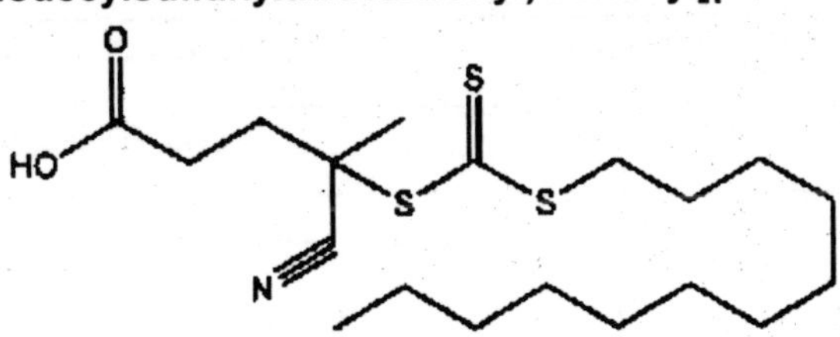

CAS 870196-80-8 **MF** $C_{19}H_{33}NO_2S_3$ **MW** 403.67

Matrix	Cat. No.	Unit
1000 µg/mL in Hexane	PLAS-RT-005S	1 mL
NEAT	PLAS-RT-005N	50 mg

Cyanomethyl dodecyl trithiocarbonate NEW

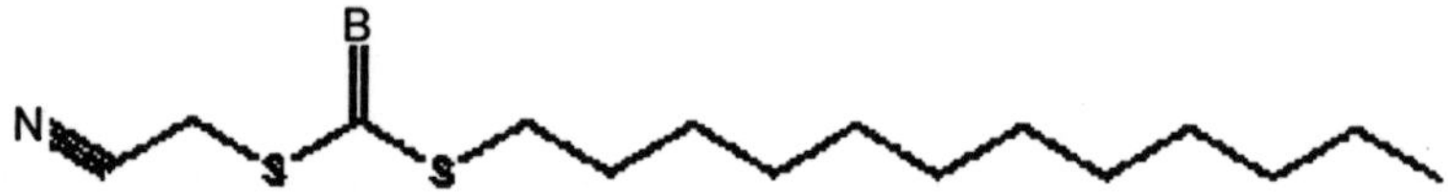

CAS 796045-97-1 **MF** $C_{15}H_{27}NS_3$ **MW** 317.58

Matrix	Cat. No.	Unit
1000 µg/mL in Hexane	PLAS-RT-006S	1 mL
NEAT	PLAS-RT-006N	50 mg

Cyanomethyl methyl(phenyl)carbamodithioate NEW

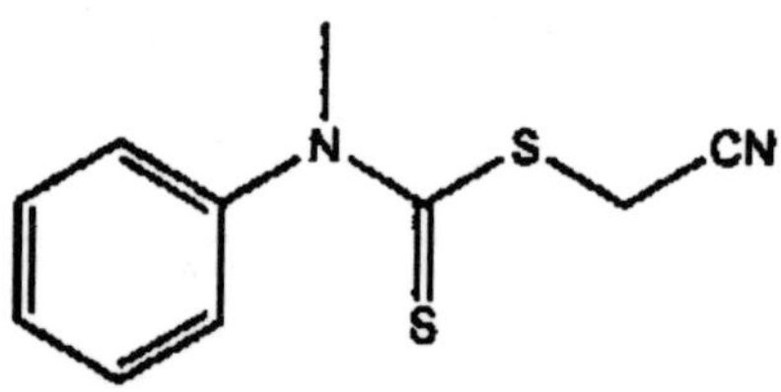

CAS 76926-16-4 **MF** $C_{10}H_{10}N_2S_2$ **MW** 222.33

Matrix	Cat. No.	Unit
1000 µg/mL in Hexane	PLAS-RT-009S	1 mL
NEAT	PLAS-RT-009N	50 mg

2-(Dodecylthiocarbonothioylthio)-2-methylpropionic acid NEW

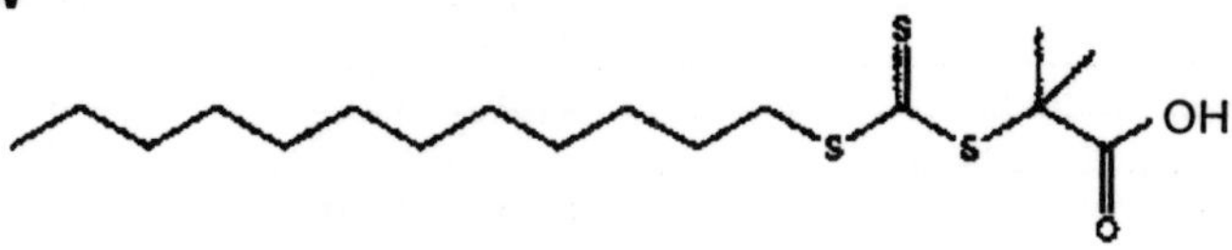

CAS 461642-78-4 **MF** $C_{17}H_{32}O_2S_3$ **MW** 364.63

Matrix	Cat. No.	Unit
1000 µg/mL in Hexane	PLAS-RT-010S	1 mL
NEAT	PLAS-RT-010N	50 mg

Bis(dodecylsulfanylthiocarbonyl)disulfide NEW

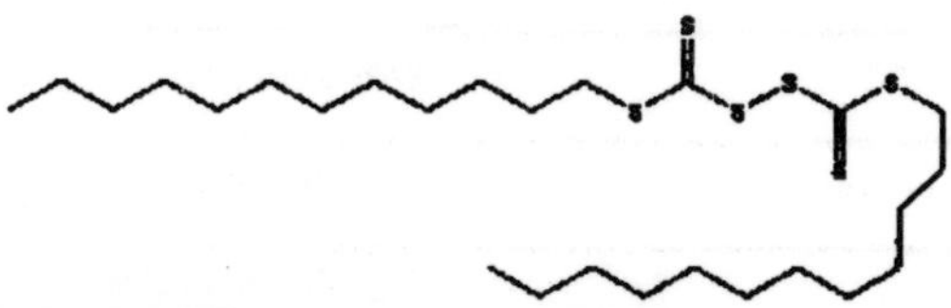

CAS 870532-86-8 **MF** $C_{26}H_{50}S_6$ **MW** 555.07

Matrix	Cat. No.	Unit
1000 µg/mL in Hexane	PLAS-RT-008S	1 mL
NEAT	PLAS-PL-008N	50 mg

Retarder AK

phthalic anhydride

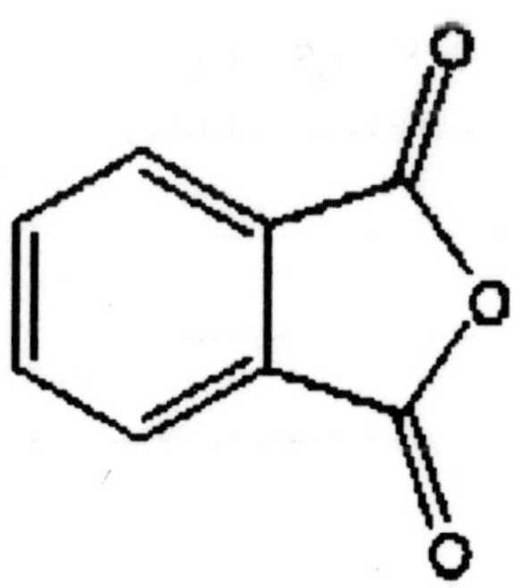

Akrochem Corporation.

CAS 85-44-9 **MF** $C_8H_4O_3$ **MW** 148.12

Matrix	Cat. No.	Unit
1000 μg/mL in Hexane: Acetone(60:40)	PLAS-RT-001S	1 mL
NEAT	PLAS-RT-001N	50 mg

Bis(thiobenzoyl) disulfide NEW

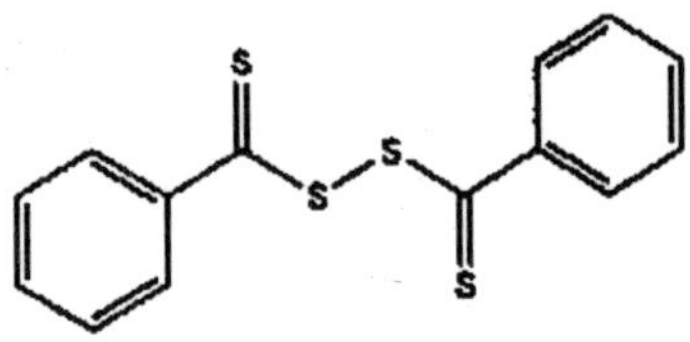

CAS 5873-93-8 **MF** $C_{14}H_{10}S_4$ **MW** 306.49

Matrix	Cat. No.	Unit
1000 μg/mL in Hexane	PLAS-RT-007S	1 mL
NEAT	PLAS-RT-007N	50 mg

STEARATES

Stearic acid and the metallic salts of this acid are used for many different applications depending on the polymer system. Stearates can act as lubricants, acid scavengers, anti-tack compounds, vulcanization promoter/accelerator, or a mold release agent.

Stearic Acid RG (rubber grade)

stearic acid

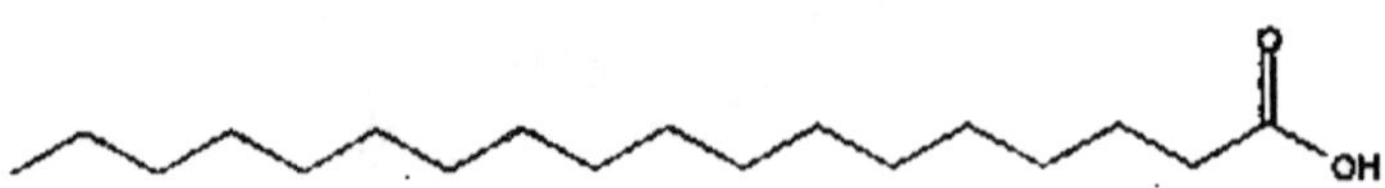

Akrochem Corporation.

CAS 57-11-4 **MF** $C_{18}H_{36}O_2$ **MW** 284.48

Matrix	Cat. No.	Unit
1000 μg/mL in Hexane	PLAS-ST-001S	1 mL
NEAT	PLAS-ST-001N	50 mg

Stearic Acid TP

stearic acid

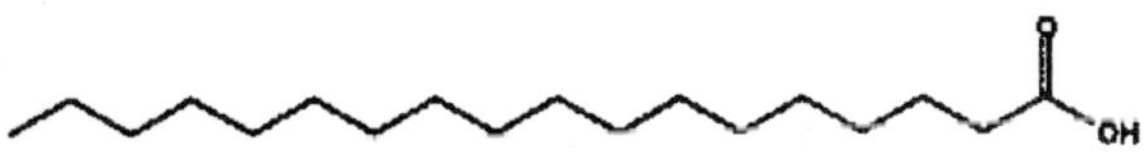

Akrochem Corporation.

CAS 57-11-4 **MF** $C_{18}H_{36}O_2$ **MW** 284.48

Matrix	Cat. No.	Unit
1000 μg/mL in Hexane	PLAS-ST-002S	1 mL
NEAT	PLAS-ST-002N	50 mg

UV STABILIZERS

UV stabilizers, or light absorbers, act to protect the plastic against UV or sunlight damage such as discoloration, cracking, brittleness, or other loss of desirable physical properties.

Typical UV Stabilizers are benzophenones, hindered amines, and benzotraizole. Also used, but not as effective, are salicylate esters, cyanoacrylates and bezilidenes.

Tinuvin® PED

2-(2-Hydroxy-5-methylphenyl)benzotriazole

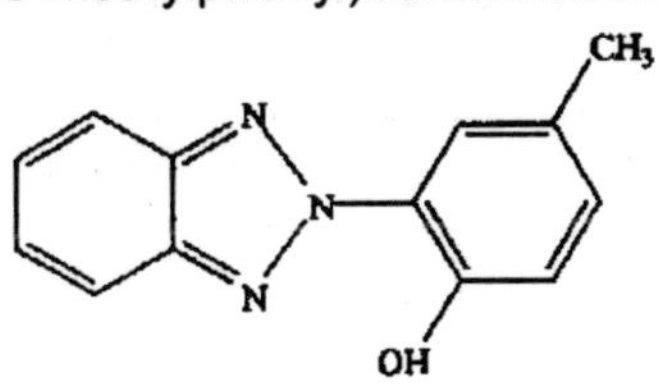

Ciba Specialty Chemicals

CAS 2440-22-4 **MF** $C_{13}H_{11}N_3O$ **MW** 225.27

Matrix	Cat. No.	Unit
1000 µg/mL in Hexane	PLAS-UV-005S	1 mL
NEAT	PLAS-UV-005N	50 mg

Uvinul® 3000

2,4-dihydroxybenzophenone

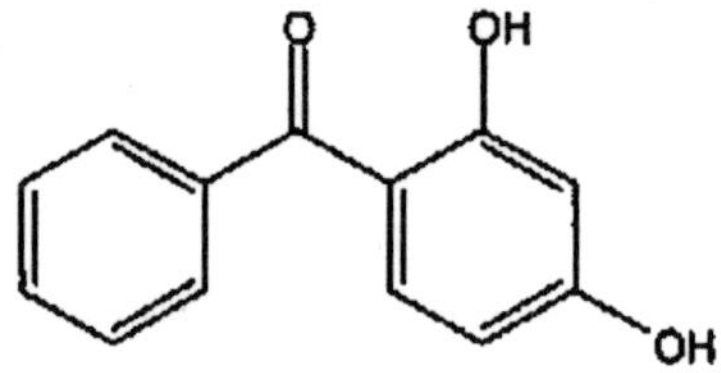

BASF Corporation

CAS 131-56-6 **MF** $C_{13}H_{10}O_3$ **MW** 214.22

Matrix	Cat. No.	Unit
1000 µg/mL in Hexane	PLAS-UV-001S	1 mL
NEAT	PLAS-UV-001N	50 mg

Uvinul® 3008

2-hydroxy-4-octyloxybenzophenone

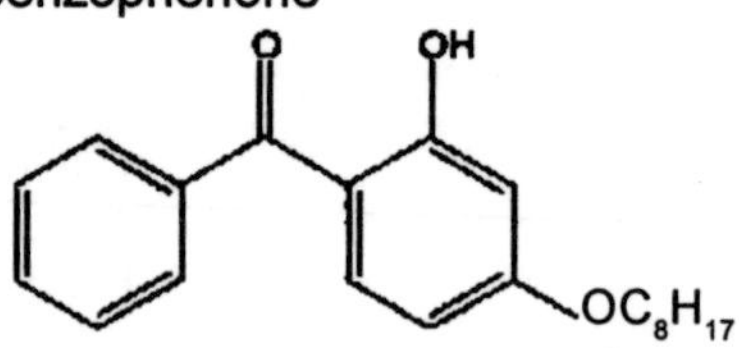

BASF Corporation

CAS 1843-05-6 **MF** $C_{21}H_{26}O_3$ **MW** 326.43

Matrix	Cat. No.	Unit
1000 µg/mL in Hexane	PLAS-UV-002S	1 mL
NEAT	PLAS-UV-002N	50 mg

Uvinul® 3040

2-hydroxy-4-methoxybenzophenone

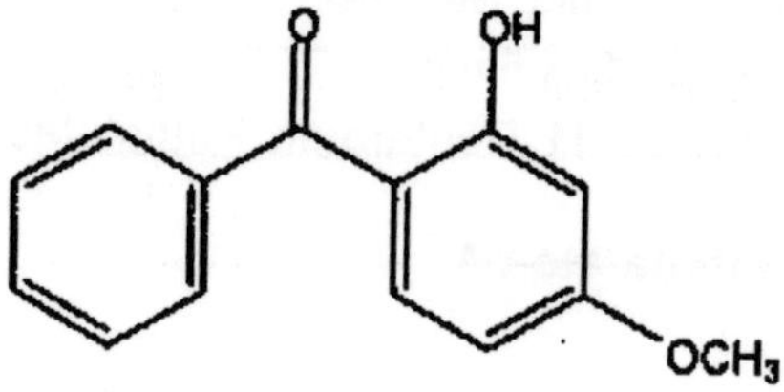

BASF Corporation

CAS 131-57-7 **MF** $C_{14}H_{12}O_3$ **MW** 228.26

Matrix	Cat. No.	Unit
1000 μg/mL in Hexane	PLAS-UV-003S	1 mL
NEAT	PLAS-UV-003N	50 mg

Uvinul® 3049

2,2-dihydroxy-4,4-dimethoxybenzophenone

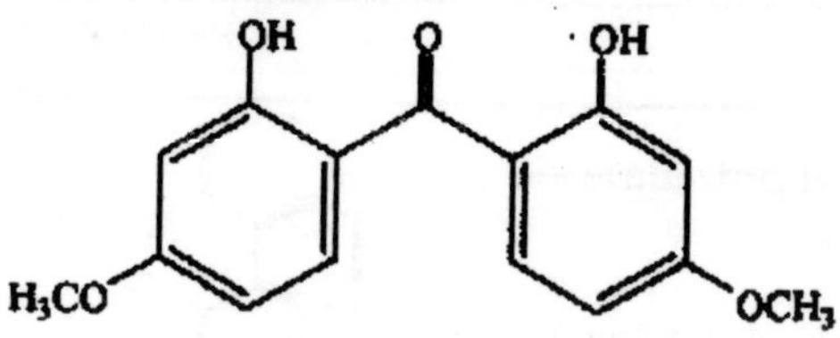

BASF Corporation

CAS 131-54-4 **MF** $C_{15}H_{14}O_5$ **MW** 274

Matrix	Cat. No.	Unit
1000 μg/mL in Hexane	PLAS-UV-004S	1 mL
NEAT	PLAS-UV-004N	50 mg

DEUTERATED COMPOUNDS

These deuterated compounds can be used as internal standards for method development for determining phtalates in environmental or other types of samples.

Deuterated Phthalate Solution Set

PHTH-D4S-SET 11 x 1 mL

Deuterated Phthalate Neat Set

PHTH-D4N-SET 11 x 5 mg

Set include 11 Deuterated Phthalates listed below:

Dibenzylphthalate-d4

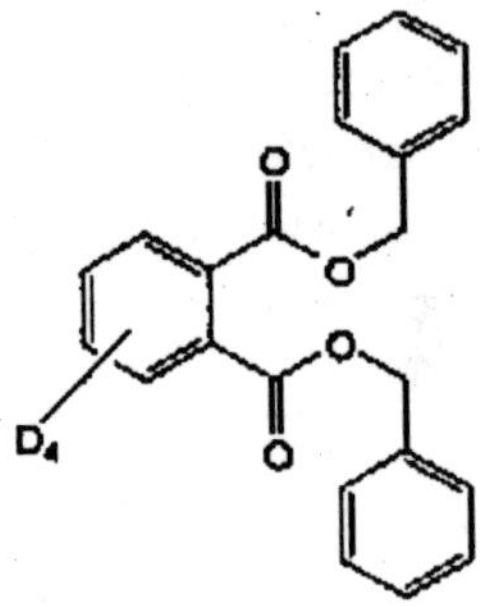

CAS MF $C_6D_4(COOCH_2C_6H_5)_2$ **MW** 350.41

Matrix	Cat. No.	Unit
1000 μg/mL in MeOH	PHTH-D4-001S	1 mL
NEAT	PHTH-D4-001N	5 mg

Di-n-butyl phthalate-d4

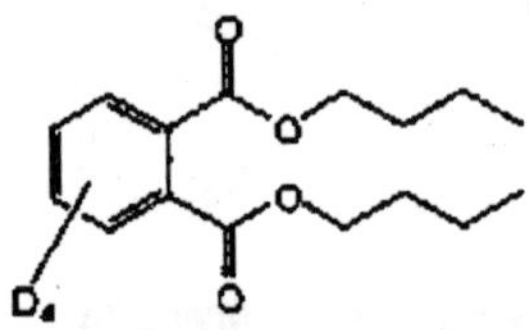

CAS 93952-11-5 **MF** $C_6D_4(COOCH_2CH_2CH_2CH_3)_2$ **MW** 282.37

Matrix	Cat. No.	Unit
1000 μg/mL in MeOH	PHTH-D4-002S	1 mL
NEAT	PHTH-D4-002N	5 mg

Di-iso-butyl phthalate-3,4,5,6-d_4

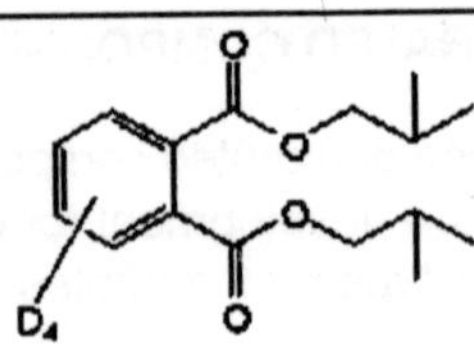

CAS 358730-88-8 **MF** $C_6D_4[COOCH_2CH(CH_3)_2]_2$ **MW** 326.43

Matrix	Cat. No.	Unit
1000 μg/mL in MeOH	PHTH-D4-003S	1 mL
Neat	PHTH-D4-003N	5 mg

Diethyl phthalate-3,4,5,6-d$_4$

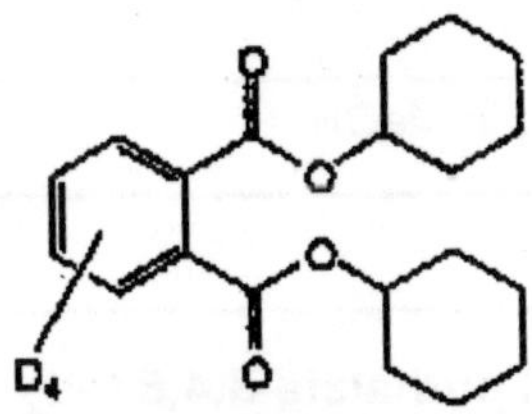

CAS 358731-25-6 **MF** $C_6D_4(COOC_6H_{11})_2$ **MW** 334.45

Matrix	Cat. No.	Unit
1000 μg/mL in MeOH	PHTH-D4-004S	1 mL
NEAT	PHTH-D4-004N	5 mg

Diethyl phthalate-3,4,5,6-d$_4$

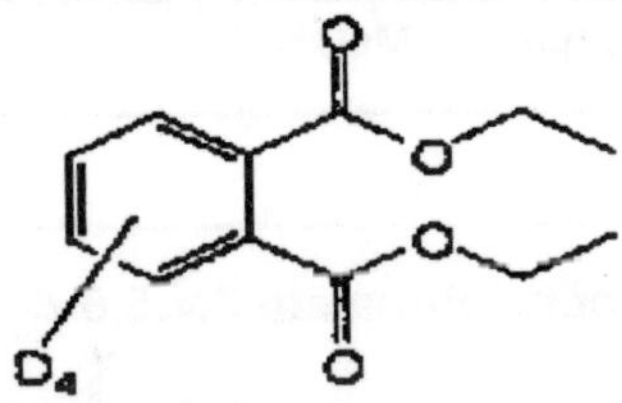

CAS 93952-12-6 **MF** $C_6D_4(COOCH_2CH_3)_2$ **MW** 226.26

Matrix	Cat. No.	Unit
1000 μg/mL in MeOH	PHTH-D4-005S	1 mL
NEAT	PHTH-D4-005N	5 mg

Di-n-hexyl phthalate-3,4,5,6-d_4

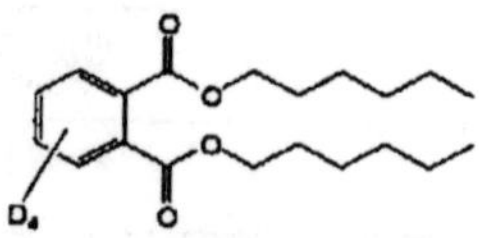

CAS N/A **MF** $C_6D_4[COO(CH_2)_5CH_3]_2$ **MW** 338.48

Matrix	Cat. No.	Unit
1000 µg/mL in MeOH	PHTH-D4-006S	1 mL
NEAT	PHTH-D4-006N	5 mg

Di-n-hexyl phthalate-3,4,5,6-d_4

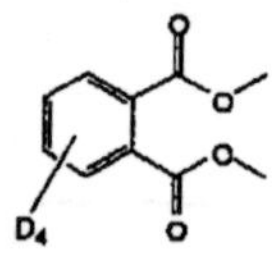

CAS 93951-89-4 **MF** $C_6D_4(COOCH_3)_2$ **MW** 198.21

Matrix	Cat. No.	Unit
1000 µg/mL in MeOH	PHTH-D4-007S	1 mL
NEAT	PHTH-D4-007N	5 mg

Di-n-octyl phthalate-3,4,5,6-d_4

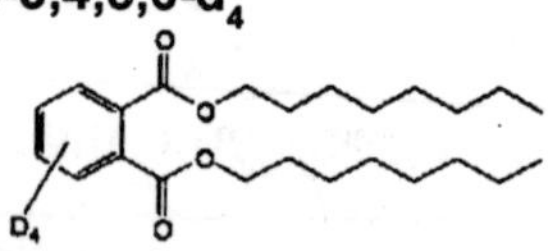

CAS 93952-13-7 **MF** $C_6D_4[COO(CH_2)_7CH_3]_2$ **MW** 394.59

Matrix	Cat. No.	Unit
1000 µg/mL in MeOH	PHTH-D4-008S	1 mL
NEAT	PHTH-D4-008N	5 mg

Di-n-pentyl phthalate-3,4,5,6-d_4

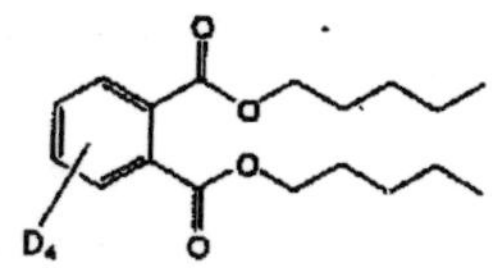

CAS 358730-89-9 **MF** $C_6D_4[COO(CH_2)_4CH_3]2$ **MW** 310.43

Matrix	Cat. No.	Unit
1000 µg/mL in MeOH	PHTH-D4-009S	1 mL
NEAT	PHTH-D4-009N	5 mg

Di-n-propyl phthalate-3,4,5,6-d_4

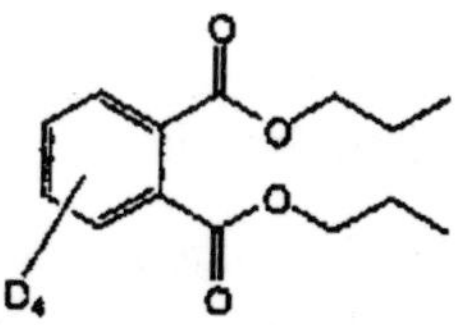

CAS 358731-29-0 **MF** $C_6D_4(COOCH_2CH_2CH_3)_2$ **MW** 254.32

Matrix	Cat. No.	Unit
1000 µg/mL in MeOH	PHTH-D4-010S	1 mL
NEAT	PHTH-D4-010N	5 mg

Bis(2-ethylhexyl) phthalate-3,4,5,6-d_4

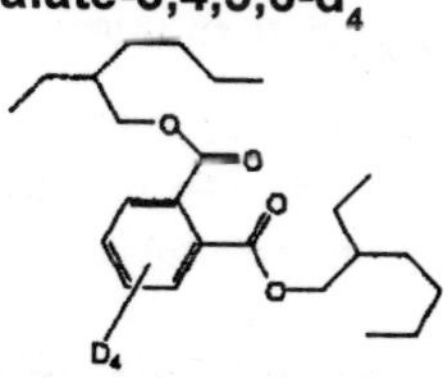

CAS 93951-87-2 **MF** $D_4[COOCH_2CH(CH_2CH_3)\ (CH_2)_3CH_3]_2$ **MW** 394.59

Matrix	Cat. No.	Unit
1000 µg/mL in MeOH	PHTH-D4-011S	1 mL
NEAT	PHTH-D4-011N	5 mg

2

Antiblock and Slip Agents

Antiblocking Agents

Antiblocking agents function by roughening the surface of film to give a spacing effect. The inherent tack of linear lowdensity polyethylene (LLDPE) and low-density polyethylene (LDPE) is a detriment when used in film where self-adhesion is undesirable. An antiblock additive is incorporated by the compounder to cause a slight surface roughness which prevents the film from sticking to itself. Years ago, efforts were made to prevent this by dusting the surface with corn starch or pyrogenic silica. This process was abandoned because of potential health concerns. Antiblocking agents are now melt-incorporated into the thermoplastic either via direct addition or by use of a master batch.

Antiblocking agents are used in polyolefin films in conjunction with slip agents in such consumer items as trash bags, shipping bags, and a variety of packaging applications. The most common polymers extruded into film include LLDPE and LDPE. Lesser amounts of highdensity polyethylene (HDPE) are used for these as well as other film applications. PE resins are used in film for their toughness, low cost and weight, optical properties, and shear sealability. Four criteria are used in the selection of an antiblocking agent, as shown in Table 2.1. While both organic and inorganic materials are used as antiblocking agents, the inorganics make up the bulk of the market. The four major types of antiblocking agents are

- Diatomaceous earth
- Talc
- Calcium carbonate
- Synthetic silicas and silicates

Antiblock Agent for Polyolefin Films

In the initial work with antiblock agents for polyethylene films, it was discovered that calcined diatomaceous earth of fine particle size (3.5 to 12 microns) worked very well as an antiblock agent. Calcined diatomaceous earth has continued to be used for this purpose for the last 35 to 40 years. Calcined diatomaceous earth contains a minimum of 63% crystalline silica and has irregularly shaped particles. The high levels of the crystalline silica in calcined diatomaceous earth have prompted a reduction of its use as an antiblock agent in polyolefin films from nearly 100% of the market to approximately 15-20% today, for reasons discussed in greater detail below.

Calcium carbonate has also been used as an antiblock agent for polyethylene films. Calcium carbonate has the advantage of being inexpensive. Calcium carbonate has the disadvantages of requiring an amount for effective antiblocking that is two to three times more than most other antiblock agents, which decreases the transparency of the resultant film. Films incorporating calcium carbonate as an antiblock agent vary in transparency from merely hazy to completely opaque. Calcium carbonate is therefore typically used as an antiblock agent for polyolefin films where clarity is not an issue, and opaque or colored films are acceptable. Calcium carbonate has irregularly shaped particles.

Microcrystalline silica has also been used as an antiblock agent. Silica had been used as an antiblock agent up until it was discovered that crystalline silica presents severe health hazards as a carcinogen. Microcrystalline silica has irregularly shaped particles and contains up to 98% crystalline silica. This ground sand or quartz also has high hardness which causes extreme metal wear in the equipment used to process the material.

Talc has also been used as an antiblock agent in polyolefin films. Talc has the benefit of requiring less material than calcium carbonate for the same level of antiblocking, and produces considerably less haze in the resultant film than calcium carbonate. However, the use of talc as an antiblock agent in polyolefin films requires special handling equipment to be able to process the talc for use as an antiblock agent, which increases overall costs. Talc has particles with a plate-shaped structure. Despite these failings, talc is now the most widely used mineral antiblock agent for LDPE and LLDPE films.

Nephylene syenite is also used as an antiblock agent in polyolefin films, despite its relative scarcity. Nephylene syenite includes no appreciable amount of quartz or crystalline silica, but has a very high hardness and is, consequently, extremely abrasive on processing and handling equipment. Nephylene syenite has a refractive index near that of polyethylene, which makes it very useful despite its relative scarcity. Currently, nephylene syenite is used in approximately ten percent of polyolefin film production applications.

Polymer producers add antiblock agents to the polymer in two different ways, near the end of the production chain. The most common way is to add the mineral and other additives "neat," i.e., mixing the antiblock agent in the appropriate percentage directly into the molten polymer as it is being produced.

A second method for adding antiblock to a polymer is to add a concentrate of the agent into the polymer. A concentrate is normally a blend of the antiblock agent and some polymer. Usually the concentrate ranges from 10% to 75% (by weight) antiblock agent, with the balance being polymer and other additives, if any. To prepare the concentrate, antiblock agent is added to an amount of the polymer so as to obtain the desired concentration of antiblock agent in polymer. The polymer is then extruded, cooled, and pelletized or granulated to form a concentrate.

Antiblock agents generally function in two ways. Antiblock agents may be present as a dusting on the surface of a film to prevent contact of the film to itself or other surfaces, thus preventing mutual adhesion. Examples of the use of an antiblock agent in such a manner include talc on surgical gloves. A second way of using an antiblock agent with a film is by intimately dispersing the agent in the polymer before the polymer is formed into the film. The antiblock agent particles extend beyond the outer surface of the polymer, thereby disturbing the planarity of the polymer film surface, thus preventing the surfaces of the film from fully contacting itself or another surface.

In contrast, minerals and other agents used as antiblock agents in polymer films are typically used in extremely small amounts, e.g., less than or equal to 1% of the polymer bulk material by weight.

Pumice has also in the past been used as an abrasive product, e.g., in abrasive soaps, etc., and polishing compounds. Pumice used in these applications is typically very coarse, includes particles over a very wide range of sizes, is used in extremely high concentrations or weight percentages, and varies considerably in both colour (although it is typically yellow) and refractive index.

The pumice used in the present method is derived from pumice stone, a naturally occurring product of volcanic origin. The pumice stone comprises a mixture of various oxides, predominantly of silicon, aluminum, iron, sodium, and potassium. Table 2.1 lists the most prevalent (by weight percent) components of a typical pumice stone which is used as the starting material for producing the pumice used in the present method . Substantially all of the oxides are chemically bound to silicon dioxide as silicates.

Table 2.1

SiO_2	Al_2O_3	Fe_2O_3	Mg	CaO	Na_2O	K_2O
73.73	11.62	1.79	0.06	0.26	4.24	4.22
P_2O_5	TiO_2	MnO	BaO	Cr_2O_3	SrO	—
0.028	0.057	0.075	0.002	0.006	<0.001	—

Unbound silicon dioxide in the mined pumice stone contains less than about 1% (by weight) crystalline silica. Accordingly, the fine pumice produced from the pumice stone also contains less than 1% (by weight), preferably less than 0.5% (by weight), of crystalline silica, therefore allowing its use in a wide variety of applications without the possibility of excessive exposure to harmful respirable crystalline silica. The pumice has a refractive index of about 1.50.

Talc antiblock compositions and method of preparation

Polyolefin films are used extensively for packaging and in film covering applications. The use of polyolefin films continues to increase as new market opportunities become available in areas where paper was traditionally used. The versatility of the film provides potentially infinite growth prospects for the product in the future. However, there is an inherent short coming in the use of plastic films that may retard its market acceptance and growth, it sticks. When plastic film is produced or used in various applications, there is a tendency for contacting layers of the film to stick together or "block", making separation of the film, opening of bags made from the film, or finding the end of the film on plastic rolls difficult. The present invention relates to polyolefin resin compositions that are specifically designed to have satisfactory antiblocking capability.

Antiblock agents are materials that are added to polyolefin resins to roughen their surface and thereby prevent layers of the plastic film from sticking, hence the term, " antiblocking agent" is applied to such materials. Although, inorganic minerals, such as, for example, diatomaceous earth, synthetic silica and talc are known to reduce blocking when added to polyolefin film resin compositions, each has both advantages and critical disadvantages.

One comparative advantage of diatomaceous earth is that it is known to be a moderately effective antiblocking agent, when used as an antiblocking agent. However, it is also known that diatomaceous earth adversely affects the film's physical properties, such as film clarity, film haze, and is very abrasive and moderately expensive and may pose a serious health threat. Synthetic silicates are known to be effective as an antiblock, however a significant disadvantage of silica is that it is very expensive. Talc, on the other hand, has found increasing use as an effective antiblock agent over diatomaceous earth and synthetic silica because of a significant cost advantage over both. However, one major disadvantage when talc is added to polyolefin film resins, is that it aggressively adsorbs other film additives, such as antioxidants, slip agents and processing aid. The absence, or reduced level of these additives in polyolefin resin compositions during production, routinely cause processing problems and raise serious film quality concerns.

For example, antioxidants are added to improve film stability, slip agents are present in the resin to improve film converting, while processing aids are employed to improve film quality, and to provide lubrication during film extrusion by eliminating melt fracture. Melt fracture is a measure of film surface uniformity, appearance and strength. Of the three additives mentioned here, processing aids are most adversely affected by the presence of antiblock agents. Although it is well known that all antiblock agents adsorb processing aids, talc antiblock agents adsorb greater levels of processing aids than either diatomaceous earth or synthetic silica antiblocks. Consequently, when resin compositions are produced having additives that include antiblock talc, it is necessary to increase the dosage of processing aids. The increased dosage adversely effects the over all production economics of the plastic film.

Therefore, what is needed is a new generation of talc antiblock agents that adsorb less process aids than either synthetic silica or diatomaceous earth.

A typical embodiment of the present method could include:

From about	To about
0.1%–1.0%	talc antiblock
0.02%–0.5%	process aid
0.05%–0.25%	slip agent
0.01%–0.5%	antioxidant
0.01%–0.25%	scavenger
0.1%–5.0%	siloxane, silane, polyether, carbon based polymer
99.7%–92.5%	polyolefin resin

A typical preferred embodiment of the present method includes:

0.5%	talc antiblock
0.15%	process aid
0.12%	slip agent
0.03%	antioxidant
0.05%	scavenger
0.10%	antioxidant
2.50%	siloxane, silane, polyether, carbon based polymer
96.55%	polyolefin resin

All percentages are based on total weight percent.

The suppliers of inorganic additives to the plastics industry market their products. *Products can also be used as antiblocking agents in polyethylene films, only a few* suppliers actively market their products for this end use.

Table 2.2: Criteria Used in Selection of an Antiblocking Agent

Specification	Function
Particle size distribution	Affects both the level of antiblock performance and the physical properties of the final film.
Surface area	Measured in square meters per gram. Affects the coefficient of friction of the film and level of wear on equipment.
Specific gravity	Indicates the relative weight of the product. Density Measures the mass/volume ratio. Affects the quality of the film

Slip Agents

Slip agents or *slip additives* are the terms used by industry for those modifiers that impart a reduced coefficient of friction to the surface of finished products. Slip agents can significantly improve the handling qualities of polyolefins and, to a lesser extent, PVC, in film and bag applications. They help speed up film production and ensure final product quality. Fatty acid amides, the primary chemical type used as slip agents, are similar to migratory antistatic agents and some lubricants with a molecule which has both a polar and nonpolar portion. These additives migrate to the surface and form a very thin molecular layer that reduces surface friction.

Slip agents are typically employed in applications where surface lubrication is desired—either during or immediately after processing. To accomplish this, the materials must exude quickly to the surface of the film. To function properly they should have only limited compatibility with the resin. Slip agents, in addition to lowering surface friction, can also impart the following characteristics:

- Lower surface resistivity (antistatic properties)
- Reduce melt viscosity
- Mold release

Slip agents are often referred to as *lubricants.* However, they should not be confused with the lubricants which act as processing aids. While most slip agents can be used as lubricants, many lubricants cannot be used as slip agents since they do not always function externally.

The major types of slip agents include:

- Fatty acid amides (primarily erucamide and oleamide
- Fatty acid esters
- Metallic stearates
- Waxes
- Proprietary amide blends

Antiblock and slip agents can be incorporated together using combination master batches which give the film extruder greater formulation control.

Anti slipping agent

PREPARATION

7.5 wt % of distilled water was added into a mixing tank. 2 wt % of polyvinylpyrrolidone (PVP K-15) was added as viscosity modifier and stirring was performed until it was dissolved completely.

The solution was heated to about 50° C. and 66 wt % of corn syrup (water content: 21.5%) and 3 wt % of maltodextrin were slowly added. When the solid contents were almost dissolved, the solution was cooled to room temperature, while continuing the stirring. Then, 1 wt % of Tween 80 and 2 wt % of sodium salicylate were added as leveling agent and antiseptic, respectively, and stirring was performed. Subsequently, 17.5 wt % of a methanol (50)/ethanol (50) solvent mixture was added. 1 wt % of dissolved glycerin was slowly added to the solution as humectant, while stirring.

Suppliers

Because of the different chemical composition of antiblocking and slip agents, few companies are involved in both. Table 2.3 presents a list of the selected global suppliers of antiblocking and slip agents.

TABLE 2.3: Selected Suppliers of Antiblocking and Slip Agents

Supplier	Type	
	Anti block	Slip
Akcros	—	x
Akzo Nobel	—	x
Allied Signal	—	x
American Ingredients	—	x
Asahi Denka Kogyo	—	x
Baerlocher	—	x
BASF	—	x
Cabot	x	—
Celite	x	—
Chemson	—	x
Clariant	—	x
Croda Universal	—	x
Cyprus Minerals	x	—
Degussa	x	—
Eastman Chemical	—	x
ECC	x	—

Supplier	Type	
	Anti block	Slip
Ferro	—	x
Guangpin Chemical	x	—
Henkel	—	x
Huels	—	x
Idemitsu Kosan	—	x
J. M Huber	x	—
Kao	—	x
Katsuta Kako	—	x
Kawaken Fine Chemical	—	x
Kawamura Kasei	—	x
Lion Akzo	—	x
Lonza	—	x
Matsumura Oil Research	—	x
Mitsui Petrochemical	—	x
Miyoshi Oil and Fat	x	—
New Japan Chemical	—	x
Nippon Fine Chemical	—	x
Nippon Kasei Chemical	—	x
Nippon Seiro	—	x
PT Sumi Asih	—	x
Petrolite	—	x
Pfizer	x	—
Sakai Chemical	—	x
Sankyo Organic Chemicals	—	x
Sanyo Chemical	—	x
Shinagawa Chemical	—	x
Struktol	—	x
Unichema	—	x
Witco	—	x
Yasuhara Chemical	—	x
Zeelan Industries	x	—

Trends and forecasts

The trend toward downgauging in PE film has favorably affected the use of slip agents. Although the value of resin decreases as films are made thinner, surface area increases, therefore, requiring higher load ings of slip agents. Both slip and antiblocking agents are expected to grow at a rate of about 4% annually over the next 5 years.

3

Antioxidants

Description

Antioxidants are used in a variety of resins to prevent oxidative degradation. Degradation is initiated by the action of highly reactive free radicals caused by heat, radiation, mechanical shear, or metallic impurities. The initiation of free radicals may occur during polymerization, processing, or fabrication.

Once the first step of initiation occurs, propagation follows:

Propagation is the reaction of the free radical with an oxygen molecule, yielding a peroxy radical. The peroxy radical then reacts with an available hydrogen atom within the polymer to form an unstable hydroperoxide and another free radical. In the absence of an antioxidant, this reaction continues and leads to degradation of the polymer. Degradation is manifested either by cross-linking or chain scissoring.

Cross-linking causes the polymer to increase in molecular weight, leading to brittleness, gellation, and decreased elongation. Chain scissoring decreases molecular weight, leading to increased melt flow and reduced tensile strength.

The function of an antioxidant is to prevent the propagation steps of oxidation. Products are classified as primary or secondary antioxidants depending on the method by which they prevent oxidation.

Primary antioxidants, usually sterically hindered phenols, function by donating their reactive hydrogen to the peroxy free radical so that the propagation of subsequent free radicals does not occur. The antioxidant free radical is rendered stable by electron delocalization. Secondary antioxidants retard oxidation by preventing the proliferation of alkoxy and hydroxy radicals by decomposing hydroperoxides to yield nonreactive products. These materials are typically used in synergistic combination with primary antioxidants.

Table 3.1 lists the chemical types of primary and secondary antioxidants and their major resin applications. Through the remainder of this chapter, antioxidants will be addressed by type based on overall chemistry. The class of antioxidant merely describes its mode of stabilization.

Amines. Amines, normally arylamines, function as primary antioxidants by donating hydrogen. Amines are the most effective type of primary antioxidant, having the ability to act as chain terminators and peroxide decomposers. However, they tend to discolor, causing staining, and, for the most part, lack FDA approval. For this reason, amines are found in pigmented plastics in nonfood applications. Amines are commonly used in the rubber industry but also find minor use in plastics such as black wire and cable formulations and in polyurethane polyols.

Preparation

The present method relates to new polymeric amines that have N-substituted 2,5-pyrrolediyl groups incorporated in the backbone. The present method also relates to a process for the preparation of such new polymeric amines, to curable resin compositions and to glued products, glued wood products in particular.

METHOD 1 (Synthesis of a Polymeric Amine)

1000 g of the olefin-carbon monoxide polymer is mixed with 370.5 g 1,2-propanediamine. The mixture is heated to 80° C. and stirred until the conversion of the primary amino group on the 1-position reached 95% (240 minutes, determined by potentiometric titration starting from 7300 mmol/kg amine to 3830 mmol/kg).

TABLE 3.1: Antioxidants by Chemical Type with Major Resin Applications

Types	Major resins	Comments
Primary Amine	Rubber, some pigmented plastics, and polyurethane polyols	Arylamines tend to discolor and cause staining.
Phenolic	Polyolefins, styrenics, and engineering resins	Phenolics are generally stain resistant and include simple phenolics (BHT), various polyphenolics, and bisphenolics.
Metal salts	Polyolefin wire and cable	These are metal deactivators used in the inner coverings next to the metal.
Secondary Organophosphite	Polyolefins, styrenics, and engineering	Phosphites can improve colour and engineering resins stability, resins but can be corrosive if hydrolyzed.
Thioester	Polyolefins and styrenics	The major disadvantage with thioesters is their odor which is transferred to the host polymer.

METHOD 2 (Curable Resin Composition)

A curable resin composition is made by protonating about 50% of the available amino groups of the above polymeric amine with acetic acid at 80° C. Water is added to achieve a 40% solids solution (the amount of water is corrected with the reaction water). The mixture is cooled to ambient temperature and 1000 g of the olefin-carbon monoxide polymer is added together with 24 g salicylic acid (catalyst). Finally, water is added for a 50% solids curable resin composition.

METHOD 1 and 2 can be carried out in a one-pot synthesis.

METHOD 3a (Wood Glue Testing EN-314)

The formulation of method 2 is applied as a 100 g/m2 single glue line onto two 20×20 cm birch wood veneer panels of 2 mm thickness. These panels were stacked with a third panel in the middle, with the wood grain of the outer layers in parallel direction and that of the centre layer in cross direction. The package was pressed for 2 minutes at 200° C at 1.2 Mpa. The triplex so formed was cooled to ambient temperature. It was then cut into sample pieces suitable for the plywood standard testing procedure EN-314. In this test, the samples are subjected to immersion in boiling water for 72 hours and subsequently exposed to a shear test when cooled down but still wet. The triplex should fail by giving wood failure at a shear level of higher than 1.0 Mpa. The samples used in the above testing gave wood failure at shear strength readings of 1.5 to 2.0 MPa.

Phenolics

The most widely used antioxidants in plastics are phenolics. The products generally resist staining or discoloration. However, they may form quinoid (colored) structures upon oxidation. Phenolic antioxidants include simple phenolics, bisphenolics, polyphenolics, and thiobisphenolics.

The most common simple phenolic is butylated hydroxytoluene (BHT) or 2,6-di-t-butyl-4-methylphenol. BHT possesses broad FDA approval and is widely used as an antioxidant in a variety of polymers. It is commonly called the "workhorse" of the industry but is losing ground to the higher molecular weight antioxidants which resist migration. The disadvantage of BHT is that it is highly volatile and can cause discoloration. Other simple phenolics include BHA (2- and 3-t-butyl-4- hydroxyanisole) which is frequently used in food applications.

Polyphenolics and bisphenolics are higher in molecular weight than simple phenolics and both types are generally nonstaining. The increased molecular weight provides lower volatility, but is generally more costly. However, the loading of polyphenolics is much less than that of the simple phenolics. The most commonly used polyphenolic is tetrakis(methylene-(3,5-di-t-butyl-4-hydroxyhydrocinnamate) methane or IRGANOX1010 from Ciba. Other important bisphenolics include: Cytec Industries' CYANOX 2246 and 425 and BISPHENOL A from Aristech, Dow, and Shell.

Thiobisphenols are less effective than hindered phenols in terminating peroxy radicals. They also function as peroxide decomposers (secondary antioxidants) at temperatures above 100°C. Typically, thiobisphenols are chosen for use in high-temperature resin applications. Users generally prefer hindered phenolics over thiobisphenols where high-temperature service is not involved.

Preparation

A three-neck reaction flask, mounted with a mechanical stirrer, thermometer, condenser and nitrogen inlet was charged with 850 parts of a styrene allyl alcohol copolymer; 447 parts of ricinoleic acid and 425 parts of acetone. The styrene allyl alcohol copolymer, a solid resin, had a hydroxyl value of 255, an equivalent weight of 220, a weight average molecular weight of 1700 and a hydroxyl group content of 7.7 moles per mole of copolymer. The mole ratio of the reactants, therefore, was one mole of styrene-allyl alcohol copolymer and 3 moles of ricinoleic acid or 7.7 equivalents of the copolymer and 3 equivalents of the acid. The mixture was heated with stirring to dissolve the resin and distill the acetone. When the temperature reached 100° C., 0.65 parts of dibutyl tin oxide were added as the esterification catalyst. The temperature was raised to 220° C. and the reaction continued until the water formed in the reaction stopped distilling and the product had an acid value of one or less. The product was cooled to 100° C. and 317.5 parts of butyl acetate were added to form an 80% solution of the product.

The new polyol solution had a Brookfield viscosity of 8,000 cps at 23° C., an acid value of 0.77, and OH value of 122.2, an equivalent weight of 459 and a volatile content of 20.3 parts percent. In comparison, an 80% solution of the unmodified styrene-allyl alcohol copolymer in butyl acetate had a Brookfield viscosity of 350,000 cps. The new polyol, therefore, had a much lower viscosity and a much higher equivalent weight then the unmodified styrene-allyl alcohol copolymer.

A mixture of 4.1 parts of 2,6-di-t-butylphenol and 1.9 parts of sulfur powder (mole ratio 1:3) was heated under refluxing for 0.5 hour in 95 percent ethanol solution containing 1.7 parts of potassium hydroxide (1.5 equivalents of KOH for 2,6-di-t-butylphenol). The mixture was neutralized by hydrochloric acid, and extracted with benzene. After evaporation of benzene, the residue was separated by column chromatography, and the mixture of 4,4'-mono- and poly-thiobis(2,6--di-t-butylphenol) was obtained. NMR measurement showed the following yield of each of the following sulfides in the mixture:

4,4'-thiobis(2,6-di-t-butylphenol) 65 percent

4,4'-dithiobis(2,6-di-t-butylphenol) 21 percent

4,4'-trithiobis(2,6-di-t-butylphenol) 5 percent

Each sulfide can be isolated by recrystallization from the mixture of ethanol solution.

Organophosphites

Acting as secondary antioxidants, organophosphites reduce hydroperoxides to alcohols, converting themselves to phosphonates. They also provide colour stability, inhibiting the discoloration caused by the formation of quinoid reaction products which are formed upon oxidation of phenolics. Tris-nonylphenyl phosphate (TNPP) is the most commonly used organophosphite followed by tris(2,4-di-tert-butylphenyl)phosphite (for example, Ciba's IRGAFOS 168). The disadvantage of phosphites is their hygroscopic tendency. Hydrolysis of phosphites can ultimately lead to the formation of phosphoric acid, which can corrode processing equipment.

Preparation

This application relates to a process for the selective synthesis of intermediates, including chloridites and dichloridites, for the synthesis of triorganophosphites.

SYNTHESIS OF PHOSPHOROCHLORIDITE 1A AND PHOSPHORODICHLORIDITE 2A

In a temperature controlled 250 ml baffled flask charged with 50 ml of 1.0 molar PCl_3 in toluene, a solution of 25 ml 2.0 molar triethylamine in toluene, and a solution of 25 ml 2.0 molar o-cresol in toluene were added separately and concurrently under vigorous stirring via a dual syringe pump over a period of 90 min. During the addition period the reaction temperature was maintained between –5° C. The ^{31}P NMR analysis showed clean transformation to the corresponding dichloridite 2a (δ 182.7) in 97% selectivity. A second 25 ml of each 2.0 molar triethylamine solution in toluene and 2.0 molar o-cresol solution in toluene were added separately and concurrently via a dual syringe pump over a period of 90 min. The ^{31}P NMR analysis showed clean transformation to the corresponding chloridite 1a (δ 161.9) in 91% overall selectivity.

Thioesters

Derived from aliphatic esters of B-thio dipropionic acid, thioesters act as secondary antioxidants and also provide high heat stability to a variety of polymers. Thioesters function as secondary antioxidants by destroying hydroperoxides to form stable hexavalent sulfur derivatives. Thioesters act as synergists when combined with phenolic antioxidants in polyolefins. The major disadvantage of thioester antioxidants is their inherent odor which is transferred to the host polymer.

Preparation

This method relates to a novel process for preparing thioesters. More particularly, the invention relates to the preparation of thioesters by reaction of an acid halide with a xanthate.

To a stirred slurry containing 0.12 moles of potassium benzyl dithiocarbonate dihydrate in 200 ml. of acetone, 0.1 moles of

2-oxo-3-benzothiazolineacetyl chloride was added in one portion. An exothermic reaction set in causing a temperature rise. After the rise in temperature subsided, the reaction mixture was stirred at 25°-30° C. for 18 hours. After 800 grams of ice water was added, stirring was continued at 0°-10° C. for 2 hours. The solid was collected by filtration, washed with water until neutral to litmus and air-dried at 25°-30° C.

Deactivators

Metal deactivators combine with metal ions to limit the potential for chain propagation. Metal deactivators are commonly used in polyolefin inner coverings in wire and cable applications where the plastic comes in contact with the metal. In effect, the deactivator acts as a chelating agent to form a stable complex at the metal interface, thereby preventing catalytic activity. The most common deactivators contain an oxamide moiety that complexes with and deactivates the metal ions. A typical product is Ciba's IRGANOX MD-1024.

Preparation

The present method provides an improved method to add a particulate deactivator to a polyethylene solution which is produced in a medium pressure solution polymerization process. More particularly the improvement comprises a process to prepare a polyethylene solution wherein ethylene is polymerized with a halogen-containing Ziegler-Natta catalyst system, at a pressure of from 3 to 35 mega Pascals ("MPa") and a temperature of from 100 to 320° C. in the presence of a solvent for said polyethylene, the improvement which comprises the injection of a particulate deactivator to said polyethylene solution subsequent to the discharge of same from said stirred reactor further characterized in that said deactivator is selected from a metal carbonate and hydrotalcite.

In a preferred embodiment, a soluble secondary deactivator is also used. In a particularly preferred embodiment, the deactivator suspension contains a polymeric "suspension enhancer" which is preferably a mixture of isobutylene polymer and a long chain carboxylic acid.

METHOD 1 Lab Screening Experiments

A series of lab-scale screening experiments were undertaken to identify materials which deactivated conventional Ziegler-Natta polymerization catalysts. A deactivator was considered for further testing if it was successful in terminating/preventing olefin polymerization and generated minimal by-products or colour. Deactivators which satisfied these criteria include water, various carboxylic acids, carbon monoxide, zinc oxide, zinc stearate, calcium stearate, dimethyl carbonate, diethyl carbonate, erucamide, glycerol monostearate and various commercially available hydrotalcites ("HT"), including those sold by Kyowa and Reheis under the tradenames DHT-4A, DHT-4, DHT-4A-2, ZHT-4A and L-55RII.

The HT materials provided particularly good results. Moreover, the use of HT materials in a commercial polyethylene product was considered feasible because similar HT materials have enjoyed commercial success when compounded into solid polypropylene resins. However, the HT materials have the undesirable characteristic of being comparatively dense particles which quickly settle out of the solvent commonly used in the solution polymerization of ethylene.

METHOD 2 Pilot Plant Trials

The use of HT, methanol ("MeOH") and nonanoic acid ("NAc") as potential deactivators was tested at a solution polymerization polyethylene pilot plant. The solution polymerization was conducted in a stirred autoclave reactor using a titanium chloride/magnesium chloride/aluminum alkyl catalyst. A large series of polymerizations were completed, resulting in a variety of polyethylene solutions exiting the stirred autoclave reactor having polyethylene concentrations of 2 to 15 weight per cent; residual chloride concentrations of up to 200 ppm and residual titanium concentrations of up to 15 ppm.

A long insulated pipe was installed between the polymerization reactor and the pressure letdown vessel. In the absence of any added deactivator, some continued polymerization is observed in this pipe (as evidenced by an increase in solution temperature and an increase in ethylene conversion). Addition of HT, MeOH or NAc (alone or in combination) in 3/1 to 7/1 molar excess (titanium basis) was sufficient to eliminate this post reactor polymerization problem. However, the use of HT alone resulted in some fouling of the process equipment (presumably from the tendency of the HT to settle out of solution).

The effect of the deactivators on UV/thermal stability (with respect to changes in colour and tensile properties) and resin corrosivity were evaluated. The most "balanced" resin properties and process considerations were obtained with HT as single deactivator as well as HT/MeOH and HT/NAc. HT is a primary deactivator in that it functions well on its own. However, it is difficult to add HT (from an operability perspective it is undesirable to add the solid particles) and, hence, it is preferred to use HT in combination with a soluble secondary deactivator. HT improves the resin colour, thermal and UV stability and suppresses resin corrosivity. Both MeOH and NAc can be used in combination and alone as a deactivator but there are concerns around process corrosion and resin corrosivity if used without HT.

RECENT DEVELOPMENTS

Some of the most significant new product development trends in antioxidants are as follows:

"Lactone" stabilizers are a new class of materials that are reputed to stop the autoxidation process before it starts. These products, which are derivatives of the benzofuranone family, act as C-radical scavengers in combination with primary and secondary antioxidants.

These blends (Ciba's HP) claim to be particularly effective in hightemperatureand high-shear processing.

A new phosphite secondary antioxidant, based on butyl ethyl propane diol, reputedly yields high activity, solubility, and hydrolytic stability in a range of polymers. This would allow the producer to use lower levels of additives to achieve similar results.

Antioxidants (AO) in the form of pellets are challenging the granule forms. Advantages include low-dusting, easy flowing, and lower-cost systems. Most major AO suppliers are now marketing these product forms.

Selected suppliers are promoting hindered amine light stabilizers for the combined use as antioxidants.

Suppliers

There are over 70 suppliers of antioxidants worldwide. Numerous suppliers offer both primary and secondary antioxidants to complete their product line. However, very few actually manufacture both primary and secondary antioxidants, since the products are based on different manufacturing routes, processes, and feedstock sources. As a result, it is quite common in this industry to resell products produced by another company. Table 3.2 displays selected suppliers of antioxidants by type.

Trends and forecasts

The overall growth of antioxidants in plastics will be influenced by the following factors:

Growth of the polyolefin industry, especially polypropylene.

Increased price competition as patents expire; this will force some suppliers to accept lower margins and/or to segment their customer base and concede lower margin accounts to selected competitors. Continued premiums will be possible for technical innovation where unique products bring value to the market. Examples include:

- Higher processing temperature performance
- New chemistry (for example, hydroxyl amines) replacing phenolicbased
- systems, avoiding potential toxicity and colour issues
- Higher molecular weight AOs to reduce volatility during processing
- Better long-term stability
- Equal performance at lower loading levels
- More economical product forms and blends

Over the next 5 years, consumption of antioxidants is expected to grow somewhat evenly around the world at a rate of about 5%/year.

TABLE 3.2: Selected Antioxidant Suppliers

Supplier	Type					
	Amine	Phenolic	Organo-phosphite	Thioester	Metal deactivator	Other
1	2	3	4	5	6	7
3V Sigma	—	X	—	—	—	—
Akcros (Akzo)	—	X	X	X	—	—
Albemarle	—	X	—	—	—	—
Albright and Wilson	—	—	X	—	—	—
Asahi Denka Kogyo	—	X	X	X	—	—
Asia Stabilizer	—	X	X	—	—	—
Bayer	X	X	X	—	—	—
Cambrex	—	X	—	—	—	—
Chang-Chun Petrochemical	—	X	—	X	—	X
Ciba Specialty	—	X	X	X	X	X
Clariant	—	X	X	—	—	—
Coin Chemical Industrial	—	X	—	—	—	—
Cytec Industries	—	X	—	X	—	—

Dai-ichi Kogyo Seiyaku	—	X	—	—	—	X
Daihachi Chemical Ind.	—	—	X	—	—	—
Dongbo S.C.	—	—	X	X	—	—
Dover Chemical	—	—	X	—	—	—
Eastman Chemical Products	—	X	X	—	—	—
Everspring Chemical	—	Y	—	—	—	—
Fairmount Chemical Company	—	X	—	—	X	—
Ferro Corporation	—	X	X	—	—	X
GE Specialty Chemical	—	—	X	—	—	X
Goodyear Tire and Rubber	X	X	—	—	—	—
Great Lakes Chemical	X	X	X	X	—	X
Hampshire Chemicals	—	—	—	—	—	—
Han Nong Adeka	—	X	—	—	—	—
Harwick Chemical Corporation	—	x	—	—	—	—
Honshu Chemical	—	x	—	—	—	—
Johoku Chemical	—	—	X	—	—	—
Kawaguchi Chemical Industry	—	X	X	—	—	
Kolon Industries	—	—	X	—	—	—
Maruzen Petrochemical	—	X	X	—	—	—
Mayzo	—	X	—	X	—	—
Morton International	—	—	—	—	—	—

1	2	3	4	5	6	7
Musashina Geigy	—	X	X	—	—	—
Nan Ya Plastics	—	—	—	—	—	—
Nanjin Chemical Plant	—	X	X	—	—	—
Nippon Oil and Fats	—	X	—	X	—	—
Orient Chemical	—	X		—	—	—
Ouchi Shinko Chemical	—	X	X	—	—	—
PMC	—	X	—	—	—	—
R. T. Vanderbilt	X	X	—	X	—	—
Raschig Corporation	—	X	—	—	—	—
Reagens	—	—	X	X	—	—
Rhodia	—	X	—	—	—	—
Sakai Chemical Industry	—	—	X	—	—	—
Sankyo Chemical	—	X	X	—	—	—
Sanyo Chemical	—	X	—	—	—	—
Schenectady Chemicals	—	X	—	—	—	—
Seiko Chemical	—	X	—	—	—	—
Solutia	—	X	—	—	—	—
Song-Woun	—	X	—	X	—	—

Sumitomo Chemical	—	X	X	X	—	—
Taiwan Ciba Geigy	—	X	—	—	—	—
Tiyoda Chemical	—	X	—	—	—	—
Ueno Fine Chemicals	—	X	—	—	—	—
Uniroyal Chemical	X	X	X	—	X	—
UOP Biological & Food Products	—	X	—	—	—	—
Witeo Corporation	X	X	X	—	—	—
Yoshitomi	—	X	X	X	—	—

4

Antistatic Agents

Description

Plastics are inherently insulative (typical surface resistivities in the range of 10^{12} to 10^{14} Ω/square) and cannot readily dissipate a static charge. The primary role of an antistatic agent or antistat is to prevent the buildup of static electrical charge resulting from the transfer of electrons to the surface. This static electricity can be generated during processing, transportation, handling, or in final use. Friction between two or more objects (for example, the passage of copy paper over a roller) is usually the cause of static electricity. Typical electrostatic voltages can range from 6000 to 35,000 V.

When the unprotected plastic is brought into contact with another material, loosely bound electrons pass across the interface. When these materials are then separated, one surface has an excess charge, while the other has a deficiency of electrons. In most plastics the excess charge will linger or discharge, causing the following problems:

- Fire and explosion hazards
- Poor mold release
- Damage to electrical components
- Attraction of dust

Antistats function to either dissipate or promote the decay of static electricity. Secondary benefits of antistat incorporation into polymer systems include improved processability and mold release, as well as better internal and external lubrication. Therefore, in certain applications, antistatic agents can also function as lubricants, slip agents, and mold release agents.

This discussion will focus on chemical antistats and excludes inorganic conductive additives such as carbon black, metal-coated carbon fiber, and stainless steel wire. Chemical antistatic additives can be categorized by their method of application (external and internal) and their chemistry. Most antistats are hydroscopic materials and function primarily by attracting water to the surface. This process allows the charge to dissipate rapidly. Therefore, the ambient humidity level plays a vital role in this mechanism. With an increase in humidity, the surface conductivity of the treated polymer is increased, resulting in a rapid flow of charge and better antistatic properties. Conversely, in dry ambient conditions, antistats which rely on humidity to be effective may offer erratic performance.

External Antistats

External, or topical, antistats are applied to the surface of the finished plastic part through techniques such as spraying, wiping, or dipping. Since they are not subjected to the temperatures and stresses of plastic compounding, a broad range of chemistries is possible. The most common external antistatic additives are quaternary ammonium salts, or "quats," applied from a water or alcohol solution.

Because of low temperature stability and potential resin degradation, quats are not normally used as internal antistats. However, when topically applied, quats can achieve low surface resistivities and are widely used in such short-term applications as the prevention of dust accumulation on plastic display parts. More durable applications are not generally feasible because of the ease with which the quat antistat coating can be removed from the plastic during handling, cleaning, or other processes. For longer-term protection internal antistats are used.

Internal Antistats

Internal antistats are compounded into the plastic matrix during processing. The two types of internal antistats are migratory, which is the most common, and permanent.

Preparation

A known method of reducing the fixation of dust on plastic bodies is the use of antistatic agents. The literature describes antistatic agents for thermoplastics (see, for example, Gächter, Müller, Plastic Additives, Hanser Verlag, Munich, 1996, p. 749 et seq.), which limit the fixation of dust. These antistatic agents improve the electrical conductivity of the plastic moulding compositions and in this manner dissipate surface charges which form during manufacture and use. Dust particles are consequently attracted to a lesser extent, and the fixation of dust is hence reduced.

A distinction is generally made between internal and external antistatic agents. An external antistatic agent is applied to the plastic moulding after processing, an internal antistatic agent is added to the plastic moulding compositions as an additive. The use of internal antistatic agents is generally desirable for economic reasons, since no additional working steps are necessary for applying an antistatic agent after processing.

Those internal antistatic agents for thermoplastics which have been described hitherto in the literature generally have one or more of the following disadvantages:

- breakdown of molecular weight of the thermoplastic
- effectiveness only at high concentrations (>0.5%)
- turbidity in transparent thermoplastics
- insufficient effect to enable electrostatic discharge to take place, for example after injection moulding, and thus to avoid the fixation of dust
- discoloration.

Sulfonic acid salts are a class of antistatic agents frequently described for use in thermoplastics. For example JP-06228420 A 940816 describes aliphatic sulfonic acid ammonium salts in polycarbonate as an antistatic agent. However, these compounds lead to breakdown of molecular weight.

Quaternary ammonium salts of perfluoroalkylsulfonic acids are known, likewise the use thereof in thermoplastics, for example. The latter application describes quaternary ammonium salts of perfluoroalkylsulfonic acids as mould release agents for polycarbonate. The examples described in that application, however, lead in polycarbonate to marked yellowing during processing, which is undesirable in particular for transparent and white-coloured formula

Dust Test

In order to investigate the fixation of dust in a laboratory test, the injection-moulded sheets are exposed to a fluidised dust atmosphere. For this purpose a 2-litre beaker having an 80 mm-long magnetic stirrer rod of triangular section is filled to a height of approximately 1 cm with dust (coal dust/20 g activated carbon, Riedel-de Haen, Seelze, Germany, product No. 18003). The dust is fluidised with the aid of a magnetic stirrer. After the stirrer has stopped the test moulding is exposed to this dusty atmosphere for 7 seconds. Depending on the test moulding used, a greater or lesser amount of dust becomes deposited on the test mouldings.

Evaluation of the fixation of dust (visual effects of dust) is visual. Sheets showing visual effects of dust received a negative (–) score, sheets virtually free of any visual effects of dust received a positive (+) score.

Method

6.25 g neopentylamine, 28 g tributylamine and 22 g DMF are introduced into a 500 ml three-necked flask. 40.8 g methyl iodide together with 14 ml DMF are added dropwise to this mixture, and stirring continues at room temperature for 12 hours. The solution is precipitated in ethyl acetate and dried. 2.4 g of colourless crystals are obtained. Neopentylamine is obtainable from Pfaltz & Bauer, Waterbury, Conn., USA.

Migratory antistats (MAS)

Migratory antistats have chemical structures that are composed of hydrophilic and hydrophobic components. These materials have limited compatibility with the host plastic and migrate or bloom to the surface of the molded product. The hydrophobic portion provides compatibility within the polymer and the hydrophilic portion functions to bind water molecules onto the surface of the molded part. If the surface of the part is wiped, the MAS is temporarily removed, reducing the antistat characteristics at the surface. Additional material then migrates to the surface until the additive is depleted. These surface-active antistatic additives can be cationic, anionic, and nonionic compounds.

Cationic antistats are generally long-chain alkyl quaternary ammonium, phosphonium, or sulfonium salts with, for example, chloride counterions. They perform best in polar substrates, such as rigid PVC and styrenics, but normally have an adverse effect on the resin's thermal stability. These antistat products are usually not approved for use in food-contact applications. Furthermore, antistatic effects comparable to those obtained from other internal antistats such as ethoxylated amines are only achieved with significantly higher levels, typically, five- to ten-fold.

Anionic antistats are generally alkali salts of alkyl sulfonic, phosphonic, or dithiocarbamic acids. They are also mainly used in PVC and styrenics. Their performance in polyolefins is comparable to cationic antistats. Among the anionic antistats, sodium alkyl sulfonates have found the widest applications in styrenics, PVC, polyethylene terephthalate, and polycarbonate.

Non-ionic antistats, such as ethoxylated fatty alkylamines, represent by far the largest class of migratory antistatic additives. These additives are widely used in PE, PP, ABS, and other styrenic polymers. Several types of ethoxylated alkylamines that differ in alkyl chain length and level of unsaturation are available. Ethoxylated alkylamines are very effective antistatic agents, even at low levels of relative humidity, and remain active over prolonged periods. These antistatic additives have wide FDA approval for indirect food contact applications. Other nonionic antistats of commercial importance are ethoxylated alkylamides such as ethoxylated lauramide and glycerol monostearate (GMS). Ethoxylated lauramide is recommended for use in PE and PP where immediate and sustained antistatic action is needed in a low-humidity environment. GMS-based antistats are intended only for static protection during processing. Even though GMS migrates rapidly to the polymer surface, it does not give the sustained antistatic performance that is obtainable from ethoxylated alkylamines or ethoxylated alkylamides.

The optimum choice and addition level for MAS additives depends upon the nature of the polymer, the type of processing, the processing conditions, the presence of other additives, the relative humidity, and the end use of the polymer. The time needed to obtain a sufficient level of antistatic performance varies. The rate of buildup and the duration of the antistatic protection can be increased by raising the concentration of the additive. Excessive use of antistats can, however, lead to greasy surfaces on the end products and adversely affect printability or adhesive applications. Untreated inorganic fillers and pigments like TiO_2 can absorb antistat molecules to their surface, and thus lower their efficiency. This can normally be compensated for by increasing the level of the antistat. The levels of antistat for foodcontact applications are regulated by the U.S. Food and Drug Administration (FDA).

Permanent antistats

The introduction of permanent antistats is one of the most significant developments in the antistat market. These are polymeric materials which are compounded into the plastic matrix. They do not rely on migration to the surface and subsequent attraction of water to be effective. The primary advantages of these materials are:

- Insensitivity to humidity
- Long-term performance
- Minimal opportunity for surface contamination
- Low offgassing
- Colour and transparency capability

There are two generic types of permanent antistats: hydrophilic polymers and inherently conductive polymers. *Hydrophilic polymers* are currently the dominant permanent antistats in the market. Typical materials that have been used successfully are such polyether block copolymers as PEBAX from Atochem. Typical use levels for these materials are in excess of 10%. B.F. Goodrich is supplying compounds utilizing their permanent antistat additive, STAT-RITE. Office automation equipment, such as fax and copier parts, is the principal application for permanent antistats based on hydrophilic polymers. The most common resins are ABS and high-impact polystyrene (HIPS).

Another approach to achieving permanent antistatic properties is through the use of inherently conductive polymers (ICP). This technology is still in the early development stages. The potential advantages of ICP include achieving higher conductivity in the host resin at lower additive loading levels than can be achieved with hydrophilic polymers. The principal ICP technology to date is polyaniline from Zipperling-Kessler and Neste. This material is a conjugated polymer composed of oxidatively coupled aniline monomers converted to a cationic salt with an organic acid and is frequently described as an organic metal. Other approaches to ICPs include neoalkoxy zirconates from Kenrich Petrochemical and polythiophenes from Bayer. The issues to be resolved in achieving commercial success with these materials include improved stability at elevated temperatures and reduction in their relatively high cost. ICPs are not expected to compete with other chemical additives but primarily with carbon black or other conductive fillers.

Permanent antistatic properties can be readily obtained with such particulate materials as carbon black. However, these materials are inappropriate for applications where colour and/or transparency capability is important. Also, particulate additives can negatively affect the physical properties of the final part and contribute to contamination in electronic applications also known as sloughing.

Suppliers

The antistatic additive market is served by fewer than 50 suppliers. The major suppliers include Akzo, Witco, Henkel, Elf Atochem, Kao, and Clariant. Table 4.1 lists some of the more prominent suppliers and the types of antistatic agents offered.

TRENDS AND FORECASTS

Continuing increases are expected in the markets for electronic components, devices, and equipment. Plant modernization activities will increase requirements for automated production machinery. Improvement in communication will continue to promote sales of items such as facsimile machines, personal computers, and cellular telephones. This will provide more opportunities for antistatic agents for static and electromagnetic interference control. Globally antistatic agents are expected to grow at a rate of 5 to 6% per year over

TABLE 4.1: Selected Suppliers of Antistatic Agents

Supplier	Type			
	Quats*	Amines	Fatty acid esters	Other†
Akzo Nobel	—	×	×	—
Bayer	—	—	—	×
Ciba Specialty Chemicals	—	—	—	×
Clariant	—	×	×	—
Cytec Industries	×	—	—	—
Elf Atochem	—	—	—	×
Henkel Corporation	—	—	×	—
ICI Americas	—	×	—	—
Kao Corporation	—	×	×	—
Lion Akzo	×	—	—	—
Lonza	×	—	×	—
NOF Corp.	—	—	×	—
Sanyo Chemical	×	—	—	—
Witco	×	×	×	—

*Quaternary ammonium compounds.

†"Other" category includes aliphatic sulfonates, fatty amides, and polymeric antistats.

5

Biocides

Description

Biocides are additives that impart protection against mold, mildew, fungi, and bacterial growth to materials. Without biocides, polymeric materials in the proper conditions can experience surface growth, development of spores causing allergic reactions, unpleasant odors, staining, embrittlement, and premature product failure. It is important to note that the biocide protects the material, not the user of the final product.

In general, in order for mold, mildew, and bacterial growth to develop, the end product must be in an environment that includes warmth, moisture, and food. Specifically, if the environment includes soil where microbes and bacteria abound, protection against bacterial growth is needed. If the end product has a water or moist environment, protection from fungi may be the most important feature. Environmental conditions overlap and many biocides are effective over a broad range.

Biocides, also referred to as antimicrobials, preservatives, fungicides, mildewcides, or bactericides, include several types of materials that differ in toxicity. OBPA (10, 10 -oxybisphenoxarsine) is the most active preservative of those commonly used for plastics. Amine-neutralized phosphate and zinc-OMADINE (zinc 2-pyridinethianol-1-oxide) have a lower activity level but are also effective. In the United States all biocides are considered pesticides and must be registered for specific applications with the U.S. Environmental Protection Agency (EPA).

The effectiveness of a biocide depends on its ability to migrate to the surface of the product where microbial attack first occurs. Most biocides are carried in plasticizers, commonly epoxidized soybean oil or diisodecyl phthalate, which are highly mobile and migrate throughout the end product. This mobility results in the gradual leaching of the additive. If significant leaching occurs, the product will be left unprotected. The proper balance between the rates of migration and leaching determines the durability of protection.

The majority of biocide additives are used in flexible PVC. The remaining portion is used in polyurethane foam and other resins. PVC applications using biocides include flooring, garden hoses, pool liners, and wall coverings, among others. The use level of biocide additives depends on the efficacy of the active ingredient. OBPA, the most active, requires approximately 0.04% concentration in the final product. Less active ingredients, such as n-(trichloro-methylthio) phthalimide, require a loading of 1.0% in the final compound to achieve a similar level of protection.

Biocides are generally formulated with a carrier into concentrations of 2 to 10% active ingredient. They are available to plastics converters, processors, and other users in powder, liquid, or solid pellet form. The carrier, as noted previously, is usually a plasticizer, but it can also be a resin concentrate such as PVC/PVA (polyvinyl acetate) copolymer or polystyrene. For example, OBPA, the most common biocide active ingredient, is typically purchased as a dispersion in a plasticizer at a concentration of 2% active ingredient.

Of the hundreds of chemicals that are effective as biocides, only a few are used in plastic applications. After OBPA, the most common group of active ingredients are 2-n-octyl-4-isothiazolin-3-one, 4, 5-dichloro-2-n-octyl-4-isothiazolin-3-one (DCOIT), zinc OMADINE, trichlorophenoxyphenol (TCPP or TRICLOSAN), N trichloromethylthio- 4-cyclohexene-1,2-dicarboximide (CAPTAN), and N-(trichloromethylthio) phthalimide (FOLPET).

Preparation

The present method relates to novel vehicles for introducing one or more compounds of the phenoxarsine family of biocides into starting mixtures which can be utilized in manufacturing processes for plastic materials

Method

A number of materials are subjected to the following procedure to determine which, if any, might be suitable as co-solvents for OBPA and diisodecyl phthalate.

In each procedure, a mixture is prepared by combining 5.0 g of 10, 10'-oxybisphenoxarsine with 45.0 g of diisodecyl phthalate and 50 g of a material of interest. The mixture is heated to a temperature in the range of 90-100° C. with stirring until it appears to be a single, clear liquid phase. The mixture is permitted to cool to room temperature (in the range of 22-25° C.) and samples of the cooled mixture are taken and stored for five days at room temperature, in a refrigerator for five days at 4° C. and in a freezer for five days at –13° C.

Suppliers

There are two tiers of biocide suppliers to the plastics industry: those who sell active ingredients and those who provide formulated products, both of which are shown in Table 5.1. The active ingredient manufacturer typically does not produce formulated biocides and formulators do not typically synthesize active materials.

The major formulated plastic biocide suppliers are Akcros Chemicals (owned by Akzo) and Morton International. Other suppliers of formulated biocide products include Ferro, Huels, Olin, and Microban. Akzo-Nobel, Ciba, and Rohm and Haas are the major suppliers of active ingredients.

Trends and forecasts

Biocides for plastics are growing at about 7% per year. OBPA, which currently holds the largest market share of all the biocides, is a mature market, growing at half that rate. Other biocides, such as isothiazolin and TCPP, will grow at a much faster rate than OBPA. Most of this growth in biocides is attributed to increased consumer awareness. The end-use customers are now demanding that nontraditional biocide applications, like door handles, hospital chair rails, garden hoses, and blue ice packs, incorporate biocides to "protect" them from germs. Consumers seem, in some cases, to be misinformed about the true function of a biocide since it is intended to protect the plastic, not the consumer. Suppliers need to be cautious regarding product claims to avoid misinformation. However, this increased awareness does appear to be a long-term trend and not solely a fad.

TABLE 5.1: Selected Suppliers of Active Ingredients and Formulated Biocides for Plastics

Supplier	Type	Active(A)/ formulated(F)
Akcros (Akzo)	OBPA	F
Akzo Nobel	OBPA	A
Allied Resinous Products	Triclosan	F
Ciba Specialty	Triclosan	A
Creanova Folpet,	Captan	A,F
Ferro	Isothiazolin	F
Microban	Triclosan	F
Morton	OBPA, Isothiazolin, and Triclosan	F
Olin Zinc	OMADINE	A, F
Rohm and Haas	Isothiazolin	A
Sanitized, Inc.	Triclosan	F
Thomson Research	Triclosan	F
Witco	OBPA	F
Zeneca	Isothiazolin	F

6

Chemical Blowing Agents

Description

The term blowing agent in the broadest sense denotes an inorganic or organic substance used in polymeric materials to produce a foam structure. There are two major types of blowing agents: physical and chemical.

Physical blowing agents

Physical blowing agents are volatile liquids or compressed gases that change state during processing to form a cellular structure within the plastic matrix. The gases or low-boiling liquids that are dissolved in the resin, evaporate through the release of pressure or the heat of processing. The compounds themselves do not experience any chemical changes. Cell size is influenced by the pressure of the gas, the efficiency of dispersion, melt temperature, and the presence of nucleating agents. The most common gases used are carbon dioxide, nitrogen, and air. The liquid blowing agents are typically solvents with low boiling points, primarily aliphatic hydrocarbons and their chloro- and fluoro- analogs.

The blowing agents should be soluble in the polymer under reasonably achievable conditions but excessive solubility is not desirable. The permeability of the gas within the polymer is also significant, as is the volume of gas released per unit weight of agent. This latter measure is called the blowing agent efficiency, and is an important yardstick for all types of materials. Effective blowing agents should yield at least 150 to 200 cm^3 of gas (measured at standard temperature and pressure) per gram of agent.

Physical blowing agents comprise over 90% of the market. They are heavily used in thermoset foams, especially polyurethanes, polyesters, and epoxies. These additives also have some application in such lowdensity thermoplastics as polystyrene. Until recently, fluorocarbons had the highest consumption among the liquid physical blowing agents. Because of environmental concerns, the market is shifting to alternative blowing agents, primarily partially halogenated chlorofluorocarbons.

Chemical blowing agents

Chemical blowing agents (CBAs) are products that decompose at high temperature. At least one of the decomposition products is a gas, which expands the plastics material to give a foam structure. The amount and type of the blowing agent influence the density of the finished product and its pore structure. Two types of pore structures are possible: open and closed cell. Closed-cell plastics have discrete, self-contained pores which are roughly spherical. Opencelled plastics contain interconnected pores, allowing gases to pass through voids in the plastic.

Factors that determine the formation of a fine-celled plastic foam with a regular cell structure are the particle size of the blowing agent, dispersion properties of the plastics processing machine used, decomposition rate of the blowing agent, and the melt viscosity of the resin processed. CBAs are mainly solid hydrazine derivatives. The gas formation must take place in a temperature range close to the processing temperature range of the polymer. In addition, the decomposition products must be compatible with the polymer. Typically, these additives decompose over a relatively narrow temperature range. CBAs can be mixed with the polymer at room temperature, requiring no special processing equipment. In most operations, they are self-nucleating and are stable under normal storage conditions. In addition, CBAs may be reformulated with such other additives as blowing agent catalysts or nucleating agents. Blowing agent catalysts lower the temperature of decomposition for the CBAs while nucleating agents provide sites for formation of a cell in the foamed plastic.

Blowing agents are used in plastics for several reasons: weight reduction, savings in cost and material, and achievement of new properties. The new properties include insulation against heat or noise, different surface appearance, improved stiffness, better quality (removal of sink marks in injection molded parts), and/or improved electrical properties.

CBAs may also be subdivided into two major categories, endothermic and exothermic. *Exothermic blowing* agents release energy during decomposition, while endothermic blowing agents require energy during decomposition. In general, endothermic CBAs generate carbon dioxide as the major gas. Commercially available exothermic types primarily evolve nitrogen gas, sometimes in combination with other gases. Nitrogen is a more efficient expanding gas because of its slower rate of diffusion through polymers compared to carbon dioxide.

Exothermic blowing agents

Once the decomposition of exothermic blowing agents has started, it continues spontaneously until the material has been exhausted. As a result, parts that are being foamed with this type of agent must be cooled intensely for long periods of time to avoid postexpansion.

Azodicarbonamide (AZ)

The most widely used exothermic CBA is azodicarbonamide. In its pure state, this material is a yellow-orange powder, which will decompose at about 390°F. Its decomposition yields 220 cm^3/g of gas, which is composed mostly of nitrogen and carbon monoxide with lesser amounts of carbon dioxide and, under some conditions, ammonia. The solid decomposition products are off-white, which not only serves as an indicator of complete decomposition but also does not normally adversely affect the colour of the foamed plastic. Unlike many other CBAs, AZ is not flammable. In addition, it is approved by the FDA for a number of food-packaging uses. AZ can be used in all processes and with most polymers, including PVC, PE, PP, PS, ABS, and modified polyphenylene oxide (PPO).

Preparation

Azodicarbonamide compounds as a class have been found capable of inhibiting the formation of fog in a silver halide photographic emulsion when contacted therewith. By "contacted" as used herein is meant that the azodicarbonamide is placed in fog-inhibiting association with the emulsion. For example, the azodicarbonamide may be incorporated within the emulsion, or in an adjacent layer, or in various photographic processing (e.g., developer) baths or the like. It has been found that the selection of the R_1 - R_4 groups in the above-described formula does not greatly vary the capacity of the compounds to inhibit fog. Examples of compounds representative of the various classes of substituted azodicarbonamides are as follows:

Modified AZ

Modified AZ systems have been developed which offer improved performance and increase versatility in a wide variety of applications. Each system has a formulated cell nucleation system (usually silica) and gas yield is approximately the same as unmodified AZ. Modified types are also available in several particle size grades. The simplest form of modified AZ is a paste. It is composed of a plasticizer, which forms the liquid phase, and may also contain dispersing agents and catalysts. Its principal field of application is the expansion of PVC plastisols. The agents facilitate the dispersion of the blowing agent when it is stirred into the PVC plastisol, while catalysts lower the decomposition temperature.

Other modified AZs have been developed for the manufacture of integral-skin foams by extrusion and injection molding. These contain additives that modify the usual decomposition process of AZ and suppress the formation of cyanuric acid, which causes plateout on the surfaces of molds, dies, and screws. The additives used include zinc oxide and/or silicic acid (a colloidal silica) with a very low water content. The additives also act as nucleating agents, producing a cell structure that is both uniform and fine-celled.

There are also grades that have been flow-treated. This type contains an additive to enhance the flowability and dispersability of the powder. These grades are very useful in vinyl plastisols, where complete dispersion of the foaming agent is critical to the quality of the final foamed product.

Another method of modifying AZ is to mix it with such other CBAs as those from the sulfonyl hydrazide group. These "auxiliary" blowing agents decompose at lower temperatures than AZ, broadening the decomposition range.

Sulfonyl hydrazides

Sulfonyl hydrazides have been in use as CBAs longer than any other type. The most important sulfonyl hydrazide is 4,4 -oxybis (benzenesulfonyl hydrazide) (OBSH). OBSH is the preferred CBA for low-temperature applications. It is an ideal choice for the production of LDPE and PVC foamed insulation for wire where it does not interfere with electrical properties. In addition, it is capable of cross-linking such unsaturated monomers as dienes. Additional applications include PVC plastisols, epoxies, phenolics, and other thermosetting resins. Like AZ, it is approved by the FDA for food-packaging applications and is odorless, nonstaining, and nontoxic.

Preparation:

The present method is related to sulfonyl hydrazide derivatives notably for use as pharmaceutically active compounds, as well as pharmaceutical formulations containing such sulfonyl hydrazide derivatives. In particular, the present method is related to sulfonyl hydrazide derivatives displaying a substantial modulatory, notably inhibitory activity of the JNK (Jun-Kinase) function or pathways respectively, and which are therefore particularly useful in the treatment and/or prevention of disorders of the autoimmune and the neuronal system. The present method is furthermore related to novel sulfonyl hydrazide derivatives as well as to methods of their preparation.

4-chloro-N-[(5-{[2-(2{-[4-(1,3-dithiolan-2-yl)phenyl]-1, 3-thiazol-4-yl}carbonyl)hydrazino] sulfonyl}thien-2-yl)methyl]benzamide 1

4-Chloro-N-thiophen-2-ylmethyl-benzamide 1a

A solution of 4-chlorobenzoyl chloride (0.114 mol) in 50 ml dry

CH_2Cl_2 is added over 30 min to a stirred solution of 2-amino-methylthiophene (0.137 mol) and $^iPr_2$ Net (0.25 mol) in CH_2Cl_2 (200 ml) at 0° C. A white solid is formed and the reaction is allowed to warm to room temperature over 1 h. The mixture is diluted with 200 ml of CH_2Cl_2, washed twice with HCl aq. (0.1N) and dried over $MgSO_4$. Evaporation of the solvents afforded 28 g (98%) of the title benzamide as a white solid: mp 153-54° C., 1 H NMR ($CDCl_3$) δ 7.9 (d, J = 8.67 Hz, 2H), 7.58 (d, J = 8.67 Hz, 2H), 7.44 (dd, J = 3.77, 1.13 Hz, 1H), 7.22 (d, J = 5.27 Hz, 1H), 7.16 (dd, J = 3.39, 5.27 Hz, 1H), 6.62 (br d, 1H), 4.98 (d, J = 5.65 Hz, 2H).

5-({[1-(4-Chloro-phenyl)-methanoyl]-amino}-methyl)-thiophene-2- sulfonyl chloride 1b

A solution of the thiophene 1b (10 g, 40 mmol) in CH_2Cl_2 (500 ml) is treated with a solution of chlorosulfonic acid (20.1 ml, 198 mmol) in CH_2Cl_2 (80 ml) at –80° C. The reaction mixture is allowed to reach r.t. over 5 h. The mixture is poured on ice and quickly extracted with CH_2Cl_2. The organic layer is dried over $MgSO_4$ and the solvent is evaporated to dryness to yield 8.8 g (63%) of the title sulfonyl chloride as a white powder which is used without further purification: mp 133-35° C., 1 H NMR (DMSO-d6) δ 9.21 (t, J=6.4 Hz, 1H), 7.87 (d, J=8.67 Hz, 2H), 7.53 (d, J=8.67 Hz, 2H), 6.91 (d, J=3.39 Hz, 1H), 6.77 (d, J=3.39 Hz, 1H), 4.53 (d, J=3.77 Hz, 2H).

4-chloro-N-[(5-{[2-({2-[4-(1,3-dithiolan-2-yl)phenyl]-1, 3-thiazol-4-yl}carbonyl)-hydrazino] sulfonyl}thien-2-yl)methyl]benzamide 1

A solution of sulfonyl chloride 1b (1.0 equivalents), 2-[4-(1,3-Dithiolan-2-yl)phenyl]-1,3-thiazole-4-carbohydrazi de (1.1 equivalents), and pyridine (1.2-2 equivalents) in $CHCl_3$ is heated to reflux for 2 h. Filtration over SiO_2(CH_3CN) and evaporation yielded 80% of the desired sulfonyl hydrazide 1.

Upon using the procedure described in the above example 1 and the appropriate starting material and reagents, the following additional sulfonyl hydrazide derivatives of formula 1 could be obtained. (If the product crystallises during the reaction, it is obtained. (If the product crystallises during the reaction, it is collected by filtration).

N'-(4-{[3-chloro-5-(trifluoromethyl)pyridin-2-yl]amino} butanoyl)-5-[(1,3-dioxo-1,3-dihydro-2H-isoindol-2-yl)methyl]thiophene-2-sulfonohydrazide 18 N-(Thiophen-2-ylmethyl)-isoindole-1,3-dione 18a

A solution of 2-aminomethyl-thiophene (2.1 ml, 20.5 mmol) in $CHCl_3$ (25 ml) is treated with phthalic anhydride (3.0 g, 20.5 mmol) at r.t. for 5 min, then at reflux for 20 min, whereupon a white powder precipitated out. This powder is collected by filtration and dried in vacuo to give N-thiophen-2-ylmethyl-phthalamic acid (4.42 g, 83%) as white crystals. An aliquot of this phthalamic acid (2.13 g, 8.12 mmol) is dissolved in MeOH (12 ml), treated with H_2SO_4 (440 μl, 8.25 mmol) and heated to reflux for 1.5 h, whereupon a white powder precipitated out. This powder is collected by filtration and dried in vacuo to give 1.38 g (70%) of the title phthalimide as white crystals: ^1H NMR (DMSO-d 6) δ7.92-7.82 (m., 4H), 7.42 (dd, J=5.1, 1.2 Hz, 1H), 7.08 (dd, J=4.0, 0.8 Hz, 1H), 6.95 (dd, J=5.1, 3.5 Hz, 1H), 4.92 (s, 2H).

5-(1,3-Dioxo-1,3-dihydro-isoindol-2-ylmethyl)-thiophene- 2-sulfonyl chloride 18b

A solution of the thiophene 18a (821 mg, 3.37 mmol) in 1,4-dioxane (8.0 ml) is treated with $ClSO_3H$ (1.0 ml, 15.0 mmol) at r.t. for 4 h. the mixture is poured in water (20 ml), and washed with CH_2Cl_2 (2 × 50 ml). The organic layer is discarded. The aqueous layer is diluted with $NaHCO_3$ aq. sat. (100 ml.), treated with TBAF (1.0M in THF, 4.0 ml, 4.0 mmol), and extracted with CH_2Cl_2 (3 × 35 ml). The organic layer is dried ($MgSO_4$) and evaporated to give the corresponding tetrabutylammonium sulfonate intermediate (857 mg, 45%) as a colorless oil. A solution of this tetrabutylammonium sulfonate (174 mg, 0.308 mmol) in CH_2Cl_2 (3.4 ml) is treated with triphosgene (46 mg, 0.154 mmol) and DMF (20 μl, 0.259 mmol) for 1.5 h. The reaction mixture is filtered of silica gel, eluting with EtOAc/cyclohexane 1:2, and evaporated to give 81 mg (77%) of the title sulfonyl chloride as white crystals which were used without further purification

4-(3-Chloro-5-trifluoromethyl-pyridin-2-ylamino)-butyric acid hydrazide 18c

A mixture of γ-aminobutyric acid (8.18 g, 79.3 mmol), 2,3-dichloro-5-(trifluoromethyl)-pyridine (11.0 ml, 79.3 mmol), triethylamine (27.6 ml, 198.3 mmol) and methanol (270 ml) is heated at 104° C. in a Parr autoclave (450 ml vessel) with mechanical agitation for 3 h. Evaporation, addition of CH_2Cl_2 (200 ml), and filtration allowed to remove the unreacted, insoluble γ-amino-butyric acid (2.5 g). Evaporation, addition of t-BuOMe (200 ml), and filtration allowed to remove most of the $Et_3N.HCl$ salt (4.4 g). The ether solution is filtered through a silica gel plug and concentrated to afford the crude N-substituted γ-aminobutyric acid as its triethylammonium salt. This crude is esterified to the corresponding methyl γ-aminobutyrate by heating to reflux for 1.5 h in methanolic H_2SO_4 (1.9M H_2SO_4 in MeOH, 50 ml). Concentration to about 30 ml, addition of EtOAc (100 ml) and cyclohexane (100 ml), washing ($NaHCO_3$ sat.; H_2O; brine), drying (Na_2SO_4) and evaporation afforded 13.8 g (59%) of 4-(3-Chloro-5-trifluoromethyl-pyridin-2-ylamino)-butyric acid, methyl ester as a colorless oil: ^1H NMR ($CDCl_3$) δ8.18 (d, J=0.9 Hz, 1H), 7.53 (d, J=2.2 Hz, 1H), 5.54-5.42 (br. t, J=6 Hz, 1H), 3.61 (s, 3H), 3.51 (q, J=6.8 Hz, 2H), 2.35 (t, J=7.2 Hz, 2H), 1.92 (quint, J=7.0 Hz, 2H).

A solution of the methyl ester prepared above (5.61 g, 19.0 mmol) in 80% aqueous hydrazine (7 ml) and MeOH (14 ml) is heated to reflux for 2 h. The reaction mixture is diluted with EtOAc (250 ml). The unreacted hydrazine is extracted with a minimum amount of water (3 × 25 ml) and oxidized with bleach. The organic layer is dried (Na_2SO_4), concentrated to 50 ml, and poured into a crystalliser containing 150 ml of cyclohexane. The desired hydrazide rapidly crystallized, and filtration after 2 h afforded 4.24 g (76%) of the title acyl hydrazide as pale yellow needles: ^1H NMR (DMSO-d6) δ8.96 (br. s, 1H), 8.32 (br s, 1H), 7.94 (d, J=2.1 Hz, 1H), 7.25 (t, J=5.5 Hz, 1H), 4.51 (s, 2H), 3.40 (q, J=6.6 Hz, 2H), 2.07 (t, J=7.6 Hz, 2H), 1.88 (quint, J=7.2, 2H); MS m/z 297 (M+H).

N'-(4-{[3-chloro-5-(trifluoromethylpyridin-2-yl]amino} butanoyl)-5-[(1,3-dioxo-1,3-dihydro-2H-isoindol-2-yl)methyl] thiophene-2-sulfonohydrazide 18

A solution of the sulfonyl chloride 18b (71 mg, 0.208 mmol), the acyl hydrazide 18c (64 mg, 0.216 mmol) and pyridine (30 μl, 0.373 mmol) in $CHCl_3$ (1.0 ml) is stirred overnight at r.t. Filtration over SiO_2 (CH_3CN) and evaporation gave 110 mg (88%) of the title compound as a colorless powder: ^1H NMR (DMSO-d6) 10.03 (d, J=3.2 Hz, 1H), 9.94 (d, J=3.2 Hz, 1H), 8.33-8.29 (br. s, 1H), 7.95-7.79 (m, 5H), 7.43 (d, J=3.8 Hz, 1H), 7.23 (br. t, J=5.6 Hz, 1H), 7.12 (d, J=3.8 Hz, 1H), 4.94 (s, 2H), 3.27 (q, J=6.4 Hz, 2H), 2.01 (t, J=7.4 Hz, 2H), 1.61 (quint, J=7.[1]Hz, 2H); MS m/z 602 (M+H).

N-[(5-{[2-(4-{[3-chloro-5-(trifluoromethyl)pyridin-2-yl] amino}butanoyl)hydrazino] sulfonyl}thien-2-yl)methyl]-4-nitrobenzamide 19 Diallyl-thiophen-2-ylmethylamine 19a

A solution of 2-aminomethyl-thiophene (51.4 g, 956 mmol) and i-Pr_2 net (140 g, 1081 mmol) in CH_2Cl_2 (1 *l*) was placed in a 3-l flask equipped with a condenser and an efficient magnetic agitation. Allyl bromide (115.7 g, 454 mmol) was added, whereupon the moderately exothermic reaction spontaneously reached the reflux temperature after 2 h. The mixture was stirred overnight (16 h), washed ($NaHCO_3$ sat.; brine), dried ($MgSO_4$), and concentrated. The resulting oil was filtered over silica gel (EtOAc:hexane 1:4). The filtrate was concentrated and the filtration was repeated to afford 70.3 g (80%) of the title diallylamine as a brown-yellow oil, clean by NMR: ^1H NMR ($CDCl_3$) δ7.25 (br. d, J=5.9 Hz, 1H), 6.98 (br. dd, J=5.1, 2.8 Hz, 1H), 6.94-0.92 (m, 1H), 5.99-5.86 (m, 2H), 5.29-5.18 (m, 4H), 3.85 (s, 2H), 3.16 (dd, J=6.3, 0.9 Hz, 4H).

5-Diallylaminomethyl-thiophene-2- sulfonyl chloride 19b

A solution of the allyl-protected thiophene 19a (6.2 g, 32.1 mmol) in Et_2O was cooled to –70° C. by means of an acetone/ dry ice bath. A solution of t-BuLi in pentane (21.38 ml, 1.5M, 32.1 mmol) was added over 2 min whereupon the internal temperature momentarily rose to –50° C. and the mixture turned orange. After 10 min., SO_2 was bubbled for 2 min, which led to the immediate formation of a thick precipitate. The reaction was allowed to reach 0°C, and a suspension of NCS (4.63 g, 32.1 mmol) in THF (20 ml) was added, whereupon the slurry turned purple. After 45 min at r.t., the mixture was filtered over SiO_2, eluting with EtOAc. Evaporation, dilution with EtOAc:hexane 1:5 and filtration over SiO_2 gave 5.0 g (53%) of the title sulfonyl chloride 19b as a pale brown oil which was used without further purification.

5-Diallylaminomethyl-thiophene-2-sulfonic acid, N'-[4-(3-chloro-5-trifluoromethyl-pyridin-2-ylamino)-butan oyl]-hydrazide 19c

A solution of the sulfonyl chloride 19b (1.2 g, 4.11 mmol), the acyl hydrazide 18c (1.00 g, 3.38 mmol), and pyridine (300 μl, 3.71 mmol) in chloroform (30 ml) was heated to reflux for 2 h. Dilution with EtOAc (100 ml), washing (half-saturated brine; brine), drying (Na_2SO_4), and chromatography (EtOAc; cyclohexane 1:2-1:1) gave 1.69 g (89%) of the title sulfonyl hydrazide as a colourless oil: ^1H NMR ($CDCl_3$) δ9.73 (s, 1H), 8.22 (s, 1H), 7.50 (d, J=2.1 Hz, 1H), 7.37 (d, J=3.6 Hz, 1H), 7.30-7.20 (br. s, 1H), 6.70 (d, J=3.0 Hz, 1H), 7.73-5.57 (m, 2H), 5.46 (t, J=6.0 Hz, 1H), 5.14.95 (m, 4H), 3.59 (s, 2H), 3.36 (q, J=6.7 Hz, 2H), 2.92 (d, J=6.7 Hz, 4H), 2.08 (dd, J=6.3, 6.9 Hz, 2H), 1.73 (quint., J=6.6 Hz, 2H); MS m/z 552 (M+H).

5-(aminomethyl)-N'-(4-{[3-chloro-5-(trifluoromethyl)py ridin-2-yl]amino}butanoyl)thiophene-2-sulfonohydrazide 19d

Procedure A. A solution of the bisallylamine 19c (4.0 g, 7.25 mmol), N,N'-dimethylbarbituric acid (NDMBA 2.8 g, 18.1 mmol), and $Pd(PPh_3)_4$ (148.8 mg, 0.13 mmol) in CH_2Cl_2 was de-gassed by bubbling argon for 10 min. The reaction was stirred for 3 h at r.t. whereupon the desired amine 19d precipitated as its NDMBA salt. The mixture was diluted with EtOAc (200 ml) and hexane (200 ml) and washed with water (3 × 50 ml). The combined aqueous phases were freeze-dried, dissolved in a minimal amount of MeOH and chromatographed (SiO_2, CH_2Cl_2 : EtOAc : NH_4OH aq 80 : 20: 5). The chromatography was repeated twice and gave 2.3 g (67%) of the free amine 19d, which was dissolved in refluxing EtOAc (80 ml) and cooled to –18° C. to afford 1.7 g (50%) of 19d as a white powder: ^{1}H NMR (DMSO-d6) δ10.02-9.85 (br. s, 1H), 8.248.19 (br. s, 1H), 7.85 (d, J=2.0 Hz, 1H), 7.32 (d, J=3.8 Hz, 1H), 7.20 (t, J=5.7 Hz, 1H), 6.82 (d, J=3.8 Hz, 1H), 5.3-4.3 (br. s, 2H), 3.80 (s, 2H), 3.23 (q, J=6.7 Hz, 2H), 1.96 (t, J=7.5 Hz, 2H), 1.57 (quint, J=7.2 Hz, 2H); MS m/z 472 (M+H).

Procedure B. Alternatively, a solution of the bisallylamine 19c (9.55 g, 17.3 mmol) and NDMBA (5.55 g, 35.5 mmol) in CH_2Cl_2 (195 ml) was degassed by bubbling argon for 10 min. Then, $Pd(PPh_3)_4$ (980 mg, 0.85 mmol) was added and the mixture was stirred for 16 h at 23° C. The mixture was concentrated to a gum, dissolved in hot (60° C.) water, and the aqueous phase was washed with a mixture of EtOAc (200 ml) and tBuOMe (200 ml). The organic layer was extracted with more water (2×100 ml). The aqueous phases were individually concentrated on a rotary evaporator, whereupon a gum quickly separated from the mixture. The gum was removed, the aqueous phases were combined, and evaporation was continued to dryness to give 8.8 g (79%) of the NDMBA salt of the title amine, as a white, crisp powder, which could be used without further purification.

N-[(5-{[2-(4-{[3-chloro-5-(trifluoromethyl)pyridin-2-yl] amino}butanoyl)hydrazino]- sulfonyl}thien-2-yl)methyl]-4-nitrobenzamide 19

A 20 mg/ml solution of the 2-aminomethyl-thiophene 19d in pyridine: CH_2Cl_2 1 : 4 was cooled to –40° C. and treated for 1 h with 0.8 equiv. of 4-nitrophenyl sulfonyl chloride. The reaction mixture was brought to room temperature over 30 min. Evaporation, dilution in CH_3CN, filtration over a SiO_2 pad, and evaporation afforded the desired amide in typically 50% yield. ^{1}H NMR (DMSO-d6) δ10.05 (d, J=3.3 Hz, 1H), 9.90 (d, J=3.3 Hz, 1H), 9.59 (t, J=5.8 Hz, 1H), 8.32 (d, J=8.8 Hz, 2H), 8.32-8.29 (br. s, 1H), 8.08 (d, J=8.8 Hz, 2H), 7.91 (d, J=2.0 Hz, 1H), 7.43 (d, J=3.8 Hz, 1H), 7.22 (t, J=5.6 Hz, 1H), 7.06 (d, J = 3.8 Hz, 1H), 4.66 (d, J = 5.8 Hz, 2H), 3.28 (q, J = 6.4 Hz, 2H), 2.04 (t, J=7.4 Hz, 2H), 1.64 (quint., J = 7.1 Hz, 2H).

N-[(5-{[2-(4-{[3-chloro-5-(trifluoromethyl)pyridin-2-yl] amino}butanoyl)hydrazino] sulfonyl}thien-2-yl)methyl]-2-hydroxybenzamide 20

Procedure A. A mixture of 3-acetoxybenzoic acid (8.1 mg, 0.0450 mmol), 5-aminomethyl-thiophene 18d (22.3 mg, 0.0473 mmol), 1-hydroxybenzotriazole (HOBt, 4.7 mg, 0.0348 mmol), and N-(3-dimethylaminopropyl)-N'-ethylcarbodiimide (EDC, 8.5 mg, 0.0443 mmol) was dissolved in DMF (0.6 ml) and stirred overnight at r.t. Work-up (AcOEt/H_2O; brine/Na_2SO_4), concentration, filtration over a silica gel plug (EtOAc) and evaporation gave the intermediate 3-acetoxybenzamide, which was deacetylated by stirring in MeOH (2 ml) and Et_3N (0.4 ml) for 1 h at 55° C. Evaporation gave 28.5 mg (103%) of the title 3-hydroxy-benzamide as a colorless oil.

Procedure B. A solution of the crude NMDBA salt of 18d (3.2 g, "5.1 mmol"), salicylic acid (987 mg, 7.14 mmol), HOBt (966 mg, 7.14 mmol), and EDC (1.37 g, 7.14 mmol) in DMF (69 ml) was stirred for 1 h at 23° C. The mixture was diluted with EtOAc (700 ml) and washed (3×H_2O; brine). The aqueous layers were back-extracted with EtOAc (250 ml). The combined organic layers were concentrated and chromatographed (EtOAc:cyclohexane 1:1→2:1) to give 2.18 g (73%) of the title 3-hydroxybenzamide, which was further purified by preparative reverse-phase HPLC(H_2O: CH_3CN 70 : 40 δ25:75 over 35 min, Rt = 31 min) to give 1.50 g (50%) of a white powder: m.p. 174.5-175.5° C. ^1H NMR (DMSO-d6) δ10.03 (s, 1H), 9.75-9.65 (br. d, 1H), 9.15 (t, J=6.0 Hz, 1H), 8.33-8.29 (br. s, 1H), 7.93 (d, J=2.0 Hz, 1H), 7.42 (d, J=3.8 Hz, 1H), 7.27-21 (m, 4H), 7.01 (d, J=3.8 Hz, 1H), 6.91 (dt, J=7.1, 2.2 Hz), 4.59 (d, J=5.8 Hz, 2H), 2.69 (q, J=7.0 Hz, 2H), 2.04 (t, J=6.9 Hz, 2H), 1.67 (quint, J=7.1 Hz, 2H). 13 C NMR (DMSO-d6) δ169.65, 167.57, 158.49, 154.79, 149.06, 142.54 (q, J=4 Hz, C-C-CF_3), 136.39, 132.80, 131.61, 126.91, 124.82, 122.93 (q, J=271 Hz, CF_3), 117.66, 116.22, 114.01, 112.91, 112.01 (q, J=33 Hz, C-CF_3), 39.19, 36.62, 29.42, 23.35. 19 F NMR (DMSO-d6) δ59.52(s). M/Z APCI: 592 (M+1), 590 (M–1). Anal. HPLC: Rt = 6.22 min (method a).$C_{24}H_{23}F_3N_4O_7S_3$ Calc.: C: 44.63%. H, 3.8%. N, 11.83%. Found: C, 44.68%, H, 3.59%, N: 11.90%.

Sulfonyl Semi-carbazides

Sulfonyl semicarbazides are important CBAs for use in high-temperature applications. TSS (p-toluene sulfonyl semicarbazide) is in the form of a cream colored crystalline powder. Its decomposition range is approximately 440 to 450°F with a gas yield of 140 cm^3/g, composed mostly of nitrogen and water. TSS is flammable, burning rapidly when ignited and producing a large amount of residue. TSS is used in polymers processed at higher temperatures such as ABS, PPO, polyamide (PA), and HIPS.

Preparation

This method relates to a novel process for manufacturing sulfonyl semicarbazide compounds.The following examples will serve to illustrate the practice of the method in more detail.

METHOD I: Preparation of p-toluene sulfonyl semicarbazide

Charged a 1 liter flask with

35.6 g sodium p-toluene sulfinate (anhydrous) (0.2 mole)

23.2 g (0.2 mole) azodicarbonamide

800 ml water

The mixture was stirred. The colour of the azodicarbonamide was discharged in 15 minutes as the temperature of the mix rose slightly (26° to 27°C.). The contents of the flask foamed slightly and developed a weakly alkaline reaction (pH paper). The mix was stirred without heating for a total of one hour and was then filtered, washed well with water and dried. Yield = 44.2 g. (98% of theory). Dec. 237°-238°C.

METHOD II : Preparation of benzene sulfonyl semicarbazide

A 500 ml. flask equipped with a magnetic stirrer was charged with 16.4 g. (0.1 mole) of sodium benzene sulfinate, 11.6 g. (0.1 mole) of azodicarbonamide and 300 cc of water. The mixture was stirred at ambient temperature for one hour. The colour of the azodicarbonamide disappeared and a white product was formed.

The material was filtered off, washed with water and dried. There was obtained 20.0 g. of benzene sulfonyl semicarbazide which decomposed sharply at 225°C.

METHOD III

Suspended 22.35 g. of barium p-toluene sulfinate (0.05 mole) and 11.6 g. azodicarbonamide (0.1 mole) in 200 ml water. Stirred for 1½ hours. The yellow colour disappeared. The white solid was filtered off, washed well with water and dried at 60°C. Yield of p-toluene sulfonyl semicarbazide, 22.2 g. (98% of theory). MP. 237°C.

A portion of the filtrate when acidified with dilute hydrochloric acid produced bubbles of CO_2.

Addition of dilute sulfuric acid to a portion of the filtrate gave a heavy precipitate of barium sulfate.

METHOD IV

Prepared a sample of potassium p-toluene sulfinate by adding 6.6 g of 85% potassium hydroxide to 15.6 g. (0.1 mole) of p-toluene sulfinic acid in 100cc water. Then 11.6 g (0.1 mole) of azodicarbonamide was added and the mixture stirred until the yellow colour was completely discharged (1½ hours). Ammonia was detected in the space above the reaction mixture. The white solid was filtered off, washed with water and dried. Yield of p-toluene sulfonyl semicarbazide was 20.6 g. This melted with decomposition near 232°C. An additional half gram of the substance was obtained by acidification of the filtrate with dilute hydrochloric acid (CO_2 was produced also).

METHOD V

Mixed 17.5 g. calcium p-toluene sulfinate (0.05 mole) and 11.6 g azodicarbonamide (0.1 mole) in 200cc water. Stirred the mixture for ½ hour. The mixture thickened and the colour soon disappeared. An addition of 150 cc more water was made. The colorless product was filtered, washed with water and dried. Yield of p-toluene sulfonyl semicarbazide was 21.5 g., MP 233°C. (dec).

METHOD VI

A suspension of magnesium p-toluene sulfinate in water was prepared by adding a solution of 24.65 g. (0.1 mole) of $MgSO_4 \cdot 7H_2O$ in 200 cc water to a solution of 42.8 g. (0.2 mole) of sodium p-toluene sulfinate dihydrate in 500 cc water. The salt separated as the mix was stirred over five minutes. Then, 23.2 g (0.2 mole) of azodicarbonamide was added to the suspension of the magnesium salt and 150 cc more of water was added. The colour of the stirred mixture was discharged in ½ hour. The white solid was filtered off, washed with water and dried. Yield of p-toluene sulfonyl semicarbazide was 44.7 g. This melted with decomposition at 235°C.

METHOD VII: Preparation of p-Toluene sulfonyl semicarbazide from p-toluene sulfonyl chloride

Into a 3 litre beaker equipped with mechanical stirred, pH meter and thermometer was charged 126 g. (1.0 mole) of sodium sulfite and 750 ml. water. The sodium sulfite dissolved. Then 190.6 g (1.0 mole) of p-toluene sulfonyl chloride was added all at once. The pH started to drop and a solution of 80 g. (2.0 mole) of sodium hydroxide in 500 ml. of water was added at a rate to keep the pH between 7-8. Once the pH stabilized, it was allowed to rise to 10. This solution of sodium p-toluene sulfinate was used in the following manner:

A 4-liter beaker equipped with mechanical stirrer was charged with 1500 ml. of water and 116 g. (1.0 mole) of azodicarbonamide. The suspension of the yellow solid was stirred as the sodium p-toluene sulfite solution (1.0 mole) was added over a period of 10 minutes. The yellow colour of the azodicarbonamide was discharged and a white product was formed. This was stirred for an additional ½ hour and was then filtered, washed well with water and dried at 60°C. Yield, 214 g. (93.4% of theory). The material decomposed at 240°C. and gave an infrared spectrum identical to an authentic sample of p-toluene sulfonyl semicarbazide.

Dinitropentamethylene tetramine (DNPT)

Dinitropentamethylene tetramine is one of the most widely used CBAs for foamed rubber. Its use is limited in plastics because of its high decomposition temperature and the unpleasant odor of its residue. DNPT is a fine yellow powder that decomposes between 266 and 374°F, producing mainly nitrogen and a solid white residue.

Endothermic blowing agents

Endothermic CBAs are used primarily in the injection molding of foam where the rapid diffusion rate of carbon dioxide gas through the polymers is essential. This allows postfinishing of foamed parts right out of the mold without the need for a degassing period. Nucleation of physically foamed materials, especially those used for food packaging, has become a well-established application area for endothermic CBAs.

Sodium borohydride ($NaBH_4$)

Sodium borohydride is an effective endothermic blowing agent because its reaction with water produces 10 to 20 times the amount of gas produced by other CBAs that give off nitrogen. Sodium borohydride must be blended with the polymer to be foamed to prevent reaction with water during storage.

Sodium bicarbonate ($NaHCO_3$)

Sodium bicarbonate decomposes between 212 and 284°F giving off CO_2 and H_2O and forming a sodium carbonate residue. Its gas yield is 267 cm^3/g. At 287°F or higher, decomposition becomes more rapid, facilitating its use as a blowing agent for such higher-temperature thermoplastics as styrenic polymers.

Polycarbonic Acid

Polycarbonic acid decomposes endothermically at approximately 320°F and gives off about 100 cm^3/g of carbon dioxide. Further heating will release even more gas. In addition to being used as the primary source of gas for foaming in some applications, this class of materials is frequently used as a nucleating agent for physical foaming agents.

Preparation

The powdered endothermic blowing agent of the present method is produced by blending a surface treated polycarboxylic acid and a surface treated inorganic carbonate. The surface treatment of these materials can be performed in a high intensity mixture at a temperature range of between about 72° C. and about 135° C., with a preferred temperature being about 80° C. The preferred level of surface treatment is from about 0.1% to about 10%, and most preferably about 3% for the polycarboxylic acid and about 3% for the inorganic carbonate. The formation of the surface treatment within this preferred range has been found to be effective in avoiding premature reaction resulting from water absorption.

In surface treating the polycarboxylic acid, a typical laboratory batch is prepared by adding about 1500 grams of polycarboxylic acid, e.g., anhydrous citric acid to a 10 liter Henschel mixer or other suitable high intensity mixer. The polycarboxylic acid is mixed at about 1500 rpm and heated until a temperature of about 80° C. is reached. Any heating means such as hot water flowing through a water jacket surrounding the mixer may be used to attain the desired temperature. After reaching the desired temperature about 15.2 grams of a surface treating compound such as glyceryl monostearate is added to the heated polycarboxylic acid and mixing is continued at about 1500 rpm and about 80° C. for an additional period of time of approximately five minutes. After five minutes the mixing speed is reduced to about 900 rpm and the mixture is alloweed to cool below about 60°. Thereafter the surface treatment of the polycarboxylic acid is complete and the mixture is unloaded.

In surface treating the inorganic carbonate, about 3500 grams of an inorganic carbonate, e.g., dry sodium aluminum hydroxy carbonate, is charged into a 10 liter Henschel mixer. The inorganic carbonate is mixed at a speed of about 1500 rpm and heated by a suitable means such as a hot water jacket until a temperature of about 80° C. is reached. After reaching the proper temperature about 108.2 grams of a surface treating compound such a glyceryl monostearate, is added to the inorganic carbonate and mixing is resumed at about 1500 rpm for about five minutes while the temperature is maintained at about 80° C. After the required mixing, the mixing speed is reduced to about 900 rpm and the mixture is allowed to cool below about 60° C. Thereafter, the inorganic carbonate has been sufficiently surface treated and may be unloaded from the mixer.

In preparing a large scale batch of the above surface treated components, about 200 pounds of polycarboxylic acid, e.g. citric acid, was charged into a 200 liter Henschel mixer. The polycarboxylic acid was mixed until a temperature of about 68° C was reached. In this case neither steam nor hot water was needed to raise the temperature. When the polycarboxylic acid reached a temperature of about 68° C. two pounds of a surface treating component, e.g., glyceryl monostearate, was added to the mixer. Mixing continued until the temperature reached about 72° C. after which mixing was continued for an additional period of time of about 5 minutes. Thereafter the mixture was allowed to cool to below about 60° C. and was unloaded from the mixer. The batch surface treatment procedure was repeated for the inorganic carbonate using about 150 pounds of dry inorganic carbonate, e.g., sodium aluminium hydroxy carbonate, and about 4.5 pounds of the surface treating component, e.g., glyceryl monostearate.

The present endothermic blowing agents are prepared by blending together the surface treated polycarboxylic acid and the surface treated inorganic carbonate. In a preferred embodiment about 1029 grams of surface treated inorganic carbonate, e.g., sodium aluminum hydroxy carbonate, was placed into a 10 liter Henschel mixer together with about 1471 grams of surface treated polycarboxylic acid, e.g., citric acid. The mixture was mixed at about 1500 rpm for a period of time of about five minutes. Thereafter the mixing speed was reduced to about 900 rpm for a short period of time and unloaded from the mixture.

In the above discussion, the preferred polycarboxylic acid used was citric acid. However, for purposes of the present invention, other suitable carboxylic acids include those of the formula:

HOOC—R—COOH

where R is an alkylene group of 1 to about 8 carbon atoms which may also be substituted by one or more hydroxy groups or keto groups and may also contain unsaturation. Also included are salts and half salts. Preferred polycarboxylic acids include citric acid, fumaric acid, tartaric acid, sodium hydrogen citrate and disodium citrate.

The preferred inorganic carbonate utilized in the invention is sodium aluminum hydroxy carbonate. However, acceptable results are also achieved by also using sodium bicarbonate as well as alkali and alkaline earth metal carbonates generally.

In the above examples glyceryl monostearate was utilized as the preferred surface treatment compound. However, surface treatment can be carried out utilizing any reagent which renders the polycarboxylic acid and the inorganic carbonate hydrophobic. In this regard, suitable surface treating components found useful for purposes of the present invention included various monoglycerides, stearic acid and silane coupling agents in addition to the above glyceryl monostearate.

In combining the surface treated polycarboxylic acid and the surface treated inorganic carbonate to produce the blowing agent the weight ratio of these two components needs to be determined based on the desired structure and composition of the final foam product to be produced. Typically, the weight ratio of surface treated polycarboxylic acid to surface treated inorganic carbonate may vary from about 0.010 to about 99.00. However, the weight ratio is preferably maintained between about 1.00 and about 5.00.

The endothermic blowing agent is preferably used by incorporating it into a polymeric concentrate which is used to produce film products. In one embodiment according to the present invention the polymeric or plastic concentrates were prepared at loading levels of from about 5% to about 50% in a single or twin screw extruder utilizing normal techniques known to those schooled in the art of plastic compounding. The extruder must, however, be operated below about 149° C. in order to keep the endothermic blowing agent from foaming prematurely.

In these polymeric or plastic concentrates citric acid may be replaced by other polycarboxylic acids such as fumaric acid, tartaric acid and sodium hydrogen citrate which have higher degradation temperatures and will allow higher extrusion temperatures. The novel interaction between the polycarboxylic acid and the inorganic carbonate controls the composition and the volume of the above gases which serve to foam a plastic for foamed products.

The application areas for these endothermic products include polyvinyl chloride, polyolefins, engineering resins, polystyrene, polyphenylene oxide and other polymeric systems. These foamed products display excellent weight reduction and drop weight impact properties and are outlined in the following examples given by way of illustration only. Other uses for the present novel blowing agent include, for example, its use as a propellant generator in aerosol containers.

As described in detail above, the present method involves an endothermic blowing agent which is a mixture of a polycarboxylic acid and an inorganic carbonate, wherein the polycarboxylic acid and the inorganic carbonate each have been surface treated with a component that prevents water from being absorbed thereby.

When properly surface treated, the level of surface treatment of the polycarboxylic acid and the inorganic carbonate is between about 1.0 and 5.0 percent by weight. In a preferred embodiment the level of surface treatment of said polycarboxylic acid is about 1.0 percent by weight and the level of surfaced treatment of said inorganic carbonate is about 3.0 percent by weight.

The ratio of the polycarboxylic acid and the inorganic carbonate may vary over a wide range and will be determined by the final desired products. Generally, the weight ratio of the surface treated polycarboxylic acid to the surface treated inorganic carbonate is between about 0.10 and about 99.00, with a more desired weight ratio being between about 1.00 and about 5.00.

As further discussed in detail above, the present method also involves a method of making the endothermic blowing agent. Generally, this method involves the steps of:

(a) heating a dry powder of polycarboxylic acid to a temperature of between about 68° C. and about 80° C. and adding thereto a surface treating component to form a surface treated polycarboxylic acid;

(b) heating a dry powder of an inorganic carbonate to a temperature of between about 68° C. and about 80° C. and adding thereto a surface treating agent to form a surface treated inorganic carbonate and;

(c) mixing together the surface treated polycarboxylic acid

and the surface treated inorganic carbonate to form the endothermic blowing agent.

In this method, each of the steps is preformed in a high intensity mixer in which the components are agitated.

The endothermic blowing agent is ideally incorporated into a polymeric concentrate that is used for producing foamed products. The polymeric concentrate includes both the endothermic blowing agent and a polymer reaction mixture. Particular polymer reaction mixtures are those that may be used to produce polymers of polyvinyl chloride, polyolefins, engineering resins, polypropylene and polystyrene.

Finally, the present method involves foamed polymeric products that have been produced by both the above blowing agent and the above discussed polymeric concentrate. Such products may be made by processes that involve either extrusion, calendering, injection molding, coating, expansion casting or rotational molding.

METHOD

A 25% concentrate of endothermic blowing agent was prepared in ethylene-vinyl acetate using a 30 millimeter twin screw extruder. The concentrates were let down to 0.5% active blowing agent in polypropylene. Plaques (4"×4"×1/4") were then foamed in a 50 ton Newbury injection molder at 200° C. Table 6.1 sets forth the excellent weight loss and impact properties. Comparisons are made with other commercially available blowing agents.

Suppliers

There are fewer than 50 suppliers of primary chemical blowing agents worldwide. Most of the leading companies have built their chemical blowing agent business over at least 20 years of experience. Many of the chemical blowing agents suppliers sell their complete product line in a single region and export only selected products. There are no suppliers of chemical blowing agent that have a leading position in all three major regions of the world. Many of the major chemical blowing agents producers are located in the Asia/Pacific region. There are a few dozen chemical blowing agent producers in China alone. Due to the poor logistics in China, the shipment of the chemicals is rather costly, so most of the companies there supply locally.

TABLE 6.1: Selected Suppliers of Chemical Blowing Agents

Supplier	Type				
	AZ*	TSS†	OBSH‡	DNPT§	Other
Bayer	×	—	—	—	—
Boehringer Ingelheim	—	—	—	—	—
Dong Jin Chemical	×	×	×	×	×
Eiwa Chemical Industry	×	×	×	×	×
Elf Atochem	×	—	—	—	—
Jiangmen Chemical Factory	×	—	—	—	—
Juhua Group	×	—	—	—	—
Kum Yang	×	×	×	—	—
Otsuka Chemical	×	—	—	—	—
Sankyo Kasei	×	×	×	×	—
Shanghai Xiangyang Chemical Industry Factory	×	—	—	×	—
Toyo Hydrazine Industry	×	—	—	—	×
Uniroyal Chemical (Crompton & Knowles)	×	×	×	×	—
Yonhua Taiwan Chemical	×	—	—	—	—
Zhenjiang Chemical Industry Factory	×	—	—	—	—
Zhuxixian Chemical Industry Factory	×	—	—	—	—

*AZ—azodicarbonamide.

†TSS—p-toluene sulfonyl semicarbazide.

‡OBSH—4,4'-oxybis (benzenesulfonyl hydrazide).

§DNPT—dinitropentamethylene tetramine.

The leading supplier of chemical blowing agents in North America is Uniroyal Chemical. Bayer is the leading supplier of chemical blowing agents in Europe followed by Dong Jin. Asia/ Pacific, the largest consuming region, has numerous suppliers, many selling only in that area of the world. The leading suppliers in this region typically manufacture in more than one country. For example, Dong Jin Chemical and Otsuka Chemical have primary manufacturing locations in Korea and Japan, respectively, but also produce in Indonesia through joint venture partnerships. A list of selected major suppliers of chemical blowing agents globally by type is shown in Table 6.1.

Trends and Forecasts

A major concern for producers of AZ type blowing agents is the shortage of the raw material hydrazine. There are few companies globally that manufacture hydrazine and there is currently an insufficient supply to satisfy market demand. However, many leading suppliers like Bayer, Otsuka, and Dong Jin are planning to expand globally. For example, Bayer is doubling its capacity by the year 2000. Its big advantage over most of the leading suppliers, with the exception of Elf Atochem and Otsuka, is that it is backward integrated into hydrazine. Long term, the global expansion of backward integrated CBA suppliers should resolve the hydrazine supply issue. The annual growth rate globally for chemical blowing agents over the next 5 years is in the 5% per year range.

7

Coupling Agents

Description

Coupling agents are additives used in reinforced and filled plastic composites to enhance the plastic-filler-reinforcement interface to meet increasingly demanding performance requirements. In general, there is little affinity between inorganic materials used as reinforcements and fillers and the organic matrices in which they are blended. With silicate reinforcements (glass fiber or wollastonite), silane coupling agents act by changing the interface between the dissimilar phases. This results in improved bonding and upgraded mechanical properties.

By chemically reacting with the resin and the filler or reinforcement components, coupling agents form strong and durable composites. Coupling agents significantly improve mechanical and electrical properties for a wide variety of resins, fillers, and reinforcements. In addition, they act to lower composite cost by achieving higher mineral loading.

Fiberglass reinforcement for plastics is the major end use of coupling agents. Thermoset resins, such as polyester and epoxy, account for approximately 90% of coupling agent consumption. Kaolin clay, wollastonite, and glass fiber are the leading fillers or reinforcements chemically treated with coupling agents. Coupling agents are either purchased and applied by the glass fiber or inorganic filler manufacturer or by the compounder for incorporation into the composite system

Another important market for silane coupling agents is in the crosslinking of polyolefins. In this market silanes are growing at the expense of organic peroxides. Silanes and titanates, along with several mino product types, make up the coupling agent market.

Silanes

Silanes comprise more than 90% of the plastic coupling agent market. They can be represented chemically by the formula Y–Si(X)$_3$ where X represents a hydrolyzable group such as ethoxy or methoxy and Y is a functional organic group which provides covalent attachment to the organic matrix. The coupling agent is initially bonded to the surface hydroxy groups of the inorganic component by the Si(X)$_3$ moiety-either directly or more commonly via its hydrolysis product, Si(OH)$_3$. The *Y* functional group (amino, methoxy, epoxy, etc.) attaches to the matrix when the silane-treated filler or reinforcement is compounded into the plastic, resulting in improved bonding and upgraded mechanical and electrical properties. Table 7.1 lists four different silane chemistries and their related composite systems.

TABLE 7.1: Silane Chemistries and Related Composites

Silane type	Resin	Filler or reinforcement
Amino	Phenolic	Alumina
	Phenolic	Silicon carbide
	Acrylic	Clay
	Nylon	Clay
	Nylon	Wollastonite
	Furan	Sand
Epoxy	Epoxy	Alumina trihydrate
Methacrylate	Polyester	Mica
Vinyl	PVC	Clay
	PVC	Talc
	EPDM	Clay

Preparation

This method relates to novel silane compounds, more particularly to a silane compound which is used as a starting material (monomer) of polysilane to be used as a precursor of electro-conductive- and photoconductve-materials, photo-reactive materials such as photoresists, polymerization initiators and silicone carbide-based ceramics and which is useful for chemical vapor deposition.

Method 1: 2,4-dimethyl-3-trichlorosilylpentane

A one-liter autoclave equipped with a stirrer was charged in a nitrogen atmosphere with 55 grams (0.56 mol) of 2,4-dimethyl-3-pentene, 148 grams (1.1 mol) of trichlorosilane and 17 grams (70 mmols) of 1,1'-azobis(cyclohexane-1-carbonitrile) and the mixture was reacted at a temperature of 130° C. for 4 days. The resulting reaction mixture was purified by distillation thereby obtaining 117 g (0.50 mol) of 2,4-dimethyl-3-trichlorosilylpentane. The structure of the resulting product was identified by ^{1}HNMR.

Yield

89% Boiling point: 110-120° C./80 mmHg; ^{1}HNMR Spectrum (in $CDCl_3$); 2.29 (m, 2H, .tbd.CH, J=4.0, J=7.0); 1.38 (t, 1H, CHSi, J=4.0); 1.17, 1.14 (d×2, 12H, $-CH_3$, J=7.0); Mass Spectrum $C_7H_{15}SiCl_3$ Calc'd: C 35.99, H 6.47, Si 12.02, Cl 45.52; Found: C 36.22, H 6.41, Si 12.17, Cl 45.20.

Method 2: 2,4-dimethyl-3-silylpentane

A one-liter four-necked flask equipped with a stirrer, a reflux cooling tube and a dropping funnel was charged with 50 grams (1.3 mol) of lithium aluminum hydride and one liter of diethylether under a nitrogen atmosphere. The mixture was added with droplets of a mixture of 117 grams (0.50 mol) of 2,4dimethyl-3-trichlorosilyl-pentane obtained in Medhod 1 and 200 ml of diethylether over 2 hours with stirring. After completion of the dropwise addition, the mixture was reacted on heating under reflux for 2 hours.

After completion of the reaction, the resulting mixture was added with droplets of 40 ml of water as being cooled with ice and then added with one liter of diluted hydrochloric acid and 500 ml of diethylether in turn, followed by three times-washing with 500 ml water after separating the organic phase. Thereafter, the organic phase was dehydrated with anhydrous magnesium sulfate and filtered out. The filtrate was purified by distillation thereby obtaining 39 grams (0.30 mol) of 2,4-dimethyl-3-silylpentane. The identification of the structure of the resulting product was conducted by ^{1}H-NMR.

Yield

·60% Boiling Point: 125-1228° C./; 1 H-NMR Spectrum (in $CDCl_3$); 3.44 (d, 3H, —SiH_3, J=4.0); 1.91 (oxtet, 2H, .tbd.CH, J=6.6); 0.97, 0.95 (d×2, 12H, –CH 3 , J=6.6); Mass Spectrum $C_7H_{19}Si$ Calc'd: C 64.52, H 13.92, Si 21.55; Found: C 64.81, H 13.75, Si 21.44;

Method 3: 3,5-diethyl-4-trichlorosilyheptane

A one-liter autoclave equipped with a stirrer was charged in a nitrogen atmosphere with 77 grams (0.50 mol) of 3,5-diethyl-3-heptene, 134 grams (1.0 mol) of trichlorosilane and 24 grams (0.1mol) of 1,1'-azobis(cyclohexane-1-carbonitrile) and the mixture was reacted at a temperature of 130° C. for 5 days. The resulting reaction mixture was purified by distillation thereby obtaining 80 grams (0.28 mol) of 3,5-diethyl-4-trichlorosilylheptane. The structure of the resulting product was identified by ^{1}H-NMR.

Yield

55% Boiling point: 130-135° C./10 mmHg; ^{1}H-NMR Spectrum (in $CDCl_3$); 2.21-2.39 (m, 2H, .tbd.CH); 1.65-1.83 (m, 8H, CH_2); 1.38 (t, 1H, CHSi, J=4.1); 1.14, 1.07 (t×2, 12H, --CH_3, J=6.8); Mass Spectrum $C_{11}H_{23}SiCl_3$ Calc'd: C 45.60, H 8.00, Si 9.69, Cl 36.71; Found: C 45.29, H 8.13, Si 9.85, Cl 36.73;

Method 4: 3,5-diethyl-4-silylheptane

A one-liter four-necked flask equipped with a stirrer, a reflux cooling tube and a dropping funnel was charged with 27 grams (0.71 mol) of lithium aluminum hydride and 500 ml of diethylether under a nitrogen atmosphere. The mixture was added with droplets of a mixture of 80 grams (0.28 mol) of 3,5-diethyl-4-trichlorosilylheptane obtained in Medhod 3 and 100 ml of diethylether over 2 hours. After completion of the dropwise addition, the mixture was reacted on heating under reflux for 2 hours with stirring.

After completion of the reaction, the resulting mixture was added with droplets of 30 ml of water as being cooled with ice and then added with 500 ml of diluted hydrochloric acid and 500 ml of diethylether in turn, followed by three times-washing with 500 ml water after separating the organic phase, Thereafter, the organic phase was dehydrated with anhydrous magnesium sulfate and filtered out. The filtrate was purified by distillation thereby obtaining 28 grams (0.12 mol) of 3,5-diethyl-4-silylpentane. The identification of the structure of the resulting product was conducted by ^{1}H-NMR.

Yield

43% Boiling Point: 92-98° C./20 mmHg; ^{1}H-NMR Spectrum (in $CDCl_3$); 3.46 (d, 3H, SiH_3, J=4.0); 2.02 (m, 2H, .tbd.CH); 1.55-1.80 (m, 8H, CH_2); 1.02, 0.97 (t×2, 12H, --CH_3, J=6.8); 0.71-0.82 (m, 11H, CHSi); Mass Spectrum $C_{12}H_{28}Si$ Calc'd: C 71.91, H 14.08, Si 14.01; Found: C 71.58, H 14.10, Si 14.32.

Method 5: 3,5-dimethyl-4-trichlorosilylheptane

A one-liter autoclave equipped with a stirrer was charged in a nitrogen atmosphere with 76 grams (0.60 mol) of 3,5-dimethyl-3-heptene, 161 grams (1.2 mol) of trichlorosilane and 29 grams (0.12 mol) of 1,1'-azobis(cyclohexane-1-carbonitrile) and the mixture was reacted at a temperature of 130° C. for 5 days. The resulting reaction mixture was purified by distillation thereby obtaining 92 grams (0.35 mol) of 3,5-dimethyl-4-trichlorosilylheptane. The structure of the resulting product was identified by ^{1}H-NMR.

Yield

58% Boiling Point: 100-110° C./40 mmHg; ^{1}H-NMR Spectrum (in $CDCl_3$); 2.21-2.39 (m, 2H, .tbd.CH); 1.55-1.76 (m, 8H, CH_2); 1.43 (t, 1H, CHSi, J =4.1); 1.08 (d, 6H, --CH_3, J=6.8); 1.05 (t,

6H, --CH_3, J=6.8); Mass Spectrum C_9H_{19} $SiCl_3$ Calc'd: $C_{41.31}$, $H_{7.32}$, $Si_{10.73}$, $Cl_{40.64}$; Found: $C_{41.86}$, $H_{7.78}$, $Si_{10.21}$, $Cl_{40.15}$.

Method 6: 3,5-dimethyl-4-silylheptane

A one-liter four-necked flask equipped with a stirrer, a reflux cooling tube and a dropping funnel was charged with 33 grams (0.83 mol) of lithium aluminum hydride and 500 ml of diethylether under a nitrogen atmosphere. The mixture was added with droplets of a mixture of 92 grams (0.35 mol) of 3,5-dimethyl-4-trichlorosilylpentane obtained in Medhod 5 and 100 ml of diethylether over 2 hours with stirring. After completion of the dropwise addition, the mixture was reacted on heating under reflux for 2 hours.

After completion of the reaction, the resulting mixture was added with droplets of 40 ml of water as being cooled with ice and then added with 500 ml of diluted hydrochloric acid and 500 ml of diethylether in turn, followed by three times-washing with 500 ml water after separating the organic phase. Thereafter, the organic phase was dehydrated with anhydrous magnesium sulfate and filtered out. The filtrate was purified by distillation thereby obtaining 22 grams (0.12 mol) of 3,5-dimethyl4-silylpentane. The identification of the structure of the resulting product was conducted by ^{1}H-NMR.

Yield

40% Boiling Point: 90-95° C./100 mmHg; ^{1}H-NMR Spectrum (in $CDCl_3$); 3.44 (d, 3H, --SiH_3 , J=4.0); 1.93 (m, 2H, .tbd.CH); 1.70-1.82 (m, 8H, —CH_2); 1.01 (d, 6H, --CH_3, J=6.6); 0.95 (t, 6H, --CH_3, J=6.7); 0.77-0.83 (m, 1 H, –CHSi); Mass Spectrum $C_9H_{22}Si$ Calc'd: C68.26, H14.00, Si17.74; Found: C68.55, H13.82, Si17.63.

Method 7: 2-methylcyclopentylsilane

A one-liter autoclave equipped with a stirrer was charged in a nitrogen atmosphere with 65 grams (0.79 mol) of 1-methylcyclopentene, 242 grams (1.79 mol) of trichlorosilane and 29 grams (0.12 mol) of 1,1'-azobis(cydohexane-1-carbonitrile) and the mixture was reacted at a temperature of 120° C. for 3 days. The resulting reaction mixture was purified by distillation thereby obtaining 148 grams of 3,5-dimethyl-4-trichlorosilylheptane.

Thereafter, a one-liter four-necked flask equipped with a stirrer, a reflux cooling tube and a dropping funnel was charged with 60 grams (1.6 mol) of lithium aluminum hydride and one liter of diethylether under a nitrogen atmosphere. The mixture was added with droplets of a mixture of 148 grams (0.68 mol) of 2-methylcyclopentyltrichlorosilane and 80 ml of diethylether over 3 hours with stirring. After completion of the dropwise addition, the mixture was reacted on heating under reflux for 2 hours.

After completion of the reaction, the resulting mixture was added with droplets of 80 ml of water as being cooled with ice and then added with 500 ml of diluted hydrochloric acid and 500 ml of diethylether in turn, followed by three times-washing with 500 ml water after separating the organic phase. Thereafter, the organic phase was dehydrated with anhydrous magnesium sulfate and filtered out. The filtrate was purified by distillation thereby obtaining 28 grams of *cis*-2-methylcyclopentylsilane represented by the formula ##STR17## and 16 grams of trans-2-methylcyclopentylsilane represented by the formula ##STR18## Each of the resulting product was identified in structure by ^{1}H-NMR.

***cis*-2-methylcyclopentsilane**

Boiling Point: 115-116° C. (atmospheric pressure); ^{1}H-NMR Spectrum (in $CDCl_3$); (the assignment was identified by two-dimensional NMR Spectrum); H-1 : 1.34-1.40 (m, 1H); H-2 : 2.25 (m, 1H); H-3, H-5: 1.69-1.78 (m, 2H); H-3': 1.25-1.32 (m 1H); H-4: 1.86-1.92(m, 1H); H-4', H-5': 1.50-1.59 (m, 2H); H-6: 3.48 (d, 3H, J 1 .5 =4.0); H-7: 0.96 (d, 3H, J 2 .7 =6.0 Hz); Mass Spectrum $C_6H_{14}Si$ (cis form) Calc'd : C 63.07, H 12.35, SI 24.58; Found: C 62.81, H 12.48, Si 24.71.

trans-2-methylcyclopentylsilane

Boiling Point: 105-108° C.; 1 H-NMR Spectrum (in $CDCl_3$); (the assignment was identified by NMR Spectrum) H-1: 0.65-0.76 (m, 1H); H-2: 1.68-1.74 (m, 1H); H-3: 1.81-1.87 (m, 1H); H-3': 1.11-1.17 (m, 1H); H-4; H-4': 1.55-1.67 (m, 2H); H-5: 1.91-1.97 (m, 1H); H-5': 1.41-1.48 (m, 1H); H-6: 3.50 (d, 3H, J 1 .5 =4.0); H-7: 1.04 (d, 3H. J 2 .7 =6.0); Mass Spectrum $C_6H_{14}Si$ (trans form) Calc'd: C 63.07, H 12.35, Si 24.58; Found: C 62.74, H 12.56, Si 24.70.

Method 8 : 2,6-dimethylcyclohexyltrichlorosilane

A one-liter autoclave equipped with a stirrer was charged in a nitrogen atmosphere with 39 grams (0.35 mol) of 1,3-dimethylcyclohexene, 94 grams (0.69 mol) of trichlorosilane and 18 grams (74 mmol) of 1,1'-azobis(cydohexane-1-carbonitrile) and the mixture was reacted at a temperature of 130° C. for 3 days. The resulting reaction mixture was purified by distillation thereby obtaining 69 grams (0.28 mol) of 2,6-dimethyl-4-cyciohexyltrichlorosilane, The structure of the resulting product was Identified by ^{1}H-NMR analysis.

Yield

80% Boiling Point: 130-135° C./80 mmHg; ^{1}H-NMR Spectrum (in $CDCl_3$); 2.28-2.50; 1.15-2.03 (m, 9H); 1.13 (d, 3H, J=7.0, --CH_3); 1.09 (d, 3H, J=7.0, --CH_3); Mass Spectrum $C_8H_{15}SiCl_3$ Calc'd: C 39.12, H 6.15, Si 11.43, Cl 43.30; Found: C 38.96, H 6.24, Si 11.18, Cl 43.62.

Method 9: 2,6-dimethylcyclohaxylsilane

A one-liter four-necked flask equipped with a stirrer, a reflux cooling tube and a dropping funnel was charged with 25 grams (0.66 mol) of lithium aluminum hydride and 500 ml of diethylether under a nitrogen atmosphere. The mixture was added with droplets of a mixture of 69 grams (0.28 mol) of 2,6-dimethylcydohexyl-trichlorosilane obtained in Medhod 8 and 100 ml of diethylether over 2 hours with stirring. After completion of the dropwise addition, the mixture was reacted on heating under reflux for 2 hours.

After completion of the reaction, the resulting mixture was added with droplets of 40 ml of water as being cooled with ice and then added with 300 ml of diluted hydrochloric acid and 300 ml of diethylether in turn, followed by three times-washing with 500 ml water after separating the organic phase. Thereafter, the organic phase was dehydrated with anhydrous magnesium sulfate and filtered out. The filtrate was purified by distillation thereby obtaining 34 grams (0.24 mol) of 2,6-dimethylcyclohexylsilane in which three types of isomers are present. The identification of the structure of the resulting product was conducted by ^{1}H-NMR.

Yield

85% Boiling Point: 88-98° C./100 mmHg; ^{1}H-NMR Spectrum (in $CDCl_3$); (The assignment was identified by two-dimensional NMR Spectrum.) 3.52, 3.46, 3.42 (d×3, --SiH_3 , J 1.7 =4.0, ratio 0.07/1.0/0.2); 1.95-2.08 (m, 1H); 1.63-1.77 (m, 3H); 1.40-1.60 (m, 5H); 0.90-1.03 (m, 6H, --CH 3); Mass Spectrum $C_8H_{18}Si$ Calc'd: C 67.52, H 12.75, Si 19.73; Found: C 67.28, H 12.91, Si 19.81.

Furthermore, the 2,6-dimethylcyclohexylsilane thus obtained was purified with use of a fractionating tower thereby obtaining 10 grams (70 mmol) of *cis*-trans-2,6-dimethylcyclohexylsilane represented by the formula ##STR19##

Boiling Point: 94-96° C./100 mmHg; ^{1}H-NMR Spectrum (in $CDCl_3$); (The assignment was identified by two-dimensional NMR Spectrum.); H-1,5: 1.00 (m, 2H, J 1 .6 =9.0, J 1 .2 =4.2); H-2: 2.03(m,1H); H-3,3': 1.46 (m, 2H); H-4: 155 (m, 1H); H-4': 1.50 (m, 1H); H-5': 1.67 (m, 1H); H-6: 1.72 (m, 1H); H-7: 3.47 (d, 3H, J 1 .7 =3.0); H-8: 0.98 (d, 3H, J 2 .8 =7.2); H-9: 0.93 (d, 3H, J 6 .9 =6.6).

Method 10: 2,5-dimethylcyclopentyltrichlorosilane

A one-liter autoclave equipped with a stirrer was charged in a nitrogen atmosphere with 49 grams (0.51 mol) of 1,3-dimethylcyclopentene, 138 grams (1.0 mol) of trichlorosilane and 24 grams (0.1 mol) of 1,1'-azobis(cyclohexane-1-carbonitrile) and the mixture was reacted at a temperature of 130° C. for 3 days. The resulting reaction mixture was purified by distillation thereby obtaining 85 grams (0.37 mol) of 2,5-dimethylcyclopentyl-trichlorosilane. The structure of the resulting product was identified by ^{1}H-NMR analysis.

Yield

73% Boiling Point: 120-125° C./85 mmHg; ^{1}H-NMR Spectrum (in $CDCl_3$); 2.12-2.42; 1.11-2.09 (m, 7H); 1.08 (d, 3H, J=7.0 Hz, --CH_3); 1.05 (d, 3H, J=7.0 Hz, --CH_3); Mass Spectrum $C_7H_{13}SiCl_3$ Calc'd: C 36.30, H 5.66, Si 12.13, Cl 45.92; Found: C 35.90, H 5.38, Si 12.44, Cl 46.28.

Method 11: 2,5-dimethylcyclopentylsilane

A one-liter four-necked flask equipped with a stirrer, a reflux cooling tube and a dropping funnel was charged with 35 grams (0.92 mol) of lithium aluminum hydride and 500 ml of diethylether under a nitrogen atmosphere. The mixture was added with droplets of a mixture of 85 grams (0.37 mol) of 2,5-dimethylcydopentyl-trlchlorosilane obtained in Medhod 10 and 100 ml of diethylether over 2 hours with stirring. After completion of the dropwise addition, the mixture was reacted on heating under reflux for 2 hours.

After completion of the reaction, the resulting mixture was added with droplets of 50 ml of water as being cooled with ice and then added with 300 ml of diluted hydrochloric acid and 300 ml of diethylether in turn, followed by three times-washing with 500 ml water after separating the organic phase. Thereafter, the organic phase was dehydrated with anhydrous magnesium sulfate and filtered out. The filtrate was purified by by distillation thereby obtaining 28 grams (0.22 mol) of 2,5-dimethylcyclopentylsilane. The identification of the structure of the resulting product was conducted by ^{1}H-NMR.

Yield

59% Boiling Point: 80-92° C./100 mmHg; 1 H-NMR Spectrum (in $CDCl_3$); (The assignment was identified by two-dimensional NMR Spectrum.); 3.53, 3.48, 3.43 (d×3, --SiH_3, 0.13/1.0/0.3); 2.02-2.23 (m, 1H); 1.60-1.80 (m, 2H); 1.25-1.57 (m, 4H); 0.90-1.10 (m, 6H, --CH_3); Mass Spectrum $C_7H_{16}Si$ Calc'd: C 65.54, H 12.57, Si 21.89; Found: C 65,27, H 12.69, Si 22.04.

Method 12: 2-tert-butylcyclopentyltrichlorosilane

A one-liter autoclave equipped with a stirrer was charged in a nitrogen atmosphere with 50 grams (0.40 mol) of 1-tert-butylcyclopentene, 108 grams (0.80 mol) of trichlorosilane and 20 grams (82 mmol) of 1,1'-azobis(cyclohexane-1-carbonitrle) and the mixture was reacted at a temperature of 130° C. for 3 days. The resulting reaction mixture was purified by distillation thereby obtaining 62 grams (0.24 mol) of 2-tert-butylcyclopentyltrichlorosilane. The structure of the resulting product was identified by ^{1}H-NMR.

Yield

60% Boiling Point: 150-160° C./20 mmHg; ^{1}H-NMR Spectrum (in $CDCl_3$); 2.25-2.40 (m, 1H); 1.20-2.10 (m, 7H); 1.12, 1.05 (s, 9H, CH_3); Mass Spectrum $C_9H_{17}SiCl_3$ Calc'd : C 41.63, H 6.60, Si 10.82, Cl 40.96; Found: C 41.14, H 6.38, Si 10.96, Cl 41.52.

Method 13 : 2-tert-butylcyclopentylsilane

A one-liter four-necked flask equipped with a stirrer, a reflux cooling tube and a dropping funnel was charged with 23 grams (0.61 mol) of lithium aluminum hydride and 400 ml of diethylether under a nitrogen atmosphere. The mixture was added with droplets of a mixture of 62 grams (0.24 mol) of 2-tert-butylcyclopentyl-trichlorosilane obtained in Medhod 10 and 50 ml of diethylether over one hour with stirring. After completion of the dropwise addition, the mixture was reacted on heating under reflux for 2 hours.

After completion of the reaction, the resulting mixture was added with droplets of 30 ml of water as being cooled with ice and then added with 200 ml of diluted hydrochloric acid and 300 ml of diethylether in turn, followed by three times-washing with 500 ml water after separating the organic phase. Thereafter, the organic phase was dehydrated with anhydrous magnesium sulfate and filtered out, followed by purification by distillation thereby obtaining 32 grams (0.20 mol) of 2-tert-butylcyclopentylsilane in which two types of isomers are present. The identification of the structure of the resulting product was conducted by ^{1}H-NMR.

Yield

85% Boiling Point: 100-110° C./80 mmHg; ^{1}H-NMR Spectrum (in $CDCl_3$); (The assignment was identified by two-dimensional NMR Spectrum.); 3.47, 3.54 (d×3, --SiH_3, J=3,9); 1.73-1.87 (m, 1H, H-2); 1.50-1.75, 1.17-1.42, 0.71-0,80 (m, 7H); 1.05, 0.97 (s, 9H); Mass Spectrum $C_9H_{20}Si$ Calc'd: C 69.14, H 12.89, Si 17.96; Found: C 68.86, H 12.93, Si 18.21.

Titanates

Titanates are used primarily as dispersing aids for fillers in polyolefins to prevent agglomeration. Titanium-based coupling agents react with free protons at the surface of the inorganic material, resulting in the formation of organic monomolecular layers on the surface. Typically, titanate-treated inorganic fillers or reinforcements are hydrophobic, organophilic, and organofunctional and, therefore, exhibit enhanced dispersibility and bonding with the polymer matrix. When used in filled polymer systems, titanates claim to improve impact strength, exhibit melt viscosity lower than that of virgin polymer at loadings above 50%, and enhance the maintenance of mechanical properties during aging.

Preparation

This method relates to a method for producing aluminum titanate in the form of a powdered primary material, ready for making aluminum titanate ceramics, by conventional ceramic techniques. The method also relates to a method for producing the mixed oxide powder from spent pickle liquor from titanium production by adding aluminum scrap or alumina salts to the same, or equally from aluminum or titanium scrap dissolved in acidic mixture, in both cases by complete recovery of the acids and production of the oxides, which after thermal treatment give the aluminum titanate material.

Method 1

A solution consisting of 25 g Al/l (0.85 mol/l) and 20.5 g Ti/l (0.43 mol/l) in HF of 2 mol/l and HNO_3 of 2 mol/l is transferred to the reactor (1 in the drawing) by means of a pump and sprayed into a heated hot gas zone at a temperature of 400° C. The acid recovery by means of this system, described in the drawing, was approx. 90% of HF and HNO_3. This model solution of the typical metal content of Ti which reflects the usual spent pickling acids in titanium metal pickling, of 20-30 g Ti/l, and acid contents of 2-3 weight percent HF and approx. 15 weight percent HNO_3, has been chosen to match a real case. For technical purposes, i.e. if scrap is used instead of a spent pickling acid, also higher concentrations of up to 100 g/l Al and 82 g/l Ti can be used instead, because of the excellent solubility of both metals in the described HF/HNO_3 acid mixture.

Method 2

Titanium Ti (0.43 mol/l) equals 20.5 g/l dissolved in HF (2 weight percent) and HNO_3 (15 weight percent) and 320 g/l $Al(NO_3)_3.9H_2O$ salt, dissolved in water, are combined and transferred into the reactor, in the way as described in Method 1. The decomposition reaction within the reactor can take place in the temperature range of in between 300° to 600° C. It should be mentioned that the higher the temperature of the thermal decomposition of the solution, the higher the NOx content of the flue gas to be formed which thereafter has to be denoxed.

Method 3

The powders formed by the process described in Medhod 1 and Medhod 2 are of white colour with a powder bulk density of inbetween 0.3-0.4 g/ccm, and a specific surface area (B.E.T) of inbetween 30-40 m^2/g and a usual humidity of 1-2%, which of course is dependent on the reactor temperature. The powder particle size distribution after a thermal decomposition of the solution at 400° C. gives a mean particle size of 20-22 micrometer, which is also typical for a very fine spray dried powder. The crystallographic analysis of such a powder usually reveals the crystallographic phases of α-Al_2O_3 , β-Al_2O_3 , TiO_2 (anatase), AlOOH (boehmite) and sometimes also already and spontaneously formed tialite, Al_2TiO_5

Method 4

Subsequent reaction sintering of such a powder described in Medhod 3 at a fast temperature cycle time in a rotary kiln, at 1350° C (up to 1500° C.) in its hot zone, and at a contact time in the hot zone of two hours up to four hours, usually leads to 100% Tialite, Al_2TiO_5, of the orthorhombic structure Cmcm, with a specific surface area (B.E.T.) of 2 m^2/g to 4 m^2/g and a particle size distribution of around 20 microne mean particle size. This powder can be ball milled to a mean particle size of 2 to 6 microbes.

Method 5

To make a final ceramic from the powder obtained in Medhod 4, the powder was compressed in a uniaxial working hand press, at room temperature, at 100 to 150 MPa to tablets, which had a green (unsintered) density of 2.0 g/ccm up to 2.1 g/ccm. These tablets were then subsequently transferred to a muffle to be sintered at 1500° C. for 1 hour. After sintering the tablets had a density of 2.9 g/ccm to 3.0 g/ccm. Crystallographically the tialite tablets remain unchanged. No decomposition was observed. The so formed ceramic was tested on its mechanical and thermal stability to give the following values: thermal shock stability (1550°/20° C.) by immediate water quenching: a minimum of 3 cycle times; thermal conductivity (W/MoK): 2.0; thermal expansion coefficient (10 exp 6/degr.C): 2.0; modulus of rupture (MOR) in (MPa) 20-40.

Suppliers

Table 7.2 presents a list of selected suppliers of coupling agents. The two leading suppliers in North America are Witco and Dow Corning. Worldwide, Witco is the leading supplier with a strong presence in Europe, in Asia/Pacific (through a distribution agreement), as well as in North America.

TABLE.7.2: Selected Suppliers of Coupling Agents

Supplier	Type		
	Silane	Titanate	Other
Aristech Chemical	-	-	x
Degussa	x	-	-
Dow Corning	x	-	-
Kenrich Petrochemicals	-	x	x
PCR	x	-	-
Rhodia	x	x	x
Shin-Etsu Chemical	x	-	-
Sivento	x	-	-
Uniroyal	-	-	x
Witco	x	-	-

Trends and Forecasts

The coupling agent market follows the growth of its three major uses: fiberglass reinforced plastics, plastics compounding, and mineral filler pretreatment. The latter two markets, although smaller than the reinforced polyester area, are leading the growth, which is running at about 6%/year globally.

8

Flame Retardants

Description

Flame retardants are in a unique position among plastics additives in that they are both created by regulations and yet are threatened by other regulations. The huge $2.3 billion industry was created over the years by various industry, federal, and state statutes, which aimed to protect people from fire and smoke situations. Indeed, the Underwriters Laboratories (UL), whose standards are integral to the success or failure of flame retardants, were created by the insurance industry. Without these regulations, the plastics industry, which accounts for 85 to 90% ($2 billion) of the global sales of flame retardants, wouldn't use these products because they are expensive and lower the physical properties of the plastics in which they are employed. On the other hand, environmental and toxicity concerns now have regulators looking at the important halogenated and antimony- based synergist flame retardants that have been developed over the years. Any regulations which limit the use of such products will again change the industry and force producers to develop a new generation of products.

Flame-retardant additives for plastics are essential safety materials. The transportation, building, appliance, and electronic industries use flame retardants in plastics to prevent human injury or death and to protect property from fire damage. Fundamentally, flame retardants reduce the ease of ignition smoke generation and rate of burn of plastics. Flame retardants can be organic or inorganic in composition, and typically contain either bromine, chlorine, phosphorus, antimony, or aluminum materials. The products can be further classified as being reactive or additive.

Reactive flame retardants

Reactive flame retardants chemically bind with the host resin. Additive types are physically mixed with a resin and do not chemically bind with the polymer. Flame retardants are used at loading levels from a few percent to more than 60% of the total weight of a treated resin. They typically degrade the inherent physical properties of the polymer, some types significantly more than others. Since flame retardants work by minimizing at least one of the requirements for a fire to exist, namely, fuel, heat energy, and oxygen, they also may be classified in another way as follows:

- *Char formers*. Usually phosphorus compounds, which remove the carbon fuel source and provide an insulating layer against the fire's heat.
- *Heat absorbers*. Usually metal hydrates such as aluminum trihydrate (ATH) or magnesium hydroxide, which remove heat by using it to evaporate water in their structure.
- *Flame quenchers*. Usually bromine or chlorine-based halogen systems which interfere with the reactions in a flame.
- *Synergists*. Usually antimony compounds which enhance performance of the flame quencher.

Resin formulators and compounders must select a flame retardant that is both physically and economically suitable for specific resin systems and the intended applications. It is common to formulate resins with multiple flame-retardant types, typically a primary flame retardant plus a synergist such as antimony oxide, to enhance overall flame-retardant efficiency at the lowest cost. Several hundred different flame-retardant systems are used by the plastics industry because of these formulation practices. Flame retardants consumed in plastics are a diverse group of chemical types and are classified in the major groups, shown in Table 8.1.

TABLE 8.1: Flame-Retardant Types and Typical Products

Types	Typical products
Brominated	Reactive
	Tetrabromobisphenol A (TBA)
	Brominated polyols
	Tetrabromophthalic anhydride
	Additive
	Decabromodiphenyl oxide (DBDPO)
	TBA derivatives
	Hexabromocyclodecane/dodecane
	Hexabromodiphenoxyethane
	Brominated polystyrene
Phosphate esters	Halogenated
	Pentabromodiphenyl oxide/phosphate ester mixtures
	Tris (chloropropyl) phosphate (TCPP)
	Tris (chloroethyl) phosphate (TCEP)
	Tridichloroisopropyl phosphate (TDCPP)
	Nonhalogenated
	Triaryl phosphates
	Alkyldiaryl phosphates
	Trialkyl phosphates
Chlorinated	Chlorinated paraffins—liquid
	Chlorinated paraffins—resinous
	DECHLORANE PLUS
	Chlorendic anhydride/HET Acid
	Bromochloroparaffins
Alumina trihydrate	—
Antimony oxides	Antimony trioxide
	Antimony pentoxide
	Sodium antimonate

Types	Typical products
Other flame retardants	Inorganic phosphorus
	Ammonium polyphosphate
	Red phosphorus
	Melamines
	Melamine crystal
	Melamine cyanurate
	Melamine phosphates
	Magnesium hydroxide
Molybdenum compounds	
Zinc borate	

Brominated Hydrocarbons

Brominated hydrocarbons represent the highest dollar volume among all flame retardants used worldwide. The major additive types are decabromodiphenyl oxide (DBDPO) and derivatives of tetrabromobisphenol A (TBA). The major reactive type is TBA itself. Significant amounts of TBA are also used to make additive types. Typically, brominated compounds are used with a synergist such as antimony oxide in a 3:1 (brominated compound-synergist) ratio. A variety of plastic resins use brominated flame retardants, with HIPS, ABS, and PC being the most prominent resins using these additive types. Epoxies for microchips and circuit boards and unsaturated polyesters are the most important applications for reactives.

Preparation

This method provides, *inter alia*, a significant improvement in a process for preparing tetrabromobisphenol-A whereby a tetrabromobisphenol-A predominant product having a reduced amount of impurities is formed. The process comprises:

(a) dissolving bisphenol-A in a methanol solvent containing up to about 5 weight percent water, wherein the ratio of methanol to bisphenol-A ranges from about 25 to about

43 moles of methanol per mole of bisphenol-A based on the total amount of methanol used and the total amount of bisphenol-A to be brominated;

(b) adding to the solution in (a) from about 3.9 to about 4.2 moles of bromine per mole of bisphenol-A to be brominated while maintaining a reaction temperature in the range of from about 0° to about 40° C.;

(c) after the bromination is substantially complete, precipitating the tetrabromobisphenol-A thus formed; and

(d) purifying the precipitated tetrabromobisphenol-A so as to obtain a product predominant in tetrabromobisphenol-A containing less than about 20 ppm total ionic impurity.

Accordingly, it has been discovered that the amount of reaction solvent relative to the bisphenol-A to be brominated and the amount of water in that solvent has a beneficial impact on the quality of product that can be produced. It has also been found that such brominated product can be further purified by contacting the precipitated product with a quality enhancing amount of treated water, and heat treating the contacted product at a temperature and for a period of time which are sufficient to form a product having less than 20 ppm total ionic impurity and a reduced amount of organic impurity.

The improved process of the present method provides, for the first time, a method for the production of a product predominant in tetrabromobisphenol-A (TBBPA) on a large scale at high yield having greatly reduced ionic and organic impurities. By greatly reduced is meant the ionic impurity in the recovered and dried product is preferably less than about 30 ppm, more preferably less than about 20 ppm, and most preferably less than about 10 ppm and the organic impurity is less than about 2 wt. %. For purposes of this invention, "total ionic impurity" means any of one or more of compounds represented by MBr wherein M is hydrogen, a metal, or an alkali or alkaline earth metal ion selected from the group consisting essentially of Ba, Ca, Fe, K, Na, Mg, and Mn. In a preferred embodiment, the ionic impurity is predominantly HBr (i.e. greater than about 50% by weight HBr). Organic impurities in the product reduced by the process of this method include phenols; brominated phenols; alkylphenols; bromoalkylphenols; brominated alkylphenols; brominated bromoalkylphenols; mono-, di-, and tri-bromobisphenol-A; and the like.

The process of this method may be used to reduce the total ionic impurity content of a TBBPA predominant product before or after drying the product. It is particularly preferred, to separate the product from the reaction mass prior to contacting the product with a quality enhancing amount of treated water and heat treating the product. Alternatively, the product may be dried and ground to a powder having an average particle size of about 70 microns or less before contacting the product with treated water and heat treating the product. It is recognized, however, that the product may be dried and heat treated essentially simultaneously.

METHOD : Temperature below 40° C.

In a 500 mL 4-neck flask fitted with a -10° C. Friedrichs condenser, thermometer, mechanical stirrer and addition funnel with a dip tube and cooled in an ice bath was placed the amount of methanol and bisphenol-A indicated in Table 8.2. In runs 1 and 2, the methanol contained 11 wt. % water. In runs 3 and 4, the methanol contained 4 wt. % water. While stirring, the reaction mass was maintained at the temperatures indicated for each run in Table below . Bromine was added through the dip tube to the reaction mass over the period of time indicated in Table 2. After completion of the bromine addition, the reaction mass was cooked at the temperature indicated for up to 3 hours and the percent yield of methyl bromide formed during the cook period was determined.

The amount of methyl bromide thus formed was determined by the use of gas chromatographic analysis according to the following procedure. Samples were removed by applying nitrogen pressure through the condenser and catching samples as the liquid rose up the diptube. Samples were taken directly into a cold mixture of 10 ml iso-octane and 10 ml water. The sample was immediately capped with a septum cap, shaken and the iso-octane layer analyzed on a 30 meter DB-5 capillary column, split injection, at 80°C. isothermal using an internal standard.

Phosphate esters

The *phosphate esters* are divided into halogenated and nonhalogenated types. The halogenated compounds, typically chloroalkyl esters, are used widely in polyurethane foam. The nonhalogenated products, with the triaryl phosphates being the most common, are used as flame retardants in engineering plastics and as flame retardants or plasticizers in PVC. There are also significant quantities of phosphate esters used outside of plastics in textile and lubricant applications. Confusion sometimes exists in the PVC category as to whether these products should be called plasticizers or flame retardants. Typically, phosphate esters are not used with a synergist.

Preparation

A preferred class of phosphate esters is when w=2. However, inasmuch as the synthesis of the phosphates results in a mixture of phosphates of different degrees of esterification, and thus conventional separation methods must be employed to obtain the preferred class of esters, mixtures of phosphate esters in which a major portion of the ester molecules have a w value of 2 constitute the most desirable product for practical use.

The preferred water solubilizing cationic ions are alkali metals such as sodium, potassium and lithium, ammonium; alkyl substituted ammonium such as methylammonium, ethylammonium, diethylammonium, triethylammonium, n-propylammonium, methyl-diethylammonium, and the like; hydroxyalkyl-substituted ammoniums such as ethanolammonium, diethanolammonium, triethanolammonium, bis(3-hydroxypropyl)ammonium and the like; cycloalkyl-substituted ammoniums such as cyclohexylammonium, methylcyclohexylammonium and the like; aryl substituted ammoniums such as phenyl ammonium, benzylammonium and the like; and heterocyclic ammoniums such as pyridinium, morpholinium and the like.

Method 1 : Preparation of Ammonium Bis [4-heptafluoroisopropoxy-3,3,4,4-tetrafluorobutyl] Phosphate.

A solution of 50.0g (0.152 mole) of 4-heptafluoroisopropoxy-3,3,4,4-tetrafluorobutanol and 6.0g (0.075 mole) of pyridine in 65g of anhydrous diethyl ether was slowly added to an agitated solution of 11.5g (0.075 mole) of phosphorous oxychloride in 85g of diethyl ether containing 6.0g (0.075 mole) of pyridine maintained at 15°-20° C. The reaction mixture was refluxed for 4 hours at 37° C., filtered, and the filtrate concentrated. There was recovered 47.6g of bis[4-heptafluoroisopropoxy-3,3,4,4-tetrafluorobutyl] phosphochloridate:

$[(CF_3)_2CFOCF_2CF_2CH_2CH_2O]_2POCl$

Analysis for $C_{14}H_8F_{22}ClPO_5$:

Calculated: C, 22.68; H, 1.08; F, 56.57; P, 4.18.

Found: C, 22.70; H, 1.05; F, 57.02; P, 3.98.

The phosphochloridate thus obtained (41.6g) was heated with 5.0g of pyridine and 6.5 g of water to 100° C. for 2 hours. After the mixture cooled, 10g of dilute hydrochloric acid was added with agitation. The organic layer was extracted with ether, separated, washed with water, dried and stripped of ether and other volatiles. There was recovered 40.5g of bis[4-heptafluoroisopropoxy-3,3,4,4-tetrafluorobutyl]hydroge n phosphate:

$[(CF_2)_2CFOCF_2CF_2CH_2CH_2O]_2POOH$

Analysis for $C_{14}H_9F_{22}O_6P$:

Calculated: C, 23.27; H, 1.24; F, 57.92.

Found: C, 24.02; H, 1.29; F, 56.95.

The hydrogen phosphate thus obtained (38g) was dissolved in 35g of dry ether, and the solution was treated with ammonia gas at about 35° C. for about 5 hours. The ammonium bis[4-heptafluoroisopropoxy-3,3,4,4-tetrafluorobutyl] phosphate was precipitated as a white crystalline solid. Melting point was 115°-120° C.

$[(cf_3)_2cfocf_2cf_2ch_2ch_2o]_2po(onh_4)$

analysis for $C_{14}H_{12}F_{22}NPO_6$:

Calculated: C, 22.70; H, 1.62; F, 56.57; N, 1.89

Found: C, 22.82; H, 1.65; F, 57.12; N, 1.98

Method 2 : Preparation of Diammonium 4-heptafluoroisopropoxy-3,3,4,4-tetrafluorobutyl Phosphate.

A solution of 100g (0.30 mole) of 4-heptafluoroisopropoxy-3,3,4,4-tetrafluorobutanol and 12.0g (0.15 mole) of pyridine in 130g of anhydrous diethyl ether was slowly added to an agitated solution of 46.0g (0.30 mole) of phosphorous oxychloride in 170g of ether containing 12.0g (0.15 mole) of pyridine and maintained at 15°-20° C. The reaction mixture was refluxed at 37° C. for 3 hours filtered and the filtrate concentrated. There was recovered 109g of 4-heptafluoroisopropoxy-3,3,4,4-tetrafluorobutylphosphoryl dichloride:

$(CF_3)_2CFOCF_2CF_2CH_2CH_2OPOCl_2$

Analysis for $C_7H_4F_{11}Cl_2PO_3$:

Calculated: C, 18.76; H, 0.89; F, 46.75; P, 6.43.

Found: C, 19.25; H, 1.24; F, 47.50; P, 6.20

The phosphoryldichloride (98g) was heated with 40g of pyridine and 36g of water at 80° C. for 2 hours. After the mixture cooled, 50g of dilute hydrochloric acid was added with agitation. The organic layer was extracted with ether, separated, washed with water, dried, and stripped of ether and other volatiles. There was recovered 57g of 4-heptafluoroisopropoxy-3,3,4,-4-tetrafluorobutyl dihydrogen phosphate:

$(CF_2)_2CFOCF_2CF_2CH_2CH_2OPO(OH)_2$

Analysis for $C_7H_6F_{11}PO_5$:

Calculated: C, 20.48; H, 1.46; F, 50.97; P, 7.55

Found: C, 21.12; H, 1.54; F, 51.61; P, 7.68.

The dihydrogen phosphate thus obtained (15g) was dissolved in 150g of anhydrous ether and the solution was treated with ammonia gas for 3 hours. The diammonium 4-heptafluoroisopropoxy-3,3,4,4-tetrafluorobutyl phosphate: $(CF_3)_2CFOCF_2CF_2CH_2$—$CH_2OPO(ONH_4)_2$ precipitated as a white crystalline solid and was filtered off.

Melting Point: 180°-185° C.

Analysis for $C_7H_{12}F_{11}N_2PO_5$:

Calculated: C, 18.91; H, 2.70; F, 47.29; P, 6.98.

Found: C, 19.29; H, 2.17; F, 48.12; P, 6.85.

Method 3 : Preparation of Ammonium Bis(8-heptafluoro-isopropoxy-3,3, to 8,8-dodecafluorooctyl) Phosphate.

Using the procedure of Method 1,8-heptafluoroisopropoxy-3,3 to 8,8dodecafluorooctanol was reacted with phosphorous oxychloride in the presence of pyridine to yield bis(8-heptafluoroisopropoxy-3,3, to 8,8-dodecafluorooctyl) phosphochloridate. Hydrolysis yielded bis(8-Heptafluoroisopropoxy-3,3, to 8,8 -dodecafluorooctyl hydrogen phosphate. This product was treated with ammonia gas to form ammonium bis(8-heptafluoroisopropoxy-3,3, to 8,8-dodecafluorooctyl phosphate.

Melting Point: 175°-180° C,:

$[(cf_3)_2cfo(cf_2cf_2)_3ch_2ch_2o]_2po(onh_4)$

analysis for $C_{22}H_{12}F_{38}NPO_6$:

Calculated: C, 23.20; H, 1.06; F, 63.28; P, 2.72

Found: C, 24.12; H, 1.15; F, 64.97; P, 2.92.

Method 4: Preparation of Ammonium Bis[13-heptafluoro-isopropoxy-12,12,13,13-tetrafluorotridecyl] phosphate.

Using the procedure of Method 1, 13-heptafluoroisopropoxy-12,12,13,13-tetrafluorotridecanol was reacted with phosphorous oxychloride in the presence of pyridine to yield bis(13-heptafluoro-isopropoxy-12,12,13,13-tetrafluorotridecyl)phosphochlori date. Hydrolysis yielded bis[13-heptafluoroisopropoxy-12,12,13,-tetrafluorotridecyl]h ydrogen phosphate. This product was treated with ammonia gas to form Ammonium bis(13heptafluoroisopropoxy-12,12,13,13-tetrafluorotridecyl) phosphate, a grease-like material:

$[(CF_3)_2CFOCF_2CF_2(CH_2)_{11}O]_2PO(ONH_4)$

Analysis for $C_{32}F_{22}H_{48}NPO_6$:

Calculated: C, 38.7; H, 4.88; N, 1.42.

Found: C, 37.5; H, 4.75; N, 1.92.

Method 5

Using the procedure of Method 2, 13-heptafluoroisopropoxy-12,12,13,13-tetrafluorotridecanol was reacted with phosphorous - heptafluoroisoproxy-in the presence of pyridine to yield 13-heptafluoroisopropoxy-12,12,13,13 -tetrafluorotridecyl phosphoryl dichloride. Hydrolysis yielded 13-heptafluoroisopropoxy-12,12,13,13-tetrafluorotridecyl hydrogen phosphate. The product was treated with ammonia gas to yield diammonium (13-heptafluoroisopropoxy-12,12,13,13-tetrafluorotridecyl) phosphate.

Melting Point: 205°-210° C:

$(cf_3)_2 cfocf_2cf_2(ch_2)_{11}opo(onh_4)_2$

analysis for $C_{20}F_{19}H_{30}O_5N_2P$:

Calculated: C, 31.2; H, 3.92; N, 3.64.

Found: C, 31.1; H, 3.47; N, 3.10.

Method 6: Preparation of Diammonium 17-heptafluoroisopropoxy-12-12, to 17,17-dodecafluoroheptadecyl phosphate.

Using the procedure of Method 2, 17-heptafluoroisopropoxy-12,12, to 17,17-dodecafluoroheptadecanol was reacted with phosphorous oxychloride in the presence of pyridine to yield 17-heptafluoroisopropoxy-12,12, to 17,17-dodecafluoroheptadecyl-phosphoryldichloride. A benzene solution of the phosphoryldichloride was treated with the calculated amount of pyridine and an excess of water at 60° for 2 hours. The liquid phase was decanted off and the dihydrogen phosphate was washed with water, and dried by azeotroping with benzene. Ammonia gas was then bubbled into the boiling benzene for 2 hours, which yielded diammonium 17-heptafluoroisopropoxy-12,12 to 17,17-dodecafluoroheptadecyl phosphate.

Melting Point 175°-210°C.

$(cf_3)_2cfo(cf_2cf_2)_3(ch_2)_{11}opo(onh_4)_2$

analysis for $C_{20}F_{19}H_{30}O_5N_2P$:

Calculated: C, 31.2; H, 3.92; N, 3.64

Found: C, 31.8; H, 3.57; N, 3.24.

Method 7: Preparation of Ammonium bis (19-heptafluoroiso-propoxy-12,12, to 19,19-hexadecafluorononadecyl) phosphate.

Using the procedure of Method 1, 19-heptafluoroisopropoxy, 12,12 to 19,19-hexadecafluorononadecanol was reacted with phosphorous oxychloride in the presence of pyridine to yield bis-(19-heptafluoroisopropoxy-12,12 to 19,19-hexadecafluorononadecyl) phosphochloridate. Hydrolysis yielded bis(19-heptafluoroisopropoxy 12,12- to 19,19-hexadecafluorononadecyl)hydrogen phosphate. This product was treated with ammonia gas to form ammonium bis-(19-heptafluoroisopropoxy-12,12 to 19,19-hexadecafluorononadecyl) phosphate.

Melting Point: 150°-175°C.

$[(cf_3)_2cfo(cf_2cf_2)_4(ch_2)_{11}o]_2poonh_4$

analysis for $C_{44}F_{46}H_{48}O_6PN$

Calculated: C, 33.1; H, 3.1; N, 0.88

Found: C, 32.8; H, 2.8; N, 0.99

Method 8 : Preparation of Diammonium 19-heptafluoro-isopropoxy-12,12, to 19,19-hexadecafluorononadecyl phosphate.

Using the procedure of Method 6, 19-heptafluoroisopropoxy-12,12 to 19,19-hexadecafluorononadecanol was reacted with phosphorous oxychloride in the presence of pyridine to yield 19-heptafluoroisopropoxy-12,12 to 19,19-hexadecafluorononadecyl-phosphoryldichloride. A benzene solution of the phosphoryldichloride was treated with the calculated amount of pyridine and an excess of water at 60° for 2 hours. The liquid phase was decanted off and the dihydrogen phosphate was washed with water and dried by azeotroping with benzene. Ammonia gas was then bubbled into the boiling benzene for 2 hours, which yielded diammonium 19-heptafluoroisopropoxy-12,12, to 19,19-hexadecafluorononadecyl phosphate.

Melting Point: 200°-220° C.

$(cf_3)_2cfo(cf_2cf_2)_4(ch_2)_{11}opo(onh_4)_2$

analysis for $C_{22}F_{23}H_{27}O_5PN_2$:

Calculated: C, 31.0; H, 3.16; N, 1.64.

Found: C, 32.0; H, 3.4; N, 1.74.

Chlorinated hydrocarbons

Three major product types comprise the Chlorinated hydrocarbons.

The largest volume, but lowest performance category, is the chlorinated paraffins. These products, like the phosphate esters, are used as flame retardants or plasticizers for PVC and in polyurethane foams. There are both liquid and resinous types with the liquids being larger in the previous applications. The resinous types are used in polyolefins, unsaturated polyesters, and some HIPS. The second category is the DECHLORANE PLUS product sold by Occidental. This is a higher-performance product used primarily in polyolefin wire and cable and nylon. The third category is the chlorendic anhydride/acid (HET acid) reactive product which is used in unsaturated polyesters. Like the brominated products, the chlorinated products (other than the HET acid) are used with antimony oxide synergists.

Preparation

The following feed materials are intimately admixed and passed in line 16 to thermal chlorination reactor 20: 87.47 lb. mols per hr. of superheated chlorine vapor at 25°C.; 68.63 lb. mols per hr. methyl chloride vapor and 255.72 lb. mols per hr. recycle streams consisting of 186.4 lb. mols per hr. methyl chloride, 41.02 lb. mols per hr. hydrogen chloride, and 28.3 lb. mols per hr. methylene chloride. Reactor 20 is maintained at an operating pressure of about 110 psig and the maximum temperature attained in the reactor is 425°C. Reaction takes place in the reactor which provides a retention time of about 12 seconds. No free or unreacted chlorine is found in the reactor exit gas which is flowed to quench column 30. A liquid stream collected in tank 50 is introduced to quench tank 30 via line 34 in an upper portion thereof. The temperature at the bottom of quench vessel 30 is maintained at about 120°C. while the effluent vapor at the top of quench vessel 30 is at a temperature of about 100°C. Indirect water cooling is effected in condenser 40 to cool the vaporous material in line 38 to a temperature of about 40°C. Refrigerant cooling is effected to achieve a temperature of about 10°C. in condenser 42 and a temperature of about -12°C. in condenser 44. The terminal pressure of the gaseous material at the exit end of condenser 44 is about 100 psig.

The uncondensed material in line 66 has the following flow composition: 90.39 lb. mols per hr. hydrogen chloride; 13.56 lb. mols per hr. methyl chloride; and 0.01 lb. mols per hr. methylene chloride. Material in line 66 is admixed with 72.24 lb. mols per hr. of superheated methanol. The combined vapor is then fed to methanol hydrochlorination reactor 70 containing an activated alumina catalyst. Reaction heat is removed by a boiling heat transfer fluid contained in the jacketted side of reactor 70. In this example, the reaction effluent is reduced in temperature by passing through a conventional heat exchange recovery system 74. All of the water of reaction is removed from the process as about 22 wt % hydrochloric acid via line 75. The methyl chloride product, plus any excess hydrogen chloride vapor, saturated with water, is dried in multi plate drying column 90 which is counter currently irrigated with concentrated sulfuric acid. The dried methyl chloride-hydrogen chloride containing stream is passed to a low temperature condenser 92 in which methyl chloride is condensed and fed to the partial chlorination process in line 94. Any non-condensable hydrogen chloride present is withdrawn in line 93.

When maximum methylene chloride production is desirable, a low chlorine ratio and a single chlorination reactor, e.g., 20, is preferably employed with the excess methyl chloride acting as a diluent to control reaction temperature. When it is desirable to maximize the chloroform to methyl chloride product ratio via methyl chloride substitution chlorination, two reaction zones arranged in series can be employed. A diluent such as carbon tetrachloride or perchloroethylene can be employed when higher chlorinated products are desired in a one or a two reactor system.

Hydrogen chloride production resulting from the formation of chloroform or carbon tetrachloride during the substitution chlorination of methyl chloride can be recovered, controlled or removed in accordance with any one of the following preferable methods:

1. Hydrogen chloride can be recovered as a gaseous anhydrous HCl from the partial chlorination plant, e.g., from 66 line in the drawing. If liquid HCl is desired, a compressor is installed on the recovery system exit of the partial chlorination plant, e.g., between condenser 44 and separator 45, which compresses the HCl — CH_3Cl vapor to at least about 150 psig. This gas is then cooled and fed to a fractionation column which, with benefit of a refrigerated reflux condenser returns liquid HCl reflux under at least about 150 psig to the top of the fractionator. The fractionator is, thus, (with sufficient sieve trays above the feed point) made capable of delivering substantially pure HCl overhead. By providing sufficient trays below the feed point the fractionator can produce a bottoms product of essentially pure CH_3Cl for return to the proper point in the partial chlorination process, e.g., 60 or 62.

2. By installing a refrigerated CCl_4 (or C_2Cl_4) absorption system on the exit of the recovery system, (line 66) of the partial chlorination plant, it is also possible to obtain high quality hydrogen chloride off gas from the partial chlorination plant. The CCl_4 (or C_2Cl_4) underflow from the absorption column, containing CH_3Cl, and some HCl is then fed to a multiplate stripping column whereby HCl and CH_3Cl can be removed as overhead product and returned to the chlorination reactor. Lean CCl_4 (or C_2Cl_4) underflow is watercooled, then refrigerant cooled and returned to the absorber.

3. Hydrogen chloride resulting from the production of chloroform or carbon tetrachloride in the partial chlorination process can be employed in the methanol hydrochlorination process to produce excess methyl chloride, thereby keeping the overall HCl production in balance.

4. Hydrogen chloride resulting from the production of chloroform or carbon tetrachloride in the partial chlorination process can be allowed to flow through the methanol hydrochlorination plant unreacted. It can then be removed as follows:

   a. By compression and fractionation as described in Item 1 above. In this case the compressor and fractionator is located in the recovery system of the methanol hydrochlorination following the sulfuric acid drying column 90.

b. By refrigerated CCl_4 or C_2Cl_4 scrubbing which, in this case, is located in the recovery system of the methanol hydrochlorination following the sulfuric acid drying column 90.

In all above cases, separation of hydrogen chloride is effected in high quality and under anhydrous conditions

Antimony Oxide

A variety of antimony compounds, including antimony trioxide, antimony pentoxide, and sodium antimonate, are combined under the category of *antimony oxides.* These are synergists used in a 1:3 ratio with halogenated flame retardants in typical formulations.

Preparation:

A furnace (10) is provided for the reaction, by combustion, of antimony sulfide with essentially pure oxygen. The oxygen is fed into the burner or combustion chamber (11) (Fig. 8.1). The antimony sulfide is fed through hopper (12) into the burner. The antimony sulfide and oxygen react in the burner and the vaporized combustion products are then directed into the furnace chamber 15. Discharge conduit (13) leads the combustion products comprising sulfur dioxide and antimony oxide (Sb_2O_3) from the furnace to a quench or cooling means (20). Molten slag is discharged from the furnace at (14). In the quench zone the stream of sulfur dioxide vapor and antimony oxide are rapidly cooled to form antimony oxide particles which are conveyed in the sulfur dioxide stream. After quenching the temperature is further reduced in a cooler (30) which conveys the mixed stream to the baghouse (40) where the solids are separated from the sulfur dioxide gas. The solid antimony oxide is discharged through the star valves (41). The sulfur dioxide is conveyed by conduit (42) to a further cooler and liquifier (50) wherein a portion of the sulfur dioxide stream is discharged at (51) to product and the remainder is recycled by recycle pipe (60) to the quench means (20). If desired, the cooler (50) may include chillers to liquify the sulfur dioxide at atmospheric pressure or

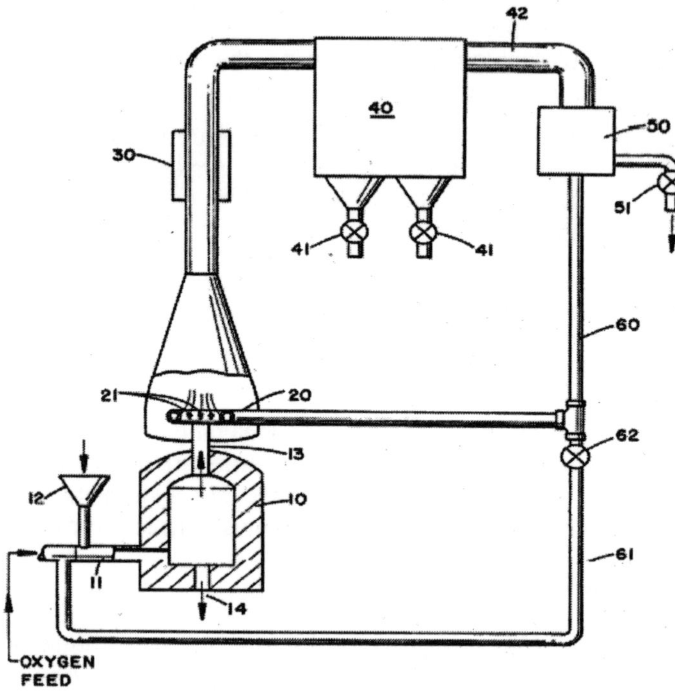

Fig. 8.1

liquefaction may be accomplished by means of a compressor.

The reaction taking place in furnace (10) is as follows:

$$2Sb_2S_3 + 9O_2 \rightarrow 2Sb_2O_3 + 6SO_2$$

Sulfur dioxide is a colorless liquid with a density of 1.46 at its boiling point, which at atmospheric pressure is minus 10° C. (15° F.). Antimony oxide is a white powder which the handbook shows to have a boiling point of 1570° C. and a melting point of about 650° C. Antimony sulfide (stibnite) is a black crystalline compound.

In the practice of the present method, the antimony sulfide is preferably in a finely divided state, substantially all of it being of a size able to pass through a 200 mesh screen and desirably about 75% of it passing through a 325 mesh screen. The temperature within the combustion chamber is desirably about 1800° F. to about 2000° F. Depending upon the purity of the antimony sulfide and the quantity of slag contained therein, it may be desirable to recycle combustion products, antimony oxide and/or sulfur dioxide, through the combustion chamber to control furnace temperature. Such recycle of sulfur dioxide may be by conduit or pipe (61), the quantity being controlled by valve (62).

The quenching means is a device designed to achieve rapid mixing between the combustion stream and a coolant stream at substantially lower temperature. For example, the gaseous discharge (13) from the furnace may lead combustion products through a ring (20) having orifices (21) on its interior and adapted to direct streams of coolant into the combustion stream. The quantity of coolant is controlled to reduce the temperature of the combustion products to 900° to 1000° F. The stream of antimony oxide and sulfur dioxide is further cooled in cooler (30) before entering the baghouse (40). In this regard, the temperature of the gaseous stream entering the baghouse is caused to be sufficiently low so that the filter bags are not adversely affected. As a practical matter, a temperature of 200° F. is quite satisfactory and some filter fabrics can tolerate higher temperature.

From the foregoing, it is clear that a unique method and apparatus have been provided which find utility in the production of antimony oxide from antimony sulfide.

Aluminum Trihydrate

Aluminum trihydrate is a low-priced commodity that is used at high loadings (up to 50 to 60% on the plastic) as a flameretardant filler. It is only effective in plastics processed at lower temperatures. Acrylics, polyolefins, PVC, and unsaturated polyesters are the major users. Fully one-third of all ATH is used outside of plastics as a flame retardant in elastomers, carpet backings, and textiles. The major aluminum companies make the basic white hydrate product and sell it to processors who tailor the product for the plastics industry.

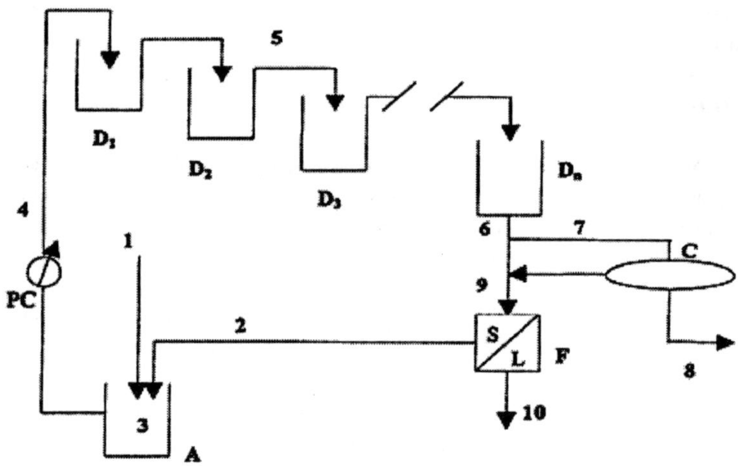

Fig. 8.2

Preparation

The pregnant aluminate liquor **1** , with an Rp close to 1.2 and a caustic concentration between 140 and 180 g of Na_2O/l, is mixed with alumina trihydrate **2** recycled at the end of precipitation and impregnated with crystallized liquor. The pregnant slurry **3** thus formed has an Rp close to 1.0. After 15 minutes residence in the seed tank A, the slurry **4** is entrained under the effect of pump PC to the series of precipitators D **1** , D **2** , D **3** , . . ., Dn. A part **7** of the slurry is separated from the crystallized slurry **6** so as to obtain classified alumina trihydrate **8** by classification C, to be used in the final treatment (washing, calcination, etc.). The other part **9** is filtered F, the filtered crystallized liquor **10** is further concentrated for recycling for further digestion of the bauxite, whereas the filtrate is alumina trihydrate **2** used as a seed and mixed with the pregnant aluminate liquor **1** .

OTHER FLAME RETARDANTS

Inorganic phosphates

Inorganic phosphates consist of ammonium polyphosphate and red phosphorus. The ammonium polyphosphate product is primarily used in intumescent coatings and rubber as well as plastics. Red phosphorus is used as a flame retardant in coatings and nylon.

Preparation

Our method relates to an improved process for the preparation of ammonium polyphosphates, and more particularly it relates to a direct method for the preparation of long-chain, substantially water-insoluble, highly condensed, crystalline ammonium polyphosphates from ammonium phosphates. We have found that the crystalline modification of long-chain ammonium polyphosphate obtained is dependent upon the temperature of the condensation and the particular phosphate charged. In our process, the starting material is heated in the range between 250° and 400°C; therefore, the ammonium polyphosphates yielded by this process have melting point characteristics such that heating to as great as 400°C will not cause same to melt, albeit it may cause a crystalline modification of the polyphosphate product. At about 275°C a mixture of Forms I and II is usually obtained. Crude monoammonium orthophosphate condensed to a mixture of Forms I, II, and V at about 250°C. If added to a bed of excess Form I, ammonium orthophosphate is condensed to Form I by heating at about 250°C. Ammonium pyrophosphate gives quantitative yields of Form II at about 300°C; but ammonium tripolyphosphate is condensed to Form I at that temperature. The time of heating employed with range from about 1 hour to 16 hours, depending upon the particular ammonium phosphate being condensed. We have determined that a good practice of our invention employs a time interval of usually about 4 hours to 8 hours for the condensation of monoammonium orthophosphate. No advantage is realized in heating any of the ammonium phosphates for more than 16 hours.

Method

Pulverized reagent monoammonium orthophosphate (N-P_2O_5-K_2O 12.1-61-7-0) was added from a calibrated powder feeder to a tumbling bed of previously prepared long-chain crystalline ammonium polyphosphate (50.0 grams) at 250°C at rates of 24.9, 25.0, and 9.3 grams per hour for periods of 0.83, 1.00, and 2.25 hours while passing a sweep gas (1446, 1440, and 3871 ml/gm raw material) consisting of a mixture of ammonia and nitrogen and containing 50.0, 66.7, and 16.7 percent ammonia, respectively, through the reactor which consisted of an electrically heated 600-ml stainless steel beaker mounted on a shaft rotating at 48 r.p.m. and tilted at about 45°. The product was a granular free-flowing solid consisting of a mixture of approximately equal amounts of Forms I and II long-chain crystalline ammonium polyphosphate. Yields, chemical analyses, and operating conditions are shown under runs 1, 2, and 3 in Table 8.2.

Melamines

Melamines consist of melamine crystal, which is used to impart flame-retardant properties to flexible polyurethane foam in upholstery applications, and melamine salts, such as melamine phosphates and melamine cyanurates, used in intumescent coatings and some plastics.

Preparation

The method relates to crystalline melamine, more in particular to multicrystalline melamine powder.

Melamine is prepared in various ways on an industrial scale. Methods exist which ultimately involve the crystallization of melamine from an aqueous solution, a process exists in which melamine is obtained directly from a gaseous phase, and a method exists which involves the synthesis of melamine at high pressure (7-25 MPa), and where the melamine melt obtained thereby is sprayed in an ammonia atmosphere and is cooled, said crystalline powder lending itself to being used as such without further purification steps.

Process

Melamine melt having a temperature of 360° C. and a pressure of 18 MPa is treated with 0.8 kg of ammonia per kg of melamine. The melamine is then introduced, via a spraying device, into a high-pressure vessel at an outflow velocity greater than 100 m/s and very rapidly cooled with liquid ammonia which is likewise sprayed into the vessel. The temperature in the vessel is 233° C. The high-pressure vessel is designed as a rotating drum provided with a wall which can be cooled, and provided with a gas inlet. The ammonia pressure in the vessel varies between 5.4 and 8.2 MPa. After 1 minute the product is cooled to ambient temperature. The cooling step to 200° C. took 5 minutes. When the melamine powder has a temperature of about 180° C., all the NH_3 is released and air is metered into the vessel. The end product has the following properties:

specific surface area:	1.2 m^2/g
level of oxygen-containing components:	0.12 wt %
colour (APHA):	10
99.3 wt % of melamine	
0.4 wt % of melam	
<0.1 wt % of melem	
concentration of ammonia	50 ppm

Comparative Example

Melamine melt of 400° C., held in a vessel under an ammonia pressure of 13.6 MPa, is rapidly cooled to ambient temperature by the vessel being brought into contact with a mixture of ice and water. The end product contains 1.4 wt % of melam and 0.4 wt % of melem. The specific surface area is 0.3 m^2/g.

Magnesium hydroxide

Magnesium hydroxide is finding increasing use as a replacement for ATH. It is a good smoke suppressant and its price is coming down relative to ATH.

Preparation

To simulate the large scale mixer/settlers shown in FIG. 8.3, laboratory studies were carried out in a series of separated agitated reactors and settlers. The reactor vessels were each of 5 liters capacity with a facility for gravity overflow to the appropriate settler which had facilities for pumping out of settled sludge and for gravity overflow of clarified sea water.

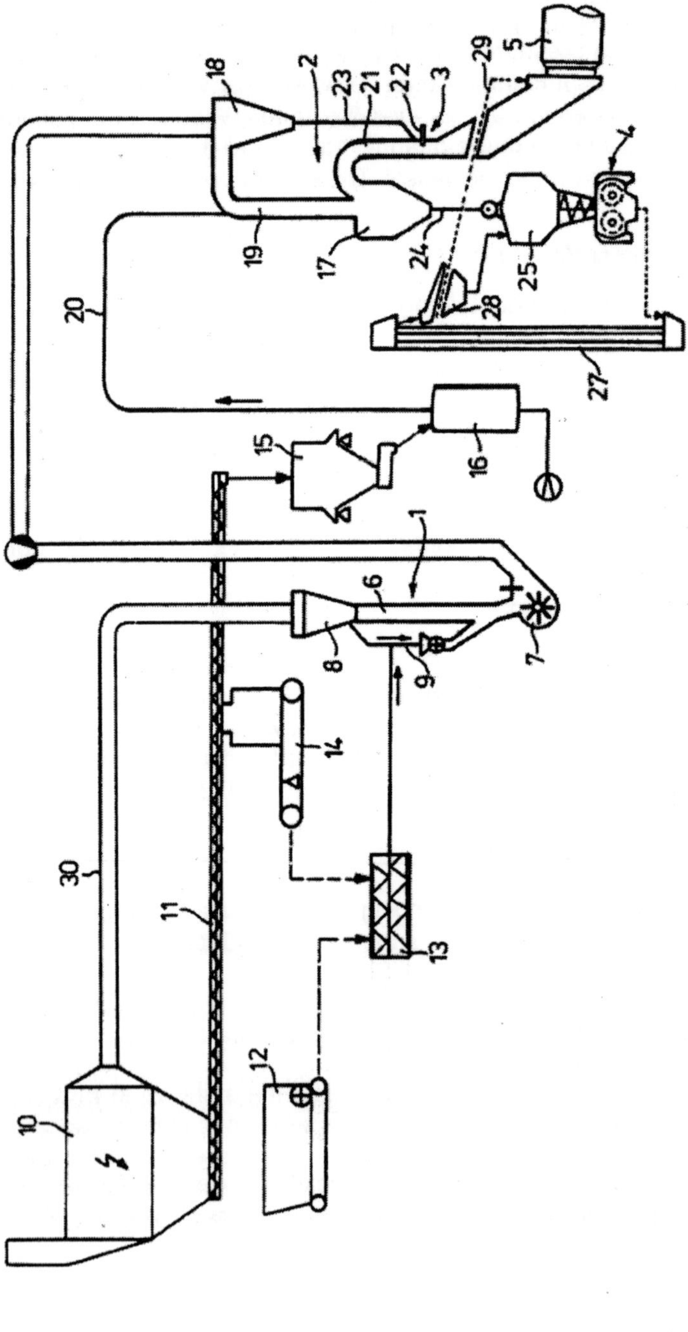

Fig. 8.3

Sea water (I) from the North Sea containing 15.4 ppm B_2O_3 and 2.15 gMgO/l. in the form of Mg^+ + ions was treated with sulphuric acid to reduce the CO_2 content to about 10 ppm, and pumped into the first of the deboronation stages (A) as indicated in FIG. 8.3 at a rate of 4 liters/minute. Simultaneously magnesium hydroxide slurry already prepared by precipitation from seawater was pumped via line 5 into the final stage (D). Prior to commencing this continuous process, each of the stages had been charged with the same seawater and adsorbing magnesium hydroxide to give a magnesium hydroxide concentration in each stage of 5 gMgO/l. With the advent of the continuous process the seawater progressed at a rate of 4 liters/minute through the deboronation stages (A) - (B) - (C) - (D), whilst the adsorbing magnesium hydroxide progressed in a manner countercurrent to the sea water from stage (D) - (C) - (B) - (A). The rate of addition of adsorbing $Mg(OH)_2$ slurry to stage D and the rate of transfer of adsorbing $Mg(OH)_2$ slurry from (D) - (C), (C) - (B), (B) - (A), and finally the rate at which the $Mg(OH)_2$ was pumped out of the process was such that the overall ratio of adsorbing $Mg(OH)_2$ being added to (D), to the Mg^{++} ions present in the seawater was 1.67:1 when both are expressed as MgO.

Molybdenum compounds

Molybdenum compounds include such products as molybdic oxide or ammonium and metal molybdates and are used in PVC and carpet backings. These products are good smoke suppressants and have been looked at as replacements for antimony oxides.

Preparation

A) Preparation of the Novel Molybdenum Oxide

The reaction apparatus consisted of a glass flask having a glass inlet tube which was connected directly to an electrically heatable tube reactor having a gas supply, from which one line led to a cyclone and two 30-l vessels and then to a waste gas disposal means.

Forty gram of molybdenum hexacarbonyl were heated to 80° C in the glass flask while passing over 120 l/h of nitrogen. At the same time 350 l/h of air were passed through the tube reactor heated to an internal temperature of 230° C.

The molybdenum hexacarbonyl vaporized and decomposed by the airstream to molybdenum oxide was deposited in finely divided form in the cyclone and in the 30-l vessels.

Five gram of blue molybdenum oxide, having a mean particle size of 20 nm and a molybdenum content of 63% by weight were obtained.

B) Coloristic Evaluation of the Novel Molybdenum Oxide

0.5 g of molybdenum oxide was stirred in 5.0 g of a polyester mixed finish having a solids content of 21% by weight and was dispersed for 2 minutes with 5 mm glass beads in a Red Devil apparatus. High-hiding coatings of the pigmented finishes were then produced on a black and white cardboard using a knife coater (100 μm wet film thickness).

The film was dried and the CIELAB values were then measured using a Multiflash M 45 Gonio spectrophotometer from Optronik (Berlin) at an angular difference of 25° and 95° relative to the gloss angle. The stated colour values (L, a*, b*,) are based on the standard illuminant D 65 and a viewing angle of 25°. L corresponds to the lightness, a*, to the red or green component and b* to the blue or yellow component. H is the colour angle and C* the chroma. Measurements were carried out against a white background on samples coated once.

The following measured values were obtained:

Angle°	H	C*	L	a*	b*
25	266.45	11.94	35.73	-0.74	-11.92
75	267.58	19.70	20.63	-0.83	-19.68

C) Use of the Novel Molybdenum Oxide as a Charge Controlling Agent

1. Preparation of the Toner

I. a polyester resin toner (SPAR® II polymer resin; from Xerox, USA) and

II. a styrene/acrylic resin toner (PICCOTONER® 1221 polymer resin; from Hercules, USA) were used as starting materials for the toner preparation.

In each case 140 g of the polymer resin were melted at 100° C in a Duplex MKD 0.6 laboratory kneader. After the addition of 60 g of carbon black PRINTEX® 150 T (from Degussa), kneading was carried out for a further 3 hours at 100° C. The kneaded material was removed and was diluted with resin free of carbon black.

For this purpose, 33.3 g of the kneaded material were added to 166.7 g of polymer resin free of carbon black and melted at 100° C. in the kneader. After kneading had been carried out for 2 hours at 100° C., the kneaded material was removed, cooled, and milled for 2 minutes in an A 10 analytical mill. The coarse fraction (particle size>36 ìm was removed by sieving. The useful fraction could be further increased by further milling of the coarse fraction and sieving again.

The molybdenum oxide was applied to the polymer resin by mixing

a) 99 parts by weight of polymer resin and one part by weight of molybdenum oxide,

b) 98 parts by weight of polymer resin and two parts by weight of molybdenum oxide or

c) 97 parts by weight of polymer resin and three parts by weight of molybdenum oxide for one hour in a glass vessel on a roller stand.

2. Preparation of the Developers and Testing

For the preparation of the developers, the toners treated with molybdenum oxide were each mixed with a spherical steel carrier (TC 101, from Pometon, Maerne, Italy) in a weight ratio of 97:3 and were activated in a glass vessel on a roller stand.

After 10, 30, 60 and 120 minutes, samples were taken in each case and their electrostatic charge was determined in a Q/m meter (from Epping, Neufahrn).

For this purpose, 2.5 g of each developer were weighed into a hard-blow-off cell which was coupled to an electrometer and into which sieves of mesh size 40 ìm had been inserted. By blowing off with an airstream, the toner powder was completely removed while the carrier particles were held back in the measuring cell by means of the sieves. The carrier charge, which corresponds to the charge on the toner particles with the opposite sign, was then determined and, by reweighing, was based on the weight of the blown-off toner.

Zinc Borate

Zinc borate is the major boron compound used as a flame retardant in plastics. It competes with antimony oxide when antimony prices are high. The largest application for boron compounds as a flame retardant is in cellulose insulation. The flame-retardant categories and the major plastics where they are used are summarized in Table 8.2

Preparation

The hydrated zinc borate of this method has the formula $4ZnO.B_2O_3.H_2O$. It is a crystalline solid having very slight water solubility and having a dehydration temperature which begins at about 415° C. with a rapid loss occurring above 425° C. Such a high dehydration temperature makes this composition especially useful as an additive for polymers requiring high processing temperatures such as the polysulfones, polyamide-imides, polyketones, polyetherketones and polyarylates. The water solubility of the compound is considerably lower than that of other known hydrated zinc borates.

The zinc borate hydrate of this method can be readily prepared by a variety of methods. The presently preferred method of production comprises the reaction of zinc oxide with a near stoichiometric amount of boric acid (2:1 mole ratio) in water at an elevated temperature, according to the equation

$$4ZnO+2B(OH)_3 \rightarrow 4ZnO.B_2O_3.H_2O + 2H_2O.$$

The reaction preferably takes place near the boiling point of the mixture and is promoted by the presence of previously prepared product seed. The concentration of the initial reaction mixture should be greater than about 5% by weight of starting reagents in order to provide a reasonably rapid reaction rate. Preferably, reaction mixtures in the 10-20% by weight range are employed, since they require only a few hours of refluxing in water to go to completion. It is also preferred that a slight molar excess (approximately 5%) of boric acid is used in order to provide complete consumption of zinc oxide in the reaction. The desired hydrated zinc borate product is readily separated from the cooled reaction solution by filtration and dried to give the desired crystalline product. It has also been found that more consistent results are obtained when boric acid is added to the zinc oxide in boiling water in at least two separate portions, thereby maintaining the pH of the reaction mixture above about 5.5, and the reaction mixture is efficiently stirred or mixed during the reaction period.

Other methods for preparing the hydrated zinc borate of this method include hydrolysis of the zinc borate $2ZnO.3B_2O_3.3.5H_2O$ in a refluxing aqueous slurry. It has been found that the concentration of the starting material in the aqueous slurry must be less than about 5% in order to produce a complete reaction. At least five days of continuous reflux at atmospheric pressure of a 5% slurry of starting material is required to give complete hydrolysis. Reflux of the reaction mixture containing free boric acid for an excessive period of time (such as for one month) will convert the zinc borate to the compound $6ZnO.5B_2O_3.3H_2O$ which was previously reported as a product of the hydrothermal reaction of zinc oxide and boric acid at 165° C.

The zinc borate of this method may also be prepared by reacting $2ZnO.3B_2O_3.3.5H_2O$ with a stoichiometric amount of zinc oxide in refluxing water. This reaction is also facilitated by the presence of seed crystals of previously prepared zinc borate $4ZnO.B_2O_3.H_2O$. In some cases, the reaction appears to be catalyzed by the presence of zinc ion such as supplied by a small amount of zinc chloride or zinc sulfate.

A fourth method for preparing the $4ZnO.B_2O_3.H_2O$ of this method is by reaction of sodium tetraborate with a zinc salt such as zinc sulfate and zinc oxide in boiling water, for example, according to

TABLE 8.2: Flame-Retardant Types—Major Plastics Applications

Type	Major resins	Comments
Brominated (additive types)	ABS, engineering resins, HIPS, urethane foam	Typically used with antimony synergist; DBDPO is most common product used.
Brominated (reactive types)	Epoxies, unsaturated polyesters	Major use in printed circuits and microchips; TBA is representative product.
Organic phosphate esters	Engineering resins, PVC, urethane foams	Halogenated types typically used in urethane foam; nonhalogenated types used in PVC and engineering resins; synergists not used with phosphate esters.
Chlorinated hydrocarbons	Engineering resins, polyolefins, PVC, urethane foams	Chlorinated paraffins used in PVC as plasticizer/flame retardant and in urethane foam; higher-performance types used in polyolefin wire/cable and engineering resins.
Antimony oxide	ABS, engineering resins, HIPS, polyolefins, PVC	Synergist used with brominated and chlorinated flame retardants.

Aluminum trihydrate (ATH)	Acrylic (counters and panels), polyolefins, PVC, unsaturated polyesters, urethane	Used at high loadings in plastics with low process temperatures; significant foams uses outside of plastics
Inorganic phosphates	Nylon, unsaturated polyesters, polyolefins	Consists of ammoniumphosphates and red phosphorus; uses outside of plastics in textiles and intumescent coatings.
Melamines	Nylon, polyolefins, urethane foam	Mainly melamine crystal for flexible urethane foam; some melamine salts (cyanurates, phosphates) used in plastics and intumescent coatings.
Magnesium hydroxide	Polyolefins, PVC	Replacement for ATH in wire/cable applications; good smoke suppressent.
Molybdenum compounds	PVC	High-priced replacement for antimony oxide; used in some PVC wire/cable.
Zinc borate	Cellulose insulation, miscellaneous other plastics	Replacement for antimony oxide.

the equation

$$Na_2B_4O_7.5H_2O + ZnSO_4.7H_2O + 7H_2O+7ZnO \rightarrow 2(4ZnO.B_2O_3.H_2O) + Na_2SO_4+10H_2O.$$

The presence of about 5% seed product facilitates the reaction which goes to completion within a few hours.

Process

200 Grams of $2ZnO.3B_2O_3.3.5H_2O$ (0.460 mol) was added to 4.5 L of deionized (DI) water and boiled under reflux for six days. During this time the pH of the reaction solution gradually decreased from 7.8 to about 4.5. The reaction slurry was then filtered, washed with DI water and air dried to give 92.2 g (97% yield) of product, $4ZnO.B_2O_3.H_2O$ having the following analysis:

	Calc.	Found
ZnO	78.79	78.35
B_2O_3	16.84	17.04
H_2O	4.36	4.88

Driving Forces

In addition to cost and performance demands, the plastics market for flame retardants is driven by a number of competing forces ranging from fire standard legislation and toxicity regulations to price situations, performance, and other market factors. These combined factors have resulted recently in significant shifts in demand for the major types of flame retardants. Further, large numbers of new flame retardants have emerged, designed for both traditional and specialty niche markets. Recent acquisitions, joint ventures, and alliances by flameretardantm producers have also created constant change in this market. The largest area of activity is in nonhalogenated flame retardants because of environmental concerns associated with the halogen-based products.

Most flame-retardant suppliers, even those making halogenated types, are focusing their product research and development on nonhalogenated products. Since the impact of this research on the markets for halogenated products is still beyond 5 years, halogenated flame retardants are still expected to show a healthy growth pattern at least through 2010. New halogenated products are still being introduced.

The environmental scrutiny that has impacted halogenated flame retardants has primarily focused on brominated diphenyl oxides such as DBDPO. There is concern that these compounds release dioxins when burned. Activity has primarily been in Europe. Currently there are no legislative bans or limits on halogenated flame retardants anywhere in the world, and there are not any on the near-term horizon. However, there are some voluntary bans on selected brominated compounds (particularly DBDPO and related types) in some of the "green" countries of Europe. In many cases, these brominated products are replaced by other brominated products that are not under immediate suspicion. This pressure is primarily political and is coming basically from the Green Parties in northern Europe (Scandinavia), Germany, and The Netherlands. In these countries, voluntary Eco-labels (ecology) have been developed for branded consumer products. In Scandinavia, the label is named White Swan, while in Germany and The Netherlands, the name Blue Angel is used. This trend has gained a substantial following from the environmental movement to eliminate chlorofluorocarbons (CFCs) and other chlorinated materials, augmented by the parallel movement against plasticizers in PVC cling film packaging. These trends in Europe are translatable to the other parts of the world. There is some activity in Japan and Canada, and within a 5- to 10-years time span, some impact could be felt in the United States. Eventually, this movement could lead to regulations on halogenated products around the world. Down the road, the need and the market exists for nonhalogenated approaches to the flame retarding of plastics. All the major flameretardant companies, including those making halogenated types, are working in the area. Viable, nonhalogenated flame-retardant products do exist, but customers are reluctant to sacrifice the cost/performance advantage of brominated products. Organic phosphate, inorganic phosphorus, melamine salts, and inorganic metal hydrate approaches seem to be the major directions being followed to develop nonhalogenated alternatives.

Suppliers

There are at least 100 suppliers worldwide that are involved in some phase of the flame-retardant business. Most suppliers are involved in only one type of flame retardant, although in the past 2 years, the major brominated supplier (Great Lakes) and the major chlorinated supplier (Occidental) have both acquired an antimony oxide synergist supplier. Some of the major suppliers are basic in raw materials, such as bromine, phosphorus, or alumina, but others buy these materials. Backward integration into raw materials seems to be more prevalent on the brominated side with all three major producers (Great Lakes, Dead Sea Bromine, and Albemarle) integrated back to bromine. This is likely to be a criteria for long-term success on the brominated side. Brominated and chlorinated flame retardants are sold throughout the world by the major producers or their affiliates. The phosphorus flame retardants are more likely to be sold through regional producers particularly in the Asia/Pacific region. Antimony oxide producers, other than Anzon, are regional, although most of the crude material is sourced from the same place, namely, China. ATH is produced by the major aluminum companies, but is upgraded and treated by other processors who sell to the plastics industry. A global listing of the major flame-retardant suppliers is provided in Table 8.3. Included are the types that each supplies.

Trends and Forecasts

The flame-retardant business has historically outpaced many segments of the plastics additives business as new regulations on fire protection were enacted. This trend will continue, especially in Asia/Pacific, Latin America, Africa, and the Middle East, since regulations regarding fire safety are in their infancy in these regions. Growth in North America, Europe, and Japan will still be healthy but lag behind the other regions. The global market for flame retardants in plastics should grow at a rate of 5%/year over North America and Europe will see growth in the 3 to 4%/year range while Asia/Pacific (for example, Japan) and the rest of the world will grow at 2 or 3 times the North America/Europe rate. In spite of continued commentary on the undesirability of halogenated compounds, brominated flame retardants are still expected to pace the growth of the overall flame-retardant market over Other than in Europe, the growth rate should exceed 5% in all regions. Phosphate ester growth has slowed down in North America and Europe, but rapid growth in the other regions will push overall growth to about 4%/year. The chlorinated flame retardants are suffering in Europe and will likely grow slowly, if at all, worldwide during the period. Antimony oxide growth will not keep pace with brominated flameretardant growth, but still should increase at a rate of 3%/year worldwide. ATH will show a healthy 5%/year growth as it replaces halogen-based products where it can. Look for some rapid growth in the other flame-retardant categories, particularly melamines, inorganic phosphates, and magnesium hydroxide. The latter is replacing ATH in some applications, and the melamine salts and inorganic phosphates are potential replacements down the road for halogenated compounds. Technologically, efforts will continue to focus on halogen and antimony oxide replacements. Smoke suppression and higher heat stability are also hot topics in the general flame-retardant area. From a competitive standpoint, the acquisition of an antimony oxide business by two major halogenated flame-retardant suppliers is a trend worth watching. Historically, companies have been content to compete within one type, but now more horizontal integration, particularly among products which are used together, might be the way to go. Also, continued efforts by major suppliers to increase their operations in the growing markets of Asia/Pacific and the rest of the world is not to be discounted. All in all, it will be another period of rapid change in the world of flame retardants over the next 5 years.

TABLE 8.3: Selected Suppliers of Flame Retardants in Plastics

Supplier	Type					
	Brominated hydrocarbons	Phosphate esters	Chlorinated hydrocarbons	Antimony oxides	ATH	Others
Ajinomoto Company	—	×	×	—	—	—
Akzo Nobel	—	×	—	—	—	×
Albemarle Corporation	×	—	—	—	—	—
Albright & Wilson	—	×	—	—	—	×
Alcan Chemicals	—	—	—	—	×	×
Alcoa	—	—	—	—	×	—
Aluchem	—	—	—	—	×	—
Aluminum Pechiney	—	—	—	—	×	—
Amspec Chemical	—	—	—	×	—	—
Asaha Glass	×	—	×	—	—	—
Asahi Denka Kogyo	—	—	×	—	—	—
Bayer	—	×	—	—	—	×
Campine	—	—	—	—	—	—
Climax Performance Materials	—	—	—	—	—	×
Courtaulds	—	×	—	—	—	—

Custom Grinders	—	—	—	—	—	x
Daihachi Chemical	—	x	—	—	—	—
Daiichi Kogyo Seiyaku	x	—	—	—	—	—
Dainippon Ink & Chemicals	x	—	—	—	—	—
Dead Sea Bromine	x	—	—	—	—	x
Dover Chemical	x	—	x	—	—	—
Dow Chemical	—	—	—	—	—	x
DSM	—	—	—	—	—	x
Elf Atochem	x	—	—	—	—	—
Ferro Corporation	x	—	x	—	—	—
FMC Corporation	—	—	—	—	—	—
Great Lakes Chemical/ Anzon	x	x	—	x	—	—
ICI	—	—	x	—	—	—
Industry Chimiche Caffaro	—	—	x	—	—	—
J.M. Huber	—	—	—	—	x	x
Kyowa Chemical Industry	—	—	—	—	—	x
Manac	—	—	—	—	—	—
Martin Marietta	—	—	—	—	—	x

Supplier	Type					
	Brominated hydrocarbons	Phosphate esters	Chlorinated hydrocarbons	Antimony oxides	ATH	Others
Martinswerke (Lonza)	—	—	—	—	x	x
Melamine Chemicals	—	—	—	—	—	x
Mikuni Smelting & Refining	—	—	—	—	—	—
Mines de la Lucette	—	—	—	—	—	—
Mitsubishi Gas Chemicals	—	—	—	—	—	—
Morton International	—	—	—	—	—	x
Nabaltec	—	—	—	—	x	—
Nihon Seiko	—	—	—	x	—	—
Nippon Chemicals	—	—	—	—	—	—
Nyacol Products	x	—	—	x	—	—
Occidental/Laurel	—	—	x	x	—	—
Sherwin Williams	—	—	—	—	x	x
Showa Denko	—	—	x	—	x	—
Société Industrielle et Chimique	—	—	—	x	—	—
Solutia	—	x	—	—	—	x

Stibiox	—	—	—	x	—	—
Sumitomo Chemical	—	—	—	—	x	—
Sumitomo Metal Mining	—	—	—	x	—	—
Teijin Chemicals	x	—	—	—	—	—
Tosoh	x	—	x	—	—	—
U.S. Borax & Chemical	—	—	—	—	—	x
United States Antiomy Sales	—	—	—	x	—	—
Velsicol	—	—	x	—	—	—
Witco	—	—	x	—	—	—

9

Heat Stabilizers

DESCRIPTION

Heat stabilizers are used to prevent the thermal degradation of resins during periods of exposure to elevated temperatures. Almost all heat stabilizers are used to stabilize PVC, polyvinylidene chloride (PVDC), vinyl chloride copolymers (for example, vinyl chloride/vinyl acetate), and PVC blends (for example, PVC and ABS). Thermal degradation is prevented not only during processing but also during the useful life of the finished products.

There are three major types of primary heat stabilizers, which include:

- Mixed metal salt blends
- Organotin compounds
- Lead compounds

Heat stabilizers belong to one of the two major classes: primary heat stabilizers and secondary heat stabilizers. When heated, chlorinated vinyl resins liberate HCl which causes further polymer degradation and discoloration. *Primary heat stabilizers* function both by retarding this dehydrochlorination and by reacting with liberated HCl to delay progressive degradation.

When mixed metal salts are used as primary heat stabilizers, metallic chlorides are formed by the reaction with labile Cl. These materials have a destabilizing effect that sometimes result in colour formation in the resin. To prevent this, *secondary heat stabilizers or costabilizers* are used to scavenge liberated HCl from the PVC resin or to react with the metallic chloride by-products of the primary mixed metal stabilizers.

Of less importance are antimony mercaptides, which find occasional use as low-cost replacements for organotins. The organotin and lead stabilizers are usually present as the only heat stabilizers in the resin formulation. However, the mixed metal stabilizers are used in combination with secondary heat stabilizers. The secondary heat stabilizers are usually organophosphites and epoxy compounds, but polyols and beta diketones are also used. The major types of primary heat stabilizers, along with their end uses are summarized in Table 9.1.

PRIMARY HEAT STABILIZERS

Mixed metal stabilizers

Mixed metal stabilizers are primarily used in flexible or semirigid PVC products. The most common are barium/zinc (Ba/Zn) metal salts. Typical liquid barium, cadmium, and zinc stabilizer products consist of such salts as octoates, alkylphenolates, neo decanoates, naphthenates, and benzoates. Typical solid barium, cadmium, and zinc stabilizer products consist of the salts of such fatty acids as stearates or laurates. Generally, Ba/Cd products provide the best thermal stability, followed by Ba/Zn and finally Ca/Zn. However, Ba/Cd stabilizers have come under increased environmental and Occupational Safety and Health Administration (OSHA) pressure and are being replaced by cadmium-free products that are usually Ca/Zn and Ba/Zn. Several Ca/Zn stabilizers have been approved by the FDA for use in food-contact applications.

Preparation

The present method is directed to vinyl halide resin compositions containing a mixed metal stabilizer, a hydrotalcite and antimony trioxide in an amount to confer increased heat stability to such compositions.

A. Vinyl Halide Resin

The vinyl halide resin employed is most commonly a

TABLE 9.1: Major Primary Heat Stabilizers

Type	Major end use	Comments
Mixed metal		
Barium/cadmium	Flexible and semirigid PVC applications	Cadmium-based stabilizers are under pressure to be replaced because of toxicological problems.
Barium/zinc	Flexible and semirigid PVC applications	This is the most common type of heat stabilizer benefiting from the cadmium replacement.
Calcium/zinc	Flexible PVC—food-contact applications	Many of these products are sanctioned by the FDA under Title 21, *Code of Federal Regulations*. This will benefit from the trend away from lead.
Organotin Butyl	Rigid PVC	Provides excellent heat stability. Most versatile organotin stabilizer.
Methyl	Rigid PVC—particularly for pipe	Very effective stabilizer on a costperformance basis. Some of these products are sanctioned by the DA under Title 21, *Code of Federal Regulations* for food-contact applications.

Octyl	Rigid PVC—food-contact applications	Several of these products are sanctioned by the FDA under Title 21, *Code of* Federal Regulations.
Lead	Wire and cable	Excellent insulation properties.

homopolymer of vinyl chloride, i.e., polyvinyl chloride. It is to be understood, however, that this invention is not limited to a particular vinyl halide resin such as polyvinyl chloride or its copolymers. Other halogen-containing resins which are employed and which illustrate the principles of this method include chlorinated polyethylene, chlorosulfonated polyethylene, chlorinated polyvinyl chloride, and other vinyl halide resin types. Vinyl halide resin, as understood herein, and as appreciated in the art, is a common term and is adopted to define those resins or polymers usually derived by polymerization or copolymerization of vinyl monomers including vinyl chloride with or without other comonomers such as ethylene, propylene, vinyl acetate, vinyl ethers, vinylidene chloride, methacrylate, acrylates, styrene, etc. A simple case is the conversion of vinyl chloride H_2 C—CHCl to polyvinyl chloride $(CH_2CHCl—)_n$ wherein the halogen is bonded to the carbon atoms of the carbon chain of the polymer. Other examples of such vinyl halide resins would include vinylidene chloride polymers, vinyl chloride-vinyl ester copolymers, vinyl chloride-vinyl ether copolymers, vinyl chloride-vinylidene copolymers, vinyl chloride-propylene copolymers, chlorinated polyethylene, and the like. Of course, the vinyl halide commonly used in the industry is the chloride, although others such as bromide and fluoride may be used. Examples of the latter polymers include polyvinyl bromide, polyvinyl fluoride, and copolymers thereof.

B. Antimony Trioxide Stabilizer System

Antimony trioxide, as indicated above, has been found to be synergistically operative in combination with a mixed metal stabilizer and a hydrotalcite. As explained above, mixed metallic carboxylates involving calcium/zinc or barium/zinc blends alone and in combination with other stabilizers such as beta-diketones, phosphite salts and phenolic antioxidants have been used. The metal stabilizer is a mixed metal salt of a carboxylate acid, advantageously of a C_8-C_{24} carbon chain monocarboxylic acid such as lauric, oleic, stearic, octoic, or similar fatty acid salts. Mixed metal salts of such acids, and their preparation, are familiar to those skilled in the art to which this present invention pertains. However, it would not have been expected that antimony trioxide, a hydrotalcite and alkaline earth/zinc carboxylate blends would have provided enhanced heat stabilization in accordance with this invention. Hydrotalcites disclosed in U.S. Pat. Nos. 4,085,088 and 4,299,759 and in copending application Ser. No. 945,011, filed Sep. 15, 1992, are suitable for use and their disclosures are incorporated herein by reference.

Process

The following composition (phr) was prepared on a 2-roll mill at 350° F.: PVC 100, diisodecyl phthalate (DIDP) 45, calcium terephthalate 0.75, a hydrotalcite of the approximate formula $Mg_{0.55}Zn_{0.15}Al_{0.3}OH(CO_3)_{0.15}$ sold as "Alcamizer 4", 1.2 dibenzoylmethane 0.06, calcium hydrogen phosphite 0.33, zinc laurate 0.21, barium laurate 0.39, and octadecyl 3-(3,5-di-t-butyl-4-hydroxphenyl) propionate phenolic antioxidant 0.06. Compositions such as this (with typical addition of low levels of filler and pigment, as noted above) have the potential to replace compositions, they provide equivalent processability and, in most respects, equivalent properties. They have, in addition, the advantage of not containing an ingredient having chronic toxicity to workers or the environment, such as lead-based stabilizers.

Organotin heat stabilizers

Organotin heat stabilizers are used primarily for rigid PVC applications. Individual products usually consist of methyltin, butyltin and octyltin mercaptides, maleates, and carboxylates. Organotin stabilizers may be divided into sulfur-containing and sulfur-free products. Sulfur-containing products (mercaptides) provide excellent overall stabilization properties but suffer from odor and crossstaining problems. The nonsulfur organotins, such as the maleates, are less efficient heat stabilizers but do not suffer from odor problems and provide better light stability. Generally, butyl and methyltins have been used when toxicity is not a concern. Some octyltin mercaptoacetates and maleates, and to a lesser extent methyltin mercaptoacetates, have FDA approval for use in food-contact applications.

Preparation

This method relates to the preparation of certain new organotin trihalides, which are particularly useful for conversion into organotin stabilizers for polyvinyl chloride or other polymers. In the synthesis of organotin compounds the formation of a tin-carbon bond constitutes a necessary step. A known method of forming such a bond is the Grignard route by the reaction

$$SnCl_4 + 4RMgCl \rightarrow R_4Sn + 4\ MgCl_2$$

where

R = alkyl or substituted alkyl.

Process

To a 500 ml, 3 neck flask fitted with a stirrer, thermometer, reflux condenser and gas inlet tube and placed in an ice/salt cooling bath were charged 80 g of anhydrous stannous chloride, 36.3 g of methyl acrylate and 150 ml of dimethoxyethane as polar solvent. To the stirred solution were added 36 g of gaseous hydrogen chloride over a period of 2 hours, the temperature being maintained at 20° C. After this time the solvent was removed on a flash evaporator and the residue was extracted with 100 ml of toluene. The extract obtained was distilled off in vacuo at 100° C. and 4 mm Hg pressure to leave 117 g of a pale residue which crystallized on cooling. By elemental analysis and infrared spectroscopy it was found that a product of the composition melting point 70° C., boiling point 174° C. (4 mm Hg) had been obtained in 89% yield, based on tin.

Lead Heat Stabilizers

Lead heat stabilizers are used primarily for wire and cable applications. Here they provide cost-effective stabilization while offering excellent electrical insulation properties. Most lead stabilizers are water-insoluble, an advantage in UL-approved electrical insulation applications. Lead stabilizers may be either organic- or inorganic-based products. Selected organic products consist of dibasic lead stearates and phthalates, while some inorganic lead products are tribasic lead sulfate, dibasic lead phosphite, and dibasic lead carbonate. There is increasing pressure to replace lead with other products. However, no suitable cost-effective replacement for lead stabilizers in primary cable insulation applications has been found.

Preparation:

For purposes of convenience this preferred silicate substrate will be hereinafter referred to as talc.

In the process for preparing the stabilizers of this method, the talc is first mixed with water under agitation until a homogeneous slurry is obtained. The talc must be uniformly dispersed in the water to insure that individual particles of the talc will complex with the basic lead compounds to be formed in the subsequent steps of the process. If the slurry is not uniform, the final product will be a mixture of talc complexed particles and uncomplexed talc particles which cannot be easilty separated. The amount of water used in making the talc slurry is not cirtical but should be sufficient to accommodate a uniform talc dispersion. Generally, from 0.5 to 15 ml of water for each gram of talc is sufficient.

After the talc-water slurry becomes homogeneous, powdered litharge is transferred to the slurry with the aid of additional water to form a talc-litharge slurry. Other methods of forming the talc-litharge slurry can be utilized as for example by separately forming a talc slurry and a litharge slurry and combining the two or by forming a litharge slurry and dispersing the talc in the slurry. However, it is preferred to first form a uniform talc slurry followed by the addition of powdered litharge. The weight of powdered litharge to be added to the talc slurry is preferably from 1/3 to three times the weight of talc in order to achieve a final product containing from 25 to 75 percent of basic lead compound.

Although the litharge can be added to the talc slurry in many ways such as by predispersing it in water and slowly adding this predispersion to the talc slurry followed by addition of water, it is preferred to wet-bolt the powdered litharge using water through a screen having a mesh size of from between 80 to 100. This insures removal of large size agglomerates of litharge which may be difficult to disperse or break up in the slurry. To the so formed litharge-talc slurry is added a catalyst such as acetic acid to aid in the conversion of litharge to the basic lead compounds after the addition of reactive acid. Other acids which form soluble lead salts such as propionic acid, sulfonic acid and lactic acid can also be used as the catalyst.

Acetic acid is preferred since it is inexpensive and readily available

The amount of acetic acid generally required for the catalysis of the litharge is from 0.003 to 0.004 g for each gram of litharge based on 100 percent acetic acid. Using 10 percent aqueous acetic acid 0.035 to 0.045 ml are required.

The amount of reactive acid to be used depends on the type of basic lead compound to be produced. Low amounts of acid relative to the amount of litharge used gives compounds of higher basicities and higher amounts of acid give lower basicities. However, all basic lead compounds complexed with talc according to this invention can be produced by using from 1/5 to 1/2 equivalent of reactive acid per mole of litharge. When using mixtures of acids the total number of equivalents of acid in the mixture must be from 1/5 to 1/2 the number of moles of litharge. The acid can be added in its pure form or diluted with water.

The reactive acid should be added slowly to the talclitharge slurry with stirring to insure temperature control and prevent agglomeration of the slurry particles. It may be added at room temperature or at elevated temperatures if desired. Generally, the reactive acid is added over a period of from 1 to 4 hours. After addition of the acid the slurry may be heated to between 50° to 75°C to insure complete reaction. The stabilizer is then recovered by filtration of the reacted slurry after which it is dried to remove water. When using water-insoluble organic acids as the reactive acids e.g., stearic acid, to prepare the corresponding basic lead organic carboxylate-talc composites it is necessary to add a base such as monoethanolamine to the talc-litharge slurry to solubilize the acid. The acid is then added as an emulsion in water using a suitable emulsifying agent to disperse the acid.

It has been found that many other silica based substrates such as hydrous silica, hydrous calcium silicate, non-hydrous crystalline calcium silicate and and diatomaceous silica do not form composites with the basic lead compounds of this invention.

In order to more fully describe the instant method, the following methods are given. All products prepared according to the methods showed excellent utility as stabilizers for polyvinyl chloride resins.

Process

This process illustrates the preparation of a stabilizer comprising talc complexed with a mixture of tribasic lead sulfate and dibasic lead phosphite wherein the weight ratio of tribasic lead sulfate to dibasic lead phosphite is 3:1 and the amount of talc comprises 50 percent of the weight of the stabilizer.

Exactly 1000 g of a talc containing 31 percent of MgO and 62 percent of SiO_2 and having an MOH hardness of 1.0 was added to 7200 ml water with stirring to form a slurry. This slurry was stirred for 30 minutes in an 11 × 10 inches stainless steel vessel equipped with a 2 blade 5 inches diameter propeller. To this slurry was added 926.7 g of litharge together with 300 ml of water. Next 18 ml of 10 percent acetic acid was added. The soformed catalyzed slurry was then heated to 50°C and a mixture of 27.96 g of phosphorous acid (100 percent) and 75.65 g of sulfuric acid (100 percent) in 50 ml of H_2O was added to the stirred slurry dropwise over a period of one hour while maintaining a reaction temperature of 50°-55°C. The slurry was stirred for an additional hour at 50°-55°C after which the slurry was filtered and the solid filter cake was dried 20 hours at 80°C. The yield of product was 2025.

The stabilizer was next tested in a chemically blown vinyl-foamed plastisol wherein 6 g of the stabilizer was dispersed in 5 g of an epoxy plasticizer, 95 g of dioctyl phthalate plasticizer and 100 g of a polyvinyl chloride resin. About 2 g of a blowing agent was also added. The stabilizer was easily dispersed in the plasticizer using a Hobart Homomixer at low to medium speed. In order to determine the viscosity stability of the plastisol, Brookfield viscosity readings were taken after one day and one week. At the end of 1 day the Brookfield viscosity of the plastisol was 2100 cps at 2 RPM at 25°C and 1980 cps at 20 RPM at 25°C. At the end of one week the viscosity was 2500 cps at 2 RPM and 2470 cps at 20 RPM at 25°C indicating excellent viscosity stability. The plastisols were also checked again for dispersability properties by observing evidence of settling or agglomeration on the stabilizer. No settling or agglomeration was found.

Antimony

Antimony compounds are effective at low concentrations as primary heat stabilizers in rigid PVC applications. They have

National Sanitation Foundation (NSF) acceptance for use in potable PVC water pipe. A disadvantage of antimony compounds is their poor light stability.

Preparation

Antimony Pentafluoride from Antimony Trioxide

67.74 g of Antimony trioxide (Sb_2O_3) was carefully added to 113.61 grams of 49.1 wt % HF solution and the mixture stirred to complete solution of the Sb_2O_3. A small amount of insoluble material separated out and the bulk solution was decanted from this residual precipitate and associated liquid (1.27 grams).

180.01 grams of this solution was transferred to a 250 mL round bottomed flask and about 1% excess of 30 wt % H_2O_2 solution (53.17 grams) added slowly such that the temperature was maintained between 60°-80° C. When addition was complete the temperature was increased to 90° C. for approximately 15 minutes.

The liquid was distilled under atmospheric pressure to leave a residue of 139.52 grams which analyzed approximately $H(H_2O)_{3.82}SbF_6$.

96.87 grams of this residue was vacuum distilled to a pot temperature of 130° C. 25 mm Hg. to remove 21.84 grams of distillate and leave a residue of approximate composition $H(H_2O)_{1.1}SbF_{4.23}O_{0.63}(OH)_{0.51}$, a fluorine deficient product.

Treatment with anhydrous HF and subsequent vacuum distillation at 75 mm Hg to a 150° C. pot temperature gave a residue product corresponding to $H(H_2O)_{1.84}SbF_{5.6}(OH)_{0.4}$.

21.24 grams of this concentrate were placed in a 300 mL aluminum pressure vessel, 7.40 grams of anhydrous HF added and 250 psig of COF_2 pressure applied (15.26 g). The reaction was warmed to 150° C. and held at this temperature for 80 minutes. The final gas analysis was N_2 = 3.2%, CF_4 = 1.5% CO_2 = 89.1% COF_2 = 6.3% indicating complete reaction. After venting the gas pressure, the remaining liquid was flashed over at reduced pressure and collected in two fractions.

SECONDARY HEAT STABILIZERS

Alkyl/aryl organophosphites

Alkyl/aryl organophosphites are often used with liquid mixed metal stabilizers in the stabilization of PVC resin. They prevent discoloration by functioning as chelators of such by-products as barium chloride from the primary heat stabilizers. The use of phosphites as secondary heat stabilizers has many additional benefits. They reduce the melt viscosity, which contributes to smoother and easier processing, and also function as antioxidants. The liquid organophosphates are usually formulated with the liquid-metal stabilizers and sold as convenient one-package systems. Solid mixed metal stabilizers do not contain liquid organophosphites. Typical organophosphites used for heat stabilization include didecylphenyl, tridecyl, and triphenyl phosphites.

A few organophosphite products have been given FDA approval for flexible and rigid vinyl applications. An example is tris (nonylphenyl) phosphite (TNPP).

Preparation

In general, the present method is based on the discovery that hydrolytically stable phosphite compositions may be prepared from crude tetrahydroabietyl alcohol. The phosphites may be synthesized by the transesterification of triphenyl phosphite with an excess of a crude, tetrahydroabietyl alcohol, more specifically a product designated ABITOL® available from Hercules, Inc. Other synthesis may also be used.

ABITOL is a commercial product containing about 80% tetrahydroabietyl alcohol with the remainder being mixture of organic materials, some very complex and difficult to identify chemically. It is made by hydrogenating the rosin acids portion from crude, tall oil fatty acid, the major portion of which is abietic acid. The manufacturer of the crude product provides a hydroxyl number which translates to an apparent molecular weight by hydroxyl equivalence. The apparent molecular weight for the ABITOL® product used in the examples was 365.

The method may best be understood with reference to the following process.

Process

Tris tetrahydroabietyl phosphite was prepared by transesterifying triphenyl phosphite with 10% excess ABITOL. A reactor was charged with 1204.5 g ABITOL (3.3 mols), 310 g triphenyl phosphite (1 mol) and 2 g sodium methylate as catalyst. The reaction mixture was heated under an inert gas to 120° C. and then a vacuum was gradually applied to remove the phenol produced in the reaction. Heating and application of vacuum were continued until reaching 195°-200° C. to less than 1 mmHg during which time the last of the phenol, the excess ABITOL and the non-alcohol components of the Abitol were removed, a total of 390 g of distillate.

The residue was dissolved in n-heptane and filtered through a precoat of Celite. The reaction product was then stripped to 120° C <1 mmHg vacuum. Total recovery was 1100 g. or 98% of theoretical yield.

When this product was exposed to 80% relative humidity at ambient temperature, the weight gain was insignificant, thus indicating no hydrolysis. The acid value increased from 0.1 to 2 in a period of 3000 hours. For purposes of comparison, tristearyl phosphite, in a similar test, showed an acid value increase from 0.5 to 27.7 in 352 hours.

Epoxy Compounds

Epoxy compounds function both as plasticizers and stabilizers in flexible and semirigid PVC. As stabilizers, epoxies react with liberated HCl. In addition, they react with the polymer chain at labile-chlorine sites—either directly or catalytically by increasing the reactivity of the labile-chlorine site with metal salt stabilizers. Most epoxy stabilizers are derived from unsaturated fatty oils and fatty acid esters. Epoxidized soybean and linseed oils and epoxy tallate are commonly used products. Epoxy tallate also increases light stability. Epoxy compounds can be formulated with metallic liquid stearates and, thus, can be sold to compounders as a one-package system if a constant ratio of stabilizer-to-epoxy is acceptable. However, since these epoxy compounds are also plasticizers, the balance of the formulation must be adjusted for this effect.

Preparation

High molecular weight epoxy resins made from epoxy compounds of the present method have improved resistance to water and are less susceptible to water induced impairment of performance.

Reinforced composite materials may be made with suitable reinforcing materials by known techniques, using the epoxy compounds of the present invention in any of the above combinations to form the polymer matrix.

Process

Preparation of 3-(trifluoromethyl)-N,N-bis(2,3-epoxypropyl)aniline

A solution of 3-(trifluoromethane)aniline (48.3 g) and trifluoromethane sulphonic acid (2 g) in benzene was prepared. To this solution was added 110 g epichlorhydrin and the whole was stirred and heated at about 70° C. for about 24 hours. The product was cooled to about 10°-15° C. and 2 g of benzyltriethylammonium chloride was added, followed by a solution consisting of 60 g of sodium hydroxide in 75 g of water. The reaction was allowed to proceed at about room temperature. The mixture was finally heated at about 70° C. for 1/2 hour. Water was then added and the product extracted with ether. Distrillation gave 41 g of 3-(trifluoromethyl)-N,N-bis(2,3-epoxypropyl)aniline, having a boiling point of 109°-111° C./0.07 Torr.

Beta diketones

Beta diketones are secondary heat stabilizers used in combination with Ca/Zn and Ba/Zn metallic heat stabilizers to improve initial colour. Beta diketones usually require the presence of other secondary heat stabilizers such as epoxidized oils and organophosphates.

Preparation

Organo-Metallic Compound

The organo-metallic compound used in the composition of this method is a beta diketonate of a metal capable of reacting to form an oxide of the metal on contacting a heated surface, i.e., surface having a temperature of about 900°-1200° F. The metal is selected from those having an atomic number from 22 to 92, preferably a transition metal, and most preferably a metal of the first transition series, having an atomic number of from 22 to 29. Such metals include uranium, thorium, erbium, cerium, platinum, antimony, tin, tungsten, titanium, cobalt, iron, chromium, copper, manganese and nickel. The metal is believed to chelate with the carbonyl oxygens of the beta diketonate to form a compound having the structure: where x and y are equal and y stands for the oxidation state of the transition metal and x stands for the number of ligands chelated with the transition metal.

The following process show the preparation of various coating compositions disclosed in the method and their application in pyrolytically coating glass substrates.

Process

A mixed ferric-chromium acetyl acetonate solution was prepared as follows: 100 grams of ferric acetyl acetonate and 26.6 grams of chromium acetyl acetonate were dissolved in 874 grams, 633 milliliters, of a solvent comprising 20 percent by volume methylene chloride, 35 percent by volume trichloroethylene and 45 percent by volume perchloroethylene. The mixed solvent was nonflammable as determined by spraying the solution into a natural gas flame of a Bunsen burner. The weight ratio of iron to chromium was 80:20 and the total metal in solution was 2 percent by weight based on total weight of the solution. The solution was then sprayed with a hand spray gun on a flat glass substrate which was preheated to a temperature of about 1100° F. The coating composition pyrolyzed to give a substantially transparent, gold-colored coating having a uniform thickness of about 450-500 Angstroms.

Polyfunctional Alcohols

Polyfunctional alcohols are secondary heat stabilizers used in combination with mixed metal products. They function by forming complexes that deactivate the metallic chloride by-products of the primary stabilizers.

Preparation:

This method relates to polyfunctional ethylenically unsaturated polymers.

Civil engineering and industrial coating applications require environmentally safe resin systems that are curable at ambient temperatures to provide polymeric coatings exhibiting good impact and wear resistance, as well as chemical and moisture resistance. Concrete structures, e.g., require coatings that exhibit such properties even where shrinkage-induced cracks occur in the underlying structure. Acrylate-based coating compositions have provided a balance of stability and fast cure (even at low temperatures) but have required the use of significant quantities of low molecular weight monomers that have sometimes presented an inhalation risk and an environmental hazard.

Acrylate-based compositions have also been widely used in the radiation curing industry, where significant quantities of low molecular weight monomers have been added to a polyfunctional polymer or oligomer in order to effect viscosity reduction. This has often resulted in an impairment of the peformance of the resultant radiation cured coatings, as the desirable properties of the base polymer or oligomer have tended to be diminished by the effect of the monomer.

Thus, there exists a continuing need in the art for polyfunctional polymers or oligomers that exhibit improved viscosities and that can be cured alone or in combination with only small amounts of low molecular weight monomer(s) to provide durable, impact-resistant polymer coatings

Process

5.0 moles (1110 g) of isophorone diisocyanate (IPDI, NCO equivalent weight of 111) was placed in a 5 liter, four-necked flask equipped with a thermometer, a mechanical stirrer, an inert gas inlet, and a reflux condenser. Then 2.0 OH equivalents (2,126 g) of polycarbonatediol (OH equivalent weight of 1063, available as Desmophen® C 200 from Bayer, Leverkusen) was added to the flask in three portions, so as not to exceed a reaction temperature of 60° C. Two NH equivalents (418 g, 1 mole) of N,N'-(butyl-1,4-

diyl)-bis-tetraethyl aspartic ester were then added slowly in four portions, and the resulting mixture was held at 50° C. for 2 hours. The mixture was allowed to cool to 23° C., and the isocyanate concentration of the mixture was measured by titration according to DIN 53 185. A calculated equimolar amount (with 10% excess) of 2-hydroxyethylmethacrylate (HEMA), corresponding to 6.6 moles (858 g) was added using a dropping funnel. The resulting mixture was then maintained at 50° C for 8 hours. The residual NCO in the resulting methacryloyl- polyfunctional polyurethaneurea product was measured (using the di-(n-butylamine) titration method according to DIN 53 185) and found to be less than 0.1%. The product was placed in glass bottles for storage.

2,2-dimethoxy-1,2-diphenylethane-1-one was added to the product (0.5 parts by weight based on 100 parts of product, Irgacure® 651 UV photoinitiator available from Ciba-Geigy, Lautertal, Germany), and the resulting mixture was stirred well. The mixture was then cured using a high intensity UV light source (UV H-bulb equipment available from Eltosch GmbH, Hamburg, Germany) emitting radiation at wavelengths of 220-440 nm and having an intensity of 110 mJ/cm^2. Films or thick samples of the cured mixture were prepared and tested.

Suppliers

There are over 100 suppliers of primary heat stabilizers. The majority of these companies use heat stabilizers as their core product and serve the PVC industry with other additives such as lubricants and organophosphite stabilizers. Many specialty suppliers sell their complete product line in a single region and export selected products. There are no suppliers of heat stabilizers that have leading positions in all three major regions of the world. A major change among suppliers of heat stabilizers took place recently with Witco's acquisition of Ciba's heat stabilizer business in exchange for Witco's epoxy and adhesives businesses. In addition, Akzo recently acquired the remaining half of the Akcros joint venture, a major heat stabilizer supplier. A global list of selected suppliers of heat stabilizers is shown in Table 9.2.

TABLE 9.2: Selected Heat Stabilizer Suppliers

Supplier	Type		
	Mixed metal	Organotin	Lead
Akzo	×	×	×
Asahi Denka Kogyo K.K.	×	×	—
Baerlocher	×	—	—
BASF	×	×	×
Cardinal Chemical	—	×	—
Chemson	×	×	×
Clariant/Hoechst	×	—	—
Dainippon Ink and Chemicals	×	×	—
Elf Atochem	×	×	—
Ferro	×	×	×
Hammond Lead	—	—	×
Kolon Chemical	×	—	×
Kyodo Chemical	×	×	—
Morton International	—	×	×
Nan Ya Plastics	×	×	×
Nanjing Chemical Factory	×	×	×
NOF	×	—	—
OMG	×	—	—
Reagens SpA	×	×	×
Sakai Chemical	×	×	×
Tokyo Fine Chemical	×	×	—
Witco	×	×	—

Trends and Forecasts

There are several heat stabilizer products that have received environmental scrutiny in selected regions of the world. The European Directives banning the use of cadmium-based stabilizers, due to the effect on human health and the environment, has successfully limited their global use. This forced the industry to find cadmium-free alternatives. Ba/Zn and Ca/Zn are being substituted in the short term. The Ca/Zn material is much less effective but benefits from having two almost nontoxic components that have worldwide approvals. Organotins will experience long-term growth at the expense of Cd. Lead is being phased out in selected regions of the world. However, this will occur over a long period of time.

In response to the concerns regarding the use of heavy metals, producers are developing reduced metal and metal-free organic stabilizer systems. One reduced metal system is based on selected difunctional epoxides and zinc compounds and is reported to perform comparably to commercial lead-based systems. Completely organic (metal-free) heat stabilizer systems are under development by all major producers. One system undergoing commercial testing is based on heterocyclic ketone compounds (the pyrimidindione ring) with HCl scavenging co-stabilizers. Although relatively insignificant in the present heat-stabilizer business, current environmental pressure might permit materials of this type to achieve 5 to 10% market penetration within the next 5 years

The growth of heat stabilizers is dependent on PVC growth. Rigid PVC applications are expected to grow at a faster rate than flexible PVC applications worldwide. This indicates organotins will experience higher growth than mixed metals. Over the next 5 years, heat stabilizers are expected to grow at a rate of 6% per year paced by the Asia/Pacific and the developing regions of the world.

10

Impact Modifiers

DESCRIPTION

Impact modifiers are used in a wide variety of thermoplastic resins to absorb the energy generated by impact and dissipate it in a nondestructive fashion. The behavior and definition of impact modifiers are complex. The selection of an impact modifier is dependent on compatibility, physical solubility, impact performance, and cost. Impact modifiers are primarily used in PVC, engineering resins, and polyolefins. The use levels of impact modifiers vary widely depending upon the modifiers, matrix type, and properties desired. The major types are shown in Table 10.1 along with the resins in which they are primarily used.

Methacrylate-butadiene-styrene (MBS)

Methacrylate-butadiene-styrene represents the highest volume of the styrenic type impact modifiers. This modifier is used in transparent packaging applications due to its clarity. Rigid applications include film, sheet, bottles, credit cards, and interior profiles. MBS has limited use in exterior applications due to poor ultraviolet (UV) stability. Methacrylate/acrylonitrile-butadiene- styrene (MABS) is closely related to MBS, but has minor use in the industry and has been completely replaced by MBS in North America.

TABLE 10.1: Major Types of Impact Modifiers by Resin

Type	Resin					
	PVC*	PE**	PP†	PA‡	PET/PBT§	Other
MBS (methacrylate butadiene styrene)	×	—	—	—	—	—
MABS (methacrylate/acrylonitrilebutadiene-styrene)	×	—	—	—	×	—
ABS (acrylonitrile-butadiene-styrene)	×	—	—	—	×	—
CPE (chlorinated polyethylene)	×	×	×	—	—	—
EVA (ethylene vinyl acetate)	×	—	—	—	—	—
PMMA (polymethylmethacrylate)	×	—	—	—	—	×
EPDM (ethylene propylene diene monomer)	×	×	×	—	—	—
EPR (ethylene propylene rubber)	×	×	×	—	—	—
SBR (styrene butadiene rubber)	—	—	—	—	—	×
Others	—	—	—	—	—	—
Maleated EPDM	—	—	—	×	×	—
Maleated PP and PE	—	—	—	×	×	—
PUR (Polyurethane)	—	—	—	—	—	×
SAN-g-EPDM	—	—	—	—	×	—

*PVC—polyvinylchloride. **PE—polyethylene. †PP—polypropylene. ‡PA—polyamide. §PET—polyethylene terephthalate; PBT—polybutylene terephthalate.

Preparation

The MBS polymer is dried from a latex which is polymerized sequentially so as to produce a graft polymer, the first stage being a rubbery polymer of butadiene, either alone or with one or more ethylenically unsaturated monomers such as methacrylates, acrylate, or styrene, the latter being most preferred. Optionally, one or more polyunsaturated cross-linking monomers are present in addition to butadiene.

The first stage, or "rubber" stage, i.e. the butadiene-containing stage, is preferably at least about 70% and more preferably at least about 75% with the balance being at least one subsequent stage.

The preferred fumed silica is produced by vapor phase hydrolysis of silicon tetrachloride at high temperatures, usually around 1100° C, and is an amorphous material having a small particle size (about 0.007 to 0.05 microns) and a large surface area (about 50 to 390 m^2-g^{-1}). Silicas of this nature are wettable but can be made hydrophobic by silanization. Both forms are useful in the process of the method .

Possibly other inert particulate material than fumed silica could be useful in the invention, especially if the inert particulate material has a particle size of about 0.007 to 1.5 microns and a surface area of about 1 to 400 m^2 -g^{-1} ; for example, aluminum silicate, calcium carbonate, carbon black, titanium dioxide, polymethyl methacrylate, zinc oxide, and infusorial earth.

Process

A. Preparation of rubbery polymer latex

A stainless steel autoclave with an agitator and several entry ports is charged with 5 parts of a diphenyl oxide sulfonate emulsifier in 2688 parts of de-ionized water and 4.9 parts of sodium formaldehyde sulfoxylate and brought to pH=4. The autoclave is evacuated and 2297 parts of butadiene, 96.8 parts of styrene, 12 parts of cumene hydroperoxide, and 24.6 parts of divinylbenzene are added and caused to react at 70° C. over 9 hours. An additional 36.9 parts of emulsifier is also added. At the end of the reaction period no further pressure drop is observed, the residual pressure is vented and the latex is strained to remove gum.

B. Preparation of the graft polymer

To 500 parts of latex prepared in the preceding paragraph is added 34 parts of styrene followed by 0.068 parts of sodium formaldehyde sulfoxylate dissolved in 52 parts of de-ionized water and 0.136 parts cumene hydroperoxide. One hour after completion of the exotherm 35 parts of methyl methacrylate, 0.352 parts of butylene dimethacrylate, 0.035 parts sodium formaldehyde sulfoxylate dissolved in 10 parts deionized water and 0.070 parts of cumene hydroperoxide are added and caused to react to completion.

C. Isolation of the graft polymer

The resultant polymer latex has a butadiene/styrene rubber content of 77.5% by weight, with an overall butadiene content of 73.6%.

Isolation of the latex as prepared in A and B, supra, in a spray dryer by atomization in the presence of air as the drying medium with varying levels of fumed silica added by suspending in the gaseous drying medium demonstrates the advantages of the invention.

Acrylonitrile-butadiene-styrene (ABS)

Acrylonitrile-butadiene-styrene is used in a variety of resins, with about 60% in PVC. The primary ABS applications are in automotive parts, credit cards, and packaging. ABS, like MBS, is not suitable for outdoor applications unless it is protected by a UV-resistant cap. ABS, although compatible with MBS, suffers from the disadvantage of not being regarded as an industry standard.

Preparation

The starting reaction mixture is a mixture of monomers comprising 65 to 90% of a styrenic compound, usually styrene, and 35 to 10% of an unsaturated nitrile, usually acrylonitrile, and an amount of elastomer corresponding to about 7 to 15% by weight based on the weight of the monomers mixture. The elastomer most often used in a polymer of 1,4-diene, typically polybutadiene, polyisoprene or a mixture of there two elastomers. Other rubbery compositions or copolymers of butadiene and vinyl compounds, such as for example, butadiene-styrene copolymers, also may be used. The starting rubber must be soluble in the mixture of styrene and acrylonitrile monomers.

The mixture of monomers and rubber form a homogeneous phase which is subjected to a partial mass-copolymerization step under vigorous stirring. This copolymerization is carried out in the presence of p-chlorobenzoyl peroxide as a free radical generating initiator and dithiobis-(benzothiazole) as a chain transfer agent. The amount of initiator is generally between 0.01 and 2%, preferably between 0.1 and 0.2% by weight, based on the total weight of rubber and monomers. The amount of dithiobis-(benzothiazole) may vary; for example, amounts as low as 0.001% by weight of the total rubber and monomers used and as high as 1% by weight of the rubbers and monomers or even more may be used. It is noted, however, that no substantial improvement in properties occurs when amounts in excess of 5% are used. The amount of dithiobis-(benzothiazole) is generally between 0.05 and 1% and preferably 0.05% to 0.5% by weight of the rubber and monomers employed. The thermal stability of p-chlorobenzoyl peroxide is higher than the thermal stability of benzoyl peroxide or other peroxy initiators. The half-lifes (in hours) are the following:

	50° C	70° C	100° C.
Benzoyl peroxide	220	13	0.36
p-chlorobenzoyl peroxide	310	18	0.50

Consequently, the polymerization rate is lower in the presence of p-chlorobenzoyl peroxide and the control of the polymerizartion temperature is easier. Further, it has been found that the reaction mixture is less viscous when the mass copolymerization is carried out in the presence of p-chlorobenzoyl peroxide. This reaction mixture therefore is more easily stirred, and the thermal exchange and the control of temperature are better than in similar processes using other initiators.

The mass copolymerization is carried out in the absence of air or oxygen which are inhibitors. This copolymerization therefore is performed under an inert atmosphere, preferably under nitrogen.

The reaction mixture is first a continuous phase consisting in elastomer dissolved in the monomers. After a certain degree of conversion of the monomers, a second phase is formed, consisting in styrene-acrylonitrile copolymers dissolved in the monomers. As a result of the evolution of the copolymerization, the volume of said second phase, which is dispersed as small drops in the first phase, increases and finally is more dominant than the volume of the first phase. At this point, a phase inversion occurs. The continuous phase is now the phase consisting in styrene-acrylonitrile copolymers dissolved in the monomers and the discontinuous phase, which is dispersed in the continuous phase, is composed of elastomer dissolved in the monomers.

The mass copolymerization is carried out until 10% to 30% conversion of the monomers. At this point, the viscosity of the reaction mixture is generally between 10,000 and 100,000 centipoises (at 65° C.), this viscosity varying with the elastomer content of the mixture. Such conditions are suitable for continuing the polymerization by suspension polymerization. The product obtained after partial mass-polymerization is mixed with water and an aqueous dispersion of a suspending agent or colloid protector. The suspending agent preferably is selected from the water insoluble inorganic compounds, for example, phosphates, Al_2O_3, ZnO, magnesium silicate which is easily and completely eliminated from the ABS resin beads. Preferably, calcium hydroxyapatite is employed. This compound may be prepared from trisodium phosphate and calcium chloride.

It is also advantageous to perform the suspension polymerization step in the presence of a surface-active agent of non-ionic type or anionic type. The amount of a surface-active agent varies with the nature of such agent and with the nature of the suspending agent. When hydroxyapatite is used as a suspending agent and sodium dodecylbenzenesulphonate is used as the surface-active agent, the amount of surface-active agent is between about 0.1 and 0.4 per liter of water in the aqueous phase of the reaction mixture. When the amount of surface-active agent is outside the above values, the beads of ABS resin have a larger than desired diameter which is detrimental to the future working of the resin. Further, in some instances, it is impossible to obtain a suspension of the organic mass in water under such circumstances.

In order to have a particularly efficient suspending agent, the reaction mass resulting from the particle mass polymerization is mixed with water, and the aqueous dispersion of suspending agent is added and then the surface-active agent, for instance the sodium dodecylbenzenesulphonate. In this way, the suspending agent is not in the presence of a high concentration of surface-active agent and consequently, it does not absorb too large an amount of surface-active agent and therefore, does not become too lipophilic which avoids its absorption in the organic mass.

The suspension polymerization step is carried out at a temperature of between 75° and 150° C. According to a preferred embodiment of the present invention, the suspension polymerization step is first carried out at a temperature of between 75° and 125° C. and the temperature is then increased about 15° to 25° C. when the beads of ABS resin have acquired a specific weight higher than that of the aqueous phase. The polymerization is carried out at such increased temperature for a period of about 2 to 4 hours.

The process of the present method may be carried out in the type of equipment which is currently used for polymerizing styrene or for producing ABS resin. Both steps of the process can be successfully performed in the same reactor. However, if desired, two reactors may be employed, one for the mass copolymerization and the other for the suspension polymerization.

Process

23.27 kg of styrene, 9.50 kg of acrylonitrile, 4.916 kg of rubber (Stereon 703A of Firestone Tire and Rubber Co.), 0.07 kg of dithiobis-(benzothiazole) as chain transfer agent, 1.133 kg of tricresyl phosphate as plasticizer and 0.475 kg of water were introduced into a reactor. The mixture was stirred under a nitrogen atmosphere and then heated up to 94° C. Next, 14.4 g of p-chlorobenzoyl peroxide were added. A mass-polymerization step was carried out under a nitrogen atmosphere with stirring.

In a separate container, a dispersion of suspending agent was prepared by mixing 15.4 kg of water, 0.59 kg trisodium phosphate, 0.79 kg of calcium chloride and 0.0403 kg of calcium oxide. The reaction mixture obtained by the mass-copolymerization and having a viscosity of 96,000 centipoises was admixed with 30.8 kg of water and the above described dispersion of suspending agent. Then, 0.289 kg of an aqueous solution containing 2.5% of the sodium salt of dodecylbenzene-sulphonic acid and 0.0245 kg of cumene peroxide at 40% were added to the mixture. The suspension polymerization step was then carried out at a temperature of 116° C. When the beads of ABS resin began to settle out, 32.7 g dicumyl peroxide was added and the mixture was heated at 135° C. and maintained at such temperature for an additional 3 hours

Acrylics

Acrylics are similar to MBS and ABS but have butyl acrylate or 2-ethyl-hexyl acrylate graft phases. Acrylics offer greater resistance to UV degradation and are used primarily in PVC siding, window profiles, and other applications calling for weather resistance. Due to growth in the building and construction industry, acrylics are experiencing the highest growth rate.

Preparation

The acrylic compositions of the present method are prepared by mixing the particles with the polymethyl methacrylate which will form the matrix of the composition and any additional materials as necessary for a particular application. The materials can be mixed in any suitable manner as will be evident to one skilled in the art. Preferably, the materials are mixed at room temperature for about 15 to 30 minutes. The compositions are then cured by any suitable procedure which will be evident to those skilled in the art from present disclosure. However, a preferred means for curing the material consists of allowing the mixture to stand at about 82° C. for about 20 minutes and then at about 125° C. for about 7 minutes.

After curing, the acrylic compositions may then be used to prepare articles such as spas and bathware by thermoforming. Suitable thermoforming processes are well known in the art and the present invention is not limited to any one type of thermoforming process.

Process

Particle Production

White and black polymer particles were prepared using a bulk polymerization process. The following ingredients were used for the white particles and black particles, respectively.

	Weight (g)
White Particles	
methyl methacrylate	2099.50
n-butyl acrylate	405.00
ethylene glycol dimethacrylate	18.90
lauryl mercaptan	12.61
TINUVIN®-P	0.27
AEROSOL® OT	0.23
LAUROX®	1.49
t-butyl peroxylacetate	0.10
50% TiO_2 dispersion in butyl methacrylate	162.00
Black Particles	
methyl methacrylate	2229.03
n-butyl acrylate	405.00
ethylene glycol dimethacrylate	18.90
lauryl mercaptan	12.61
TINUVIN®-P	0.27
AEROSOL® OT	0.23
LAUROX®	1.43
t-butyl peroxylacetate	0.10
10% dispersion of carbon black in methyl methacrylate	27.00
15% phthallo cyanine blue in butyl methacrylate	5.40
monomethyl ether of hydroquinone	0.03

Note: TINUVIN-P® is a UV stabilizer available from CibaGeigy. AEROSOL® OT is a surfactant available from Witco Chemical. LAUROX® is a solution of lauryl peroxide available from Witco Chemical.

The ingredients were mixed in a one gallon disposable plastic bottle. The mixture had a viscosity of approximately 1cP as measured with a Brookfield RVTDV-11 Viscometer. The mixture was then degassed under 23 inches of vacuum with a water aspirator in a 2000 ml vacuum flask. After degassing, the mixture was transferred to a 2 mil thick nylon bag which was fitted with a thermocouple and sealed.

The nylon bag and its contents were then placed in a Fisher Class 86A Safety Oven and taken through the heating steps set forth in Table 10.2.

TABLE 10.2

Temperature (°C.)	Duration (mins)
Ambient to 61	30
hold at 61	60
61 to 56	5
hold at 56	900
56 to 75	5
hold at 75	60
75 to 100	5
hold at 100	60
100 to 130	5
hold at 130	120
130 to ambient	30

After cooling to ambient temperature, the bag and thermocouple were removed and discarded. The resultant polymer was ground and sieved with a standard wirecloth sieve. Sieve fractions between 600 and 250 microns (>30<60) were isolated along with particles smaller than 250 microns (Fines).

Acrylic Sheet Production

The black and white polymer particles were mixed as follows:

white >30 <60	6.83 grams
white Fines	4.37 grams
black >30 <60	6.71 grams
black Fines	1.09 grams

39.0 grams of the polymer particle mixture was mixed with the ingredients necessary to form the matrix set forth below:

	weight (g)
ethylene glycol dimethacrylate	0.51
lauryl mercaptan	0.42
syrup of partially polymerized MMA	89.4
n butyl acrylate	8.62
methyl methacrylate	199.04
50% T_iO_2 dispersion	0.68
10% Carbon Black dispersion	0.07
t-butyl peroxy neocanoate	1.11
Vazo® 64	0.075
Tinuvin®-P	0.03
Aerosol® - OT	0.036
monomethyl ether of hydroquinone	0.006

These ingredients were mixed for 30 minutes in a glass bottle at a temperature of 20° C. After mixing, the material was poured into a glass cell. The mixture was allowed to polymerize at 82° C for 20 minutes and then at 125° C. for 7 minutes. The material was then allowed to cool to ambient temperature. After cooling, a smooth, high gloss, void free plaque was obtained.

Chlorinated polyethylene (CPE)

Chlorinated polyethylene modifiers are most commonly used in pipe, fittings, siding, and weatherable profiles. CPE modifiers compete primarily with acrylics in siding applications. CPE can be used in resins other than PVC, for example, PE and PP.

Preparation

The polyethylene becomes elastomeric when chlorine atoms are incorporated into the polymer which lessens the degree of crystallinity of the polymer. The polyethylene can be chlorinated at elevated temperatures, usually about 60°-100° C., with gaseous chlorine or a chlorine-generating material. This process can be carried out in solution in an inert solvent, i.e., inert to the reactants, or in a suspension in an inert nonsolvent or without a solvent. These processes are usually conducted in the presence of conventional free-radical initiators, such as organic peroxides or aliphatic azo compounds. When the chlorination is conducted in an inert solvent, suitable solvents include chlorinated solvents, aromatic hydrocarbons and, specifically, carbon tetrachloride, tetrachloroethane, chloroform, chlorobenzene and trifluoro-chloroethane, or mixtures thereof. Suspension chlorination of the polyethylene is usually conducted in water. The amount of gaseous chlorine or chlorine-generating material that is used in the process must be sufficient to incorporate into the polyethylene about 20-28% by weight, preferably 22-26% by weight, chlorine. If less than about 20% by weight chlorine is incorporated into the polymer the crystallinity is undesirably high and if more than about 28% by weight chlorine is incorporated into the polymer the crystallinity is unacceptably low.

When polyethylene is chlorinated in the presence of sulfur dioxide and/or sulfuryl chloride, or if the reactions are conducted sequentially, sulfonyl chloride groups are introduced into the polymer. The sulfonyl chloride groups that are introduced into the elastomer do not significantly alter its physical properties, but allows the elastomer to be crosslinked or cured, usually with polybasic metal oxides, especially litharge (PbO), magnesium oxide, or polybasic metal salts of weak acids, such as tribasic lead maleate. The amount of sulfur in the form of sulfonyl chloride groups in the elastomer is from about 0.2-2% by weight, usually about 1% by weight.

The chlorinated polyethylene or chlorosulfonated polyethylene elastomers are characterized as having: a molecular weight distribution of about 6-13, as determined by the ratio of Mw/Mn where Mw represents the weight average molecular weight and Mn represents the number average molecular weight, a chlorine content of about 20-28% by weight, a Mooney viscosity value, determined according to ASTM D 1646-81, ML (1+4) at 100° C. of 15-36. The percent elongation of the chlorosulfonated polyethylene compounded with nonreinforcing fillers, at 60° C., or at a temperature which is just above the melting point of the elastomer, and determined according to ASTM D 412, shows the extraordinarily high percent elongation obtained with the elastomers made using the conditions of the present process, as compared to chlorosulfonated polyethylenes known in the art. Similar results can be obtained with chlorinated polyethylene of the same chlorine level containing the same compounded ingredients, and tested just above its melting point e.g., about 70° C. The percent elongation of the elastomers were measured at 60° C. and determined according to ASTM D 412, at a draw rate of 50 cm. per minute when the chlorosulfonated polyethylenes were compounded with the ingredients.

The high amount of elongation without rupturing or breaking a sheet of the uncured elastomer at a temperature just above its melting point is an important characteristic. The uncured chlorinated polyethylene elastomers which are usually compounded with fillers, acid acceptors, plasticizers, pigments, processing aids and the like can be fed to forming equipment and, for example, film can be conveyed and drawn down without rupturing or breaking the stock, which commonly occurs with elastomers made according to the teachings of the prior art. This permits one to conduct the forming process at higher rates. It also provides for the preparation of a wider range of films or sheet sizes, and it reduces the amount of manual labor required to prepare these formed products.

The chlorinated polyethylene elastomers described herein are especially useful in the uncured compounded condition as roofing film and pond and pit liners.

Process

A stirred autoclave was charged with 18.16 kg of carbon tetrachloride and 1.35 kg of linear polyethylene having a density of 0.960 g/cc, a flow rate of 4.2 grams per 10 minutes and a molecular weight distribution ratio of Mw/Mn of 11. The autoclave was closed and heated to 109° C. and pressurized to 25 psig

(0.29 MPa) to dissolve the polyethylene. A feed of initiator solution (1% 2,2'-azobis-[2-methylpropanenitrile] in chloroform) was begun and maintained at a rate of 3 ml per minute throughout the remainder of the reaction. The temperature was reduced to 105° C. and a chlorine feed was begun and a total of 0.38 kg of chlorine was passed into the reaction over a period of 72 minutes. After 30 minutes from initiation of the reaction a feed of sulfuryl chloride was begun and 600 ml was added over a period of 20 minutes. After the addition of chlorine was complete, the pressure on the reactor was released and the sample was degassed at 100°-75° C. A stabilizer solution of 1% Epon 828 epoxy resin (condensation product of epichlorohydrin and bisphenol A with a neutralization equivalent of 180) in CCl_4 was added in an amount of 2.7 kg. The solution was filtered and the polymer was isolated by drum drying. The chlorosulfonated polyethylene product contained 23.6% Cl and 1.07% S, and the Mooney viscosity was 21. The Mw/Mn ratio was unchanged at 11.

Ethylene vinyl acetate (EVA)

Ethylene vinyl acetate modifiers have minor usage compared to other types of impact modifiers. EVA finds use in limited segments of the flexible PVC sheet business.

Preparation:

Broadly, the method pertains to a process for the preparation of ethylenevinyl acetate copolymers in which

(a) ethylene and vinyl- acetate are introduced to a polymerization zone;

(b) said ethylene and vinyl acetate are reacted in the presence of a free radical catalyst in said polymerization zone at elevated pressures and temperatures;

(c) the resulting reaction mixture is passed from the polymerization zone through a pressure reduction zone into a separation zone;

(d) the reaction mixture is separated into unreacted monomer and ethylene-vinyl acetate copolymer and;

(e) the unreacted monomer is recycled to the polymerization zone,

the improvement which comprises: introducing into the reaction mixture of unreacted monomer and ethylene-vinyl acetate copolymer at a location downstream from the polymerization zone a hindered phenolic compound in amounts ranging from about 6×10^{-7} moles to about 4×10^{-5} moles of phenolic nuclei per mole of total monomer feed to the polymerization zone.

The continuous polymerization reaction can be conducted either in a tubular reaction zone or in a stirred autoclave. The concentration of vinyl acetate in the total monomer feed can range from about 0.5 weight percent to about 50 weight percent, preferably between about 1 weight percent to about 20 weight percent. The reactor conditions include pressures from about 20,000 psig to about 50,000 psig, preferably from about 23,000 to about 40,000 psig, and temperatures in the range between about 250° and about 600° F, preferably between about 400° and about 550° F. The reaction is carried out in the presence of any of the well known conventional free radical catalysts in amounts usually maintained in the range from about 0.01 to about 10 parts per 1000 parts of the copolymer product. Examples of suitable catalysts include peroxy compounds, such as t-butyl peroxide, t-butyl peroctoate, t-butyl perbenzoate, t-butyl peracetate, t-butyl perisobutyrate and many others.

The effluent from the reaction zone, i.e. polymer product and unreacted monomer, is reduced in pressure and introduced into a so-called high pressure separation zone, which is usually maintained at a pressure in the range from about 3000 psig to about 6000 psig. Due to the inverse Joule-Thomson effect, the temperature of the effluent after the aforementioned pressure reduction will increase, resulting in temperature of about 20° to about 165° F higher than that of the effluent exiting the polymerization zone. After separation the unreacted monomer stream from the high pressure separator is usually purified by passing it through one or more condensers to remove undesired low-molecular weight by-products and through one or more filters to remove entrained polymer fines. After compression, the purified unreacted monomer is then recycled to the reactor. The copolymer product separated in the high pressure separator is introduced after further pressure reduction e.g. to a pressure in the range from about 2 psig to about 20 psig, into a low pressure separation zone, where further quantities of unreacted monomer is removed from the product.

The hindered phenolic compound is introduced into the total polymerization effluent downstream of the polymerization zone. The point of introduction may be located anywhere from immediately adjacent the reactor exit to and including the high pressure separator. Preferably, the hindered phenol is introduced into the effluent prior to pressure reduction, however, it is entirely feasible to add it into the high pressure separator. The rate of addition of the compound is very small, i.e. from about 6×10^{-7} moles to 4×10^{-5} moles of phenolic nuclei per mole of total monomer fed to the inlet of the polymerization zone. Advantageously the rate is maintained between about 2×10^{-6} and about 3×10^{-5} moles/mole.

The hindered phenolic compound can be any one of the well known additives commonly used in stabilization of polyolefins, e.g. polypropylene. The following is a partial list of hindered phenolic compounds that can be used in the process: 2,6-diisopropyl phenol, 2,6-di-t-butyl phenol, 2,6-di-t-butyl-4 methyl phenol, 2,5-di-t-amyl hydroquinone, 4 hydroxymethyl-2,6-di-t-butyl phenol, 2,2'- ethylene bis (4-methyl-6-t-butyl phenol), 4,4'-methylene bis (6-t-butyl ortho cresol), 4,4'-methylene bis (2,6-di-t-butyl phenol), 2,4,6-tri-t-butyl phenol, and the like. Other hindered phenolic compounds, which can be used in the method are the mono and polyesters of alkane polyols, wherein the ester group or groups are derived from C_2-C_7 alkanoic acids containing a terminal phenolic nucleus of the general structure shown above. Specific examples of such compounds include the esters of such polyols as ethylene glycol, propanediols, butanediols, hexanediols, heptanediols, butane triols, glycerol, neopentyl glycol, erythritol, pentaerythritol, sorbitol, and the like.

Suitable hindered phenolic compounds include also the polymeric condensation products of phenol and formaldehyde. Many other hindered phenolic compounds not specifically mentioned above can obviously be used as the additive in the process of the present method.

By practicing the method it is possible to continuously polymerize ethylene and vinyl acetate on a large scale without experiencing explosive decomposition of the polymer product. In addition, no deleterious effect on the quality of the copolymer product is experienced in this process, in fact, since decomposition of polymerized and unreacted vinyl acetate is prevented in this process, the product is exceptionally free of objectionable odor.

Process

Comparative experiments were carried out in the manner described below:

Into an autoclave equipped with a stirrer was fed a mixture of 96 wt% ethylene and 4 wt% vinyl acetate at a rate of about 1750 lbs/hours. Catalyst, t-butyl peroxide, was fed to the reactor at a rate of about 0.04 to 0.06 parts by weight per 1000 parts copolymer produced. The reactor pressure was maintained at 35,000 psig and the temperature at a maximum of 490° F. The effluent was reduced in pressure to about 4200 psig and then introduced into a high pressure separation zone. Due to the Joule-Thomson inverse effect the temperature of the effluent increased considerably, and temperatures in the range of 574° to 603° F were observed on the effluent after pressure reduction. The unreacted monomer was separated, purified and returned to the autoclave as recycle.

Ethylene propylene diene monomer (EPDM)

Ethylene propylene diene monomer is used in thermoplastic olefin (TPO) for automotive bumpers and parts as well as scattered consumer durable markets.

Preparation

The ethylene-propylene-diene monomer terpolymers of the method are suitably somewhat variable in proportions. Either monoolefin is present in a major proportion, often from about 50% by weight to about 70% by weight, preferably from about 55% by weight to about 65% by weight. The proportion of the other monoolefin is a lesser amount, e.g., from about 25% by weight to about 45% by weight with proportions from about 25% by weight to about 40% by weight being preferred. The diene monomer is present in a relatively small, although significant proportion.

Amounts of diene monomer from about 1% by weight to about 8% by weight are satisfactory.

The ethylene-propylene-diene monomer terpolymers of the method are characterized by a high degree of random polymerization as compared with EPDM polymers produced with conventional titanium-based catalysts. Expressed differently, the ethylene and propylene portions of the terpolymer are less "blocky". Due to the relatively small amount of the diene monomer present in the terpolymer, the diene monomer can be disregarded in considerations of the degree of random copolymerization. If the arrangement of ethylene and propylene moieties in the polymer chain is highly random, the location of diene monomer moieties will also be random. The highly random location of monomeric moieties in terpolymers of the method is reflected in the improved properties of the ethylene-propylene-diene monomer terpolymers including an improved processability. The terpolymers have improved green strength and reasonably high tensile strength without the necessity for carbon black being present, thereby permitting the production of white EPDM polymers.

When a growing polymer chain exhibits the same preference for reacting with one monomer as the other, a random copolymerization takes place and the two types of monomer will be found randomly along the polymer chain in relative amounts determined by the olefin feed. A strong preference for reacting with the same monomer leads to block polymers.

The disclosures of the Billemeyer text relative to copolymers are applied to the production of the present terpolymers when the role of diene monomer in the degree of random polymerization is disregarded as is discussed above. In the text, the term "monomer reactivity ratio" is defined for the rate constants r_1 and r_2 for a polymer chain terminating in a first monomer (e.g., propylene) and a second monomer (e.g., ethylene), respectively, reacting with its own monomer as opposed to reacting with the other monomer. The magnitude of the value is related to the tendency to react with the same monomer as that terminating the growing polymer chain. For example, if the value of r_1 is greater than 1, it has the significance that a chain terminating in a first monomer (M_1) prefers to react with additional first monomer. A value of r_1 less than 1 sigfnifies that the M_1 -terminating polymer chain would prefer to react with the second monomer (M_2). Corresponding considerations apply to values of r_2. This reference further describes the type of copolymerization in terms of the product of monomer reactivity ratios, i.e., r_1r_2. Although the discussion of this reference is presented in terms of free radical polymerizations of a somewhat different type, the considerations apply generally to the polymerizations leading to the terpolymers of the method when the influence of the diene monomer is disregarded. If the measured value of r_1r_2 is zero, the polymerization would be alternating, except for the occasional diene monomer moiety present. A value of r_1r_2 of 1 would represent a completely random polymerization. A value of r_1r_2 greater than 1 would indicate that a polymer is at least somewhat blocky and the higher the value of $r_1 r_2$ is determined to be, the more blocky the polymeric chain will be. In the polymerizations of the method the value of $r_1 r_2$ is determined to be, the more blocky the polymeric chain will be. In the polymerizations of the invention the value of $r_1 r_2$ will be less than about 2.1 and preferably less than about 1.7. The mathematical derivation of the r_1r_2 values is described in the above textbook reference.

The r_1r_2 value for a given polymer is traditionally determined by measuring the monomeric composition of the polymer as a function of the proportions of monomers in the feed, as is also described. An alternate and more direct method is based on the nuclear magnetic resonance (NMR) spectra of the polymer, particularly the ^{13}C-NMR spectra. The use of the r_1r_2 value is probably not a quantitative measure of the degree of random copolymerization in all cases but whenever similar molecular are used the value does give a good indication of the extent to which a polymer of at least two monomeric moieties is produced by random copolymerization.

The polymeric compositions of the method are therefore elastomeric ethylene-propylene- diene monomer terpolymers having a relatively high degree of random polymerization, i.e., a high degree of "randomness." To the elastomeric terpolymers may be added a variety of the conventional additives for this type of polymer including stabilizers, antioxidants, fillers, colorants, processing aids and mold release agents. The ethylene-propylene-diene monomer terpolymers are processable by conventional methods such as extrusion and injection molding and have established utility as a precursor of shaped parts such as automotive and electrical housings, wire and cable coatings, as construction materials and in blending applications with other polymers. The terpolymers are also crosslinked or vulcanized by reaction with conventional sulfur species. Because of the high degree of random polymerization the terpolymers are less blocky and less crystalline and more easily processable at lower processing temperatures.

An olefin polymerization procatalyst precursor was prepared by dropwise addition of a trimethoxysilane-stabilized 12% solution of magnesium methoxide in methanol to a solution of 0.5 equivalent of 2-metholresorcinol in methanol. The precursor was a crystalline compound of the formula

$$Mg_4(OCH_3)_6(CH_3OH)_{10}[1,3—(O,OH)—2—CH_3—C_6H_3]_2.$$

Partial azeotropic desolvation of this precursor was conducted by slurrying 40 g of the precursor in 300 g of cyclohexane containing 120 g of tetramethoxysilane and boiling the resulting mixture until a 20%-30% decrease in volume had occured.

The olefin polymerization procatalyst was prepared by stirring 7.8 g of the partially desolvated procatalyst precursor with 2.5 ml (8.7 mmol) of diisobutyl phthalate in 200 ml of a 50/50 by volume solution of titanium tetrachloride and chlorobenzene for 1 hour at 115° C. The resulting solids were collected by filtering the solid-containing mixture while hot. The solids were treated with two washes at 115° C. with fresh 200 ml portions of the 50/50 solution, followed by a rinse of less than 10 minutes with 100 ml of fresh 50/50 solution. The solids were then washed once with isooctane at 90° C., twice with isooctane at room temperature, and were then dried under flowing nitrogen at 40° C. The titanium content of the resulting solids was 2.72% by weight. A portion of the dry procatalyst was then made into a 5% by weight slurry in mineral oil.

A number of EPDM terpolymers were produced by using a catalyst prepared from the procatalyst slurry of Illustrative Embodiment I, triethylaluminum (TEA) as a 0.28M solution in isooctane and 2,6-lutidine as the selectivity control agent (SCA). For comparison purposes, a comparative catalyst (CC) was produced using diisobutyldimethoxysilane as the selectivity control agent.

The catalyst components were mixed in a TEA/SCA/Ti molar ratio of 0.70/0.20/0.01 and allowed to stand at ambient temperature for 20 minutes. The mixture was then injected into 2.7 liters of liquid propylene in a 1-gallon stainless steel autoclave also containing ethylene and diene termonomer. During polymerization, ethylene was added to the autoclave in a steady, continuous flow. The autoclave was then maintained at 60° C. for 90 minutes with continuous stirring and ethylene flow. The reactor was then cooled and the remaining propylene flashed. The resulting polymer was an amorphous solid. It was cut into small pieces and dried in air overnight and then for several hours under aspirator vacuum at 80° C.

Maleic anhydride grafted EPDM

Maleic anhydride grafted EPDM reacts with the matrix resin, typically nylon, to become its own compatibilizer. This type of modifier provides for excellent balance in impact, hardness, modulus, and tensile strength and is the major additive component of "super tough" nylon.

Preparation

Mixing of the maleic anhydride and copolymers can be by blending molten anhydride with copolymer in an internal mixer or extruder, or by blending finely divided dry maleic anhydride with copolymer on a well-ventilated rubber mill with concurrent or subsequent heating, such as in a hot press or mold. Temperatures necesary to achieve thermal grafting are sufficiently high to dehydrate maleic acid, forming maleic anhydride in situ. Thus, maleic acid can be compounded with the copolymer instead of maleic anhydride when such is desired. The maleic anhydride can be substituted with groups, such as bromine or chlorine, which do not unduly interfere with the graft reaction.

Preferred copolymers of ethylene, propylene, and 1,4-hexadiene are very resistant to free radical formation under high shear stress conditions and are readily mixed on conventional bulk processing equipment without gel formation Care must be exercised, however, in selecting the mixing conditions for copolymers derived from strained ring dienes such as ethylidene norbornene. Such copolymers will readily generate free radicals when sheared at low temperatures, and are preferably mixed with maleic anhydride at high temperature, such as above 90° C. to avoid appreciable gel formation.

It is generally desired to form adducts containing about 0.5 to 9 percent, and preferably about 1 to 4 percent, by weight maleic anhydride. Adducts containing such quantities of maleic anhydride have sufficient carboxylated sites for ionic curing or grafting of the copolymer. To achieve a desired degree of adduct formation within a reasonable time, high concentrations of reactants are helpful. One will generally select a polymer having about twice the amount of side-chain unsaturation as is stoichiometrically required for the desired amount of maleic anhydride incorporation. Similarly, about twice as much maleic anhydride is added as is desired in the polymer adduct. Conversion of about 40 to 50 percent of the maleic anhydride will result in copolymer adduct having the desired compositions. For example, if one desires to obtain an ethylene/ propylene/1,4-hexadiene copolymer having 2.2 weight percent maleic anhydride content, he could conveniently mix a copolymer having 0.49 moles side-chain unsaturation per kilogram of polymer with 0.49 moles maleic anhydride and heat the mixture to about 45 percent of the anhydride, thereby obtaining the desired product.

Unreacted maleic anhydride is conveniently removed from the adduct by extraction with water. During washing, a portion of grafted maleic anhydride (now a succinic anhydride) is hydrolyzed to grafted succinic acid. When the polymer adduct is used to prepare a thermoplastic elastomer, it is not necessary to regenerate the anhydride groups.

If desired, the anhydride groups are readily regenerated by heating while removing evolved water vapor. The heating can conveniently be accomplished while subjecting the graft polymers to mechanical shearing which generates at least a portion of the required heat. For instance, the graft copolymer can be processed on a rubber mill at 120° C. to regenerate anhydride groups. Alternatively, anhydride groups can conveniently be regenerated by heating sheets of the graft copolymer overnight at 115° C. in a vacuum oven. Higher heating temperatures expedite regeneration.

Unreacted maleic anhydride can also be removed from the copolymer/ maleic anhydride adduct by dissolving the adduct in a solvent which will not dissolve maleic anhydride. Such as hexane, decanting the solution, and recovering the adduct from solution. Alternatively, both adduct and unreacted maleic anhydride are dissolved in a mutual solvent, such as tetrahydrofuran,followed by precipitation of the adduct with a nonsolvent such as anhydrous acetone. Unreacted maleic anhydride remains in the acetone/ tetrahydrofuran solution.

The adducts of this method have a substantially saturated hydrocarbon backbone chain and have an inherent vicosity of at least 1.0, preferably at least 1.5, as measured on 0.1 gram graft copolymer dissolved in 100 milliliters of perchloroethylene at 30° C. The adducts have a gel content less than 5 percent, and generally less than 2 percent, as measured by weight percent adduct which is insoluble in boiling tetrahydrofuran at atmospheric pressure after 48 hours. Low gel content indicates that the adducts can readily be blended with agents such as carbon black, antioxidants, etc., using standard equipment such as a rubber mill or extruder.

The adducts have special utility in preparation of thermoplastic elastomers. In such applications the adduct is compounded with a metal salt of a weak acid and then heated to form salt aggregates between adduct molecules.

Preferred metal salt curing agents are divalent Group II A or B metal salts of weak acids. Included in this preferred group are metal oxides, such as magnesium or preferably zinc oxide, and metal salts of weak carboxylic acids, phenoxides, and â-diketonates such as calcium catecholate and magnesium acetylacetonate. Metal salts of other groups may be selected. For example, the curing agent can be sodium acetate, potassium carbonate, copper acetylacetonate, tetraisobutyltitanate, tin octoate, lead acetylacetonate, chromium acetylacetonate, nickel acetylacetonate, aluminum acetylacetonate or iron acetylacetonate.

The adduct curing rate will vary with the particular adduct, curing agent, curing temperature, intimacy of contact between adduct and curing agent, and whether the adduct cure sites are anhydride groups or carboxylic acid groups formed by opening the anhydride groups. While the curing agent will form salt aggregates with anhydride group cure sites, high temperatures such as 250° C.

are generally required to accomplish curing within a reasonable time.

More favorable curing times and temperatures can be selected, and generally a better cure can be obtained, when the grafted anhydride groups are open to make carboxylic acid groups available for curing. Compounds which perform this ring-opening function have an active hydrogen atom and are defined herein as accelerators.

Water is an excellent accelerator. In combination with metal oxide curing agents, organic acids (such as stearic acid, acetic acid, salicyclic acid, benzoic acid, and oleic acid) are also excellent accelerators since they produce water in situ during the neutralization as well as provide solubilization of the cation as discussed hereinafter. Amino acids (such as 11-aminoundecanoic acid, 6-aminohexanoic acid, and 4-aminobutyric acid) are especially preferred as they convert small residual amounts of unreacted maleic anhydride to innocuous form, removing the practical requirement that unreacted maleic anhydride be eliminated from the adduct piror to further processing. Other compounds useful as accelerator include mercaptans, thiols, phenols, alcohols, and amines.

Polyfunctional accelerators, such as diamines, are generally avoided when a thermoplastic product is desired since they may permanently cross-link the adduct, forming an intractable product.

Accelerator may be introduced in a variety of ways. For instance, the adduct gradually absorbs sufficient water vapor to cause curing, in the presence of a curing agent, even at ambient temperatures. But the quantity of water absorbed is dependent on time and temperature, long times are required for favorable curing, and adduct compositions cured in this manner do not possess predictable tensile properties.

More consistent and rapid curing is obtained by exposing compounded adduct and curing agent to a controlled atmosphere of accelerator such as steam or ammonia vapor. Alternatively, the compounded adduct can be immersed in liquid accelerator such as aqueous potassium hydroxide or ammonia. Preferably, liquid or solid accelerator is compounded with the adduct. Compounding is conveniently performed on a rubber mill or in an internal mixer concurrent with the compounding of adduct and curing agent.

Selection of optimum quantities of curing agent is within the skill of the art. The optimum quantity will vary with the metal and counterion of the curing agent, and with the nature of the accelerator. Generally, 100 percent neutralization is avoided when the only available anion for the metal is the grafted polymer carboxylate anion since intractable product can be formed. By "100 per cent neutralization" is meant formation of salt aggregates at all available curing sites.

Most curing agents are not soluble in the adduct to any appreciable extent and only a small percent of the curing agent is actually involved in curing. Unreacted curing agent generally does not greatly affect room temperature tensile properties of the cured adduct, and consequently, greater than stoichiometric quantities of curing agent are used. More efficient curing is obtained when a complexing ion is present which solubilizes the metal cation of the curing agent. For example, stearic acid may be used in conjunction with zinc oxide to greatly reduce the quantity of zinc oxide required to achieve desired tensile properties. The stearic acid acts both as an accelerator and a a solubilizing agent for the zinc cation.

Especially favorable results are obtained when compounds such as zinc acetate dihydrate, hydrated zinc acetylacetone, and hydrated zinc catecholate are used alone as a curing agent or together with zinc oxide as an accelerator. Such compounds provide water as an acclerator and also help solubilize zinc oxide. When the counterion of zinc is not volatile at curing temperatures, or when a nonvolatile anion such as the anion of stearic acid is also present, it has been found that thermoplastic elastomeric adducts are prepared even at 100 percent neutralization.

Optimum curing conditions can readily be determined for a particular formulation of adduct, curing agent, and accelerator by testing tensile properties obtained over a range of curing times and temperature. For adducts of maleic anhydride and ethylene/propylene/1,4-hexadiene copolymer, excellent cures are obtained within 30 minutes at 160° C. using 4 phr. zinc acetate with a promoter, hydrated zinc catecholate alone or in combination with zinc oxide, or zinc oxide with 4-aminobutyric acid or 11-aminoundecanoic acid. When zinc oxide with stearic acid promoter is selected for curing, equivalent cures are obtained when the curing time is extended at 160° C., although the cure is less reliable in that it depends somewhat on the heat history of the adduct. Hot mixing of the adduct and curing agents has been found to be especially beneficial in expediting cure times.

Conventional additives such as carbon black and processing oils may be compounded with the adduct prior to, concurrent, or subsequent to the compounding with the divalent metal salt of a weak acid. Antioxidants should be added if the thermoplastic elastomer will be exposed to prolonged high temperature usage.

Adducts so cured possess tensile properties comparable to those achieved by conventional sulfur-curing techniques. They are thermoplastic materials and can readily be reshaped by heating to temperatures above about 180° C. Such thermoplastic elastomers can be processed in known manner, such as by extrusion or molding, to form films, hoses, and other useful articles of commerce such as gaskets.

The adducts may also be permanently cross-linked by polyfunctional curing agents, such as diamines, to prepare an elastomer which may be used in place of conventional sulfur cured EPDM rubbers. Thus, the irreversibly cured adduct may be used in the manufacture of hoses, gaskets, shock absorbers, and the like.

In addition, the uncured adduct has readily available carboxylated sites which can be used for grafting of functional groups to the elastomeric copolymer for special applications.

In the process that follow all proportions, parts, and percentages are by weight unless otherwise indicated, and all testing is at 25° C. in accordance with ASTM standards unless otherwise indicated. Gel content is that portion of the graft copolymer, in percent, which is insoluble in boiling tetrahydrofuran at atmospheric pressure after 48 hours.

Copolymer EPHD used in the examples has a Mooney (ML-1+4/121° C.) viscosity of about 35 and the following monomer unit composition: ethylene, 61.4 weight percent; propylene, 32 weight percent, 1,4-hexadiene, 6.6 weight percent. The copolymer has about 0.5 gram mole of ethylenic unsaturation per kilogram of copolymer. The Wallace plasticity is about 28 at 100° C. The inherent viscosity, as measured on 0.1 gram copolymer EPHD dissolved in 100 milliliters of perchloroethylene at 30° C., is about 2.0.

Process

A Werner and Pfleider 53 mm twin screw extruder is assembled by end-to-end attachment of 16 barrel sections of 1/2 inch dimeter. Following a short feed section are four reaction sections (zones 1-4), one vacuum port section (zone 5), a cooling section (zone 6), and a die section. Provisions are made for the metering of molten maleic anhydride at the forward part of zone 1. The screws are composed of kneading blocks, reverse pitch screws, and transport screws arranged to generate100-200 psi pressure in zones 1-4 and no pressure in zone 5. The free volume of zones 1-5 is equivalent to two pounds of polymer at operating temperature. Zones 1-4 are preheated to 300° C., zone 5 to 260° C., and zone 6, the cross-head, and the die to 150° C.

Copolymer EPHD is fed to the extruder in the form of chips which pass a 1/2 inch screen. Maleic anhydride is metered to the extruder at an average feed rate of 4.8 percent of the polymer weight. The screw speed is 12 rpm and the vacuum port is operated at about 25 inches Hg.

The product, extruded at the rate of 6.15 lb/hr., has a maleic anhydride content of 2.23 percent as determined by a calibrated infrared method and 2.19 percent by weight as determined by titration in tetrahydrofuran with 0.1 M tetrabutylammonium hydroxide in methanol. Wallace plasticity of the product is 32 and gel content is less than about 5 per cent.

Following purification of a small sample by solution in tetrahydeofuran and precipitation with anhydrous acetone, the maleic anhydride content is 2.19 percent and 2.05 percent by weight, respectively, by infrared and titration determination. The gel content is less than about 5 percent. The inherent viscosity is 1.5 as measured on 0.1 gram of adduct dissolved in 100 milliliters of perchloroethylene at 30° C.

Suppliers

There are over 30 suppliers of impact modifiers worldwide. Most concentrate their efforts in one type of modifier as a result of their developed technologies and backward integration. Selected suppliers resell other producers' technologies in their home regions

TABLE 10.3: Selected Impact Modifier Suppliers

Supplier	Type					
	Acrylic	ABS/MBS/ MABS	EVA	EPR/ EPDM	CPE	Other
Baerlocher	×	—	—	—	—	—
Bayer	—	×	×	—	—	—
Chisso	—	—	×	—	—	—
DSM Copolymer	—	—	—	×	×	—
Dupont/Dow Elastomers	—	—	×	×	×	—
Elf Atochem	×	×	—	—	—	×
Exxon	—	—	—	×	×	×
GE Specialty Chemicals	—	×	—	—	—	—
Huels	—	—	—	—	×	—
JSR	—	—	—	—	—	×
Kaneka	—	×	—	—	—	×
Kureha	—	—	—	—	—	×
Mitsubishi Rayon	—	—	—	—	—	×
Mitsui Petrochemical	—	—	—	—	—	×
Nippon Zeon	—	—	×	—	—	×

Osaka Soda	—	—	—	—	×	—
Polysar	—	—	—	×	—	—
Rohm and Haas	×	×	—	—	—	—
Shell	—	—	—	—	—	×
Showa Denko K.K.	—	—	—	—	×	—
Sumitomo Chemical	—	×	—	×	—	—
Toyo Soda	—	—	—	×	—	—
Ube Cycon	—	×	—	—	—	—
Uniroyal	—	—	—	×	—	×

to broaden their product lines Rohm and Haas, Kaneka, and Atochem are the leading suppliers of impact modifiers worldwide. Each has strong positions in both the acrylic and MBS-related modifiers. Elf Atochem is stronger in acrylics, while Kaneka is stronger in MBS types. Rohm and Haas, including its joint venture with Kureha in the Asia/Pacific region, has a more balanced position. Table 10.3 presents the major global suppliers of impact modifiers by type.

Trends and Forecasts

The need for cost-effective materials that are strong, stiff, and ductile will continue to increase. In many cases the key to success will be the development of tailored impact modifier systems for specific resins. The EPDM market will probably see a decline over the next couple of years due to the advent of reactor-generated polypropylene. This material incorporates the impact modifier in the polymer chain and does not require a secondary compounding operation. The MBS market is decreasing partially due to PVC bottles being replaced by PET. This trend is more evident in Europe due to widespread use of water bottles. In contrast, the film and sheet market remain strong. Overall, MBS sales are heavily dependent on the future of PVC, particularly flexible PVC. Flexible PVC, comprising 15% of the total PVC market, is vulnerable to penetration by metallocene catalyzed polyolefins (for example, "super soft polypropylene"). Acrylic impact modifiers will continue to grow with the growth of rigid PVC in the construction market. Product development in this market will target improved low-temperature impact properties to reduce failures, lengthen the installation season, and lower cost.

A significant area for product development is the impact modification of engineering plastics. The replacement of such conventional materials as metal, glass, and wood by plastics has been underway for years. The applications are typically converted to engineering plastics and then lost to lower-cost polyolefins and/or vinyl type materials. Most of the "easy" applications have already converted to plastic. The remaining ones, particularly in durable goods, require new levels of strength and impact performance. Consumption of impact modifiers worldwide is projected to grow at 5%/year over the next 5 years.

11

Light Stabilizers

DESCRIPTION

Light stabilizers are used to protect plastics, particularly polyolefins, from discoloration, embrittlement, and eventual degradation by UV light. The three major classes of light stabilizers are UV absorbers, excited state quenchers, and free-radical terminators. Each class is named for the mechanism by which it prevents degradation. The major types included in each light stabilizer class may be categorized by their chemistries, as shown in Table 11.1.

BENZOPHENONE

Benzophenone UV absorbers are mature products and have been used for many years in polyolefins, PVC, and other resins. These products also have wide use in cosmetic preparations as sunscreens and protectants.

Preparation:

Method 1

95.7 g of finely pulverised aluminium chloride are suspended in 180 ml of absolute methylene chloride. While stirring and cooling, 35 g of 5-methoxybenzocyclobutene-1-carboxylic acid methyl ester, dissolved in a small amount of methylene chloride, are added dropwise in such a manner that the temperature remains below 30°C.

TABLE 11.1: Major Types of Light Stabilizers

Type	Representative chemistry
UV light absorbers	
Benzophenone	2-hydroxy-4-methoxybenzophenone
	2-hydroxy-4-*n*-octoxybenzophenone
	2,4-dihydroxy-4-*n*-dodecycloxybenzophenone
Benzotriazole	2,2-(2-hydroxy-5-tert-octylphenyl) benzotriazole
	2-(32 -tert-butyl-2-hydroxy-5-methylphenyl)-5-chlorobenzotriazole
	2-(32 ,52 -di-tert-butyl-22 -hydroxyphenyl)-52 - chlorobenzotriazole
	2-(22 hydroxy-32 -52 -di-tert amyl phenyl) benzotriazole
	2-(2-hydroxy-5-methylphenyl) benzotriazole
Phenyl esters	3,5-di-t-butyl-4hydroxybenzoic acid
	N-hexadecyl ester
Diphenylacrylates	Ethyl-2-cyano-3,3-diphenyl acrylate
	2-ethylhexyl-2-cyano-3,3-diphenyl acrylate
Excited state quenchers	
Nickel compounds	Nickel dibutyldithiocarbamate
	2,22 -thiobis (4-octylphenolato)-*n*-butylamine nickel II
Free-radical terminators	
Hindered amine light stabilizers (HALS)	Bis (2,2,6,6-tetramethyl-4-piperidinyl) *N,N*-bis(2,2,6,6-tetramethyl-4-piperidinyl)-1,6-hexane diamine polymer with 2,4,6-trichloro-1,3,5 triazine and 2,4,4-trimethyl-1,2-pentanamine

At the same temperature, 50.5 g of benzoyl chloride are added dropwise thereto and the whole is subsequently heated at reflux for 4 hours. After cooling, the reaction mixture is poured onto 600 g of ice. The organic phase is separated off and the aqueous phase is extracted 3 times with 150 ml of methylene chloride each time.

The combined organic phases are washed once with 250 ml of water, dried over magnesium sulphate and concentrated by evaporation. The excess benzoyl chloride is distilled off under a high vacuum and the residue is crystallised from ether/petroleum ether. 4-benzoyl-5-hydroxybenzocyclobutene-1-carboxylic acid methyl ester is obtained in the form of yellow crystals having a melting point of 75°-76° C.

Method 2

14 g of 4-benzoyl-5-hydroxybenzocyclobutene-1-carboxylic acid methyl ester are dissolved in 150 ml of ether and the solution is added to 62 ml of 2N aqueous sodium hydroxide solution and 25 ml of water. This mixture is vigorously stirred for 1 hour at room temperature. The ether phase is separated off and extracted once with 75 ml of water. The aqueous phase is washed once with 75 ml of ether. The combined aqueous phases are rendered acidic with 2N aqueous hydrochloric acid and extracted 3 times with 100 ml of methylene chloride each time. The combined methylene chloride extracts are dried over magnesium sulphate and concentrated by evaporation. Crystallisation of the residue from ether/petroleum ether yields 4-benzoyl-5-hydroxybenzocyclobutene-1-carboxylic acid in the form of yellow crystals having a melting point of 167°-169° C.

Method 3

26.6 g of finely pulverised aluminium chloride are suspended in 60 ml of methylene chloride. While stirring and while cooling slightly, 9.61 g of 5-methoxybenzocyclobutene-1-carboxylic acid methyl ester, dissolved in a small amount of methylene chloride, are added dropwise at room temperature. After stirring for 30 minutes at room temperature, 15.85 g of o-fluorobenzoyl chloride are added dropwise thereto and the resulting reaction mixture is heated at reflux for 4 hours. After cooling, the reaction mixture is poured onto ice and extracted thoroughly with methylene chloride. The combined organic phases are washed with water, dried over magnesium sulphate and concentrated by evaporation. The yellow oily residue (20 g) is chromatographed over 400 g of silica gel with methylene chloride. Fractions 7-16 (50 ml fractions) are combined and concentrated. The residue is crystallised from ether/ petroleum ether. 4-(o-fluorobenzoyl)-5-hydroxybenzocyclobutene-1-carboxylic acid methyl ester is obtained in the form of yellow crystals having a melting point of 59°-61° C.

Method 4

12.1 g of 4-(m-chlorobenzoyl)-5-hydroxybenzocyclobutene- 1-carboxylic acid methyl ester are dissolved in 120 ml of ether; 100 ml of 2N aqueous sodium hydroxide solution are added and the whole is stirred well for 15 minutes at room temperature. The ether phase is separated off and washed with water. The strongly yellow-coloured aqueous phase is washed with ether. The combined aqueous phases are rendered acidic with concentrated hydrochloric acid and extracted thoroughly with methylene chloride. The combined methylene chloride extracts are dried over magnesium sulphate and concentrated by evaporation. Crystallisation of the residue from ether/petroleum ether yields 4-(m-chlorobenzoyl)-5-hydroxybenzocyclobutene-1-carboxylic acid in the form of yellow crystals having a melting point of 138°-139° C.

Method 5

28.26 g of aluminium trichloride are suspended in 70 ml of dichloromethane and, over a period of 15 minutes, 10.19 g of 5-methoxybenzocyclobutene-1-carboxylic acid methyl ester are added dropwise at from 20° to 30°. Stirring is carried out for 30 minutes, 20.8 g of m-methylthiobenzoyl chloride are added dropwise over a period of 20 minutes and the whole is stirred for 4 hours at room temperature, poured into a mixture of 200 g of ice, 20 ml of concentrated hydrochloric acid and 200 ml of water, stirred for 30 minutes and extracted by shaking twice with 50 ml of dichloromethane each time and once with 50 ml of a mixture of trichloromethane and methanol (3:1). The organic phases are combined, washed twice with water, dried over magnesium sulphate, treated with kieselguhr and concentrated by evaporation. Chromatography over silica gel using hexane/ethyl acetate (4:1) as eluant yields 4-(m-methylthiobenzoyl)-5-hydroxybenzocycl-obutene-1-carboxyl ic acid methyl ester in the form of a yellow oil.

Method 6

In a manner analogous to that described in Method 5, starting from 37.12 g of aluminium trichloride, 13.42 g of 5-methoxy-benzocyclobutene-1-carboxylic acid methyl ester and 26.05 g of o-methylthiobenzoyl chloride there is obtained 4-(o-methylthi-obenzoyl)-5-hydroxybenzocyclobutene-1-carboxyl ic acid methyl ester in the form of a viscous yellow oil.

Method 7

In a manner analogous to that described in Method 5, starting from 26.6 g of aluminium trichloride, 9.61 g of 5-methoxybenzo-cyclobutene-1-carboxylic acid methyl ester and 17.56 g of p-cyanobenzoyl chloride there is obtained 4-(p-cyanobenzoyl)-5-hydroxybenzocyclobutene-1-carboxylic acid methyl ester having a melting point of 113°-114° C.

Method 8

In a manner analogous to that described in Method 5, starting from 26.6 g of aluminium trichloride, 9.61 g of 5-methoxy-benzocyclobutene-1-carboxylic acid methyl ester and 20.95 g of 2,4-dichlorobenzoyl chloride there is obtained 4-(2,4-dichloro-benzoyl)-5-hydroxybenzocyclobutene-1-carboxyl ic acid methyl ester having a melting point of 99°-100° C.

Method 9

In a manner analogous to that described in Method 5, starting from 26.6 g of aluminium trichloride, 9.61 g of 5-methoxy-benzo-cyclobutene-1-carboxylic acid methyl ester and 20.95 g of 3,4-dichlorobenzoyl chloride there is obtained 4-(3,4-dichlorobenzoyl)-5-hydroxybenzocyclobutene-1-carboxyl ic acid methyl ester having a melting point of 95°-96° C.

Method 10

5.71 g of 4-(o-methylthiobenzoyl)-5-hydroxybenzocyclobutene-1-carboxyl ic acid methyl ester are dissolved in 70 ml of ether; 45 ml of 2N sodium hydroxide solution are added and stirring is carried out for 1 hour at room temperature. The aqueous phase is separated off and the ether phase is extracted by shaking twice with 25 ml of water each time. The aqueous phases are combined, acidified with 2N hydrochloric acid and extracted three times with 50 ml of dichloromethane each time. The extracts are combined, washed with water, dried over magnesium sulphate and concentrated by evaporation. After recrystallisation of the residue from dichloromethane/hexane, 4-(o-methylthiobenzoyl)-5-hydroxybenzo-cyclobutene-1-carboxyl ic acid is obtained having a melting point of 177°-178° C.

Method 11

In a manner analogous to that described in Method 10, starting from 4.9 g of 4-(m-methylthiobenzoyl)-5-hydroxybenzocyclobutene-1-carboxylic acid methyl ester there is obtained 4-(m-methyl-thiobenzoyl)-5-hydroxybenzocyclobutene- 1-carboxylic acid having a melting point of 122°-124° C.

Method 12

3.0 g of 4-(α-hydroxybenzyl)-5-hydroxybenzocyclobutene-1-carboxylic acid are dissolved in 30 ml of dichloromethane and over a period of 10 minutes, while stirring, 30 g of pyridinium dichromate in 100 ml of dichloromethane are added dropwise thereto. Stirring is then carried out for 7 hours at room temperature, and the mixture is decanted off from the black residue, filtered over silica gel, concentrated to dryness by evaporation and crystallised from ether/hexane. 4-benzoyl-5-hydroxybenzocyclobutene-1-carboxylic acid is obtained having a melting point of 167°-169° C.

The starting material can be manufactured, as follows:

3.84 g of 5-methoxybenzocyclobutene-1-carboxylic acid methyl ester are dissolved in 20 ml of dichloromethane, the whole is cooled to 0° C and there are added dropwise thereto at from 0° to 5° C firstly 3.16 g of titanium tetrachloride over a period of 3 minutes and then 3.83 g of dichlorodimethyl ether (Cl_2CHOCH_3) over a period of 20 minutes. The whole is then stirred for 5 minutes at from 0° to 5° C, gradually heated to room temperature and then stirred for 15 minutes at 35° C. The mixture is then left to cool to room temperature and poured onto 25 g of ice; the organic phase is separated off, the aqueous phase is then shaken three times with 10 ml of dichloromethane each time and the organic phases are combined, washed three times with 15 ml of ice-water each time, dried over magnesium sulphate, concentrated to dryness by evaporation and chromatographed over silica gel using dichloromethane as eluant. 4-formyl-5-methoxybenzocyclobutene-1-carboxylic acid methyl ester is obtained in the form of a colourless oil.

1.6 g thereof are dissolved in 25 ml of ether; 19 ml of 2N sodium hydroxide solution are added and the whole is stirred vigorously for 20 minutes at room temperature. The ether phase is separated off and the aqueous phase is acidified slightly with 2N hydrochloric acid, extracted by shaking twice with 50 ml each time of a mixture of dichloromethane and ethyl acetate (4:1), washed with a small amount of ice-water, dried over magnesium sulphate and concentrated to dryness by evaporation. 4-formyl-5-methoxybenzocyclobutene-1-carboxylic acid is obtained in the form of a yellowish oil.

0.91 g thereof is dissolved in 5 ml of tetrahydrofuran and the solution is added dropwise to a freshly prepared, boiling solution of phenylmagnesium bromide (prepared from 0.39 g of magnesium and 2.51 g of bromobenzene in 10 ml of tetrahydrofuran). The whole is heated at reflux while stirring for 90 minutes, left to cool to room temperature and there are added thereto 20 g of ice and then saturated ammonium chloride solution until the turbidity disappears. The organic phase is separated off and the aqueous phase is extracted by shaking twice with ethyl acetate. The organic phases are combined, washed in succession with 40 % sodium bisulphite solution, saturated sodium bicarbonate solution and water, dried over magnesium sulphate and concentrated by evaporation. 4-(á-hydroxybenzyl)-5-methoxybenzocyclobutene-1-carboxylic acid is obtained which has a melting point of 143°-146° and which can be converted in a manner analogous to that described in Example 20 into 4-(á-hydroxybenzyl)-5-hydroxybenzocyclobutene-1-carboxylic acid.

Benzotriazole

Benzotriazole UV absorbers are highly effective in hightemperature resins such as acrylics and polycarbonate. They also find extensive use in areas outside plastics such as coatings.

Preparation

A mixture of 2.0 g (10 mmol) of 6,6-difluoro-[1,3]dioxolo[4,5-f]-1H- benzotriazole and 40 ml of absolute tetrahydrofuran is admixed at room temperature, with stirring, with 0.3 g (10 mmol) of sodium hydride (80% pure) and is then stirred for 10 minutes at room temperature. 1.9 g (10 mmol) of 3,5-dimethylisoxazole-4-sulphonyl chloride are then added and the mixture is stirred for 16 hours at 60° C. For work-up, the reaction mixture is poured into 20 ml of water. The resulting mixture is extracted twice, each time with 50 ml of ethyl acetate. The combined organic phases are dried over sodium sulphate and concentrated under reduced pressure. The remaining residue is chromatographed on silica gel with methylene chloride as mobile phase. 2.7 g (75% of theory) of 1-(3,5-dimethylisoxazole-4-sulphonyl)-6,6-difluoro-[1,3]diox olo[4,5-f]-benzotriazole are obtained in this manner in the form of a colourless solid of melting point 120-123° C.

Benzoates and Salicylates

Benzoates and salicylates such as 3,5-di-tbutyl-4hydroxy-benzoic acid n-hexadecyl ester, function by rearranging to 2-hydroxybenzophenone analogs when exposed to UV light to perform as UV absorbers.

Nickel Organic Complexes

Nickel organic complexes protect against degradation caused by UV light via excited state quenching. These deactivating metal ion quenchers stop the energy before it can break any molecular bonds and generate free radicals. Nickel complexes are primarily used in polyolefin fiber applications. Some examples of nickel complexes are nickel dibutyldithiocarbamate and 2,22 thiobis (4-octylphenolato)-n-butylamine nickel II which are also used in agricultural film because of their resistance to pesticides.

Preparation

Poly(2-vinylpyridine) powder was prepared at about 50°-70°C from a 90:10 by weight mixture of 2-vinylpyridine and commercial divinylbenzene using azo-bis-isobutyronitrile as a catalyst yielding a heavily crosslinked solid polymer having a molecular weight in excess of one million.

Two grams of this powder were added to a 125 milliliter flask. To this flask was also added 30 milliliters of ethylene glycol monomethyl ether.

To another flask was added 0.24 grams of nickel dichloride hexahydrate and 15 milliliters of ethylene glycol monomethyl ether. When all of the nickel salt had dissolved, this solution was added to the flask with the polymer. It was then warmed with stirring for about 15 minutes and then filtered. The solid was then dried for four hours at 140°C while at 0.1-0.25 mm. A dry, dark blue powder was recovered

A 0.5 gram quantity of the above-prepared nickel- complexed solid polymer was charged into a dry 7-ounce reaction flask together with 20 milliliters of chlorobenzene. Propylene was pressured in at 5 psig and 3 milliliters of a one molar solution of ethylaluminum dichloride and chlorobenzene was added. The reaction was allowed to proceed at essentially room temperature for about 45 minutes with stirring. An additional 3 milliliters of the ethylaluminum dichloride solution had been added after 10 minutes of the reaction period.

The reaction was stopped by the addition of 20 milliliters of water. The organic layer was decanted and distilled, yielding 18.3 grams of C 6 olefins. A sample of the olefin dimer product was hydrogenated and then analyzed by gas-liquid chromatography showing the presence of 69.0 weight percent 2-methylpentane, 26.8 weight percent n-hexane, 3.4 weight percent of 2,3-dimethylbutane, and 0.8 weight percent 3-methylpentane.

This run demonstrates that the solid catalyst system of this invention is very effective for the dimerization of propylene to hexenes.

Hindered Amine Light Stabilizers (HALS)

Hindered amine light stabilizers are the newest type of UV light stabilizer. They were introduced in 1975 by Ciba and Sankyo. HALS do not screen ultraviolet light, but stabilize the resin via free-radical termination. HALS are used at lower levels than benzophenones and benzotriazoles, and are widely used in polyolefins for their cost-effectiveness and performance. The successful growth of HALS has been directly related to their substitution for benzophenones and benzotriazoles in many applications as well as their blending with benzophenones

Preparation

Method I: Attachment of N-(2,2,6,6-tetramethyl-4-piperidinyl-N'-aminooxamide to Octadecene-Maleic Anhydride Copolymer

Into a 1.5 liter jacketed reactor were added 18.15 g of PA-18 (octadecene-maleic anhydride copolymer) and 200 grams of xylene. The reactor was equipped with a Teflon mechanical stirrer, Dean Stark trap and reflux condenser, thermometer and nitrogen sparge. The mixture was heated to reflux by circulating hot oil through the reactor jacket while passing nitrogen through the hot solution. To the hot solution was slowly added 10.0 grams (0.04 mole) of N-(2,2,6,6-tetramethyl-4-piperidinyl)-N'-aminooxamide (Reactive Stabilizer A). The neck of the flask was rinsed down with an additional 80 grams of xylene and the reaction mixture azeotroped for 21/2 hours. A small sample of the solution was withdrawn at this point and placed on infrared (IR) salt plates and an IR scan run. The IR scan showed the anhydride band at 1780 cm^{-1} has been almost completely converted to an imide band at 1740 cm^{-1} indicating the reaction was essentially completed. The reaction mixture was cooled and discharged into a liter of methanol. A white precipitate formed. The white precipitate was filtered off, washed with fresh methanol, and dried in a vacuum oven at 50° C overnight.

Method II : Attachment of 3-(2,2,6,6-tetramethyl-4-piperidinylamino)propionhydrazide to Octadecene-Maleic Anhydride Copolymer

Into a 500 ml 3-neck round bottom flask was added 80 grams of xylene. The flask was equipped with a magnetic stirrer, thermometer, nitrogen sparge, Dean Stark trap, and reflux condenser. The flask was placed in an oil bath and warmed to about 80° C. Then 10.3 grams of PA-18 (octadecene-maleic anhydride copolymer) were added and the mixture was heated to

130° C. to dissolve the polymer. To the the hot solution was slowly added 6.0 grams (0.024 mole) of 95% 3-(2,2,6,6-tetramethyl-4-piperidinylamino)propionhydrazide (Reactive Stabilizer F). The reaction was sparged with nitrogen and the neck of the flask rinsed down with an additional 30 grams of xylene. The reaction mixture was heated to reflux and azeotroped for 2 hours. The reaction was monitored by withdrawing small samples of the solution and following the conversion of the anhydride band at 1780 cm^{-1} to the imide band at 1740 cm^{-1}. Reaction was completed during the two hour period and the solution was cooled and precipitated into a liter of methanol. The precipitated polymer was filtered, washed with fresh methanol, and dried in a vacuum oven at 50° C overnight. The dry product weighed 12.13 g.

Method III: Attachment of Hydrazido Substituted Hindered Amine Light Stabilizers to Maleic Anhydride Copolymers

The indicated equivalents of copolymer (based on maleic anhydride) were weighed into a 250 ml 3-neck flask. The flask was equipped with a Dean-Stark trap containing a water cooled reflux condenser, a magnetic stirring bar, thermometer, and ground glass stopper. Approximately 130-150 ml of xylene were added to the flask and the flask was heated in an oil bath to 120°-140° C. The particular HALS hydrazide was slowly added in the indicated amount over 2-5 minutes by momentarily removing the stopper and adding small portions of the hydrazide in short intervals. The reaction mixture was then heated to reflux and the xylene azeotroped for 1-5 hours depending on the reactivity of the particular hydrazide. The reaction was monitored by following the water that azeotroped over in the Dean-Stark trap and by periodically withdrawing samples of the reaction mixture and running infrared spectra on the samples. The conversion of the anhydride peak of the copolymer at 1780 cm^{-1} to the imide peak around 1730-1740 cm^{-1} indicated qualitatively the extent of reaction. After the reflux period was completed, the reaction mixture was cooled below 90° C. If the product was insoluble in the hot xylene, the mixture was filtered; the filter cake was washed with hexane (SMAs) or methanol (PA-18) and air dried on a watch glass. If the product was soluble or partially soluble in the xylene, the xylene was stripped off on a rotary evaporator under reduced pressure. The last portion of xylene was driven off by heating the flask with a heat gun. Upon completion of the stripping, the product was scraped out of the flask and pulverized in a mortar with a pestle. The pulverized product was then dried to a constant weight on a watch glass.

Tg's were determined in some cases on a Perkin Elmer 7 Series Thermal Analysis System DSC using a nitrogen purge and heating at a rate of 20° C./minute.

Method IV: Attachment of Hydrazido Substituted Hindered Amine Light Stabilizers to Dylark™ SMA Copolymers

In these method, the indicated equivalents of a Dylark™ SMA copolymer were slowly added to a hot solution of xylene (130 ml) in a 3-neck 250 ml flask. The flask was equipped with a Dean-Stark trap containing a water cooled reflux condenser, a magnetic stirring bar, thermometer, and ground glass stopper. After all the Dylark had dissolved in the hot solution, the indicated amounts of Jeffamine M-360, if any, were added and allowed to react 15 minutes before adding the indicated HALS hydrazide. In both cases where the Jeffamine M-360 was added, the polymer remained in solution and there was a reduction in the infrared peak at 1780 cm^{-1} (anhydride) and the formation of an imide peak at 1740 cm^{-1}. Upon addition of HALS hydrazides A or G the reaction mixture immediately gelled up while the polymer remained in solution upon addition of the acetylated HALS hydrazide H. All the reactions were refluxed for 2 hours after the addition of the HALS hydrazide, cooled below 50° C. and precipitated into 1 to 11/2 liters of methanol. The methanol-xylene solution was decanted off and the polymer was ground up in 300 ml of fresh methanol in a Waring blender. The polymer was filtered off and air dried on a watch glass overnight. An infrared scan was run on the product to insure the anhydride portion of the copolymer had reacted with the hydrazide portion of the hindered amine light stabilizer.

Method V

Methods were run similar to Method I except the reactor size and amount of xylene used varied with the reaction scale. The PA-18 was diluted with xylene and heated to 120° C. or above. The HALS hydrazide was slowly added to the PA-18 solution by removing the reactor stopper temporarily and adding the hydrazide in small portions. The Hydrazide rapidly reacts with the PA-18 to form the amic acid and then converts over to the imide at a slower rate above 120° C. If the hydrazide is added too quickly or all at once, it forms a very viscous gel of the relatively insoluble amic acid and stirring becomes difficult or impossible. Therefore, it is wise to add the hydrazide over a period of time allowing most of the amic acid that forms to convert over to the imide before adding more hydrazide. The imidization can be monitored by the water that azeotropes over. After the hydrazide addition and the imidization were completed (no more water azeotroping), the xylene solution was cooled below 90° C. The product was isolated by evaporating off the xylene on a rotating evaporator under reduced pressure or by precipitating the product out of the xylene by the addition of 4-5 volumes of methanol and filtering off the precipitated polymer.

Suppliers

There are about 40 suppliers of light stabilizers worldwide. Some of these companies also produce antioxidants and PVC heat stabilizers. Of these 40 or so suppliers, only Ciba Specialty Chemicals is a significant player in every region of the world with the broadest product line of light stabilizers. Selected global suppliers of light stabilizers are given in Table 11.2.

Trends and Forecasts

The entrance of Great Lakes into the European light stabilizer market with a series of acquisitions has been the most significant restructuring that has occurred in the light stabilizer market. This move has accelerated the trend toward a more competitive market in these materials. Growth in the light stabilizer business is strongly dependent on the growth of the polyolefin applications. Polyolefins account for about three-quarters of the total global consumption of light stabilizers in plastics. Polyolefins, particularly PP, are replacing metals, engineering plastics, and styrenics in automotive and other applications, further increasing the volume of stabilizers consumed.

The use of nickel-containing stabilizers is decreasing in the marketplace, particularly in North America, due to potential toxicity

TABLE 11.2: Selected Light Stabilizer Suppliers

Supplier	Type			
	HALS	Benzotriazole	Benzophenone	Others
3V Sigma	×	—	×	—
Akcros (Akzo)	—	×	×	—
Asahi Denka Kogyo	×	×	×	—
Asia Stabilizer	—	×	×	—
BASF	×	—	×	×
BF Goodrich	×	—	—	—
Chemipro Kasei Kaisha	—	×	×	×
Ciba Specialty Chemicals	×	×	×	×
Clariant	×	×	×	×
Cytec Industries	×	×	×	—
Dai-ichi Chemical Industries	—	—	—	×
Dainippon Ink and Chemicals	—	—	—	×
Eastman Chemical	—	—	—	×
Elf Atochem	×	—	—	—
Everlight Chemical Industrial	×	×	×	—
Fairmount Chemical	—	×	—	—

Ferro	—	—	×	×
Great Lakes Chemical	×	×	×	—
Honshu Chemical	—	—	×	—
Iwaki Seiyaku	—	—	—	×
Johoku Chemical	—	×	—	—
Kolon Industries	—	—	×	—
Korea Fine Chemicals	—	—	×	—
Kyodo Chemicals	—	×	×	×
Liaoyang Organic Chemical	×	—	—	×
Mitsubishi Petrochemical	—	—	—	×
Musashino Geigy	×	×	—	—
Nissan Ferro Organic Chemical	—	—	—	×
Osaka Seika Chemical Ind.	—	×	×	—
Sakai Chemical Industry	—	—	—	×
Sankyo	×	—	×	—
Shipro Kasei	—	×	×	×
Shonan Kagaku Kogyo	—	—	×	—
Sumitomo Chemical	—	×	×	×
Witco	—	—	×	—
Yashiro Seiyaku	—	—	—	×
Yoshitomi Fine Chemicals	×	×	×	—

concerns. In Europe, nickel continues to be used in agricultural film applications. Design efforts are focusing on down-gauging of exterior plastic parts for weight and cost reduction. This will place increased value on light stabilization to maintain adequate performance at thinner wall sections. HALS will experience the strongest growth due to their widespread use in polyolefins and their cost-effectiveness and performance. Benzotriazoles and benzophenones, however, are more effective than HALS in vinyl and engineering plastics.

Significant product development work is being done in HALS technology to produce higher-performance products in polyolefin systems. Low molecular weight alkoxy substituted amine systems and higher molecular weight HALS stabilizers significantly improve the performance of pigmented TPO parts with regard to colour and gloss retention. HALS are being promoted by selected suppliers as effective light stabilizer with excellent capabilities as antioxidants. In some cases, these materials are comparable to well-established antioxidant products such as Ciba's IRGANOX 1010. Suppliers continue to improve on the physical forms of light stabilizers. For example, Cytec is introducing a flake form light stabilizer which reduces dusting and increases the shelf life of the products.

Consolidation is expected to continue due to margin pressures caused by regulatory issues such as FDA compliance, toxicological testing, environmental compliance, and the continual need for capital investment. This trend may be most apparent in the Asia/Pacific region where there are a large number of small suppliers. Globally, light stabilizers should grow at a rate of 7% per year over the next 5 years, with the less developed regions in Asia/Pacific, Latin America, and Africa leading the way. This robust growth parallels the growth of polyolefins, particularly polypropylene/TPO, and engineering resins into more exterior applications replacing metal and painted plastic.

12

Lubricants and Mould Release Agents

DESCRIPTION

Lubricants

Lubricants represent a broad class of materials that are used to improve the flow characteristics of plastics during processing. Besides this primary task of improving flow properties, lubricants can act as melt promoters, antiblock, antitack, and antistatic agents as well as colour and impact improvers. They can be used in conjunction with metal release agents and heat stabilizers. Lubricants are widely used in packaging film to prevent sticking to the metal processing equipment. Lubricants can improve efficiency by lowering the resin melt viscosity, resulting in reduced shear and equipment wear, increased rate of production, and decreased energy consumption. Selection of lubricants is dependent upon the type of polymer as well as the process by which it is manufactured. The method of selection is easier when the manufacturing process is fully developed. Lubricant choices for new processes require careful experimentation.

The selection process is driven by the lubricant's compatibility with the hot resin, lack of adverse effects on polymer properties, good transparency, regulatory approval, and the balance of other additives in the polymer. The amount of lubricant used can also affect the final polymer properties. Overlubrication can cause excessive slippage and underlubrication can cause degradation and higher melt viscosities. The two general classifications of lubricants are internal and external.

External lubricants

External lubricants do not interact with the polymer but function at the surface of the molten polymer between the polymer and the surface of the processing equipment and are generally incompatible with the polymer itself. These lubricants function by coating the process equipment and reducing friction at the point of interface. They delay fusion and give melt control and the desired polymer flow to such applications as rigid PVC pipe, siding, and window frames.

Internal lubricants

Internal lubricants are usually chemically compatible with the polymer and act by reducing friction between polymer molecules. They reduce van der Waals forces, leading to lower melt viscosity and lowering energy input needed for processing.

Several chemicals are used as both internal and external lubricants since lubricants can function at several different points during polymer processing. When used during the blending portion of processing, they are usually waxy substances that coat the surface of resin pellets allowing easier movement through the cold portions of the processing equipment. As the polymer mix is heated, the lubricant softens, melts, and penetrates the polymer. The rate of penetration is dependent upon the solubility of the particular lubricant in the specific polymer.

Metallic stearates

Metallic stearates are the most widely used lubricants. They are utilized predominantly in PVC, but also find use in polyolefins, ABS, polyesters, and phenolics. The primary disadvantage of metallic stearates is their lack of clarity. Calcium stearate, the most common metallic stearate, is primarily used as an internal lubricant, but in PVC applications, it provides external lubricant and metal release characteristics while also acting as a heat stabilizer.

Preparation

There is provided an improved alkaline earth metal stearate composition and related method of preparation, wherein a substantial portion of the stearate is in the dihydrate form. Methods of making metallic salts of fatty acids are well known in the art. The "double decomposition" method involves a two-step process. First, the fatty acid is reacted with at least one base in a basic aqueous solution, typically at least one alkali hydroxide to form an alkaline soap. Second, at least one aqueous metallic salt solution is added to the soap to form metallic salts of the corresponding fatty acid.

Conventional pharmaceutical preparation of alkaline earth metal stearates, for example magnesium stearate and calcium stearate, typically utilize this method. The stearic acid reacts with an alkali hydroxide, for example NaOH, to form the sodium soap, which then reacts with an alkaline earth metal salt, for example magnesium chloride, as shown below:

$$2CH_3(CH_2)_{16}COOH+2NaOH\rightarrow \quad (1)$$

$$2C_{18}H_{35}O_2Na+MgCl_2\rightarrow \quad (2)$$

$$C_{36}H_{70}O_4Mg+2NaCl \quad (3)$$

Stearate compositions produced by this method exhibit great variation in quality and properties. It is known that commercially available stearic acid typically contains palmitic acid also. While pure stearic acid does have limited availability, the purification is not feasible on an industrial scale.

Method 1

A magnesium stearate composition containing a variable ratio of discrete monohydrate and dihydrate polymorphs is manufactured from a "soap solution" via precipitation, as is well known in the art. The salt of this illustrative example is formed by mixing of at least one fatty acid and at least one strong base, NaOH and a magnesium salt, $MgSO_4$. In the present method, the soap solution is produced from a fatty acid mixture of suitable stearic/palmitic acid composition to obtain an appreciable amount of the dihydrate form of the resulting stearate. Addition of the alkaline earth metal salt to an alkaline "soap solution" results in the precipitation of magnesium stearate containing the dihydrate phase. The precipitate is separated from the liquor, and dried to a water content of 3.5-6.0%, predominately water of hydration. A fine-particulate solid is obtained. The product is designed for use as a pharmaceutical lubricant/mould release agent, but can be used for other applications, as is known in the art.

The following is an illustrative example of an industrial manufacturing process for a product containing the desired magnesium stearate dihydrate and is not intended to limit the present invention to the production of magnesium stearate/palmitate for pharmaceutical uses:

An aqueous solution, either water or a heel from a previous batch was heated to a temperature at which the fatty acid did not congeal when introduced to the aqueous solution, as is well known. A 50% sodium hydroxide solution was added in at least a 1:1 molar ratio to the fatty acid, so that substantially all the fatty acid constituents were converted to the sodium soap. The fatty acid component was then added until the solution was slightly alkaline to phenolphthalein indicator. In this illustrative example, a fatty acid composition of about 93% by weight stearic acid to about 5% by weight palmitic acid was used.

A solution of magnesium sulfate was then added, without agitation, in an amount to substantially precipitate the sodium soap, thereby forming the magnesium stearate/palmitate. The reaction mixture was then mixed to create a homogeneous mixture and insure reaction with the magnesium sulfate, typically about 20 minutes. The reaction mixture remained heated throughout this and the remaining steps to prevent any solidification of the reaction mixture, thereby providing ease of handling. The pH was then adjusted with sodium hydroxide to precipitate any excess magnesium as MgO. An illustrative pH range is from about 9.0 to about 9.5. A solid-liquid separation was performed, and the resulting solid product was dried, and deagglomerated by suitable conventional methods. These steps and reaction conditions are well known to those skilled in the art.

This resulting product was characterized as containing a mixture of magnesium stearate and magnesium palmitate as mixed hydrates as follows:

1. The product had a loss on drying of 3.5-6.0% indicating a significant amount of the dihydrate form is present. TGA indicates 2 water loss events, one at about 60° C. and one at about 90° C., corresponding to the dihydrate and monohydrate forms respectively.
2. DSC analysis showed 2 endothermic transitions between 100°-135° C. (ca. 118° C. and 128° C. for Mg stearate) as a result of 2 pseudopolymorphs that are each derived from unique hydrates.
3. X-ray diffraction showed crystallinity (not amorphous), and exhibited a characteristic XRD pattern indicating the dihydrate form is present.

The product had regular or irregular (e.g. fragmented) platelet morphology. Other features of the manufacturing process that are considered relevant to the manufacture of magnesium stearate are obvious to those skilled in the art.

Esters

Esters, including fatty esters, polyol esters, and even wax esters, are reasonably compatible with PVC. They are also used in polystyrene and acrylic polymers. High molecular weight esters are used as external lubricants; conversely, low molecular weight esters are used as internal lubricants, although they are somewhat inefficient as either.

Preparation

The following examples demonstrate the preparation of terephthalate ester polyols of this method, polyurethane foams employing a terephthalate ester polyol and polyurethane foams which do not employ terephthalate ester polyols of this method.

Method I

A terephthalate ester polyol of this method was prepared from the following materials.

Materials	Moles
mixture of glycols, monomers and oligomers	1
glycerin	1.1
magnesium acetate	2×10^{-3}

The total amounts of the mixture, the glycerin and the magnesium acetate were added to the reactor at room temperature. The contents of the reactor were then heated with constant agitation using a continuous nitrogen sparge. The temperature of the contents of the reactor was raised to about 170° C, and a vacuum of 25 inches Hg was applied and distillation of free glycols began. The distillation of free glycols was complete at a temperature of about 210° C. The resulting product in the reactor was permitted to cool to room temperature and recovered as a terephthalate ester polyol of this invention. The resulting polyol was found to have a hydroxyl number of 365 and a viscosity (measured on a Brookfield RVT model viscometer with an RV no. 7 spindle and a speed of 4 RPM) at 25° C of 404,000 cps.

A typical mixture of glycols, monomers and oligomers used in this example, and in the following examples, was obtained from Eastman Chemical Products, Inc., Kingsport, Tennessee, and had the following analyses:

Weight Percent (± 2%)	Component Range
ethylne glycol	8
diethylene glycol	6
triethylene glycol	3
tetraethylene glycol	0
ethylene glycol monomer	14
diethylene glycol monomer	6
mixed monomers	13
oligomers	50

The mixture was determined to have number average molecular weight peaks, as measured by gel permeation chromatography, at 188 and 513, a saponification number range of from about 219 to about 316 and a hydroxyl number of about 389.

Fatty Amides

Fatty amides possess unique mould release properties. Simple primary fatty amides are used as slip and mould release agents primarily in polyolefins but also in a variety of other polymers. The more complex bis-amides, such as ethylene bis-stearamide, offer mould release as well as internal and external lubricity functions in materials such as PVC and ABS.

Preparation

The method relates to an enzyme which catalyzes a hydrolytic conversion between soporific fatty acid primary amides and their corresponding fatty acids and is designated a fatty-acid amide hydrolase (FAAH), to methods for enzymatically catalyzing such conversions, and to methods for inhibiting the enzymatic catalysis of such conversions. More particularly, the invention relates to FAAH protein, in either isolated or recombinant form, and to its use and inhibition.

SYNTHETIC PROTOCOLS

1. Cis-9,10-octadecenoamide (1:)

A solution of oleic acid (1.0 g, 3.55 mmol, 1.0 equiv.) in CH_2Cl_2 (8.9 mL, 0.4 M) at 0° C. was treated dropwise with oxalyl chloride (5.32 mL, 2.0 M solution in CH_2Cl_2, 10.64 mmol, 3.0 equiv.). The reaction mixture was stirred at 25° C. for 4 h, concentrated under reduced pressure, cooled to 0° C., and treated with saturated aqueous NH_4OH (2.0 mL). The reaction mixture was then partitioned between ethyl acetate (EtOAc) (100 mL) and H_2O (100 mL), and the organic layer was dried (Na_2SO_4) and concentrated under reduced pressure. Chromatography (SiO_2, 5 cm × 15 cm, 40-100% EtOAc-hexanes gradient elution) afforded 1 as a white solid (0.810 g, 0.996 g theoretical, 81.3%): ^1H NMR ($CDCl_3$, 250 MHz) δ 6.06 (bs, 1H, $NH_2C(O)$), 5.58 (bs, 1H, $NH_2C(O)$), 5.32 (m, 2H, CH=CH),

2.16 (t, 2H, J=7.5 Hz, $CH_2C(O)NH_2$), 2.02 (m, 4H, $CH_2CH=CHCH_2$), 1.61 (m, 2H, $CH_2CH_2C(O)NH_2$), 1.29 (b s, 14H, alkyl protons), 0.87 (t, 3H, CH_3); FABHRMS (NBA/NaI m/e 282.2804 ($C_{18}H_{35}NO + H^+$ requires 282.2797). The regions of the spectra that distinguish between the cis and trans isomers are the olefinic protons from δ 5.3 to 5.2 and allylic protons from δ 2.0 to 1.8. These regions identify the natural compound as cis-9,10-octadecenoamide.

2. Trans-9,10-octadecenoamide (2:)

A solution of elaidic acid (1.0 g, 3.55 mmol, 1.0 equiv.) in CH_2Cl_2 (8.9 mL, 0.4 M) at 0° C. was treated dropwise with oxalyl chloride (5.32 mL, 2.0 M solution in CH_2Cl_2, 10.64 mmol, 3.0 equiv.). The reaction mixture was stirred at 25° C. for 4 h, concentrated under reduced pressure, cooled to 0° C., and treated with saturated aqueous NH_4OH (2.0 mL). The reaction mixture was then partitioned between ethyl acetate (EtOAc) (100 mL) and H_2O (100 mL), and the organic layer was dried (Na_2SO_4) and concentrated under reduced pressure. Chromatography (SiO_2, 5 cm × 15 cm, 40-100% EtOAc-hexanes gradient elution) afforded 2 as a white solid. The regions of the spectra that distinguish between the cis and trans isomers are the olefinic protons from δ 5 5.3 to 5.2 and allylic protons from δ 2.0 to 1.8. These regions identify the compound as trans-9,10-octadecenoamide.

3. Cis-8,9-octadecenoamide (3:)

A solution of 11, synthesized infra, (0.130 g, 0.461 mmol, 1.0 equiv.) in CH_2Cl_2 (1.5 mL, 0.31 M) at 0° C. was treated dropwise with oxalyl chloride (0.69 mL, 2.0 M solution in CH_2Cl_2, 1.38 mmol, 3.0 equiv.). The reaction mixture was stirred at 25° C. for 4 h, concentrated under reduced pressure, cooled to 0° C., and treated with saturated aqueous NH_4OH (2.0 mL). The reaction mixture was then partitioned between ethyl acetate (EtOAc) (100 mL) and H_2O (100 mL), and the organic layer was dried (Na_2SO_4) and concentrated under reduced pressure. Chromatography (SiO_2, 5 cm × 15 cm, 40-100% EtOAc-hexanes gradient elution) afforded 3 as a white solid. (0.105 g, 0.130 theoretical, 80.8%): ^1H NMR ($CDCl_3$, 250 MHz) δ 5.70-5.34 (m, 4H, $H_2NC(O)$ and CH=CH), 2.21 (t, 2H, J=7.5 Hz, $CH_2C(O)NH_2$), 2.00 (m, 4H, $CH_2CH=CHCH_2$), 1.63 (m,

2H, $CH_2CH_2C(O)NH_2$), 1.47-1.23 (m, 20H, alkyl protons), 0.87 (t, 3H, RCH_3); FABHRMS (NBA/CSI m/e 414.1762 ($C_{18}H_{35}NO$ + Cs^+ requires 414.1773).

4. Cis-11,12-octadecenoamide (4:)

A solution of Δ11,12 octadecenoic acid (1.0 g, 3.55 mmol, 1.0 equiv.) in CH_2Cl_2 (8.9 mL, 0.4 M) at 0° C. was treated dropwise with oxalyl chloride (5.32 mL, 2.0 M solution in CH_2Cl_2, 10.64 mmol, 3.0 equiv.). The reaction mixture was stirred at 25° C. for 4 h, concentrated under reduced pressure, cooled to 0° C., and treated with saturated aqueous NH_4OH (2.0 mL). The reaction mixture was then partitioned between ethyl acetate (EtOAc) (100 mL) and H_2O (100 mL), and the organic layer was dried (Na_2SO_4) and concentrated under reduced pressure. Chromatography (SiO_2, 5 cm × 15 cm, 40-100% EtOAc-hexanes gradient elution) afforded 4 as a white solid.

5 Oleic acid(5:)

Oleic acid was obtained from Aldrich chemical company, CAS #112-80-1.

6. ERUCAMIDE (6:)

Erucamide was obtained from Aldrich Chemical Company, CAS #28,057-7.

7. METHYL-8-HYDROXY-OCTANOATE (7:)

A solution of suberic acid monomethyl ester (1.5 g, 7.97 mmol, 1.0 equiv.) in tetrahydrofuran (THF) (32.0 mL, 0.25M) at –20° C. was treated dropwise with BH_3THF (1M solution in THF, 7.97 mL, 7.97 mmol, 1.0 equiv.). The reaction mixture was stirred overnight and was subsequently allowed to reach room temperature. The reaction mixture was then diluted with ethyl acetate (100 mL) and quenched with methanol (10 mL) and 10% HCl (10 mL). Extraction with $NaHCO_3$ (1 × 20 mL), water (2 × 10 mL), and brine (1 × 10 mL), afforded methyl-8-hydroxy-octanoate (7) as a crude white solid.

8. Methyl-8-bromo-octanoate (8:)

A solution of crude methyl-8-hydroxy-octanoate (7, 1.24 g, 7.13 mmol, 1.0 equiv.) in CH_2Cl_2 (15 mL, 0.48 M) at 0° C. was treated successively with CBr_4 (3.07 g, 9.27 mmol, 1.3 equiv.) and PPh_3 (2.61 g, 9.98 mmol, 1.4 equiv.) and the reaction mixture was stirred at 4° C. for 10 h. The reaction mixture was then concentrated under reduced pressure and washed repeatedly with Et_2O (8×10 mL washes). The Et_2O washes were combined and concentrated under reduced pressure. Chromatography (SiO_2, 5 cm × 15 cm, hexanes) afforded 8 as a clear, colorless oil (1.25 g, 1.69 g theoretical, 74.0%): ^1H NMR ($CDCl_3$, 250 MHz) δ 3.64 (s, 3H, $C(O)OCH_3$), 3.38 (t, 2H, J=6.8 Hz, CH_2Br), 2.29 (t, 2H, J=7.4 Hz $CH_2C(O)OCH_3$), 1.83 (p, 2H, CH_2CH_2Br), 1.63 (m, 2H, $CH_2CH_2C(O)OCH_3$) 1.47-1.28 (m, 6H, alkyl protons)

9. Methyl-8-triphenylphosphoranyl-octanoate-bromide (9:)

A solution of 8 (1.25 g, 5.23 mmol, 1.0 equiv.) in CH_3CN (4.0 mL, 1.31 M) was treated with triphenylphosphine (1.52 g, 5.75 mmol, 1.1 equiv.) and stirred at reflux for 10 h. Additional triphenylphosphine (0.685 g, 2.61 mmol, 0.5 equiv.) was added to the reaction mixture and stirring was continued at reflux for 5 h. The reaction mixture was concentrated under reduced pressure and washed repeatedly with Et_2O (5×10 mL washes). The remaining residue was then solubilized in the minimum volume of CH_2Cl_2 and concentrated under reduced pressure to afford 9 as a colorless foam (2.20 g, 2.61 g theoretical, 84.3%): ^1H NMR ($CDCl_3$, 250 MHz) δ 7.82-7.51 (m, 15H, ArH), 3.70-3.46 (m, 5H, $CH_3OC(O)R$ and CH_2PPh_3), 2.13 (t, 2H, J=7.4 Hz, $CH_2C(O)OCH_3$), 1.62-1.43 (m, 6H, alkyl protons), 1.30-1.02 (m, 4H, alkyl protons); FABHRMS (NBA) m/e 419.2154 ($C_{27}H_{32}BrO_2P$—Br requires 419.2140).

10. Methyl-cis-8.9-octadecenoate (10:)

A solution of 9 (0.71 g, 1.42 mmol, 1.0 equiv.) in THF (7.0 mL, 0.2 M) at 25° C. was treated with KHMDS (3.0 mL, 0.5 M solution in THF, 1.5 mmol, 1.06 equiv.) and the reaction mixture was stirred at reflux for 1 h. The reaction mixture was then cooled to –78°C, treated with decyl aldehyde (0.321 mL, 1.71 mmol, 1.2 equiv.) warmed to 25° C., and stirred for an additional 30 min. The reaction mixture was then treated with saturated aqueous NH_4Cl and partitioned between EtOAc (100 mL) and H_2O (100 mL). The organic layer was dried (Na_2SO_4) and concentrated under reduced pressure. Chromatography (SiO_2, 5 cm × 15 cm, 0-2% EtOAc-hexanes gradient elution) afforded 10 as a colorless oil (0.290 g, 0.422 g theoretical, 68.7%): ^1H NMR ($CDCl_3$, 250 MHz) δ 5.34 (m, 2H, CH=CH), 3.65 (s, 3H, $CH_3OC(O)$), 2.29 (t, 2H, J=7.4 Hz, $CH_2C(O)OCH_3$), 2.00 (m, 4H, $CH_2CH=CHCH_2$), 1.61 (m, 2H, $CH_2CH_2C(O)OCH_3$), 1.29 (bs, 20H, alkyl protons), 0.86 (t, 3H, RCH_3).

11. Cis-8,9 octadecenoic Acid (11:)

A solution of 10 (0.245 g, 0.825 mmol, 1.0 equiv.) in THF-MeOH—H_2O (3-1-1 ratio, 4.1 mL, 0.2 M) at 0° C. was treated with $LiOH.H_2O$ (0.104 g, 2.48 mmol, 3.0 equiv.). The reaction mixture was warmed to 25° C., stirred for 8 h, and then partitioned between EtOAc (100 mL) and H_2O (100 mL). The organic layer was washed successively with 10% aqueous HCl (100 mL) and saturated aqueous NaCl (100 mL), dried, and concentrated under reduced pressure. Chromatography (SiO_2,5 cm × 15 cm, 10-30% EtOAc-hexanes gradient elution) afforded 11 as a colorless oil (0.156 g, 0.233 g theoretical, 67.0%): ^1H NMR ($CDCl_3$, 250 MHz) δ 5.34 (m, 2H, CH=CH), 2.34 (t, 2H, J = 7.4 Hz, CH_2COOH), 2.01 (m, 4H, $CH_2CH=CHCH_2$), 1.61 (m, 2H, CH_2CH_2COOH), 1.47-1.23 (m, 20H, alkyl protons), 0.87 (t, 3H, RCH_3).

12. 18-Hemisuccinate-cis-9,10-octadecenoamide (12:)

A solution of 18 (0.047 g, 0.160 M, 1.0 equiv) in CH_2Cl_2—$CHCl_3$ (3-1, 1.60 mL, 0.1M) was treated successively with Et_3N (0.045 mL, 0.320 mmol, 2.0 equiv), succinic anhydride (0.033 g, 0.320 mmol, 2.0 equiv) and DMAP (0.002 g, 0.016 mmol, 0.1 equiv), and the reaction mixture was stirred at 25° C. for 10 h. The reaction mixture was then partitioned between CH_2Cl_2 (50 mL) and H_2O (50 mL), and the organic layer was washed successively with 10% aqueous HCl (50 mL) and saturated aqueous NaCl (50 mL), dried (Na_2SO_4), and concentrated under reduced pressure. Chromatography (SiO_2, 3 cm × 15 cm, 0-10% MeOH-EtOAc) afforded 12 as a white solid (0.051 g, 0.063 theoretical, 80.3%): ^1H NMR ($CDCl_3$, 250 MHz) δ 6.95 (b s, 1H, $H_2NC(O)$), 5.72 (bs, 1H, $H_2NC(O)$), 5.34 (m, 2H, CH=CH), 4.08 (t, 3H, J=6.6 Hz,

$CH_2OC(O)R$), 2.61 (m, 4H, $ROC(O)CH_2CH_2COOH$), 2.21 (t, 2H, J=7.5 Hz, $CH_2C(O)NH_2$), 2.00 (m, 4H, $CH_2CH=CHCH_2$), 1.70-1.52 (m, 4H, $CH_2CH_2C(O)NH_2$ and CH_2CH_2OH), 1.29 (b s, 18H, alkyl protons); FABHRMS (NBA) m/e 398.2893 ($C_{22}H_{39}NO_5 + H^+$ requires 398.2906).

13. Methyl-9-bromo-nonanoate (13:)

A solution of methyl-9-hydroxy-nonanoate (1.1 g, 5.85 mmol, 1.0 equiv) in CH_2Cl_2 (30 mL, 0.2 M) at 0° C. was treated successively with CBr_4 (2.5 g, 7.54 mmol, 1.3 equiv) and PPh_3 (2.15 g, 8.19 mmol, 1.4 equiv) and the reaction mixture was stirred at 4° C. for 10 h. The reaction mixture was then concenctrated under reduced pressure and washed repeatedly with Et_2O (8×10 mL washes). The Et_2O washes were combined and concentrated under reduced pressure. Chromatography (SiO_2, 5 cm × 15 cm, hexanes) afforded 13 as a clear, colorless oil (1.02 g, 1.47 g theorectical, 69.5%): ^1H NMR ($CDCl_3$, 250 MHz) d 3.64 (s, 3H, $C(O)OCH_3$), 3.38 (t, 2H, J=6.8 Hz, CH_2Br), 2.29 (t, 2H, J = 7.4 Hz $CH_2C(O)OCH_3$), 1.83 (p, 2H, CH_2CH_2Br), 1.63 (m, 2H, $CH_2CH_2C(O)OCH_3$) 1.47-1.28 (m, 8H, alkyl protons).

14. Methyl-9-triphenylphosphoranyl-nonanoate-bromide (14:)

A solution of 13 (1.02 g, 4.06 mmol, 1.0 equiv) in CH_3CN (3.5 mL, 1.16 M) was treated with triphenylphosphine (1.17 g, 4.47 mmol, 1.1 equiv) and stirred at reflux for 10 h. Additional triphenylphosphine (0.532 g, 2.03 mmol, 0.5 equiv) was added to the reaction mixture and stirring was continued at reflux for 5 h. The reaction mixture was concentrated under reduced pressure and washed repeatedly with Et_2O (5 × 10 mL washes). The remaining residue was then solubilized in the minimum volume of CH_2Cl_2 and concentrated under reduced pressure to afford 14 as a colourless foam (1.90 g, 2.08 g theoretical, 91.3%): ^1H NMR ($CDCl_3$, 250 MHz) δ 7.82-7.51 (m, 15H, ArH), 3.70-3.46 (m, 5H, $CH_3OC(O)R$ and CH_2PPh_3), 2.13 (t, 2H, J = 7.4 Hz, $CH_2C(O)OCH_3$), 1.62-1.02 (m, 12H, alkyl protons); FABHRMS (NBA) m/e 433.2312 ($C_{28}H_{34}BrO_2P—Br^-$ requires 433.2296).

15. Methyl-18-t-butyldiphenysilyloxy-cis-9,10 octadecenoate (15:)

A solution of 14 (1.0 g, 1.95 mmol, 1.0 equiv) in THF (6.5 mL, 0.3 M) at 25° C. was treated with KHMDS (3.9 mL, 0.5 M solution in THF, 1.95 mmol, 1.0 equiv) and the reaction mixture was stirred at reflux for 1 h. The reaction mixture was then cooled to –78° C., treated with 3 (0.93 g, 2.35 mmol, 1.2 equiv), warmed to 25° C., and stirred for an additional 30 min. The reaction mixture was then treated with saturated aqueous NH_4Cl and partitioned between EtOAc (100 mL) and H_2O (100 mL). The organic layer was dried (Na_2SO_4) and concentrated under reduced pressure. Chromatography (SiO_2, 5 cm×15 cm, 0-2% EtOAc-hexanes gradient elution) afforded 15 as a colorless oil (0.82 g, 1.07 g theoretical, 76.3%): ^1H NMR ($CDCl_3$, 250 MHz) δ 7.67 (m, 4H, ArH), 7.41 (m, 6H, ArH), 5.34 (m, 2H, CH=CH), 3.65 (m, 5H, $CH_3OC(O)$ and $CH_2OTBDPS$), 2.29 (t, 2H, J=7.4 Hz, $CH_2C(O)OCH_3$), 2.00 (m, 4H, $CH_2CH{=}CHCH_2$), 1.55 (m, 4H, $CH_2CH_2C(O)OCH_3$ and $CH_2CH_2OTBDPS$), 1.29 (b s, 18H, alkyl protons), 1.04 (s, 9H, $(CH_3)_3C$).

16. 18-T-butyldiphenylsilyloxy-cis-9,10-octadecenoic Acid (16:)

A solution of 5 (0.81 g, 1.47 mmol, 1.0 equiv) in THF-MeOH-H_2O (3-1-1 ratio, 7.3 mL, 0.2 M) at 0° C. was treated with $LiOH.H_2O$ (0.188 g, 4.48 mmol, 3.0 equiv). The reaction mixture was warmed to 25° C., stirred for 8 h, and then partitioned between EtOAc (100 mL) and H_2O (100 mL). The organic layer was washed successively with 10% aqueous HCl (100 mL) and saturated aqueous NaCl (100 mL), dried, and concentrated under reduced pressure. Chromatography (SiO_2, 5 cm × 15 cm, 10-30% EtOAc-hexanes gradient elution) afforded 16 as a colorless oil (0.700 g, 0.790 g theoretical, 88.7%): ^1H NMR ($CDCl_3$, 250 MHz) δ 7.67 (m, 4H, ArH), 7.41 (m, 6H, ArH), 5.34 (m, 2H, CH=CH), 3.65 (t, 3H, J=6.5 Hz, $CH_2OTBDPS$), 2.34 (t, 2H, J=7.4 Hz, CH_2COOH), 2.00 (m, 4H, $CH_2CH{=}CHCH_2$), 1.65-1.50 (m, 4H, CH_2CH_2COOH and $CH_2CH_2OTBDPS$), 1.47-1.23 (m, 18H, alkyl protons), 1.05 (s, 9H, $(CH_3)_3C$); FABHRMS (NBA/CsI) m/e 669.2772 ($C_{34}H_{52}O_3Si+Cs^+$ requires 669.2740).

17. 18-T-butyldiphenylsilyloxy-cis-9,10-octadecenoamide (17:)

A solution of 16 (0.685 g, 1.28 mmol, 1.0 equiv) in CH_2Cl_2 (4.3 mL, 0.3 M) at 0° C. was treated dropwise with oxalyl chloride (1.92 mL, 2 M solution in CH_2Cl_2, 3.84 mmol, 3.0 equiv). The reaction mixture was stirred at 25° C. for 4 h, concentrated under reduced pressure, cooled to 0° C., and treated with saturated aqueous NH_4OH (2.0 mL) The reaction mixture was then partitioned between EtOAc (100 mL) and H_2O (100 mL), and the organic layer was dried (Na_2SO_4) and concentrated under reduced pressure. Chromatography (SiO_2, 5 cm × 15 cm, 40-100% EtOAc-hexanes gradient elution) afforded 17 as a colorless oil (0.520 g, 0.684 g, 76.0%): ^1H NMR ($CDCl_3$, 250 MHz) δ 7.67 (m, 4H, ArH), 7.41 (m, 6H, ArH), 5.70-5.34 (m, 4H, $H_2NC(O)$ and CH=CH), 3.65 (t, 3H, J=6.5 Hz, $CH_2OTBDPS$), 2.21 (t, 2H, J=7.5 Hz, $CH_2C(O)NH_2$), 2.00 (m, 4H, $CH_2CH{=}CHCH_2$), 1.65-1.50 (m, 4H, $CH_2CH_2C(O)NH_2$ and $CH_2CH_2OTBDPS$), 1.47-1.23 (m, 18H, alkyl protons), 1.05 (s, 9H, $(CH_3)_3C$); FABHRMS (NBA/CsI m/e 668.2929 ($C_{34}H_{53}O_2NSi + Cs^+$ requires 668.2900).

18. 18-Hydroxy-cis-9,10-octadecenoamide (18:)

A solution of 17 (0.185 g, 0.345 mmol, 1.0 equiv) in THF (1.1 mL, 0.31 M) was treated with tetrabutylammoniumfluoride (0.69 mL, 1.0 M solution in THF, 0.69 mmol, 2.0 equiv) and the reaction mixture was stirred at 25° C. for 2 h. The reaction mixture was then partitioned between EtOAc (50 mL) and H_2O (50 mL), and the organic layer was dried (Na_2SO_4) and concentrated under reduced pressure . Chromatography (SiO_2, 3 cm × 15 cm, 0-5% MeOH-EtOAc gradient elution) afforded 18 a white solid (0.097 g, 0.103 g theoretical, 94.6%): ^1H NMR ($CDCl_3$, 250 MHz) δ 5.65-5.34 (m, 4H, $H_2NC(O)$ and CH=CH), 3.62 (t, 3H, J=6.5 Hz, CH_2OH), 2.21 (t, 2H, J=7.5 Hz, $CH_2C(O)NH_2$), 2.00 (m, 4H, $CH_2CH{=}CHCH_2$), 1.65-1.50 (m, 4H, $CH_2CH_2C(O)NH_2$ and CH_2CH_2OH), 1.29 (b s, 18H, alkyl protons); FABHRMS (NBA) 298.2732 ($C_{18}H_{35}NO_2 + H^+$ requires 298.2746).

19. Synthesis of Compound 100

Methyl-9-t-butyldiphenylsilyloxy-nonanoate (intermediate for compound 100:). A solution of methyl-9-hydroxy-nonanoate (0.838 g,

4.46 mmol, 1.0 equiv: Aldrich) in CH_2Cl_2 (15 mL, 0.3 M) was treated successively with Et_3N (0.75 mL, 5.38 mmol, 1.2 equiv), t-butylchlorodiphenylsilane (1.28 mL, 4.93 mmol, 1.1 equiv), and DMAP (0.180 g, 1.48 mmol, 0.33 equiv), and the reaction mixture was stirred at 25° C. for 12 h. Saturated aqueous NH_4Cl was added to the reaction mixture and the mixture was partitioned between CH_2Cl_2 (100 mL) and H_2O (100 mL). The organic layer was dried (Na_2SO_4) and concentrated under reduced pressure. Chromatography (SiO_2, 5 cm × 15 cm, 0-5% EtOAc-hexanes gradient elution) afforded the intermeidate as a clear, colorless oil (1.22g, 1.831 theoretical, 64.1%): ^1H NMR ($CDCl_3$, 250 MHz) δ 7.66 (m, 4H, ArH), 7.38 (m, 6H, ArH), 3.67-3.62 (m, 5H, $C(O)OCH_3$ and $CH_2OTBDPS$), 2.30 (t, 2H, J=7.4 Hz, $CH_2C(O)OCH_3$), 1.58 (m, 4H, $CH_2CH_2OTBDPS$ and $CH_2CH_2C(O)OCH_3$), 1.28 (b s, 8H, alkyl protons), 1.05 (s, 9H, $C(CH_3)_3$)

20. Methyl-9-bromo-nonanoate (Intermediate for Compound 100:)

A solution of methyl-9-hydroxy-nonanoate (1.1 g, 5.85 mmol, 1.0 equiv) in CH_2Cl_2 (30 mL, 0.2 M) at 0° C. was treated successively with CBr_4 (2.5 g, 7.54 mmol, 1.3 equiv) and PPh_3 (2.15 g, 8.19 mmol, 1.4 equiv) and the reaction mixture was stirred at 4° C. for 10 h. The reaction mixture was then concenctrated under reduced pressure and washed repeatedly with Et_2O (8×10 mL washes). The Et_2O washes were combined and concentrated under reduced pressure. Chromatography (SiO_2, 5 cm×15 cm, hexanes) afforded the intermediate as a clear, colorless oil (1.02 g, 1.47 g theorectical, 69.5%) ^{1}HNMR ($CDCl_3$, 250 MHz) d 3.64 (s, 3H, $C(O)OCH_3$), 3.38 (t, 2H, J=6.8 Hz, CH_2Br), 2.29 (t, 2H, J=7.4 Hz $CH_2C(O)OCH_3$) 1.83 (p, 2HC H_2CH_2Br), 1.63 (m, 2H, $CH_2CH_2C(O)OCH_3$) 1.47-1.28 (m, 8H, alkyl protons).

21. 9-T-butyldiphenylsilyloxy-nonanal (Intermediate for Compound 100:)

A solution of 1 (1.25 g, 2.93 mmol, 1.0 equiv) in toluene (9.80 mL, 3.0 M) at –78° C. was treated dropwise with DIBAL-H(4.40 mL, 1.0 M solution in hexanes, 4.40 mmol, 1.5 equiv). The reaction mixture was stirred at –78° C. for 30 min. The reaction mixture was then treated dropwise with MeOH(2 mL) and partitioned between EtOAc (100 mL) and H_2O (100 mL). The organic layer was washed with 10% aqueous HCl (100 mL), dried (Na_2SO_4), and concentrated under reduced pressure. Chromatography (SiO_2, 5 cm×15 cm, 0-5% EtOAc-hexanes gradient elution) afforded 3 as a colorless oil (1.1 g, 94.9%): ^{1}HNMR ($CDCl_3$, 250 MHz) δ 9.76 (t, 1H, J=1.8 Hz, HC(O)R), 7.67 (m, 4H, ArH), 7.40 (m, 6H, ArH), 3.65 (t, 2H, J=6.4 Hz, CH_2OTBDPS), 2.41 (t of d, 2H J=1.8 and 7.3 Hz, CH_2C(O)H), 1.58 (m, 4H, CH_2CH_2OTBDPS and CH_2CH_2C(O)H), 1.29 (b s, 8H, alkyl protons), 1.05 (s, 9H, $(CH_3)_3$C); FABHRMS (NBA/CsI) m/e 529.1560 ($C_{25}H_{36}O_2Si+Cs^+$ requires 529.1539).

22. Methyl-9-triphenylphosphoranyl-nonanoate Bromide (Intermediate for Compound 100:)

A solution of 9-T-butyldiphenylsilyloxy-nonanal (1.02 g, 4.06 mmol, 1.0 equiv) in CH_3CN (3.5 mL, 1.16 M) was treated with triphenylphosphine (1.17 g, 4.47 mmol, 1.1 equiv) and stirred at reflux for 10 h. Additional triphenylphosphine (0.532 g, 2.03 mmol, 0.5 equiv) was added to the reaction mixture and stirring was continued at reflux for 5 h. The reaction mixture was concentrated under reduced pressure and washed repeatedly with Et_2O (5×10 mL washes). The remaining residue was then solubilized in the minimum volume of CH_2Cl_2 and concentrated under reduced pressure to afford the intermediate as a colorless foam (1.90 g, 2.08 g theoretical, 91.3%): ^{1}H NMR ($CDCl_3$, 250 MHz) δ 7.82-7.51 (m, 15H, ArH), 3.70-3.46 (m, 5H, CH_3OC(O)R and CH_2PPh_3), 2.13 (t, 2H, J=7.4 Hz, $CH_2C(O)OCH_3$), 1.62-1.02 (m, 12H, alkyl protons); FABHRMS (NBA) m/e 433.2312 ($C_{28}H_{34}BrO_2$ P—Br^- requires 433.2296).

23. Methyl-18-t-butyldiphenysilyloxy-cis-9,10-octadecenoate (Intermediate for Compound 100:)

A solution of (1.0 g, 1.95 mmol, 1.0 equiv) in THF (6.5 mL, 0.3 M) at 25° C. was treated with KHMDS (3.9 mL, 0.5 M solution in THF, 1.95 mmol, 1.0 equiv) and the reaction mixture was stirred at reflux for 1 h. The reaction mixture was then cooled to –78° C, treated with 3 (0.93 g, 2.35 mmol, 1.2 equiv), warmed to 25° C, and stirred for an additional 30 min. The reaction mixture was then treated with saturated aqueous NH_4Cl and partitioned between EtOAc (100 mL) and H_2O (100 mL). The organic layer was dried (Na_2SO_4) and concentrated under reduced pressure. Chromatography (SiO_2, 5 cm × 15 cm, 0-2% EtOAc-hexanes gradient elution) afforded the intermediate as a colorless oil (0.82 g, 1.07 g theoretical,

76.3%): ^{1}H NMR ($CDCl_3$, 250 MHz) δ 7.67 (m, 4H, ArH), 7.41 (m, 6H, ArH), 5.34 (m, 2H, CH=CH), 3.65 (m, 5H, $CH_3OC(O)$ and CH_2 OTBDPS), 2.29 (t, 2H, J=7.4 Hz, $CH_2C(O)OCH_3$), 2.00 (m, 4H, $CH_2CH{=}CHCH_2$), 1.55 (m, 4H, $CH_2CH_2C(O)OCH_3$ and CH_2CH_2 OTBDPS), 1.29 (b s, 18H, alkyl protons), 1.04 (s, 9H, $(CH_3)_3C$).

24. 18-T-butyldiphenylsilyloxy-cis-9,10-octadecenoic Acid (Compound 100:)

A solution of Methyl-18-t-butyldiphenysilyloxy-cis-9,10-octadecenoate (0.81 g, 1.47 mmol, 1.0 equiv) in THF-MeOH-H_2O (3-1-1 ratio, 7.3 mL, 0.2 M) at 0° C. was treated with LiOH.H_2O (0.188 g, 4.48 mmol, 3.0 equiv). The reaction mixture was warmed to 25° C., stirred for 8 h, and then partitioned between EtOAc (100 mL) and H_2O (100 mL). The organic layer was washed successively with 10% aqueous HCl (100 mL) and saturated aqueous NaCl (100 mL), dried, and concentrated under reduced pressure. Chromatography (SiO_2, 5 cm×15 cm, 10-30% EtOAc-hexanes gradient elution) afforded 100 as a colorless oil (0.700 g, 0.790 g theoretical, 88.7%): ^{1}H NMR ($CDCl_3$, 250 MHz) δ 7.67 (m, 4H, ArH) 7.41 (m, 6H, ArH), 5.34 (m, 2H, CH=CH), 3.65 (t, 3H, J=6.5 Hz, CH_2 OTBDPS), 2.34 (t, 2H, J=7.4 Hz, CH_2COOH), 2.00 (m, 4H, $CH_2CH{=}CHCH_2$), 1.65-1.50 (m, 4H, CH_2CH_2COOH and CH_2CH_2 OTBDPS), 1.47-1.23 (m, 18H, alkyl protons), 1.05 (s, 9H, $(CH_3)_3C$); FABHRMS (NBA/CsI) m/e 669.2772 ($C_{34}H_{52}O_3Si+Cs^+$ requires 669.2740).

Fatty Alcohols

Fatty alcohols are used primarily in rigid PVC. Because of their compatibility and internal and external lubricant capabilities, they are chosen where clarity is important.

Preparation

The fatty alcohol is an important intermediate of various chemical products/household goods, demand therefor is significantly increasing in recent years, and there are extensive studies on processes producing the same at low cost while maintaining its qualities. Generally, the fatty alcohol is produced in the presence of a hydrogenation catalyst by catalytically reducing a starting material such as naturally occurring fat and oil, a fatty acid or a fatty acid ester, with hydrogen to form a crude fatty alcohol and then refining this product by distillation.

Generally, distillation residues generated in this distillation step have been disposed of so far, or, a part of the residues have been recovered and mixed with a starting fatty acid and returned to the hydrogenation step.

In the fatty alcohol produced from a fatty acid ester through catalytic reduction, there remain a small amount of the unreacted fatty acid ester, and such fatty acid ester has a vapor pressure near to that of the fatty alcohol and is thus hardly separated therefrom. For the purpose of decomposition and removal of such unreacted ester, the addition of an alkali component at the time of distillation is known. For the purpose of reducing impurities including carbonyl compounds such as aldehydes, the addition of an alkali component such as sodium borohydride or an aqueous solution of sodium hydroxide is known.

Method

Hydrogenation and Distillation

Palm kernel oil-derived fatty methyl ester (saponification value 240 mg KOH/g) was used as the starting material, and 200 g of this starting ester was subjected to hydrogenation reaction for 3 hours under the conditions of 285° C. and 24.5 MPa by circulating 5 L/min hydrogen therethrough in the presence of 3 g Cu—Cr hydrogenation catalyst (KSC-1 manufactured by Nikki Chemical Co., Ltd.) to give a crude fatty alcohol. Potassium hydroxide was added in an amount of 50 ppm (in terms of potassium) to the crude fatty alcohol, which was then subjected to distillation by charging it into a continuous distillation apparatus and heating it to a temperature of 232° C. in the top of a column at a vacuum degree of 1.6 kPa. The alkali component in the distillation residues, as determined by an atomic absorption spectrometer., was 1020 ppm.

Removal of the Alkali Component

The resulting distillation residues were charged into a stirring mixing apparatus, and hot water at 80° C. was added thereto in an amount of 90 wt % relative to the residues, which were then regulated to a temperature of 90° C. and stirred for 30 minutes. Then, the residues were adjusted to pH 2.4 with 20% aqueous sulfuric acid, and then stirred at 90° C. for 30 minutes. The residues were left at a kept temperature of 90° C. in a separatory funnel for 1 hour to separate them into an oil phase and an aqueous phase, to give distillation residues from which the alkali component had been removed. The alkali component in the distillation residues after subjection to removal of the alkali component was 2.5 ppm, indicating that 99.8% of the alkali component had been removed.

Hydrogenation Reaction of the Recovered Residues

20 g of the distillation residues from which the alkali component had been removed were added to 200 g palm kernel oil-derived fatty methyl ester (saponification value 240 mg KOH/g) and charged into a 500-mL autoclave. The total content of the alkali component in the starting fatty acid ester was 3.9 ppm. The mixture was subjected to hydrogenation reaction for 3 hours under the conditions of 285° C. and 24.5 MPa by circulating 5 L/min hydrogen therethrough in the presence of 3 g Cu—Cr hydrogenation catalyst.

1.5 hours after the reaction was initiated, the saponification value (SV) was 7.5 mg KOH/g. When the SV became 5 mg KOH/ g as a result of progress of the reaction, the amount of hydrocarbon (HC) was 0.34% (by gas chromatography).

Waxes

Waxes are non-polar and are, therefore, very incompatible with PVC which makes them excellent external lubricants for this material. Partially oxidized PE wax works well as an external lubricant for PVC by delaying fusion and is almost always combined with calcium stearate for melt flow control. Although the primary function of waxes, as well as metallic soaps, fatty acid esters, and amides is lubrication, they are in fact multifunctional, as noted previously, providing slip, antiblock, and mould release properties.

Preparation:

According to the method, there is provided a process for modifying a wax, which process comprises in a treatment step, treating a wax to form primary and/or secondary hydroxyl groups thereon, thereby to obtain a hydroxyl wax; and in an alkoxylation step, subjecting at least some of the hydroxyl groups of hydroxyl wax to alkoxylation, thereby to form a modified wax.

A wax is a linear saturated hydrocarbon having a C 20 to C 100 carbon number distribution. While the method can, at least in principle, have application to any wax, eg a polyethylene wax, it is believed that the method will have particular application to Fischer-Tropsch derived waxes.

By 'Fischer-Tropsch derived waxes' is meant waxes obtained by reacting a synthesis gas comprising carbon monoxide and hydrogen in a specific ratio, over a cobalt, iron, or cobalt/iron Fischer-Tropsch catalyst, at a temperature between 200° C. and 240° C., typically about 240° C., in a fixed or slurry bed reactor, thereby to produce a product range of mainly C 21 -C 85 paraffinic hydrocarbons; and fractionating these hydrocarbons into soft, medium and hard wax fractions, with one of these fractions then being used as the feedstock for the process of the invention. The fractionation may typically be by way of Short Path Distillation, using a temperature between 150° C. and 400° C. at a pressure between 2,0 mbar and 0,02 mbar, more preferably, a temperature between 200° C. and 350° C. at a pressure between 1,5 mbar and 0,07 mbar is used.

A wax having a carbon number distribution of C 20 to C 32, eg ave C 24, is typically deemed to be a soft wax; a wax having a carbon number distribution of C 20 to C 42, e.g. ave C 30, is typically deemed to be a medium wax; and a wax having a carbon number distribution of C 29 to C 85 is typically deemed to be a hard wax. The hard wax can in turn be fractionated into a light fraction typically having a carbon number distribution of C 29 to C 55, eg ave C 40, and a heavy fraction, typically having a carbon number distribution of C 45 to C 85, eg ave C 75 .

The modified wax obtained from the process is suitable for use as a wax emulsifier and/or is a self-emulsifiable wax.

In a first embodiment of the method, the treatment of the wax to form the hydroxyl wax, may comprise grafting the wax with allyl alcohol (CH_2 $CHCH_2$ OH). The wax may then, in particular, be the heavy fraction of a Fischer-Tropsch derived hard wax. The hydroxyl wax then comprises a wax with side chains carrying a propanol group, ie $RCH_2CH(CH_2CH_2CH_2OH)CH_2R$ where R=C 40 to C 80.

The ratio or proportion of allyl alcohol to wax may be between 0,0330 and 0,0730 g allyl alcohol/gram of wax, preferably between 0,0360 and 0,0640 g/g wax, to produce a hydroxyl wax having a hydroxyl value in the range 30 to 75 mg KOH/g.

The grafting of the wax with the allyl alcohol may be effected in the presence of a radical initiator, such as a peroxide.

This hydroxyl wax may then be reacted, in the alkoxylation step, with differing amounts or an alkoxide, typically ethylene oxide, to obtain the modified waxes, which are thus polyethoxy modified waxes when ethylene oxide is used as the alkoxide. These modified waxes typically have a HLB (hydrophilic-lipophilic balance) value between 2 and 18, and can be used as self-emulsifiable waxes, or can be used as emulsifiers for modified, ie oxidized, or unmodified Fischer-Tropsch derived hard waxes.

An emulsion comprises either a mixture of a self emulsifiable wax and water, or a mixture of an emulsifier, with a wax, such as a Fischer-Tropsch derived wax. All emulsifiers comprise a molecule comprising both hydrophilic and lipophilic groups. The HLB thus express the balance of the size and strength of the hydrophilic and lipophilic groups of an emulsifier.

HLB can also be expressed as the amount of alkoxide polymerization observed in the modified wax. Stable pressure emulsions can typically comprise a mixture of the polymer derivative and wax, typically 5% of the polyethoxy modified wax as emulsifier, can be blended with 20% of a Fischer-Tropsch wax, with the balance being water.

In a second embodiment of the method, the wax may be an oxidized wax, such as an uncatalysed auto-oxidized, ie air oxidized, Fischer-Tropsch derived hard wax or a component thereof eg the light or heavy fraction of the Fischer-Tropsch derived hard wax. The process may include, if desired, forming the oxidized wax e.g. by reacting the unoxidised wax and air in a suitable reactor, e.g. in a batch reactor.

The auto-oxidized wax will thus have oxygen-containing primary and secondary functional groups such as ketone, ester and carboxylic acid functional groups. The treatment of the oxidized wax may then include hydrogenating the oxidized wax to form the hydroxyl wax.

It was surprisingly found that the hydrogenation of the oxidized wax could be effected by means of hydrogen in the presence of a catalyst, such as a CuCr and/or a Ru/C catalyst, optionally in the presence of methanol as esterification/trans-esterification agent, and at elevated temperature and pressure. The temperature may be in the range 100° C. to 300° C., with the pressure ranging from 50 bar to 300 bar. Typically, the hydrogenation may be effected in a plug flow reactor.

Alternatively, prior to the hydrogenation of the oxidized wax, the oxidized wax may be esterified with methanol in the presence of a small amount of p-toluene sulphonic acid as catalyst to catalyze the reaction. The esterification may then be effected at a temperature in the range 100° C. to 200° C., and at a pressure in the range 0,5 to 3 bar.

This hydroxyl wax may have a hydroxyl value in the range of 30 to 150 mg KOH/g, and may have primary and secondary hydroxyl groups, with the hydroxyl value being dependent on the oxidation value of the starting material and also on the hydrogenation conditions.

In the alkoxylation step, the resulting secondary and primary hydroxyl groups on the hydroxyl wax may then be alkoxylated, eg ethoxylated, to produce a self-emulsifiable wax product or a wax emulsifier, depending on the hydroxyl value of the hydroxyl wax. Typically when 50 (mol) % to 70 (mol) % hydroxyl groups are present, a self-emulsifiable wax is obtained, and typically with hydroxyl groups from 90 (mol) % to 140 (mol) % an emulsifier is obtained.

The oxidation level of the wax and the hydrogenation conditions have a direct effect on the hydroxyl value of the resulting hydroxyl wax. This in turn has an influence on the product after reaction with the alkoxide, eg ethylene oxide. The properties of the ethylene oxide derived products range from self-emulsifiable waxes to that of an emulsifier allowing a range of 20 to 60% of unfunctionalized wax to be added to still form stable emulsions.

The ethoxylation may typically be effected in a batch reactor, in the presence of a catalyst such as sodium ethoxide, at a temperature between 100° C. and 200° C., and at a pressure between 3 bar and 6 bar.

In a third embodiment of the method, the treatment of the wax to form the hydroxyl wax, may comprise reacting the wax with a peroxide, typically hydrogen peroxide, eg in a nitrogen/air inert atmosphere, to form the hydroxyl wax. The hydroxyl wax can then be alkoxylated, eg ethoxylated, to produce a wax emulsifier and/or a self-emulsifiable wax. The wax may, in this embodiment, be a Fischer-Tropsch derived hard wax, or a light or heavy fraction thereof.

The reaction with the hydrogen peroxide may be effected (i) at a temperature between 100° C. and 300° C., more preferably between 160° C. and 175° C.; and (ii) for a period between 15 and 200 minutes, more preferably for between 45 and 130 minutes, with the reaction time depending on the reaction temperature. This results in a hydroxyl wax with a hydroxyl value of between 15 and 40 mg KOH/g. The hydroxyl Fischer-Tropsch wax can be directly ethoxylated to form the same range of products and emulsions as hereinbefore set out.

Prior to ethoxylation, the hydroxyl wax may first be subjected to propylene oxide treatment, if desired.

Hydroxyl waxes thus obtained can also be used as an end product, eg to prepare amino-amide waxes, as a textile finishing agent, as lubricants in coatings, or as lubricating coating for metals and hot-melt adhesives.

It has also surprisingly been found that the long chain, ethoxylated, heavy and light fractions of the hard wax, of the Fischer-Tropsch derived hard waxes, can find applications as emulsifiers or self-emulsifiable waxes in the textile industry, in water-based inks and in the formulation of various polishes and lubricants.

Method

300 g of Fischer-Tropsch hard wax was heated to 180° C. in a stirred autoclave. After proper purging of the autoclave with nitrogen the allyl alcohol (18, 82 g to give an hydroxyl value of 55 mg KOH/g at 90% conversion) and di(tert-butyl)peroxide (6,27 g where allyl alcohol/DTBP ratio is 3:1) mixture was added to the autoclave at 3 ml/min with stirring. The reaction mixture was left for 20 minutes (6,5 times the half-life time of DTBP) before releasing the pressure of the autoclave into a fume cupboard. The autoclave was purged with nitrogen before removing the product.

Mould Release Agents

When a plastic part tends to stick in the mould, a *mould release agent* is applied as an interfacial coating to lower the friction. Improper mould release can lead to long cycle times, distorted parts, and damaged tooling. The two types of mould release agents are internal and external.

Internal mould release agents

Internal mould release agents are mixed directly into the polymer. These materials have minimal compatibility with the polymer. The additive either migrates to the surface of the polymer and sets up a thin barrier coating between the resin and mould cavity or is present in a sufficient quantity on the surface of the polymer to reduce adhesion to the mould cavity.

External release agents

Traditionally, *external release agents* are applied by spraying or painting the surface of the mould with an aerosol, liquid, or by applying a paste. The solvent or water carrier then evaporates leaving a layer of release agent on the mould. Mould release agents are used in a variety of applications, including fiber-reinforced plastics, castings, polyurethane foams and elastomers, injection-molded thermoplastics, vacuum-formed sheets, and extruded profiles. Because each application has its own plastic, mould material, cycle time, temperature, and final product use, there is no universal release agent. Mould release selection is dependent upon all of these conditions. Release agents should ideally have high tensile strength so they are not worn by abrasive mineral fillers or glass fiber reinforcements. The agents should also be chemically resistant to decomposition and should stick to the mould to prevent interference with the final product. The major types of materials used as mould release agents are fatty acid esters and amides, fluoropolymers, silicones, and waxes.

Fatty Acid Esters and Amides

Fatty acid esters and amides do not usually interfere with the secondary finishing operations and some have hightemperature stability making them well-suited for rotational mould resins and engineering plastics.

Preparation

The polyglycerol fatty acid ester mixture according to the method can additionally be employed as a water-soluble lubricant in chemicotechnical preparations.

The polyglycerol fatty acid ester mixture according to the method can be combined without difficulty with other additives or adjuvants in ready-to-use formulations. Electrolytes and/or other surfactants and also solvents and/or diluents can preferably additionally be employed in detergents, cleaning agents and/or body shampoos. In addition, the polyglycerol fatty acid ester mixture according to the method can be used together with preservatives, perfuming compositions, colorants, pharmaceutically active compounds, pH-adjusting compositions for pH regulation, complexing agents for masking metal ions, skin-care agents and/ or thickening agents and other compounds such as colloids, active disinfectants, compounds having fungicidal, insecticidal and/or antibacterial activity, corrosion inhibitors, etc.

Method 1: Preparation of polyglycerol caprate.

A mixture of 2608 g of polyglycerol (average molecular weight: about 326 g/mole; consisting of about 30% triglycerol, about 45% tetraglycerol, about 17% pentaglycerol, and about 8% higher oligomers), 688 g=4 moles of capric acid, 5.6 g of dodecylbenzenesulfonic acid and 2.2 g of hypophosphorous acid was heated up to a maximum of 155° C. at 400 to 40 mbar during the course of about 3 h with stirring and simultaneous passage of inert gas in a 4-liter four-neck flask which was provided with a stirrer, water separator, thermometer and gas inlet tube, the water of reaction being continuously removed by distillation. On attaining an acid number of <2, the reaction mixture was cooled down to about 65° C. and unreacted contents of polyglycerol were removed as follows:

The reaction mixture was dissolved in ethyl acetate (half the amount by volume) and extracted with water. The amount of sodium hydroxide solution corresponding to the acid number was added to the water. The amount of water used for extraction was about 50% by volume of the ester employed. The total of the extracted contents of polyglycerol after removal of the solvent by distillation was about 20 wt-% of the crude ester employed. The organic phase remaining after the extraction was evaporated in vacuo (residual content of water: 10 wt-%).

Characterizing data:

Acid number	<2
Hydrolysis number	75-85
HLB	14.3

Example 2: Preparation of polyglycerol laurate.

A mixture of 886 g of polyglycerol (average molecular weight: about 326 g/mole; consisting of about 30% triglycerol, about 45% tetraglycerol, about 17% pentaglycerol, and about 8% higher oligomers), 272 g = 1.36 moles of lauric acid, 2.8 g of dodecylbenzenesulfonic acid and 1.1 g of hypophosphorous acid was heated up to a maximum of 155° C. at 400 to 40 mbar during the course of about 3 hours with stirring and simultaneous passage of inert gas in a 2-liter four-neck flask which was provided with a stirrer, water separator, thermometer and gas inlet tube, the water of reaction being continuously removed by distillation. On attaining an acid number of <2, the reaction mixture was cooled down to about 70° C. and unreacted contents of polyglycerol were removed as follows:

The reaction mixture was dissolved in ethyl acetate (half the amount by volume) and extracted with water. The amount of sodium hydroxide solution corresponding to the acid number was added to the water. The amount of water used for extraction was about 50% by volume of the ester employed. The total of the extracted contents of polyglycerol after removal of the solvent by distillation was about 31 wt-% of the crude ester employed. The organic phase remaining after the extraction was evaporated in vacuo.

Characterizing data:

Acid number	0.9
Hydrolysis number	98.4
HLB	13.0

Example 3: Preparation of polyglycerol caprylcaprate.

A mixture of 2457 g of polyglycerol (average molecular weight: about 273 g/mole; consisting of about 4% diglycerol, about 62% triglycerol, about 24% tetraglycerol, about 7% pentaglycerol, and about 3% higher oligomers), 706 g=4.5 moles of caprylic/capric acid mixture, 6.3 g of dodecylbenzenesulfonic acid and 2.5 g of hypophosphorous acid was heated up to a maximum of 155° C. at 400 to 40 mbar during the course of about 3 hours with stirring and simultaneous passage of inert gas in a 4-liter four-neck flask which was provided with a stirrer, water separator, thermometer and gas inlet tube, the water of reaction being continuously removed by distillation. Upon attaining an acid number of <2, the reaction mixture was cooled down to about 70° C., and unreacted polyglycerol was removed as follows:

The reaction mixture was dissolved in ethyl acetate (half the amount by volume) and extracted with water. An amount of sodium hydroxide solution corresponding to the acid number was added to the water. The amount of water used for extraction was about 50% by volume of the ester employed. The total amount of extracted polyglycerol after removal of the solvent by distillation was about 25 wt-% of the crude ester employed. The organic phase remaining after the extraction was evaporated in vacuo.

Characterizing Data:

Acid number	1.0
Hydrolysis number	108.9
HLB	12.3

Fluoropolymers

Fluoropolymers form a monolayer providing easy application but are expensive.

Preparation:

The fluoropolymer obtained in the present method has a cyclic structure on its main chain, and it has high chemical stability or heat resistance. Further, since a hydroxyl group blocked by a specific blocking group is introduced into a side chain, it is applicable as a base polymer of resist materials for excimer laser, which has been difficult to achieve with conventional fluoropolymers. Additionally, the fluoropolymer of the present method is applicable also to an optical fiber, an electronic member, a transparent film material, an agricultural polyvinyl chloride film, an adhesive, a fiber material, a weather-resistant coating material or the like.

Methods

Prepation Method 1: Preparation Method of chloromethyl(2-cyclohexylcyclohexyl)ether)

A 500 ml reactor made of glass was substituted by nitrogen, 46.6 g of 2-cyclohexylcyclohexanol and 200 ml of dehydrated chloroform were charged therein, and the resultant solution was stirred by a stirrer, and then 7.70 g of paraformaldehyde was added therein at the time of complete dissolution. Next, the reactor was cooled to 0 to 5° C. by ice bath, and hydrogen chloride was introduced into the solution by a bubbler. When a suspension of the solution caused by paraformaldehyde became clear and the solution became transparent, the introduction of hydrogen chloride was stopped. The lower phase was separately isolated, followed by drying by adding 28.3 g of anhydrous calcium chloride powder.

Thereafter, 48.0 g of chloromethyl (2-cyclohexylcyclohexyl) ether was obtained (the purity according to ^{1}H NMR was 87%) after distillation of the solvent.

Hereinafter, the data of ^{1}H NMR is shown: ^{1}H NMR (399.8 MHz, solvent: $CDCl_3$, standard: tetramethylsilane) δ (ppm): 0.84–2.23 (m, 20H), 3.54–4.20 (m, 1H (exo-, endo-form mixed)), 5.55–5.62 (m, 2H).

Preparation Method 2:Preparation Method of chloromethyl fenchyl ether

45.9 g of chloromethyl fenchyl ether was obtained in the same manner as in Preparation Example 1 except that 39.5 g of fenchyl alcohol was used instead of using 46.6 g of 2-cyclohexylcyclohexanol in Preparation Method1 1. The yield was 88%, and the purity according to ^{1}H NMR was 90%. Hereinafter, the data of ^{1}H NMR is shown:

^{1}H NMR (399.8 MHz, solvent: $CDCl_3$, standard: tetramethylsilane) δ (ppm): 0.87–1.68 (m, 16H), 3.32 (s, 1H (exo-, endo-form mixed)), 5.48–5.50 (m, 2H).

Preparation Method 3 :Preparation Method of chloromethyl(2-norbornanemethyl)ether)

40.6 g of chloromethyl(2-norbornanemethyl)ether was obtained in the same manner as in Preparation Method 1 except that 32.3 g of 2-norbornanemethanol was used instead of using 46.6 g of 2-cyclohexylcyclohexanol in Preparation Example 1. The yield was 90%, and the purity according to ^{1}H NMR was 90%. Hereinafter, the data of ^{1}H NMR is shown:

^{1}H NMR (399.8 MHz, solvent: $CDCl_3$, standard: tetramethylsilane) δ (ppm): 0.64–2.25 (m, 11H), 3.34–3.67 (m, 2H), 5.50–5.52 (m, 2H).

Preparation Method 4 : Preparation Method of chloromethyl(4-tert-butylcyclohexyl)ether)

37.9 g of chloromethyl(4-tert-butylcyclohexyl)ether was obtained in the same manner as in Preparation Method 1 except that 40.0

g of 4-tert-butylcyclohexanol was used instead of using 46.6 g of 2-cyclohexylcyclohexanol in Preparation Example 1. The yield was 68%, and the purity according to ^{1}H NMR was 90%. Hereinafter, the data of ^{1}H NMR is shown:

> ^{1}H NMR (399.8 MHz, solvent: $CDCl_3$, standard: tetramethyl-silane) δ (ppm): 0.85 (s, 9H), 0.98–2.11 (m, 9H), 3.60–4.02 (m, 1H(exo-, endo-form mixed)), 5.56 (s, 2H).

Preparation Method 5 :Preparation Method of chloromethyl(dicyclohexylmethyl)ether)

49.9 g of chloromethyl(dicyclohexylmethyl)ether was obtained in the same manner as in Preparation Method 1 except that 50.3 g of dicyclohexylmethanol was used instead of using 46.6 g of 2-cyclohexylcyclohexanol in Preparation Example 1. The yield was 79%, and the purity according to ^{1}H NMR was 86%. Hereinafter, the data of ^{1}H NMR is shown:

> ^{1}H NMR (399.8 MHz, solvent: $CDCl_3$, standard: tetramethyl-silane) δ (ppm): 1.40–14.4 (m, 20H), 1.45–2.06 (m, 2H), 2.81 (d, 1H), 5.46 (s, 2H).

Preparation Method 6: Preparation Method of 1,1,2,3,3-pentafluoro-4-trifluoromethyl-4-hydroxy-1,6-heptad iene)

Into a 2 L reactor made of glass, 108 g of $CF_2ClCFClCF_2C(O)CF_3$ and 500 ml of dehydrated THF were charged and cooled to 0° C. A diluted solution having 200 ml of a 2M THF solution of $CH_2=CHCH_2MgCl$ further diluted with 200 ml of dehydrated THF, was dropwise added thereto in a nitrogen atmosphere over a period of about 5.5 hours. After completion of the dropwise addition, the mixture was stirred at 0° C. for 30 minutes and at room temperature for 17 hours, whereupon 200 ml of 2N hydrochloric acid was dropwise added. 200 ml of water and 300 ml of diethyl ether were added for liquid separation, and a diethyl ether layer was obtained as an organic layer. The organic layer was dried over magnesium sulfate, followed by filtration to obtain a crude liquid. The crude liquid was concentrated by an evaporator, followed by distillation under reduced pressure to obtain 85 g of $CF_2ClCFClCF_2C(CF_3)(OH)CH_2CH=CH_2$ (60 to 66° C./0.7 kPa).

Then, into a 500 ml reactor made of glass, 81 g of zinc and 170 ml of dioxane were charged, and activation of zinc was carried out by iodine. The reactor was heated to 100° C., and a solution prepared by diluting 84 g of the above prepared $CF_2ClCFClCF_2C(CF_3)(OH)CH_2CH{=}CH_2$ with 50 ml of dioxane, was dropwise added thereto over a period of 1.5 hours. After completion of the dropwise addition, the mixture was stirred at 100° C. for 40 hours. The reaction solution was filtered and washed with a small amount of dioxane. The filtrate was distilled under reduced pressure to obtain 30 g of $CF_2{=}CFCF_2C(CF_3)(OH)CH_2CH{=}CH_2$ (36 to 37° C./1 kPa) Hereinafter, the data of ^{1}H NMR and ^{19}F NMR are shown.

^{1}H NMR (399.8 MHz, solvent: $CDCl_3$, standard: tetramethylsilane) δ (ppm): 2.74 (d, J=7.3, 2H) 3.54 (broad s, 1H), 5.34 (m, 2H), 5.86 (m, 1H).

^{19}F NMR (376.2 MHz, solvent: $CDCl_3$, standard: $CFCl_3$) δ (ppm): –75.7 (m, 3F), –92.2 (m, 1F), –106.57 (m, 1F), –112.6 (m, 2F), –183.5 (m, 1F).

Preparation Method 7 : Preparation Method of 1,1,2,3,3-pentafluoro-4-trifluoromethyl-4-methoxymethoxy-1,6-heptadiene)

Into a 10 L reactor made of glass, 758 g of $CF_2ClCFClCF_2C(O)CF_3$ and 4.5 L of dehydrated THF were charged and cooled to 0° C. 1.4 L of a 2M THF solution of $CH_2{=}CHCH_2MgCl$, was dropwise added thereto in a nitrogen atmosphere over a period of about 10.5 hours. After completion of the dropwise addition, the mixture was stirred at 0° C. for 30 minutes and at room temperature for 12 hours, whereupon 350 g of chloromethyl methyl ether was dropwise added. The mixture was further stirred at room temperature for 92 hours. 1.5 L of water was added, followed by liquid separation. A crude liquid obtained by concentrating an organic layer by an evaporator, was washed twice with 1.5 L of water. Then, it was distilled under reduced pressure to obtain 677 g of $CF_2ClCFClCF_2C(CF_3)(OCH_2OCH_3)CH_2CH{=}CH_2$ (53 to 55° C./0.17 kPa).

Then, into a 3 L reactor made of glass, 577 g of zinc and 1.3 L of dioxane were charged, and activation of zinc was carried out by iodine. Then, the reactor was heated to 100° C., and 677 g of the above prepared $CF_2ClCFClCF_2C(CF_3)(OCH_2OCH_3)CH_2CH{=}CH_2$ was dropwise added thereto over a period of 2 hours. After completion of the dropwise addition, the mixture was stirred at 100° C. for 47 hours. The reaction solution was filtered and washed with a small amount of dioxane. To the filtrate, 2.5 L of water and 1.5 L of ether were added, followed by liquid separation. An organic layer was dried over anhydrous magnesium sulfate, followed by filtration to obtain a crude liquid. The crude liquid was concentrated by an evaporator, followed by distillation under reduced pressure to obtain 177 g of $CF_2{=}CFCF_2C(CF_3)(OCH_2OCH_3)CH_2CH{=}CH_2$ (43 to 45° C./0.6 kPa) Hereinafter, the data of ^1H NMR and ^{19}F NMR are shown.

^1H NMR (399.8 MHz, solvent: $CDCl_3$, standard: tetramethylsilane) δ (ppm): 3.16 (broad, 2H), 3.44 (s, 3H), 4.95 (m, 2H), 5.22 (m, 2H), 5.92 (m, 1H).

^{19}F NMR (376.2 MHz, solvent: $CDCl_3$, standard: $CFCl_3$) δ (ppm): –72.5 (m, 3F), –92.9 (m, 1F), –106.8 (m, 1F), –109.7 (m, 2F), –183.0 (m, 1F).

Preparation Method 8 :Preparation method of Fluoropolymer Precursor

7.50 g of 1,1,2,3,3-pentafluoro-4-trifluoromethyl-4-hydroxy-1,6-heptad iene [$CF_2{=}CFCF_2C(CF_3)(OH)CH_2CH{=}CH_2$], 3.66 g of 1,4-dioxane and 16.6 g of methyl acetate were charged into a pressure resistant reactor made of glass having an internal capacity of 30 mL. Next, 0.22 g of perfluorobenzoyl peroxide was added as a polymerization initiator. The interior of the system was freeze-deaerated, and then, polymerization was carried out for 18 hours in a constant temperature shaking vessel (70° C.). After the polymerization, the reaction solution was dropwise added into hexane to reprecipitate a polymer, followed by vacuum drying at 150° C. for 15 hours. As a result, 5.40 g of a white powdery non-crystalline polymer having a fluorinated cyclic monomer unit in its main chain (hereinafter referred to as precursor polymer A) was obtained. A molecular weight of precursor polymer A was measured by GPC (THF solvent), and as calculated in terms of a polystyrene, the number average molecular weight (Mn) was 7,600, and the weight average molecular weight (Mw) was 15,000, whereby Mw/Mn=1.99. A glass transition point measured by a differential scanning calorimetry (DSC) was 152° C.

Preparation Method 9 :Preparation Method of Fluoropolymer Precursor

4.82 g of 1,1,2,3,3-pentafluoro-4-trifluoromethyl-4-hydroxy-1,6-heptad iene[CF_2=$CFCF_2$ $C(CF_3)(OH)CH_2$ CH=CH_2], 1.00 g of 1,1,2,3,3-pentafluoro-4-trifluoromethyl-4-methoxymethyloxy-1,6-heptadiene[CF_2=$CFCF_2$ $C(CF_3)(OCH_2OCH_3)CH_2$ CH=CH_2], 0.78 g of 1,4-dioxane and 15.4 g of methyl acetate were charged into a pressure resistant reactor made of glass having an internal capacity of 30 mL. Next, 0.088 g of perfluorobenzoyl peroxide was added as a polymerization initiator. The interior of the system was freeze-deareated, and then, polymerization was carried out for 18 hours in a constant temperature shaking vessel (70° C.). After the polymerization, the reaction solution was dropwise added into hexane to reprecipitate a polymer, followed by vacuum drying at 150° C. for 15 hours. As a result, 5.16 g of a white powdery non-crystalline polymer having a fluorinated cyclic monomer unit in its main chain (hereinafter referred to as precursor polymer B) was obtained. A molecular weight of precursor polymer B was measured by GPC (THFsolvent), and as calculated in terms of a polystyrene, the number average molecular weight (Mn) was 12,800, and the weight average molecular weight (Mw) was 31,000, whereby Mw/Mn=2.42. A glass transition point measured by a differential scanning calorimetry (DSC) was 140° C.

The polymer composition calculated by ^{19}F NMR and ^{1}H NMR measurements, was a monomer unit composed of 1,1,2,3,3-pentafluoro-4-trifluoromethyl-4-hydroxy-1,6-heptad iene/a monomer unit composed of 1,1,2,3,3-pentafluoro-4-trifluoromethyl-4-methoxymethyloxy-1,6-heptadiene=85.0/15.0 mol %.

Preparation method 10 :Preparation Method of Fluoropolymer Precursor

6.43 g of 1,1,2,3,3-pentafluoro-4-trifluoromethyl-4-hydroxy-1,6-heptad iene[CF_2=$CFCF_2C(CF_3)(OH)CH_2$CH=CH_2], 0.18 g of tert-butyl methacrylate, 0.93 g of 1,4-dioxane and 20.4 g of methyl acetate were charged into a pressure resistant reactor made of glass having an internal capacity of 30 mL. Next, 0.112 g of perfluoro-benzoyl peroxide was added as a polymerization initiator. The interior of the system was freeze-deaerated, and then, polymerization was carried out for 18 hours in a constant temperature shaking vessel (70° C.). After the polymerization, the reaction solution was dropwise added into hexane to reprecipitate a polymer, followed by vacuum drying at 150° C. for 15 hours. As a result, 5.28 g of a white powdery non-crystalline polymer having a fluorinated cyclic monomer unit and a monomer unit composed of tert-butyl methacrylate in the main chain (hereinafter referred to as precursor polymer C) was obtained. A molecular weight of precursor polymer C was measured by GPC (THF solvent), and as calculated in terms of a polystyrene, the number average molecular weight (Mn) was 8,300, and the weight average molecular weight (Mw) was 16,800, whereby Mw/Mn=2.01. A glass transition point measured by a differential scanning calorimetry (DSC) was 162° C.

The polymer composition calculated by ^{19}F NMR and ^{1}H NMR measurements, was a monomer unit composed of 1,1,2,3,3-pentafluoro-4-trifluoromethyl-4-hydroxy-1,6-heptad iene/a monomer unit composed of tert-butyl methacrylate=95/5 mol %.

Process

5.00 g of precursor polymer A prepared in Preparation Method 8 and 25 mL of methanol were put into a 200 mL round flask and stirred with a magnetic stirrer. After dissolving the polymer, a methanol solution of sodium hydroxide (0.31 g of sodium hydroxide is previously dissolved in 7.65 g of methanol) was added therein and stirred overnight at room temperature. After distilling the solvent, 200 mL of dehydrated THF and 1.95 g of chloromethyl(2-cyclohexylcyclohexyl)ether prepared in Preparation Example 1 were added and stirred vigorously. The above solution was stirred for three days at room temperature, and then the solvent was distilled off. A residue thus obtained was dissolved in 100 mL of diethyl ether, and 200 mL of pure water was added for liquid separation to remove a water-soluble component. After distillation of the solvent from the organic layer, the residue was dissolved in 20 mL of acetone, and it was dropwise added into hexane to reprecipitate a polymer. The polymer thus obtained was vacuum dried at 130° C. for 15 hours, and 4.20 g of a white powdery non-crystalline polymer (hereinafter referred to as Polymer 3A) was obtained.

SILICONES

Although silicones are used as both external and internal mould release agents, the primary application is as the active ingredient in external release agents. The silicone is in a solution or aqueous dispersion that is sprayed intermittently into the mould cavity between shots. A disadvantage of silicones as internal release agents is their possible interference with painting and contamination of finish surfaces.

Preparation

The present authors have now found a useful way of processing Silicone gel or other hydrolysed silicon compounds into ceramic articles which demonstrate improved physical and/or physico-chemical properties.

Process 1

45% Silicone gel of water content 45 to 50 wt. %, produced by hydrolysing higher boiling point organochlorosilanes produced in the manufacture of methylchlorosilanes by the direct process in which silicon metal was reacted with methyl chloride, was preground. 10% Al rich clay was added in solid form as binder and was mixed with the Silicone gel to form a homogenous mass. 45% alumina powder was added and the composition was mixed again to a homogenous silicon composition.

The silicon composition was pressed into shape and allowed to dry for 2 days. The resulting dry hard shapes were fired for 8 hours at 1500° C. The fired product, which had density about 1.2 g/cc, withstood application of pressure sufficient to crumble a conventional insulation brick. The fired product was hard enough to cut glass. The fired product withstood heating to 1650° C. without loss of shape. The fired product, 2 cm thick, was heated to 1500° C. and placed in a 1 cm depth of water without cracking, and was also heated to 1500° C. and dropped in an excess of cold water without cracking.

Process 2

70% of the Silicone gel was preground and mixed with 5% fumed silica and 25% ball clay and pressed and dried. The dry hard shapes were fired for 8 hours at 1300° C. The fired product had a specific gravity of about 1.0 and was highly resistant to acid attack—it was held in contact with 30% aqueous HNO_3 for more than 3 months, and also in contact with 50% aqueous H_2SO_4 for more than 3 months, without visible degradation. The melting temperature of the fired product was about 1470° C.

Process 3

Higher boiling point organochlorosilanes produced in the manufacture of methylchlorosilanes by the direct process were filtered to remove solid materials such as silicon metal, copper and iron. The filtered organochlorosilanes were hydrolysed with lime solution to produce a Silicone gel. The Silicone gel was washed with de-ionised water in a centrifuge and was separated form a heavy mineral phase. 20% of the resulting modified Silicone gel was preground and mixed with 35% clay and 45% alumina powder and pressed and dried. The clay was an alumina rich clay from Fuchs. The alumina (Al_2O_3) had the following grain distribution by wt %: 10%>90 μm; 30%>63 μm; 60%>45 μm; 80%>32 μm. The dry hard shapes were fired for 4 hours at 1450° C. The fired product retained its shape at temperatures up to 1670° C. and was suitable as a rack for support of ceramic articles during firing. The fired product also resisted molten aluminium and could be used as a mould for aluminium ingots or castings.

Process 4

25% of the modified Silicone gel of Process 3 was preground and mixed with 40% alumina and 35% clay. The mixture was pressed and dried. The dry hard shapes were fired for 4 hours at 1450° C. The fired product had an insulation value of 1.07 W/(mK) when tested according to DIN EN 993-15 at 1100° C. and was particularly suitable as refractory insulation material.

Suppliers

There are numerous suppliers of lubricants and mould release agents as a result of the variety of chemistries that perform the function of internal and external lubrication. The suppliers are generally large specialty chemical companies that sell the particular chemistry to a wide variety of end-use applications. The amount of material sold to function as a lubricant or mould release agent for plastics is typically small in comparison to each company's total sales. Table 12.1 shows the major global suppliers of lubricants and mould release agents by type.

Trends and forecasts

Other than plasticizers, lubricants come closest to being a commodity business within the plastic additives market. Since over 70% of lubricant consumption is directed at PVC for applications such as pipe, siding, and windows, demand will be highly dependent on the construction industry.

The use of lubricants with heat stabilizers, particularly lead types, in "one-pack" systems has not taken off in North America as it has in Europe. North America has focused more on the tin-based stabilizer systems, and customers still prefer buying the additives separately.

Key technology trends in lubricants include the development of high-temperature lubricants and the continuing work on lubricants that are compatible with other additives and colors in the plastic. Mould release agents are actually a different business than lubricants although there are some related chemistries at the lower end. These products are typically higher-priced formulations and are used primarily in thermoset urethanes, polyesters, and epoxies. The active ingredients are sold by silicone and fluorochemical producers such as Dow Corning, GE Silicones, Wacker, DuPont, and ICI. Overall, the lubricant and mould release businesses are growing at 4 to 5% per year worldwide.

TABLE 12.1: Selected Suppliers of Lubricants and Mold Release Agents

Supplier	Type						
	Metallic stearates	Petroleum wax	Fatty amides	Fatty esters	PE wax	Fatty acid/ alcohols	Silicones
Akcros (Akzo)	×	—	—	—	—	—	—
AlliedSignal	—	—	—	—	×	—	—
Baerlocher	×	—	—	—	—	—	—
BASF	—	—	—	—	×	—	—
Chemson	×	—	—	—	—	—	—
Clariant	—	×	—	×	×	—	—
Croda	—	—	×	—	—	×	—
Dow Corning	—	—	—	—	—	—	×
Eastman Chemical	—	—	—	×	×	—	—
Elf Atochem	×	—	—	—	—	—	—
Faci	×	—	×	—	—	—	—
Ferro	×	—	—	—	—	—	—
GE Specialty Chemicals	—	—	—	—	—	—	×

Henkel	×	—	—	×	—	×	—
Huels	—	—	—	—	×	—	—
ICI Specialty Chemicals	—	—	×	×	—	×	—
Lonza	—	—	×	×	—	—	—
Morton Plastic Additives	×	—	×	—	×	—	—
Olefina	×	—	×	×	—	—	—
Rhodia	—	—	—	—	—	—	×
Sogis	×	—	×	—	—	—	—
Wacker Silicones	—	—	—	—	—	—	×
Witco	×	×	×	×	—	×	—

13

Nucleating Agents

DESCRIPTION

Nucleating agents are used in polymer systems to increase the rate of crystallization. These agents are added to partly crystalline polymers and change the polymer's crystallization temperature, crystal spherulite size, density, clarity, impact, and tensile properties. These intentional contaminates achieve these functions by acting as sites for crystalline formation. Nucleating agents are typically added postreactor and are used primarily in injection molding applications. However, they can also be found in blow molding, sheet extrusion, and thermoforming. They are incorporated into materials such as nylon, PP, crystalline polyethylene terephthalate (CPET), and thermoplastic PET molding compounds at use levels typically below 1%, although CPET uses higher levels. The incorporation of these nucleating agents can be done in several ways, including powder mixtures, suspensions, solutions, or in the form of a masterbatch. Whichever method is used, good dispersion of the nucleating agent throughout the polymer must be achieved to provide the optimal effect. The addition of nucleating agents into polymers yields benefits such as higher productivity and improved optical properties. Nucleating agents can shorten cycle time by reducing set-up time in the mold. Care must be taken to ensure that shrinkage and impact properties are not negatively affected. With some difficult-to-crystallize thermoplastics, such as partially aromatic polyamides or PET, nucleants are needed to obtain useful parts with reasonable cycle times and mold temperatures. The optical benefits of nucleating agents are increased clarity and improved gloss. These properties improve because of an increase in the number of fine crystals. When crystals are smaller than the wavelength of visible light, the light is scattered at smaller angles, decreasing the hazy effect seen when nucleating agents are not used. When utilized to improve transparency in materials such as PP, these materials are referred to as *clarifiers or clarifying agents.* An example of how clarifiers work is depicted in Fig. 13.1.

Table 13.1: Criteria Used in Selection of an Antiblocking Agent

Specification	Function
Particle size distribution	Affects both the level of antiblock performance and the physical properties of the final film.
Surface area	Measured in square meters per gram. Affects the coefficient of friction of the film and level of wear on equipment.
Specific gravity	Indicates the relative weight of the product. Density Measures the mass/volume ratio. Affects the quality of the film

Types

Several different types of nucleating agents are used in specific polymers, as shown in Table 13.1. The four major categories of chemical nucleating agents are substituted sorbitols, low molecular weight polyolefins, sodium benzoate, and ionomer resins. In addition, a variety of mineral fillers, reinforcements, and pigments are used in nylon and other polymers. These nonchemical nucleating agents are easily dispersed, inexpensive, and typically available "on-site" since they are commonly used for their primary reinforcing and filling function.

Substituted sorbitols

Substituted sorbitols are used in polyolefins, particularly PP, for nucleation and clarification purposes. They have varying degrees of miscibility in PP and different melting points and process temperatures as well as odor. Both homopolymers and random copolymers of PP use sorbitols. Use levels range from 0.1 to 0.3% on the polymer. The FDA has regulated the use of substituted sorbitols, but has given its approval for their use in PP. These materials are used in injection molded housewares, medical devices, and protective packaging. Smaller amounts are used in blow-molded bottles.

Preparation

The present method provides recombinant SLDH. One can increase the production yield of the SLDH enzyme by introducing the gene of SLDH provided by the present method into organisms including acetic acid bacteria including the genus Gluconobacter and the genus Acetobacter. One can also produce active SLDH in microorganisms beside Gluconobacter by using the SLDH gene of the present method in combination with the ORF2 gene of the present method . The recombinant SLDH can be immobilized on a solid carrier for solid phase enzyme reaction. The present method also provides recombinant organisms. One can produce L-sorbose from D- sorbitol with the recombinant organisms. One can also produce L-sorbose from D- sorbitol even in a host organism beside acetic acid bacteria by introducing the SLDH gene in combination with the ORF2 gene of the present method

Method 1 :Determination of Amino Acid Sequences of SLDH

(1) N-terminal Amino Acid Sequence Analyses of Lysylendopeptidase-treated SLDH Polypeptides

Partial amino acid sequences of peptides No.1, 3 and 8 prepared from SLDH protein were determined. Purified SLDH of *G. suboxydans* IFO 3255 was digested with lysylendopeptidase; the reaction mixture (25 ml) contained 1.2 mM of lysylendopeptidase and 3 nmol of the SLDH protein in 100 mM Tris-HCl buffer, pH9.0, and the reaction was carried out at 37° C. for 15 hours. The resulting peptide fragments were separated by HPLC with acetonitrile/isopropanol gradient in 0.1% TFA at a flow rate of 1.0 ml/min. Elution of the peptides was monitored by UV absorbance at 214 nm, and the peak fractions were collected manually and subjected to N-terminal amino acid sequence analysis with an amino acid sequencer.

Method 2 : Cloning of Partial SLDH Gene by PCR

PCR was conducted with chromosomal DNA of *G. suboxydans* IFO 3255 and degenerate oligonucleotide DNA primers, s7 and s6R whose sequences are shown. The PCR amplification was carried out with thermostable polymerase Amplitaq, using a thermal cycler. The following reaction mixture (50 μl) was used for PCR: 200 μM of dNTPs, 10˜20 pmol of each primer (54˜288 degeneracy), 6 ng of chromosomal DNA of *G. suboxydans* IFO 3255 and 0.5 unit of the. DNA polymerase in the buffer provided from the supplier. The reaction consisted of 30 cycles of 1) denaturation step at 94° C for 1 min; 2) annealing step at 48° C. min; 3) synthesis step at 72° C. for 2 min. Consequently, 1.6 kb DNA was amplified and cloned in *E. coli* vector, pUC57/T (MBI Fermentas, Vilnius, Lithuania), which has 32 -ddT-tailed ends for direct ligation of an amplified DNA fragment to obtain a recombinant plasmid pMT20. The cloned DNA was subjected to nucleotide sequencing by the method of dideoxy-chain termination; the 1.6 kb fragment encoded the peptides No. 3 and No. 8.

Method 3 : Complete Cloning of the SLDH Gene

(1) Construction of Gene Library of *G. suboxydans* IFO 3255

The chromosomal DNA of *G. suboxydass* IFO 3255 was prepared from the, cells grown on MB agar plate for 2 days. The chromosomal DNA (160 μg) was partially digested with 20 units of Eco RI in 500 μl of reaction mixture. Portions of the sample were withdrawn at 5, 10, 15, 30, and 60 minutes and the degree of the digestion was detected by agarose gel electrophoresis. Former four portions which contained partially-digested DNA fragments were combined and subjected to preparative gel electrophoresis, (agarose: 0.6%). Fragments of 15-35 kb were cut out and electroeluted from the gel. The eluate was filtered and precipitated with sodium acetate and ethanol at –80° C. The DNA fragments were collected by centrifugation and suspended in 200 μl of mM Tris-HCl, pH8.0, buffer containing 1 mM EDTA.

In parallel, 1.8 μg of a cosmid vector pVK100 was completely digested with Eco RI and treated with calf intestine alkaline phosphatase. The linearized and dephosphorylated pVK100was ligated with 15-35 kb Eco RI fragments of the chromosomal DNA of *G. suboxydans* IFO 3255 (5g) with the ligation kit in 20 separate tubes under the condition recommended by the supplier to obtain highly polymerized DNA. The ligated DNA was then used for in vitro packaging according to the method described by the supplier. The resulting phage particles were used to infect *E. coli* ED8767, a host for the genomic library. Consequently, 4,271 colonies were obtained and all of the colonies tested (20 colonies) possessed the insert DNAs with the average size of about 25 kb.

(2) Colony Hybridization to Obtain Complete SLDH Gene

The cosmid library described above was screened to isolate the clone carrying complete SLDH gene by colony hybridization method with ^{32}P-labeled. 1.6 kb DNA of pMT20. One clone was isolated and designated pSLII, which carry about 25 kb insert in pVK100 vector. From the pSLII, 6.2 kb Pst I fragment was isolated and cloned into pUC18 to obtain plasmid PUSLIIP. The 6.2 kb Pst I fragment containing ORF2 and SLDH genes was isolated from PUSLIIP and subcloned into pCRII vector (Invitrogen Corporation, CA, USA) to produce pCRSLIIP. From the resulting plasmid, the DNA fragment containing the 6.2 kb Pst I fragment was isolated as Hind III-Xho I fragment and cloned between Hiked III and Xho I sites of pVK100 to obtain pVKSLIIP.

(3) Expression of SLDH Gene in *E. coli*

To confirm whether 6.2 kb Pst I-fragment encodes the target SLDH, cells of *E. coli* JM109 carrying pUSLIIP was subjected to Western-blot analysis with anti-SLDH antibody as described above. Immuno-positive proteins with a molecular weight of about 80 kDa were observed in the transformant, indicating that the Pst I-fragment encodes the polypeptides with the molecular weight of the intact SLDH (79 kDa +/–0.5 kDa).

(4) Construction of SLDH-deficient Gluconobacter, Strain 26A11, as the Test Strain for SLDH-activity Complementation

Transposon Tn5 mutagenesis was performed with *G. melanogenus IFO* 3293 as the parent. Tn5, a transposable element coding for Kmr, causes null mutations at random on DNA of its host organism and widely used as a mutagen in Gram-negative bacteria. The IFO 3293 was selected as the parent in the following reasons: (i) it produced L-sorbose from D- sorbitol, (ii) it showed immuno-positive polypeptide of about 80 kDa in Western-blot analysis with the antibody prepared against SLDH purified from *G. suboxydans* IFO 3255 and (iii) its frequency for generating Tn5 mutants was much higher than that of *G. suboxydans* IFO 3255.

G. melanogenus IFO 3293 was cultivated in a test tube containing 5 ml of the MB medium containing 25 g/l of mannitol, 5 g/l of yeast extract (Difco Laboratories,), 3 g/l of Bactopepton (Difco) at 30° C. overnight. *E. coli* HB101 (pRK2013) and *E. coli* HB101 (pSUP2021) were cultivated in test tubes containing 5 ml of LB medium with 50 μg/ml of kanamycin at 37° C. overnight. The cells was separately collected by centrifugation and suspended in the half volume of MB medium. The each cell suspension was mixed in the ratio of 1:1:1 and the mixture was placed on the nitrocellulose filter on the surface of MB agar plate. The plate was incubated at 27° C. overnight and the resulting cells on the filter was scraped, suspended in the appropriate volume of MB medium and spread on the selection plate (MPK plate), MB containing 10 1 μg/ml of polymyxin B and 50 μg/ml of kanamycin . The MPK plate was incubated at 27° C. for 3 to 4 days.

The resulting 3,436 Tn5 mutants were subjected to the immuno-dot blot screening with the anti-SLDH antibody. The cells of each strain were independently suspended in 50 μl Laemmli buffer consisting of 62.5 mM Tris-HCl (pH6.5), 10% glycerol, 2% SDS and 5% β-mercaptoethanol in 96-well microtiter plate and incubated at 60° C. for 2 hours. The Cell Free Extracts (CFEs) were stamped on the nitrocellulose filter and the immuno-positive samples in the CFEs were screened with AP conjugate substrate kit (Bio-RAD Laboratories, Richmond, Calif., USA). As a result, only one strain 26A 11 without positive signal in the immuno-dot blot screening was obtained.

SLDH-deficiency of the strain 26A11 was confirmed by Western-blot analysis; it expressed at most 1/500 amount of SLDH compared with its parent strain. 26A11 was not a complete SLDH-deficient strain but the strain with SLDH gene repressed by Tn5. insertion; the insertion site was found to be close to the C-terminus by determining the nucleotide sequence around Tn5-insertion point. Next, a resting cell reaction was conducted. to examine the whole SLDH activity in 26A11 and the wild Gluconobacter strains. In the potassium phosphate buffer 100 mM (pH7.0) containing 2%

D-sorbitol, 26A11 slightly converted D-sorbitol to L-sorbose, whereas the wild strains IFO 3293 and IFO 3255 completely did it in 39.5 hr at 30° C.

Low Molecular Weight Polyolefins

Low molecular weight polyolefins are primarily used in CPET for rapid crystallization of otherwise amorphous material. These products are typically sold by the CPET suppliers in a package along with the base resin. Use levels are higher than with the sorbitols and average 1 to 3% of the resin. The major application is in thermoformed dual-purpose food trays for conventional and microwave ovens. The nucleating agent promotes fast crystallization during the tray thermoforming process.

TABLE 13.2: Nucleating Agents Used in Specific Polymers

Polymer	Nucleating agents
Polyethylene terephthalate	Inert mineral fillers, chalk, clay, talc,
(PET/CPET)	silicates, carbonates, pigments Organic compounds, carboxylic acids, diphenylamine Polymers, mainly polyolefins, PE, PP, ethylene and styrene copolymers, ionomers
Polyamides (nylon)	Highly dispersed silica
	Sodium benzoate
	Talc
	Titanium dioxide
Polypropylene	Sodium benzoate
	Bis-benzylidene sorbitol
Polyethylene	Potassium stearate
	Nucleated PE or higher polyolefins

Preparation:

Method 1 :Determination of Amino Acid Sequences of SLDH

(1) N-terminal Amino Acid Sequence Analyses of Lysylendopeptidase-treated SLDH Polypeptides

Partial amino acid sequences of peptides No.1, 3 and 8 prepared from SLDH protein were determined. Purified SLDH of *G. suboxydans* IFO 3255 was digested with lysylendopeptidase; the reaction mixture (25 ml) contained 1.2 mM of lysylendopeptidase and 3 nmol of the SLDH protein in 100 mM Tris-HCl buffer, pH9.0, and the reaction was carried out at 37° C. for 15 hours. The resulting peptide fragments were separated by HPLC (column protein C-4, VYDAC, California, USA) with acetonitrile/isopropanol gradient in 0.1% TFA at a flow rate of 1.0 ml/min. Elution of the peptides was monitored by UV absorbance at 214 nm, and the peak fractions were collected manually and subjected to N-terminal amino acid sequence analysis with an amino acid sequencer.

Method 2: Cloning of Partial SLDH Gene by PCR

PCR was conducted with chromosomal DNA of *G. suboxydans* IFO 3255 and degenerate oligonucleotide DNA primers, s7 and s6R whose sequences are shown. The PCR amplification was carried out with thermostable polymerase Amplitaq, using a thermal cycler. The following reaction mixture (50 μl) was used for PCR: 200 μM of dNTPs, 10~20 pmol of each primer (54~288 degeneracy), 6 ng of chromosomal DNA of *G. suboxydans* IFO 3255 and 0.5 unit of the. DNA polymerase in the buffer provided from the supplier. The reaction consisted of 30 cycles of 1) denaturation step at 94° C. for 1 min; 2) annealing step at 48° C. min; 3) synthesis step at 72° C. for 2 min. Consequently, 1.6 kb DNA was amplified and cloned in *E. coli* vector, pUC57/T (MBI Fermentas, Vilnius, Lithuania), which has 32 -ddT-tailed ends for direct ligation of an amplified DNA fragment to obtain a recombinant plasmid pMT20. The cloned DNA was subjected to nucleotide sequencing by the method of dideoxy-chain termination; the 1.6 kb fragment encoded the peptides No. 3 and No. 8.

Method 3 : Complete Cloning of the SLDH Gene

(1) Construction of Gene Library of *G. suboxydans* IFO 3255

The chromosomal DNA of *G. suboxydass* IFO 3255 was prepared from the, cells grown on MB agar plate for 2 days. The chromosomal DNA (160 μg) was partially digested with 20 units of Eco RI in 500 μl of reaction mixture. Portions of the sample were withdrawn at 5, 10, 15, 30, and 60 minutes and the degree of the digestion was detected by agarose gel electrophoresis. Former four portions which contained partially-digested DNA fragments were combined and subjected to preparative gel electrophoresis, (agarose: 0.6%). Fragments of 15-35 kb were cut out and electroeluted from the gel. The eluate was filtered and precipitated with sodium acetate and ethanol at –80° C. The DNA fragments were collected by centrifugation and suspended in 200 μl of mM Tris-HCl, pH8.0, buffer containing 1 mM EDTA.

In parallel, 1.8 μg of a cosmid vector pVK100 was completely digested with Eco RI and treated with calf intestine alkaline phosphatase. The linearized and dephosphorylated pVK100was ligated with 15-35 kb Eco RI fragments of the chromosomal DNA of *G. suboxydans* IFO 3255 (5g) with the ligation kit (Takara Shuzo, Kyoto, Japan) in 20 separate tubes under the condition recommended by the supplier to obtain highly polymerized DNA. The ligated DNA was then used for in vitro packaging according to the method described by the supplier (Amersham Japan). The resulting phage particles were used to infect *E. coli* ED8767, a host for the genomic library. Consequently, 4,271 colonies were obtained and all of the colonies tested (20 colonies) possessed the insert DNAs with the average size of about 25 kb.

(2) Colony Hybridization to Obtain Complete SLDH Gene

The cosmid library described above was screened to isolate the clone carrying complete SLDH gene by colony hybridization method with ^{32}P-labeled. 1.6 kb DNA of pMT20. One clone was isolated and designated pSLII, which carry about 25 kb insert in pVK100 vector. From the pSLII, 6.2 kb Pst I fragment was isolated and cloned into pUC18 to obtain plasmid PUSLIIP. The 6.2 kb Pst I fragment containing ORF2 and SLDH genes was isolated from PUSLIIP and subcloned into pCRII vector (Invitrogen Corporation, CA, USA) to produce pCRSLIIP. From the resulting plasmid, the DNA fragment containing the 6.2 kb Pst I fragment was isolated as Hind III-Xho I fragment and cloned between Hiked III and Xho I sites of pVK100 to obtain pVKSLIIP.

(3) Expression of SLDH Gene in *E. coli*

To confirm whether 6.2 kb Pst I-fragment encodes the target SLDH, cells of *E. coli* JM109 carrying pUSLIIP was subjected to

Western-blot analysis with anti-SLDH antibody as described above. Immuno-positive proteins with a molecular weight of about 80 kDa were observed in the transformant, indicating that the Pst I-fragment encodes the polypeptides with the molecular weight of the intact SLDH (79 kDa +/–0.5 kDa).

(4) Construction of SLDH-deficient Gluconobacter, Strain 26A11, as the Test Strain for SLDH-activity Complementation

Transposon Tn5 mutagenesis was performed with *G. melanogenus IFO* 3293 as the parent. Tn5, a transposable element coding for Kmr, causes null mutations at random on DNA of its host organism and widely used as a mutagen in Gram-negative bacteria. The IFO 3293 was selected as the parent in the following reasons: (i) it produced L-sorbose from D-sorbitol, (ii) it showed immuno-positive polypeptide of about 80 kDa in Western-blot analysis with the antibody prepared against SLDH purified from *G. suboxydans* IFO 3255 and (iii) its frequency for generating Tn5 mutants was much higher than that of *G. suboxydans* IFO 3255.

G. melanogenus IFO 3293 was cultivated in a test tube containing 5 ml of the MB medium containing 25 g/l of mannitol, 5 g/l of yeast extract, 3 g/l of Bactopepton (Difco) at 30° C. overnight. *E. coli* HB101 (pRK2013) [D. H. Figurski, Proc, Natl. Acad. Sci. USA 76: 1648-1652, 1979] and *E. coli* HB101 (pSUP2021) (R. Simon, et al., BIO/TECHNOL. 1:784-791, 1983] were cultivated in test tubes containing 5 ml of LB medium with 50 μg/ml of kanamycin at 37° C. overnight. The cells was separately collected by centrifugation and suspended in the half volume of MB medium. The each cell suspension was mixed in the ratio of 1:1:1 and the mixture was placed on the nitrocellulose filter on the surface of MB agar plate. The plate was incubated at 27° C. overnight and the resulting cells on the filter was scraped, suspended in the appropriate volume of MB medium and spread on the selection plate (MPK plate), MB containing 10 1 μg/ml of polymyxin B and 50 μg/ml of kanamycin . The MPK plate was incubated at 27° C. for 3 to 4 days.

The resulting 3,436 Tn5 mutants were subjected to the immuno-dot blot screening with the anti-SLDH antibody. The cells of each strain were independently suspended in 50 μl Laemmli buffer consisting of 62.5 mM Tris-HCl (pH6.5), 10% glycerol, 2% SDS and 5% β-mercaptoethanol in 96-well microtiter plate and incubated at 60° C. for 2 hours. The Cell Free Extracts (CFEs) were stamped on the nitrocellulose filter and the immuno-positive samples in the CFEs were screened with AP conjugate substrate kit (Bio-RAD Laboratories, Richmond, Calif., USA). As a result, only one strain 26A 11 without positive signal in the immuno-dot blot screening was obtained.

SLDH-deficiency of the strain 26A11 was confirmed by Western-blot analysis; it expressed at most 1/500 amount of SLDH compared with its parent strain. 26A11 was not a complete SLDH-deficient strain but the strain with SLDH gene repressed by Tn5. insertion; the insertion site was found to be close to the C-terminus by determining the nucleotide sequence around Tn5-insertion point. Next, a resting cell reaction was conducted. to examine the whole SLDH activity in 26A11 and the wild Gluconobacter strains. In the potassium phosphate buffer 100 mM (pH7.0) containing 2% D-sorbitol, 26A11 slightly converted D- sorbitol to L-sorbose, whereas the wild strains IFO 3293 and IFO 3255 completely did it in 39.5 hr at 30° C.

Methods

Polyethylene, as described hereafter, was placed in a sigma blade mixer maintained at 200° F. Petroleum wax was added until it comprised 25 percent of the total weight. One part of 2,2'-methylene-bis-(4-methyl-6-t-butylphenol), an antioxidant, was added to every thousand parts of polymer and wax. Typical properties of this polyethylene are:

Specific gravity 0.940-0.942 Melt index, ASTM D1238 nil Crystalline melting point 266-268° F. Molecular weight 1,250,000

Typical physical properties of the petroleum wax are:

Melting point, ASTM D127 195° F. Viscosity SUS at 210° F. 84 Specific gravity at 60° F. 0.943 the mixing was continued until all of the wax melted and a well-mixed blend was obtained. At 200° F. the polyethylene did not melt and there was no appreciable absorption of the polyethylene by the wax. Heat to the sigma blade mixer was shut off and the blend was allowed to cool while agitation was maintained. When cooled to ambient temperature the composition was a granular, free-flowing powder consisting essentially of particles of the polyethylene coated with wax.

This powder was fed to an extruder equipped with a 1:1 compression ratio transport screw whose surface was chromium plated. The extruder was fitted with a 1/4-inch rod die whose inner surface was coated with a fluorocarbon polymer. The temperature in the front of the barrel was 220° F., the rear of the barrel 205° F., while the die was maintained at 300° F. These barrel temperatures kept the wax molten but did not melt the solid polyethylene. As the slurry was transported to the heated die, the action of the transport screw forced the slurry into the shape of the ¼-inch rod die. As the forced blend passed into the heated portion of the die the combination of heat and pressure fused the slurry into a homogeneous ¼-inch diameter rod. The fused rod emerged at a rate of about 4 grams per minute. The aforementioned extrusion was repeated using 2.5, 5.0, 10.0 and 15.0 weight percent of the wax.

Next, standard test specimens were prepared from the rods extruded as described heretofore. The specimens were prepared and tested according to ASTM D638-67T (Tentative Method of Test for Tensile Properties of Plastics). The physical properties of the extruded polyethylene and wax blends were as shown in Table 13.3.

These results indicate that the physical properties of the polyethylene and wax blends do not vary appreciably as the amount of wax varies from 2.5 to 25 weight percent.

The molecular weights of the fused polyethylene in these rods as determined by reduced viscosity in tetrahydronaphthalene at 135° C. were as follows:

Polyethylene and Molecular Weight

2.5 wt. % wax	870,000
5.0 wt. % wax	970,000
10.0 wt. % wax	870,000
15.0 wt. % wax	870,000
25.0 wt. % wax	920,000

TABLE 13.3: Physical Properties of Extruded Samples

Tensile Poly-Yield Strength	Elon-Modulus of ethylene Point, at Break gation	Elasticity, . and p.s.i	p.s.i. %	p.s.i.
2.5 wt. % wax	2,840	3,470	599	47,600
5.0 wt. % wax	2,743	3,370	565	44,730
10.0 wt. % wax	2,765	2,975	562	43,600
15.0 wt. % wax	2,770	3,141	603	47,900
25.0 wt. % wax	2,800	3,385	602	54,200

These results indicate that the molecular weights of the polyethylenes in the polyethylene and wax blends do not vary appreciably as the amount of wax varies from 2.5 to 25 weight percent.

Substantially equivalent results, as in the aforementioned specific example, are obtained when (1) other carriers are used and/or (2) the other polyolefin is used.

Sodium benzoate

Sodium benzoate is an inexpensive traditional nucleating agent used predominantly in nylon and PP homopolymer. Sodium benzoate has full FDA approval in PP and is used in food applications and pharmaceutical synthesis. Typical use levels of sodium benzoate as a nucleating agent in PP are lower than the sorbitols. The major application is in injection-molded packaging closures.

Preparation

It has now been found according to the present method that sodium benzoate is recovered in easily filterable form from the mixture of benzoic acid in an aromatic hydrocarbon solvent by adding sodium alkoxide to a solution, thereby forming a slurry of solid sodium benzoate in the aromatic hydrocarbon, and separating the sodium benzoate from the slurry. This isolation is readily carried out on a commercial scale at small expense.

Benzoic acid solutions in aromatic hydrocarbons such as benzene, toluene, or xylene are the by-product streams from various chemical processes. Such a solution, however, is most commonly encountered as the liquid effluent from toluene oxidation. This effluent contains benzoic acid, toluene, oxidation by-products and dissolved metal oxidation catalysts, ordinarily a cobalt compound, which is preferably removed from the solution prior to the precipitation.

The concentration of the benzoic acid in the liquid aromatic hydrocarbon may vary widely depending on the source. Generally, concentrations of about 5 to about 30 percent by weight of benzoic acid are found in the effluent streams, with about 5 to about 15 percent being especially suited to the invention. Such solutions readily lend themselves to crystal formation to give a granular precipitate which is easily filtered.

The sodium alkoxide of the present method is conveniently and preferably prepared by reacting sodium hydroxide with an alkanol of up to about 10 carbon atoms. Alkoxides of 1 to 6 carbon atoms are preferred, with sodium methoxide being of special interest because of its availability and effectiveness. Substantial excesses of the alkanol are not desirable in the formation of the alkoxide since the benzoate is soluble in alcohols causing a reduced yield of the precipitate, but the precipitation is usually conducted in the presence of an excess of the alcohol corresponding to the alkoxide. A mixture of caustic and alcohol having a mole ratio of 1-10 moles of alcohol per mole of caustic is preferred, with ratios of about 1.5 to about 4 moles of alcohol per mole of caustic being especially preferred.

The amount of the sodium alkoxide reacted with the benzoic acid mixture is preferably that amount which stoichiometrically reacts with the benzoic acid. This amount, however, is not critical. For the reaction of less than a stoichiometric amount of sodium alkoxide, some benzoic acid is unreacted and remains unprecipitated. For an excess, sodium alkoxide impurities are introduced into the system which may be combined with the precipitate.

The temperature of precipitation may be varied widely. Preferred temperatures are about 10° to about 75°C. with especially good results being obtained with temperatures of about 25° to about 60°C. At higher temperatures, the alcohol tends to evaporate under normal atmospheric conditions. To prevent this loss, however, pressure may be employed.

Under the reaction conditions, a preferred reaction time is about 5 to about 30 minutes. During this time the reaction mixture is stirred, but extended or vigorous stirring of the benzoic acid-sodium alkoxide mixture in some cases forms a less granular precipitate.

By the use of the present method, the sodium benzoate is obtained from an aromatic hydrocarbon solvent in a granular form which is conventionally separated on a commercial scale by simple filtration.

Method 1 : Sodium Methoxide in Methanol-Water

To 750 g. of the reaction mass from a toluene oxidation reaction which contained 13% benzoic acid in toluene along with minor by-products from the oxidation was added 29 g. of 72 percent sodium hydroxide solution which had been previously mixed with 75 g. of methanol. The reactor mass was being held at a temperature of 46°C. when the methanol-caustic mixture having a temperature of 66°C. was added to it. The temperature rose over a minute to about 60°C. and quickly cooled to 56°C. The mixture was gently stirred with a stirring rod and held for approximately 10 minutes with only occasional stirring before filtration. With an Eimco twill NY-518F filter cloth, the filtration rate was 3.16 gallons per square foot per minute. In a parallel experiment using caustic alone the filtration rate was unacceptably low, <1 gallon per square foot per minute. The product was identified as the desired sodium benzoate.

Method 2: Sodium Methoxide in Methanol-Toluene

Caustic fines were added to an azeotropic mixture of 70/30 percent by volume methanol/toluene solution to give 1 mole of sodium hydroxide per mole of methanol. This mixture was added to the toluene reactor mass to give a readily filterable precipitate of sodium benzoate.

Method 3: Sodium Methoxide in Methanol

Caustic fines were added to methanol to give 1 mole of caustic per 10 moles of methanol. This mixture was added to the toluene reactor mass to give a readily filterable sodium benzoate product. The yield, however, was lower due to the solubility of the benzoic acid in the methanol.

Method 4: Sodium Ethoxide in Ethanol

Caustic fines were added to ethanol to give 1 mole of caustic per mole of ethanol. This mixture was added to the toluene reactor mass at room temperature to give a readily filterable sodium benzoate product.

Method 5: Sodium Butoxide

In the same manner as described by the examples above, caustic fines were reacted with butanol to give a solution having 1 mole of caustic per mole of butanol. This solution was added to the toluene reactor mass at room temperature to give a readily filterable sodium benzoate product.

Method 6 : Dry Sodium Methoxide

In the same manner as described above, dry sodium methoxide was added to the toluene reactor mass. A fine precipitate was obtained which filtered better than the sodium hydroxide alone but was not as good as sodium methoxide in methanol.

In the same manner as described by the examples above, sodium hydroxide may be reacted with other alkanols, such as isopropyl alcohol, t-butyl alcohol, hexanol, octanol or dodecanol, to give a sodium alkoxide which may then be reacted with the benzoic acid in an aromatic hydrocarbon solvent, such as toluene, benzene or xylene, to give a sodium benzoate product which is easily filterable.

IONOMER RESINS

Ionomer resins are metal salts of ethylene/methacrylic acid copolymers and have a long chain semicrystalline structure. DuPont's SURLYN is the representative material. Ionomers are used as nucleating agents to control crystallization in PET molding resins. PET is processed at high mold temperatures. The ionomer provides faster crystallinity, more rapid cycle time, and good dimensional stability at elevated temperatures. The improvement rate in crystallization at lower temperatures allows the use of water-cooled molds. Typical use levels are below 1%.

Preparation

The preparation of the mini-emulsion depends on careful selection of the ingredients. The mini-emulsion is prepared by mixing water, perfluorinated hydrocarbon, fluorinated surfactant(s), ionomer, and a co-surfactant or inorganic salts. The amounts employed are 0.1-40 weight percent, preferably 0.1-20, of the perfluorinated hydrocarbon; 1-40 weight percent, preferably 0.1-25, of the surfactant and cosurfactants; 1-20 weight percent, preferably 5-15, of the ionomer; with the remainder water. This mixture is subjected to high shear mixing using methods known in the art such as mechanical shear and/or cavitation to break the oil phase into submicron size droplets. Multiple passes through such mixers may be required to obtain a mini-emulsion. The resulting mini-emulsion is neither completely transparent as observed with microemulsions, nor milky white as it is in a (macro)emulsion. Rather, it is substantially translucent, often with a slight hint of colour, for example a blue tint. Without being bound by any particular theory, the resulting mini-emulsion of perfluorinated hydrocarbons is believed to serve as mini-reactors for fluorinated monomers to enter and to be polymerized.

Method

An aqueous mini-emulsion was prepared by pre-mixing and homogenization of a mixture containing 1650 grams of deionized water, and 50 grams of 20% by weight of ammonium perfluoro octanoate (ammonium salt of perfluoro octanoic acid) aqueous solution, and 194 grams of 82.5% by weight of $CF_2 = CF—O—CF_2CF(CF_3)—O—CF_2CF_2—SO_2F$ monomer and 17.5% by weight of Fluorinert® FC-77 (a perfluorinated hydrocarbon, manufactured by 3M). A mini-emulsion was formed using the homogenizing module of a microfluidizer. An air motor using compressed air of about 40 psi sent the mixture through the homogenizing module. The whole mixture was sent through the homogenizing module six times. The final mixture was a translucent aqueous mini-emulsion of very light blue colour. The aqueous mini-emulsion was then added to a 4-liter reactor. The reactor was evacuated three times and purged each time with tetrafluoroethylene gas. The oxygen content of the aqueous solution was about 20 ppm immediately prior to admitting the tetrafluoroethylene gas.

The reactor agitation speed was set at 700 rpm throughout the reaction. The aqueous mini-emulsion was heated from its jacket to a temperature about 83° C. Then, tetrafluoroethylene gas was introduced to the pressure reactor to raise the pressure to 0.87 MPa. About 0.1 gram of ammonium persulfate pre-dissolved in 400 ml of deionized water was pumped into the reactor to start the reaction. The reaction temperature was maintained between 82 and 84° C. throughout the polymerization. The tetrafluoroethylene pressure was maintained at about this initial value for a first reaction time of about 4 minutes. The tetrafluoroethylene supply was stopped and the reaction continued without more charge of tetrafluoroethylene to the reactor. The reaction pressure went down gradually from ˜0.87 MPa initially to about 0.2 MPa during the course of the next 172 minutes. Then, the reaction temperature was lowered to below 50 degrees C. and the reaction system was evacuated to atmosphere. The reaction yielded 2333 g of an aqueous dispersion of copolymer. The total weight percent copolymer obtained by precipitation and isolation was 9.7%. The average colloidal particle size was about 131 nm.

Suppliers

Milliken is the leading producer of substituted sorbitol clarifiers in North America and Europe under the MILLAD trademark. Ciba has recently reached a joint market agreement with Roquette. This will enable the formidable Ciba marketing organization to increase significantly the market exposure of Roquette's sorbitol-based clarifiers. Significant amounts of sodium benzoate are sold to the plastics industry through distributors, who purchase from basic suppliers such as Kalama Chemical. The suppliers of low molecular weight polyolefins are the CPET resin producers such as Shell, Eastman, and ICI. AlliedSignal also offers related compounds. DuPont and others supply ionomer resins. A list of selected global suppliers can be seen in Table 13.4.

Trends and forecasts

PP, CPET, and PET molding resins, and, to some extent, nylon, account for most of the nucleating agent consumption. Approximately 10% of all PP and nearly 50% of the injection molding category is nucleated. Smaller percentages of the PP blow molding and extrusion categories use nucleating agents. Improved clarity of PP has provided the ability for replacement of PVC with PP in applications such as blisterpacks for hardware. In addition, new PP resins are being developed that use single-site metallocene catalysts (mPP). While virtually no difference exists in the processing behavior or finished product properties between conventional PP and mPP, these new materials are easier to nucleate. The use of nucleated mPP provides for a product with the higher physical properties of PP homopolymer and the clarity of nucleated random PP copolymer. There is continuing growth of nucleated PP, particularly in the blow molding and extrusion markets. CPET continues to expand in thermoforming applications, and PET molding compounds continue to penetrate electrical uses. Based on this activity, consumption of nucleating agents is likely to increase at a rate of about 6%/year globally over the next 5 years.

TABLE 13.4: Selected Suppliers of Nucleating Agents

Supplier	Type			
	Sorbitols	Sodium benzoates	LMW polyolefins	Other
AlliedSignal	—	—	×	—
Ciba/Roquette	×	—	—	—
Clariant	—	—	—	×
Cytec Industries	—	—	—	×
DuPont	—	—	—	×
Eastman Chemical	—	—	×	—
FBC	—	×	—	—
ICI	—	—	×	—
Jarchem	—	×	—	—
Kalama Chemical	—	×	—	—
Milliken	×	—	—	—
Mitsui Toatsu Chemicals	×	—	—	—
New Japan Chemical	×	—	—	—
Shell	—	—	×	—
Witco	—	—	—	×